PEOPLE'S THEATRE
IN AMERIKA

PEOPLE'S THEATRE IN AMERIKA

Karen Malpede Taylor

Preface by John Howard Lawson

Documents by the people who do it

DRAMA BOOK SPECIALISTS/PUBLISHERS

New York

ISBN: 0-910482-33-0
Library of Congress Catalog Card Number: 72-87055

To David
    because we are learning
    how to live
        and
For the Revolution
    as it lives in the work
    of the artists represented
    on these pages

ACKNOWLEDGMENTS

There is no part of this book that has not been a collaboration with people I talked or corresponded with, or whose work I read. Unless otherwise indicated in the text, all quotations are from personal letters and interviews, and I am grateful to everyone who helped in this way. At the outset I would like to thank a few people by name. Albert Bermel read much of this manuscript in many of its various stages and his comments were always insightful and often essential. Victor and Marie Basil and their family gave us the quiet of their land and log cabin in Woodstock, New York, during most of the time I was writing. Since 1970 I have been, off-and-on, one of seven persons gathering for breakfast to discuss approaches to dramatic structure. Many of this book's observations about structure could not have been made without the presence on these mornings of Annabelle Henkin, David Keller, Brenna Katz, George Mandelbaum, David Shaber, and Bernard Beckerman (whose *Dynamics of Drama* is the basis of our work). Finally, it is not possible to thank my editor Ralph Pine, my friends Jack and Sue Lawson, my brother John Malpede and my husband David Taylor, the people who believed in this book most thoroughly and who most nearly lived its creation with me.

Grateful acknowledgment is made to the following people and publications for permission to reprint their work: Julian Beck, R. G. Davis, Mordecai Gorelik, Paul Peters, Peter Schumann, George Sklar, Luis Valdez, the *New York Times*, the *Village Voice*, and *Yale/Theatre*.

PREFACE

This book is a pioneering attempt to deal with avant-garde movements in the American Theatre from the early twenties to the seventies. This history is diverse, fragmented, contradictory, but always rich in promise, always concerned with fundamental questions of dramatic art.

Karen Malpede Taylor, the first critic to examine its historical continuity and present relevance, sees the American avant-garde as radical in the true meaning of the term—pertaining to the root and function of the creative experience, radical in its changing forms, cruel but sensitive in its moral passion, revolutionary in its vision of the individual and society in constant conflict, in which both are transformed.

I have spent a good part of my life in the service of this theatre, and I believe I am still in the front rank of dissenters and activists as we move into this inscrutable decade. It would never occur to me to doubt the continuity of this fifty-year experience, because my character and identity have been shaped—and often scarred—by the struggle for an art of the vanguard, of rebels and pathfinders.

The judicious selections of documents in this book, and the writer's perceptive text provide a new perspective on the problems and unanswered questions of the present period. These questions are not new in any absolute sense. There is a *radical* concept of dramatic art which has survived the shocks and traumas of sight-and-sound experimentation. The most consistent element in the pattern is the rejection of conventional or box office values, with their false sexuality (the sexuality of TV commercials), absurd stereotypes and mechanical situations.

In 1927 I denounced the "gradual rot of stale sentiments, old jokes and dead repetitions"* in the Broadway theatre. Later Bertolt Brecht warned against the tendency to "fob us off with portable anguish" which can be "detached from its cause, transfered in toto to some other cause."** The warning is echoed by Joseph Chaikin in 1971: "My early training was for the boulevard theater. I was taught to represent other people by their stereotypes. All this has not changed . . . Boulevard

*"The New Showmanship "Program for Francis Faragoh's *Pinwheel*, Neighborhood Playhouse, February 3, 1927.
**Brecht on Theatre*, ed. and trans. John Willet, New York, 1964.

Theatre is basically to care about fictions, things or people which you don't truly care about."*

It is not my purpose here to propose "definitive" answers to complicated questions, I am not sure I know any answers. I am not even sure I can ask the right questions. I can only point out that the following pages are full of tantalizing questions and surprising insights. In stressing the book's usefulness, I hardly dare suggest that it be used as "a weapon." The word is loaded with comic (and tragic) ambiguities. This is a matter of history. It is also a matter of the use or misuse of words.

If I suggest that a work of art is a means of expanding consciousness, including the possibility of changing the world, each phrase opens a Pandora's Box of conflicting meanings. Instead of arguing these inflammable questions, I should like to offer some rough notes on my personal response to some moments of excitement, and possible revelation. These moments are in part non-verbal. But words are the only tools at my disposal. I have no laser beams, no electronic amplifiers, no holograms or fountains of light.

I share these limitations with the artists whose work has moved me. It is a basic condition of people's theatre art that its physical resources are meager. This poverty of means is one of the links between the twenties and the seventies. The artist may dream of technological miracles, but his available resources are not much more than a shoestring.

Yet there is another kind of resource—the imagination and commitment of people.

Bread and Puppet Theatre

FIRE

Lone Mountain College in San Francisco. A large square room. We have come early to get a good location. But there are no seats. About 100 people, most of them young, are sitting on the floor. We are embarrassed by our age and our preoccupation with our own comfort.

One of us returns to the young woman who took our admission at the door. She is sympathetic and efficient. Folding chairs are brought and placed in the exact center of

*Performance, vol 1., no. 1, December 1971.

the room. Men and women, and a few babies, have to move from their privileged positions to make a place for us. Everyone is friendly and our apologies seem ridiculous. Perhaps the process of sharing has begun.

THE SHARING OF BREAD

Actors distribute hunks of homemade bread. It is a simple matter. Care is taken to make sure that every spectator receives the symbolic bread.

Peter Schumann, director of the Bread and Puppet Theatre, says bread should remind us that the theatre "is not the place of commerce that you think it is . . . . It is more like bread, more like a necessity . . . . Puppets and masks should be played in the street . . . ."

We are not in the street. We might be here for a class or lecture. The only suggestion of theatre is the curtained platform in front of us. We accept the bread, not as a necessity, but as an amusing gesture. We continue to discuss its meaning as the performance begins.

Fire is a lyrical political statement, concerning the suffering of the people of Asia, the savage course of US imperialism in Vietnam, and the responsibility of all Americans. But the theme is never stressed as a narrative "situation." The robed figures are not "characters." Their identity is most fully expressed in their masks. Peter Schumann is a plastic artist, and his concept of theatre is embodied in the groping gestures, the subdued passion of these sculptured faces.

Fire becomes more explicit as it proceeds. The death of the woman in the final scene is devastatingly climactic.

The double symbolism of "fire" runs through all of human culture. Fire is the Promethean gift; it is also the reality of war, the destruction of cities. In *The Trojan Women* the women lament in the smouldering ruins of the city. Cassandra carries a lighted torch as she prophesies revenge for the crimes of the Greek conquerors. The royal child, the baby son of Andromache and Hector, is hurled to his death in the fiery ruins.

These are literary references. But they show that *Fire* is not a careless rejection of tradition. It grows from the roots

xi

of all drama. The death of the woman at the end of *Fire* is as senseless, as timely and contemporary, as the smashing of a child's body in *The Trojan Women*.

The fire-symbol is in many of my plays. In 1923, the vision of New York as a burning ruin was verbally suggested in *Roger Bloomer*. And, in 1928, the end of *The International* showed the gutted skyscrapers and the city in flames.

I made a more complex use of fire symbols in *Marching Song* in 1937. In the final moments of the play, gangsters torture the union organizer. The shadowy figures around a fire brand him with hot irons. As the organizer dies, the city goes dark. A general strike has cut off the electricity.

I believe there is a bridge between *Marching Song* and *Fire*. It is not a simple connection, and relates to the search for symbols which expand consciousness. Both plays have a quality of estrangement, of ordinary events seen in a new strange way, which is Brecht's inspired contribution to theatrical theory.

The symbols in *Marching Song* are too narrowly realistic. In *Fire* the symbolism is somewhat forced and ambiguous. There is still the unsolved problem of intense personal participation, relating the brotherhood of individuals to their capacity to transform themselves and their environment.

Open Theatre

THE MUTATION SHOW

ROYCE HALL, UCLA, 1972

Joseph Chaikin and his associates in the Open Theatre have made an impressive attempt to take the actor out of the dream-world of the proscenium.

In *Fire*, the performers are not individualized. The psyche is masked and shrouded. In the Open Theatre's recent work, the personality of the performer is open—open to the winds of change. The action consists in transformations, affecting the actor, the spectators and their mutual situation.

Mutation is a work-in-progress, co-directed by Chaikin and Roberta Sklar. I am not sure it is successful. It simply has no relationship to what we mean by a "successful" work of art.

I have vivid memories of Royce Hall which relate to my own "mutations" and the history of my generation. For me, this auditorium gives zest and savor to the performance: it is a footnote to *Processional*, a gloss on *Loudspeaker*, an ironic comment on the transformations that occurred in the late forties and fifties.

There was the *Writers' Congress* in 1943; three days of hopeful seminars and meetings were climaxed by a meeting in Royce Hall. At the end of the meeting, a student appeared in a spotlight and read AN AMERICAN WRITER'S CREDO. The crowded audience stood and repeated each phrase. The last lines were a solemn commitment: "I pledge myself to know the thought and feeling of the American people . . . . To these millions I dedicate my skill and talent, and the strength of my heart and mind."*

The CREDO was anonymous, but I wrote it. I am still moved by it, but I smile at the naive assumption concerning a "people's culture." That was before the Cold War and the witch-hunts. Who in 1972 would presume to "know the thought and feeling of the American people"?

I look around at the young faces. They understand *Mutation* but there is no clue to their specific response. I doubt whether the few people over forty in the audience can understand the production at all. It is certainly not a "program" or "credo." It is a series of improvisations built around individuals whose identities are determined by a circus freak show.

The acting technique, derived from many sources, is based in part on Viola Spolin's *Improvisation for the Theater*. She is an old friend from the thirties. She traces the origin of her "theatre games" to her work with the WPA Recreational Project in Chicago. Her method was more fully developed during the eleven years in which she directed the Young Actors' Company in Hollywood. The lack of structure in *Mutations* disturbs me. The moments of intense communication are scattered, I wonder about the limits of improvisation. Yet something is happening that may never have happened before on this spacious stage: theatre is being born.

Writers' Congress, University of California Press, 1944.

San Francisco, New Committee Theatre, 1971

THE TRIAL OF THE CATONSVILLE NINE

The burning of draft files at Catonsville, Maryland, on May 17, 1968, is a profoundly theatrical event. The trial of "criminals" is another matter. Daniel Berrigan's play follows the court record. In his introduction, Berrigan writes: "In condensing such a mass of material, it was predictable that a qualitative change would occur, almost by the law of nature, as the form emerged. And this, of course, was my hope, to induce out of the density of matter an art form worthy of the passionate acts and words of the nine."

This hope could not be realized by the dramatic presentation of the court proceedings. The performance is followed by a discussion. The casual interchange between spectators and players, with its unplanned reference to world tragedy has a theatrical substance and complexity, which was not present in the previous action on the stage.

I do not mean to diminish the stature of Daniel Berrigan's play. It has the stature of its author, a striking figure of our time. The trial shows that Berrigan and his eight companions are people of good will and integrity. But the trial cannot go beyond conventional characterization. The verdict is predictable, and so is the revelation that "justice" in capitalist society is hypocritical and cruel.

A play is not a document. The exact external record of a given situation may be "useful," and more or less "true." But it cannot portray the inner reality, the tension of being. A soul is not a torso with arms and legs.

The search for deeper reality, an expanded consciousness of self and community, follows many courses. Black Theatre, Chicano Theatre, and the theatrical ventures of other ethnic groups are engaged in exploring different areas of experience, seeking a personal identity that is rooted in the community, seeking a lost heritage that is history's promise to future generations.

I have dealt with only three occasions, my personal responses to three theatrical adventures. It is a long way from the twenties but there is a longer journey before us. The itinerary cannot be charted. There is no map, only a vision.

John Howard Lawson
Van Nuys, California
May 21, 1972

Michael Gold
PROLETARIAN ART*

The multitudes of men and women are in darkness, deep, bitter
darkness. They lie on the ground and weep, remembering the eons of
oppression. They moan in a low key, like the sweep of a vast wind.
They remember the slavery in which their forefathers lived—they remember poverty, lynching, war. It is good for them to remember this—
it keeps them humble and it makes them stern in the conviction that
such things not come again.

The darkness is slowly invaded by a faint red glow from a color
organ. The moaning changes to a more hopeful key. Tremendous bat-
teries around the field have cast a wider and more brilliant scarlet light
on the mob. It is an illumination that makes the heart leap with hope;
the people rise to their feet and move about singing a new song.

A thousand great mechanical orchestras, more wonderful than anything we know, break into mighty strains. The people chant a marvel-
ous cantata that rises to the stars like a hymn to life. Now the color
organs have burst into full flower. They throw strange patterns on the
sky; the sky is filled with a thousand clashing beautiful colors; the earth
is filled with powerful singing; not a man, woman, child or dog is
outside the communion of this night; the world is wonderful; it is the
drama of the proletarian revolution; it is the proletarian art.

*From "Prize-Fights vs Color Organs," *The Liberator*, Vol. V,
March 1922.

From what I know of the work at Spirit House in New-Ark and especially from reading Imamu Amiri Baraka's (LeRoi Jones') plays, his seems to be the exemplary black people's theatre and one that should occupy a significant place in a book like this. For several reasons, however, I have chosen not to deal with it. At this time of tremendous activity among black artists, appraisals of their radical works—because they have been written especially for black people—are best left to black critics and audiences. And the many recent anthologies and histories devoted solely to black theatre provide much more comprehensive information about this crucial part of the people's theatre movement than space allows for here.

TABLE OF CONTENTS

November 9, 1972

Dear Ralph,

Spending the summer in
northern Vermont has made added
sense of the 30s plays. The ethnic
cultures of the city streets exist
and are being turned into theatre,
but small town culture is hardly more
than a plastic reproduction of some
Madison Avenue executives' crazed
notions about what people should want.
There is a nice universality about
hamburger huts and discount houses
but this is hardly the stuff from
which theatre is made.

It's on this point that I
think the strike plays and the living
newspapers have something to teach us.
These plays attempted the habits,
hopes, jokes, prejudices, fears of the
working class before these qualities
were standardized by consumerism.
Some of this contact with their
reality has got to be recovered and
then, as was also tried in the 30s,
the reality has got to be transformed.

We must attend to the
struggles of those people who for
reasons of age or occupation are
not completely caught up in the

media enforced middle-class dream.
People doing theatre in the cities
have known for several years that
their audience exists on the streets,
in the ghettos, prisons, asylums,
schools. It's time also to reach out
to the rest of the country. In
Vermont I got a sense of vitality
from the dairy farmers around us,
from the welfare mothers and older
people we met at the low income organization and from some of the high
school students.

Remember the second meeting
Mark Hall Amitin called last spring?
Despite its incoherence, weird hostil-
ities and nonsense, it made something
amazingly clear. About no other theatre
but the radical theatre can it be said
that people, most of whom do not know
one another, meet in garages (even
performing garages) to talk long into
the night about its nature.

POLITICS ARE NO LONGER
SEPARATE FROM ESTHETICS. They do not
seem any longer to be two separate
things.

People who work in the
theatre have a tremendous opportunity right now. For the first time
we have the artistically convincing
means to accomplish our revolutionary
purpose.

2

I couldn't have under-
stood this without first going back
to the 30s. It's this concrete
knowledge of the similarities of goals
and of the painful, step-by-step
advances in techniques--from activist endings to simultaneous texts--
that gives me some hope for the future.

There is no doubt in my
mind that the most exciting and ener-
gizing element in the theatre is simultaneous text. And simultaneous text is
radical in every way. It is the
device allowing for the realization in
the theatre that inner and outer realities are in dialectical relationship
and must be considered at the same
time in order for their transformational power to be understood.

I've written in one draft
of the once proposed introduction:
"The bourgeois realism that has
dominated the theatre since the Res-
toration assumes neither people nor
social structures can be fundamentally changed. It teaches us wrongly
that the place where art illuminates
life most precisely is here where it
scrutinizes the gap between the
liberation each of us knows is hers
and the repressive pattern of our
daily existence under capitalism."

Again from the intro:
"This book as it moves from a history

3

of radical theatre in the 20s and 30s
to impressions of radical theatre as
it exists for me today is first of all
a record of how the bourgeois gap has
been narrowed in the theatre by the
substitution of activities that allow
the inner and outer man to meet, there
to effect his own and society's transformation."

Such great formality.
It can't continue once I put your
name at the top of the paper. Now
whoever reads this after you, it will
still be a personal communication.

All my best,

Karen

NEW PLAYWRIGHTS THEATRE

In 1926 radicals, isolated and impotent since the Palmer raids and general right-wing hysteria of the post-war years, had wrecked the Anarchist, Socialist and IWW movements, and liberals came to the defense of textile workers in Passaic, New Jersey, who were on strike protesting a ten percent cut in their already insufficient wages. John Dos Passos, Michael Gold, Mary Heaton Vorse, Frieda Kirchway were among the writers who went to Passaic. Back in New York they wrote bitter accounts of their experiences in their new magazine *The New Masses*. This monthly, first published in May 1926, several months after the strike began, had been in the planning stages all during the early part of the year. It was meant to revive the mixture of radical politics and artistic comment that had once made Max Eastman's and Floyd Dell's *Masses* indispensable. In its first issue the editors wrote:

> From one angle, the Passaic strike has been the most heartening event in years. It has dispelled the cloud of pessimism and defeatism that hung over the radical movement since the vast calamity of the war. It has united the different sections of the movement on vital issues.

Also in 1926 Ida Raugh, Jasper Deeter, Hugo Gellert, John Howard Lawson and other artists organized the Workers Drama League, which produced Michael Gold's mass recitation about the Passaic strike. *Strike!* opens at a board meeting chaired by a silk-hatted financier named Wealth. His shadow, Poverty, makes an unwelcome speech reminding the board members of the consequences of their actions. A chorus of workers interrupts the meeting periodically with short laments about their hunger, but they are interrupted by a young union organizer (a Communist just out of school was leading the Passaic strike) who convinces them of their power. Then the workers' chorus takes the stage from the financiers, vowing to strike and urging the audience to join them singing "The Internationale."

Gold's recitation is significant in light of the failure of earlier experiments with expressionism to find a method for effecting change. Expressionistic segments are moments of psychic reaction within the causal progression of a traditional story. In Lawson's *Roger Bloomer* (1923) the story is the commercially honored one of unrealized love. But when the story halts so that inner rebellion can be displayed, its very display proves it is powerless to alter the nature of the play's progression (linear and causal) or its world view (the inevitable separation of the lovers and confirmation of the gap between desire and fulfillment).

In *Strike!* it is the announcement of a hard fact (the ten percent wage cut) and not the revelation of their inner misery that causes the workers to desert prayers for action. The mass action is instigated by a working-class hero, a man who has already discovered (off stage) how his personal dissatisfaction is connected to the social structures around him.

Lawson considers the dream sequence at the end of *Roger Bloomer* his "farewell to expressionism." In it the hero, a typical Amerikan boy from Iowa, relives the play's plot in abbreviated, nightmare form. He again confronts the college entrance examiner, the business executive, and the judge, reconfirming his understanding of the bourgeois world as living death. His lover, Louise, has killed herself to escape this horror, but when she appears in Roger's dream she urges him to choose life: "Away! Away, ghosts of yesterday, for the young are coming, marching, marching; can't you hear the echo of their feet, can't you hear them singing a new song?"

From the personal agony of *Roger Bloomer*, Lawson turned to the jazz ensemble of *Processional!* (1925). It was the story of labor strife, prejudice and violence in a Kentucky coal mining town whose citizens were portrayed in a broadly farcical manner borrowed from vaudeville and burlesque.

6

Processional!'s socialist content was as inseparable from the theatrical style Lawson created for it as it was from his interest in the current troubles in the coal mining districts. Here was a possible new song: one that turned the energy of popular art against the cruelties of Amerikan life.

Gold, having had several plays produced by the Provincetown Players, now approached the millionaire financier and patron Otto Kahn for a subsidy. Kahn had just finished losing money on Lawson's black comedy *Nirvana*, a play that departed from the revolutionary concerns of *Processional* to describe the limits of mysticism, science and technology (each of them commonly considered panaceas in the twenties). It ran for three days. At the same time Kahn was financing Emjo Basshe's half-year residence in the deep South where he was writing a play, *Earth*, about the conflict between imposed Christianity and natural spiritualism in a remote black community.

Instead of giving Gold an individual grant, Kahn suggested that he was willing to fund an entire theatre and asked that Gold invite Lawson, Basshe, and Francis Edwards Faragoh to lunch with him to discuss the idea. Gold was already a vocal member of the Communist Party, Lawson, Faragoh and Basshe had definite anarchist and bohemian leanings, and all four were agreed on the need for a revolutionary and iconoclastic theatre in New York. The luncheon to plan their New Playwrights Theatre took place at the Bankers Club, the central gathering place for Wall Street's moguls. It was probably an intentionally ironic gesture on Kahn's part because he knew about the playwrights' radical sympathies. Gold meant to counter by attending the luncheon without socks, but Faragoh, who stole enough Bankers Club stationery to placate his creditors throughout the Depression, insisted on lending a pair of his own. Gold used to sign his letters to Kahn "your class enemy"; yet the relationship between the playwrights and their benefactor was always cordial. Kahn and the four were unlikely conspirators, but where else could a non-commercial theatre turn for funds? In fact, the *New Masses* was also founded with money from a private fortune.

At lunch Lawson suggested that Eugene O'Neill and his good friend, John Dos Passos, be invited to join the theatre. O'Neill sent Lawson a brief, cold note refusing to have anything to do with it. Dos Passos was travelling in Europe

7

and could not be reached, but he joined the theatre for its second season and became its chief propagandist. Lynn Riggs was also considered for membership, but according to Faragoh, he was "too shy to work in a group."

The most immediate incentive for a New Playwrights Theatre had been the International Theatre Exposition, organized by Jane Heap, which opened early in the year. *The Little Review* devoted an entire issue (winter, 1926) to the Exposition, and in it Otto Kahn, who was chairman of the honorary committee of sponsors, expressed his "hope" that "there may be, in the not too distant future, at least one theatre in New York devoted exclusively to youth—a stage where young America shall have its innings."

New York's Steinway Hall was decorated with scene designs for the most daring productions of theatres in Italy, Holland, Germany, Sweden, France, Poland, the USSR and the US. Caspar Nehar's working sketches for Brecht's *Edward II* and *The Drumming* [sic] *in the Night* hung along with Mordecai Gorelik's renderings for Lawson's *Processional!* and Norman Bel Geddes' design for Basshe's *Adam Solitaire*. But it was Russian experiments with constructivism, above all else, that captured the imagination of the New Playwrights. In the accompanying *Little Review* article on the Russian stage, S. Margolene identified Meyerhold as head of the left theatres in the USSR, while naming Lunacharsky, Stanislavsky and Nemirovich-Danchenko as leaders of the "academic" factions (which, though theatrically conservative, were favored by most government officials). Margolene continued:

> The new actor no longer renders his passions on the stage; rather he manifests a judgment of these passions. He weighs and criticizes them. To this end, he is equipped not only with keenly modern ideas, but also with a supple body and a sonorous voice.

The New Playwrights seized upon constructivist staging as a way to make the interior revolt of expressionism functional. (Meyerhold was equally drawn to Amerikan jazz and vaudeville, whose use in plays NPT members pioneered. In 1928 William Gropper reported from the Soviet Union in the *Daily Worker* that Meyerhold was planning productions of *Processional!* and *The Belt*, which opened the NPT's second season. The productions never materialized; though he would not be arrested until 1939, he may have already been feeling the strictures of his unpopular position.)

On February 27, 1927, Emjo Basshe supplied the Sunday drama section of the *New York Times* with a manifesto for the new theatre. It was headlined "The Revolt on 52nd St." In it Basshe called for "a theatre which is as drunken, as barbaric, as clangorous as our age." The theatre artist, he said, could no longer hide from current history:

> He stands shoulder to shoulder with the mentors of this our age: the Einsteins, Gothals, Curles, Michilsons, Edisons. He is their historian, their toastmaster and very often their clown. He accepts the clay and the model that they have ready for him. He accepts their nuts, bolts, cranes; he listens to the tune played by their acetylene torches, cutting through steel, rock, bone; he trembles as the earth trembles when their showy engines shriek and pound away. Does the earth welcome it? Probably no more than man. Protest. Clench your fists. Try to trip the paraders. Throw rotten eggs at the dynamo. The show will go on. We are in the presence of the present.

Basshe's article made up in enthusiasm what it lacked in specificity. For instance, he was uncertain whether the New Playwrights Theatre would do best to "shock" and "terrify" its audience or to act as a "therapeutic," nursing the "harrowed and haunted citizen . . . into a child of the morning." Either approach might serve because, Basshe said, "there is nothing absolute about our theatre, we are always ready to change the cloak if it shows signs of fading."

For their first season the New Playwrights rented an abandoned music hall on 52nd Street called Bims. The theatre was too large for them, and its proximity to Broadway indicated that they were still attracted by the bohemian formula of the twenties: they wished to dissociate themselves from the stupefying sensibility of capitalism and at the same time rise to fame on their ability to shock it.

Lawson's *Loud Speaker* and Basshe's *Earth* opened in March 1927 within the same week and continued in repertory throughout the early spring. Gold's *Fiesta: a comedy of the Mexican revolution*, like the first two productions, involved a large cast and ambitious staging. It was carried to dress rehearsal before the playwrights decided it was not ready to open. After the unfavorable critical reception and tiny audiences that greeted *Loud Speaker* and *Earth*, the theatre could not afford another costly failure. (*Fiesta* was subsequently staged for five weeks by the Provincetown Players in 1929.)

Loud Speaker a farce about a rich man running for governor of New York who kills himself after facing the sham of politics, employed the first open constructivist set on a US stage. Designed by Mordecai Gorelik, its wooden framework included a platform for the jazz band, which was present throughout and to whose music the actors had to negotiate their stylized movements and complicated entrances.

The production style was anti-illusionistic; the play's content proclaimed an end to sentimental illusions about life in the US.

Critics from the bourgeois press found the New Playwrights' first two productions incomprehensible. Before the theatre even opened Alexander Woollcott labelled them "the revolting playwrights," a pun that would be repeated in many unfriendly reviews. Neither of the theatrical experiments of the first season was more than marginally connected to the concerns of US radicals. The operatic pageantry of *Earth* was due as much to Basshe's bohemian fascination with all sorts of exotica, as to a desire to indict paternalistic Christianity. *Loud Speaker* was Lawson's counterpart to the political farces being staged by Meyerhold in the USSR. It was conceived primarily to show off the constructivist stage, secondarily to mock Amerikan candidates and their gullible electorate.

Though their uptown failure gave the playwrights a painfully personal, if not very altruistic, shove toward the Left, it was not until after their horror at the execution of anarchists Nicola Sacco and Bartolomeo Vanzetti that they committed themselves outright to a radical theatre. Dos Passos had been involved in defense efforts for the two since 1926. The afternoon of the execution on August 27, 1927, Dos Passos, Gold and Lawson and a number of other writers, were arrested for picketing the Massachusetts State House. Lawson says: "There is no doubt that the execution of Sacco and Vanzetti (and our trial that followed which we won) had an effect in making the NPT more openly revolutionary. But this was a basic tendency in the culture of the time."

For the second season they rented a small theatre at 40 Commerce Street, "that a bunch of London-minded aesthetes tried to rename Cherry Lane," Dos Passos remarked. They celebrated the theatre's opening by raising a red flag over its door, "a ceremony that attracted little attention," Lawson remembers. They asked for and got the Communist Party to publicize their plays in radical labor circles. Still they had ridiculous problems with audiences. Elizabeth Merrill Faragoh, who was their treasurer during this period, remembers selling blocks of tickets to organizations like the Ukranian Window Washers, who were anxious for revolutionary art but who spoke little English, and to liberal groups like the Doctors' Wives, who were off on a Village adventure, not a radical crusade.

Before the New Playwrights opened their second season in December 1927, John Dos Passos wrote an article for *New Masses* called "Towards a Revolutionary Theatre." It was the first time that the playwrights' theatrical iconoclasm was said to be integrally related to the radical reorganization of the working class:

> By revolutionary I mean that such a theatre must break with the present day theatrical traditions, not with general traditions of the theatre, and that it must draw its life and ideas from the conscious sections of the industrial and white collar working classes which are out to get control of the great flabby mass of capitalist society and mould it to their own purpose . . . . In method of presentation it will be something between a high mass in a Catholic church and Barnum and Bailey's circus, both of which are rituals stripped to their bare lines. Vigor and imagination must take the place of expensiveness and subtlety.

Dos Passos' revolutionary ardor has to be remarked upon because it did not last. By the end of the thirties he was exchanging it for militant conservatism. "Dos is only slumming," Faragoh used to tell his wife during the New Playwrights days. The play Dos Passos wrote for them, *Airways, Inc.* was, despite his *New Masses* article of the previous year,

11

straight from the realistic canon. It was full of despair, death (for the radical organizer who was its protagonist) and general lethargy about how nothing can be done. In the mid-fifties he published a mundane novel, *Most Likely to Succeed*, which caricatured members of the New Playwrights, especially his friend Jack Lawson, as being completely under the Communist Party's thumb. However, at the time neither Lawson nor any New Playwright was a Party member, except Gold (who had the least influence on theatre policy), and the relationship between NPT and the Communist reviewers ranged from cordial to heated feuding.

> The demand to change consciousness amounts to a demand to interpret reality in another way, that is, to accept it by means of another interpretation.
> —Marx & Engels

The issue at the heart of the four plays of the second season* was how increasing industrialization—the assembly line, the speed-up, economic imperialism—could be stopped from mechanizing the hearts and minds of people. It was an issue characteristic of the twenties, a decade of financial expansion and prosperity, and one that would no longer seem as urgent once the stock market crash began to throw millions of people out of work. It is also a radical issue that lends itself exceedingly well to theatrical experiment. The rhythms of oppressed and alienated labor, which are the rhythms of naturalism, can be overthrown by the dance, song, acrobatics, choral chants, and constructed scenery which were essential to the playwrights' theatricalist intentions.

Almost as an earnest of their radical will, the New Playwrights opened their second season with *The Belt* by journalist Paul Sifton. Sifton was not yet a member of the group (he would become one for the third and failing season, after Lawson and Faragoh had left for Hollywood) and his play adhered mainly to the realistic tradition they had spent so

---

Hoboken Blues by Gold strikes me as the least interesting of the four scripts and will not be discussed here. It is printed in *American Caravan: A Yearbook of American Literature*, eds. VanWyck Brooks, Alfred Kremborg, Lewis Mumford, Paul Rosenfeld, New York, 1927, pp. 548-626.

much time denigrating. But Sifton's reporting work had given him firsthand knowledge of union organizing, and *The Belt* was, as Gilbert Gabriel pointed out at the end of a damning review in the *New York Sun*:

> ... the first and only play ever seen over here which does not doom the labor theme to a defeatist ending, to a hangdog meekness at the final curtain.

Until the final act, *The Belt* explores the degradation of a single family forced to live in a company town and meet the never-ending demands of the assembly belt. The father, Jim, is physically and emotionally exhausted; the mother is a shrew who translates her miserable sex life into a craving for glamor and material possessions. Ironically, this couple and their rebellious daughter, Nance, who works as a secretary at the automobile factory, have been chosen as the perfect working class family by the company public relations experts. The father receives his service pin from the Old Man himself (Henry Ford), and newsreel cameras grind away while the mogul performs a stiff dance with the wife of his chosen worker. After this Hallmark Card celebration, Nance and her exhausted fiance Bill are discovered asleep together on the living room couch. Convinced that his daughter has been violated, the father calls his secret lodge members to the house to run Bill out of town. Nance returns from the plant with news that a speed-up is being called. Bill uses her information to save himself from a beating and to uncover the actual cause of the mens' puritanical rage—they are being emasculated by the repetitive tyranny of the belt. He urges them to march on the factory and shut it down.

Act III opens with the sterile, mechanized motions of the workers on the night shift and their depressed conversation: snide sex talk and unrealizable plans for the future. They are interrupted by the crowd of militant workers who show their new awareness by dancing and playing music! For a moment the pleasure principle triumphs, and as it liberates the mind from defeatist routine it also explodes the structure of the realistic drama by which it is surrounded but in which it is not contained. The realism of *The Belt* turns into the reality of a liberated society.

The Old Man has been notified of the frenzy in his factory.

13

He arrives on stage on top of a half-assembled auto moving down the line. He entreats his employees to return to work, but his presence ignites the violence they had momentarily transcended. They begin to destroy the factory. The police are called and Bill is arrested. The curtain falls on the ruined assembly line and the workers' pledges to continue strike action.

Basshe's *The Centuries*, the second production of the second season, is the story of the Lower East Side. It had a cast of 52 and a multi-leveled set that represented the rooms of an entire tenement house, a brothel, a synagogue, stores, a shirtwaist factory, a saloon, and the street below. Its action covers a period of fifteen years.

No definite time periods or lapses are indicated nor are seasons, months, days or hours given undue importance since their action upon the characters in their battle for life and existence . . . is no different from the other phases of their struggle. The tide and flow of their life here is so swift, so brutal and primitive that neither night, day, heat, cold nor death can have any more than a glancing effect upon the whole community.

Author's introduction

There is no formal chorus, but groups of peddlers, strikers, mourners, and housewives lift the action out of realistic and domestic confines and give it mass significance. Short scenes of conversational dialogue expand into personal lamentations which are in turn amplified by other characters or groups whose lives are being improvised at the same moment around the same general theme. This is how the linear, temporal, plot-oriented structure of bourgeois realism is destroyed. With it go ideological constructs about the insularity of the individual.

Basshe recognized several themes which determined the development of immigrants in the new world: the conflict between the old dogma, Judaism, and the new one, money; between the old order, in which the parents ruled the children, and the new order where the children support and control the parents; and between honest but impoverished work in the factories and corrupt but well-paid hustling and politicking in the ghettos. The themes are constant through-

14

out the play but the variations on them are multiple, giving *The Centuries* a richness, a wry humor, and a sympathy for the lives it comes from that is quite beautiful.

The central family, whose members embody the play's themes, is composed of the father, a lazy Shames; the mother, Chave; and two children. Gitel works in a shirtwaist factory. She falls in love with a fellow worker and they become strike leaders. Yankel steals, goes to law school, marries for money, does in the old gang and becomes ward boss of the Lower East Side. The movement in both cases is toward greater sophistication, greater, though opposite, facility in dealing with the demands of industrialized Amerika.

The play opens as this family and other victims of the Czar's pogroms huddle together in an immigrant house. They are greeted by former inhabitants of their Russian village who have been in the US several years. The honest ones explain how everybody must work and perhaps grow rich, and they suggest various jobs: carpenter, tailor, rag picker, peddler, seamstress. The dishonest one, Yoshke, hires the greenhorns out as manual laborers and pockets most of their pay. The immigrants establish a synagogue and, gathered together in it, they relive the pogrom's terror, but the noise of the sewing machines being run on the Sabbath blurs their memories of past oppression. In the room above, Gitel stitches shirts and tells her mother, "the Sabbath does not give us bread."

In Act II as Gitel leaves the shop with Reuben, her exhaustion stimulates a frantic, dream-like vision indicating both her love for him and her awakening social conscience:

We could go on working . . . on and on . . . for the machines are lullabies that keep you awake and rock you to sleep . . . go on working for ever . . . needles in fingers . . . dust, grit, smoke and all . . . you are all steel . . . I am being born . . . your body is dry like the wheel that turns and turns . . . .

[ellipses in text]

Reuben catches her and holds her, and Louis, the neighborhood pimp, asks them if they want a room for 50 cents. Louis follows Gitel home, but is stopped when her mother answers the door. In the synagogue two tramps, Zwi and Chono, mumble, along with the Rabbi, about past amorous

15

exploits. "Four wives you had, and I had three, but what is a wife to love?" The mother of Yoshke, the neighborhood's biggest hoodlum, enters the synagogue and asks that the Rabbi judge between herself and her son. He is the warped product of a fanatically religious home; she is the victim of his greed and his hate for the family—he makes her the madame at the whore house he operates. In the flat above, Gitel wakes to the screaming of the alarm clock. She begs her mother to save her from the living death of the shop. Chave answers:

> Would I bring you into the world to make you the twin of a machine? . . . The world of mothers is being judged.

From the synagogue, Elke's voice is heard:

> Would a mother bring a child into the world to tear him limb from limb? Where, then, is the blood that the loss to one is the loss to the other? The pain of one is the pain of both . . . judge between us then.

The actions of the overlapping scenes correspond. Two mothers face children who are caught in a struggle that allows neither filial love nor the fulfillment of the promise of their birth. And the language the mothers use becomes ironic because it points to the lack of correspondence between what they wish for their children and what the poverty of their lives has provided for them.

Act III intensifies the inverted order where "the young hold life and death in their hands, and honor is due them because they have captured the new world." An anonymous mother sends her daughter to work sensing that she won't return. The shirtwaist factory, crowded past safety and working at a furious pace to meet speed-up orders, catches fire (in a re-creation, by light, of the Tri-Angle Shirtwaist Fire that caused hundreds of deaths and led to early unionization of the garment trades).

Out of this devastation a strike is built. The sameness of experience that exploitation creates for the workers finally makes their united action possible. This recognition (which determines the play's structure) is verbalized by a girl striker:

16

There were many of us, but he picked me out . . . his hands were large . . . he picked me out, but we are all one, for if he had beaten another girl, the bruises would have been on my body too, for we are all one . . . I looked into his face, scarred and torn like an old sieve left out in the rain . . . I wanted to ask him "why?" but he was running away, as if I could harm him . . . .

As the strike continues, the strikers' laments are drowned out by the despair of the housewives who are watching their children starve:

> . . . there will be no more children . . . no more . . . not from me . . . all night long I've walked to kill that which is in my belly . . . I've stamped my feet on the hard sidewalks . . . I've pressed my body against the sharp corners of buildings . . . bread for those who are already born.

The strike settlement is announced on the street below and the mothers' mourning becomes a victory chorus. The play ends with a polyphonic movement, including Yankel's wedding to the ugliest but richest girl he knows (a corrupt celebration that follows his ouster of the old gang), Gitel's and Reuben's joy over the strike settlement which becomes a pledge of their love:

> Over the ruins of the Ghettos . . . over the wastes of the gangsters . . . of Rabbis we are marching . . . do you feel light?

and the elated gossip of housewives who are finally getting out of the ghetto:

FIRST WOMAN: A gas range second floor three rooms rear hot water two blocks from school and what are you going to do? . . .
It's all right . . . it's moving anyway, isn't it? As long as we get away from here. And what do you think of my next door? Moving to the Avenue!
SECOND WOMAN: What Avenue?
FIRST WOMAN: Second Avenue!
RABBI: Second Avenue.
SECOND WOMAN: But the big news is that Mrs. Boriskin is moving to the Bronx!

17

A word about Basshe's language. Its disrupted syntax, echoed phrases and exploratory sounds are familiar enough to us now—almost as though they came out of an acting workshop—but such dialogue must have been extremely difficult to perform for actors who approached it like everyday chatter. If an actress has to say, "Every time I go into that place my heart . . . I feel it . . . here . . . feel my heart . . . it is not mine . . . a sewing machine is there . . . don't you hear it? It is changing stitches now . . ." and she says it as though she were saying "I can't stand another day in that sweat shop," it sounds impossibly evasive and emotional. Yet the language, even when less than accurate, is uniquely suited to this play because it forms the cyclical verbal patterns that reflect Basshe's structural intent.

The structural antecedents of *The Centuries* are in Elizabethan drama, the last time in which plot was clearly subordinated to theme. Shakespeare's plays use variations on a theme to pass in and out from a character's emotions to his public function, and from there to a panorama of the society he inhabits. Each character's private life corresponds to social realities; harmony in one sphere results in harmony in the others. In this sense the Elizabethan vision was communal. But it was also hierarchic: perfect harmony reflected a fixed metaphysical order: God on high, Satan below; king at the top, peasants below (and bourgeoisie clawing at the middle). The world was (almost) in stasis. The notion of correspondence that Basshe dramatized in *The Centuries* is revolutionary and therefore dynamic. The material world is represented in the play by the recurring whir of the machines, the broken movements of the workers and the harshness of street life. But the material world is in constant flux, and when it changes, man's inner world also changes. As Gitel and Reuben, by leading a victorious strike, begin the long process of turning industrialization into a servant of the people, they are also transformed: "I've been born again." The workers they lead are changed, too, though in more objective ways (this is true of the play: that it always reflects from the inner life of Gitel and Reuben outward to the social realities around them). The quarrels, anger and frustration of the housewives become their joy as they talk of moving. The whir of the machines is punctuated by joyful tunes from the phonographs. At Yankel's wedding the old people dance to a

18

hired band. Outside on the street the young move freely to their own rhythms.

The Centuries leaves its characters long before they have achieved a socialist society; it ends with the housewives' hymns to their new homes, a preview of just the sort of insular family life that was impossible as long as poverty herded them together. In exchange for united strike action, Basshe offers his characters only a slightly more endurable form of capitalism. It is a contradiction that runs through people's theatre: though the revolution is the desired end, the immediate problem is to feed and house the people. But higher wages and more buying power cause them to become enmeshed in the same system they thought to overthrow.

Reviews of *The Centuries* were generally uncomprehending of the play and dissatisfied with the acting. Brooks Atkinson wrote in the *New York Times* of November 30, 1927:

[The Centuries] has subordinated story to form instead of letting the story dictate its own manner of expression. The faults are so elementary that mentioning them seems silly. Yet if "The Centuries" did not insist on putting the cart before the horse, the fun of staging a play on three levels, with ghastly chorus movements, would be entirely lost. In staging the New Playwrights have done uncommonly well. Their stage is recklessly small. By setting it with four exposed rooms and three series of stairs they make every inch of playing space earn its living. At present the New Playwrights lack intelligible plays and experienced actors*. Until they are better supplied with these two chief elements of drama, they will find their audience limited to their nervously expectant friends.

Unable to find a suitable director for the next production, *The International*, Lawson decided to direct his play himself, using most of the same actors who had been in *The Belt* when he sharply criticized the realistic staging by Edward Massey of that production. Relations were strained to begin

---

*Franchot Tone got his start acting at New Playwrights in *The Belt, The Centuries* and the lead in *The International*. Sylvia Feningston and Irwin Swirdlow were among the NPT actors who continued to work often.

with and they were complicated by the size of the production and Lawson's inexperience as a director. "I was aware of the contradiction between our economic exploitation of the actors and our desire to make them the backbone of the theatre. I knew (theoretically, at least) that the actor is the key to the theatrical experience . . . but I had a very mechanical approach to acting. I thought if I just told the actors what I wanted, they would do it. Finally, I was absolutely floored by the problem of acting and by the complexity of this production," Lawson says.

Throughout the second season the desperation must have been increasing. A single successful production would make NPT solvent and strengthen Kahn's commitment to the theatre; each playwright had to believe that his would be it. The economic tension fed their tempers and their uneasy relations with the actors—as it always does. The plays were becoming more revolutionary, but collective work was becoming impossible.

The scenery for *The International*, multiple-leveled bare platforms with scrim and sliding panels, was designed by Dos Passos. Choreography was by Don Oscar Becque, and the original score was by Edward A. Ziman. Lawson insisted his composer try to imitate the modernism of *Rite of Spring* and says the result was "loud with a little of the feeling of electronic music, but pretty uninteresting."

Processional! was the play that prefigured the aims of the New Playwrights most accurately because it dealt with the facts of US life (the Kentucky coal strike it portrayed was then in progress) in a manner that admitted entirely new emotions to the theatre. "It has a remarkable gift of pathos unique to our drama," Stark Young, who proved too genteel to continue as an admirer of people's theatre, wrote. In his preface to the play, Lawson explained:

I have endeavored to create a method which shall express the American scene in native idiom, a method as far removed from the older realism as from the facile mood of Expressionism. It is apparent that this new technique is essentially vaudevillesque in character—a development of the two-a-day and the musical extravaganza . . . . Here the national consciousness finds at least a partial reflection of itself in the mammy melody,

20

the song and dance act and the curtain of real pearls. Here the concern with a direct contact, an immediate emotional response across the footlights . . . . All around me I see the grotesques of the American language—these are Rabelaisian in their intensity . . . . Art as an escape from life is no better than morphine, rotary clubs, murder, speech-making, or any of the other methods used by hundred per-cent Americans to escape from actuality.

With *The International* Lawson meant to extend the experiment and the politics begun in *Processional!* He wanted to fuse drama, dance, music into a theatrical form that would be truly international (influenced not only by popular entertainments but by the libertine dances of Isadora Duncan, Stravinsky's triumphant *Rite of Spring*, dada, surrealism and Meyerhold) and would therefore be the best vehicle for presenting his version of the world-wide proletarian uprising. *The International* was a far less popular play than *Processional!* because a chaotic production, the bourgeois hostility to New Playwrights, and the Communist critics' quarrel with Lawson's politics stopped anybody from ever confronting the script. It is also far more ambitious and is full of the energy that belongs so distinctly to the playwright. "Pathos," yes, but also a wild contrariness, an audacity that is breathtaking and heartbreaking and which is part of Lawson the man, too, and has gotten him into plenty of trouble.

In *The Centuries* Basshe minimizes linear plot in favor of correspondences. In *The International* Lawson mocks plot by creating a wholly fantastic adventure story involving four components of the new world: a Russian Communist, a middle class intellectual, a woman revolutionary, and a lumpenproletarian who admires the masculinity of Mussolini's rule. These four go around the world, through prison, plane crash, starvation, and armed battles, always being rescued in the knick of time by improbable forces like the British imperialist army.

The International is not a serious play with some funny parts. It is a tragedy of defeated revolution—written just as Chang Kai Shek was murdering Communists in the streets and the US and England joined reactionary forces to put down a workers' strike in Shanghai—and it is a farce. It is an

21

intimate love story between an upper middle class boy, David, and a revolutionary girl, Alise, at the same time as it is a panorama of the wretched of the earth, whose symbolic center is the International Whore House, and an expose of US imperialism and the military-industrial complex.

The play employs two choruses of eight women each, who represent the people of Thibet, China, Italy, and Russia (in a scene cut from the acting version), office workers in New York, and prostitutes at Madame Miau's.

Three financiers, Fitch, Spunk, and Henley, are discussing news of oil deposits in Thibet—"a sphere of English influence jealously propagandized by the Russians." Fitch fears that oil profiteering might ignite the precarious situation in Asia. Spunk and Henley think the profits will be too great not to take that chance. Fitch's son David has contracted a lot of Marxist ideas in college. He wants a working class adventure but is persuaded to go along with Henley to Thibet. There David meets Karneski, a lone revolutionary whose rusty cannon is pointing at the capital:

> ... Wherever you Americans go, blood and money walk hand in hand, worse than the English—but you're too late here! When this machine goes off . . . and frankly I can't control it at all—the status of this dead old country will be changed . . . .
>
> A ritual my friend! Like to light a candle, speak a high word, spit upon an altar . . . a little thing in itself but in such things there lies the seed of change.

Karneski, David, Henley, Alise, and Tim, the Amerikans' pilot and a fascist sympathizer, are arrested. Henley is brutally tortured for Karneski's deed and in a fit of madness that occurs during an audience with the ruler he murders the "Living Buddha of Lhasa." It is capitalism trampling on one of its most faithful supporters, mysticism, and it causes the dying industrialist to remark: "I stumbled over a grave an' it was myself lying in it."

Alise and David make it back to New York via Paris, where David's father is meeting to discuss military aid to help crush the people's uprising. The two young people become leaders of the world-wide revolution as it spreads to the U.S.

In *Processional!* Lawson's experiments with new ways to

motivate his characters became fused with his desire to unite music and dance with drama. He hit upon a jazz form that seemed to move its characters according to their unconscious attention to its rhythm. Sadie Cohen, the woman-child emotional center of the play, is constantly dancing and swaying to rhythms she half understands but which make her go into the darkened mine with the strike leader and want to have his baby. She, like Alise, represents Lawson's recurrent fascination with the myth in *Rite of Spring*: the girl who dances herself to death to ensure a fruitful harvest.

The International is more complex; it wanders around the globe and through three possible modes of being in the world. The first is the pre-revolutionary capitalist sensibility, represented in realistic dialogue, between the financiers, between them and the French diplomats, and, in the early scenes, between David and his father.

The second mode is represented by the tangential responses of one character to another that are borrowed from surrealism and which signify a rupture in the established order, a spiritual breakdown in the conventional connections between people. The tangential response appears in *The International* at those places where characters of different classes or social experiences meet. David and his father speak tangentially toward the end of the play; they respond not to each other but to the thoughts that one person's remark sets off inside the other's head.

DAVID: I'm against you then. I choose between life and death!
FITCH: We're in danger here, here in my office above Wall Street . . . danger, do you understand?
DAVID: I saw red flags in Union Square, and signs, "Don't kill your brothers in China."
FITCH: Guns will clear the streets.

The tangential mode is used strikingly earlier in the play when the businessman Spunk comes to the International Whore House. He wants the prostitute Gussie to give him relief from his fear of impending revolution.

SPUNK: A curse is on me, the curse of a map with blood on it!
Like a bed where the world lies.
GUSSIE: Warm bed, hot bed.
Groanin in the bed!

23

SPUNK: Dance Faster . . .
  I lie between cold sheets,
  Lying on a cold bed,
  Dreaming of a map!
  I tell you, I'm tortured—
GUSSIE: I can hurt you new ways
  I can love you true ways . . .
  Jesus how it hurts, Jesus how it hurts!
  She throws herself on bed sobbing bitterly.

Later on Gussie strangles Spunk to death; the man who has treated the world as his personal whore house to be exploited at will is murdered by the object of his delight. The world revolution is personalized in one bitter act of revenge.

The third mode of response is affirmative; it allows for communal and exultant proclamations of a new age. These choral odes contain the verbal images of fertility of which Alise and the prostitutes are the dynamic symbols. Affirmation occurs when the office workers and the prostitutes respond to the pulse of the revolution. As the uprising continues in the street below, Fitch calls his workers to take dictation. They stand around him stiff and sallow-faced, writing without thinking: "Vast interests are at stake in all parts of the world . . . . Under the direction of wise generals . . . . From a steel tower in Wall Street, I speak!" David interrupts his father: "It won't do they're singing around you." Suddenly, the stenographers become aware of the street noises: "Change . . . not change . . . change (in strained, unnatural voices) Change is on us!" The rhythms of typewriters, adding machines, pencil sharpeners explode into triumphant chords, the workers begin to dance: "We are not ourselves, we are." As they move to the new rhythms they transcend their old, limited acceptance of life. They join Alise as she speaks to the prostitutes.

ALISE: Lie on a tower to conceive buildings, the will of a people upon
  you, the two rivers of a city flow into you.
FIRST CHORUS (WORKERS): We are the ground that got no seed.
SECOND CHORUS: We are the fields that got no plow . . .
  We are the whores white with shame . . .
ALISE: Mothers of something without a name!
FULL CHORUS: Give us wings.
ALISE: I give you a sword to cut the strings!
FULL CHORUS: Tell us how . . . tell us how . . .

24

ALISE: It is now . . . Now!

The Act III curtain falls on a triumphant cry. In Act IV this communal affirmation dissipates under force. The revolution is being crushed on the streets, so David, in order to keep something of it, personalizes the revolution through his love for Alise even as she denies her womanhood to personify the agony of the revolution's defeat:

If you want me, you must lie on the breasts of guns, your arms be the wings that flank the coming machines.

They die together on the barricades they have helped erect in the street, as Tim, the lumpenproletariat, steps drunkenly out of an overturned taxi:

How do I get home? Christ, for the love a'pity, where do I go home.

He is shot by US troops brought to New York to restore order.

The affirmative segments in *The International* are not wholly equal to the idea of transcendence that dictated them. The language (and most likely the music and maybe the dance as well) works mainly by simple addition, never quite managing to create the multiple psychological and physical images of fulfillment that liberation should allow. Such a complex problem could not have been solved without a close reciprocal relationship with the actors. But failure to solve it meant failing to sustain the revolution on stage, and Lawson could not do otherwise than end his play with its defeat.

The Communist press did not like *The International*. NPT had placed ads in the *Daily Worker* announcing that it was the "first Communist play to be produced in an American Theatre," but it struck their reviewer, Sender Garlin, as being full of "the intellectual confusion characteristic of most liberal minds." He objected that the workers' roles were minimized while the hero was the son of a millionaire and, further, that having the Communist Karneski fire a cannon that begins a global conflict not only put the Soviet Union in a bad light but was historically inaccurate. Joseph Freeman, a *New Masses* editor and critic, visited Lawson and they had a

25

long argument during which Lawson defended his play against charges that in it he had misconceived the nature of revolution. Dos Passos wrote the *Worker* to say that Garlin's review "seemed to be written from the same angle as those in the capitalist press, the angle of contemporary Broadway 'realism.'" Lawson was strongly committed to the theatrical style of the piece and knew it could not be judged according to realistic standards; yet he also felt himself in a contradictory position of "trying to abolish Broadway narrative values, and yet falling into the giant trap of romanticism."

It is possible that the distaste of Garlin and Freeman for the play was motivated by their knowledge of the Russian Communist Party's slow drift toward socialist realism and the corresponding decline in Meyerhold's prestige. Although these events were beginning to take shape in 1927, it is just as probable that their dislike for *The International* was stirred by a chaotic production that went far toward emphasizing every deficiency in the play.

Subsequent to the failure of *The International*, Lawson went through a period of "grave uncertainty" about what to write next (and where to get it produced*) that corresponded to the dilemma of many artists who, by the late twenties, sensed the twin disasters of fascism and economic collapse,

---

*Lawson earned his living in Hollywood and supplied the Group Theatre and Broadway with three plays (*Success Story, The Pure in Heart, Gentlewoman*) which continued to focus on radical themes while being cast in the realistic-romantic modes the commercial theatre preferred. At one time Harold Clurman thought Lawson was "the hope" of the Group, but, in fact, their favored styles were almost diametrically opposed. Lawson's labor play, *Marching Song*, was produced by the Theatre Union in 1937. Until his death at age forty, Basshe continued to work around the theatre, as stage manager for the Theatre Guild and author of two short plays that were produced at one of the regular radical theatre nights during the thirties. He also wrote a full-length play, *Doomsday Circus*; it was never produced in New York. Faragoh became a successful screen writer until he was blacklisted in 1951; he never worked in the industry again and died at the end of the decade. His sensitive play about child labor, *Sunup to Sundown*, was produced on Broadway in 1938, directed by Joseph Losey. Gold stopped writing plays and devoted himself to journalism. He became the staunchest US supporter of socialist realism and his criticism, under the pressure of the Depression and the hope of a radical victory, becomes more and more strident and less constructive. His very good proletarian novel, *Jews Without Money*, was published in 1930.

26

and wondered just how useful their art would be in getting people through them:

> I wrote a one page outline for a play that echoes the political concerns of *The International* and includes some of what became *Success Story*. A man tries to kill himself by jumping out of an office window. Something breaks his fall and he ends up in a hospital full of glass and it's uncertain whether he'll live or die. He has an ether dream in which a voice comes to him and says: "If you live you will have to go through fascism and another world war and the suffering of millions of people and death and disaster. Do you want to live or die?" He says: "I want to live." That's all I could figure out about the play. And in a way that's plenty.

John Dos Passos

DID THE NEW PLAYWRIGHTS THEATRE FAIL?*

"In the face of these results which may be important in the history of the theatre, even important politically, and which were achieved in the midst of tremendous difficulties both human and cultural, one may fairly say that the failure of our enterprise is relatively unimportant."**

This is a good text on which to hang a summing up of what the New Playwrights Theatre did and did not accomplish.

In the first place, I think you can cross out political results. The American mind of all classes and denominations is too accustomed to keeping art or ideas in separate watertight compartments. Their influence on action is infinitesimal and only to be measured in generations and major emotional movements.

Now so far as the results in the theatre! I don't feel that the various people who have worked with and for the New Playwrights Theatre at different times need to be ashamed of their work or to feel that they wasted their time.

Loudspeaker, in spite of many crudities, was a fairly successful attempt to put a political farce into three dimensions, to break down the pictureframe stage and to turn a stream of satire on the audience vigorously and unashamedly. It was fairly natural that the audience, being used to the conventions of the picture frame and to the carefully pigeonholed distinctions of farce, musical comedy, drama, didn't like it. Hatred of novelty is one of the main characteristics of the human

---

*The New Masses, August 1929.

**This is a quotation from an article by Erwin Piscator about the failure of the Volksbuhne in Germany, which was translated by Anna Rochester and had appeared in *The New Masses* of the previous month.

27

organism. But if you want a new theatre, there's nothing to do but to have one and to let the audience recover its equilibrium as it can. You can't make an omelet without breaking eggs.

Earth was not a very successful production, but it was important as the incubator for the method of treating a play like a musical composition that was later so successful in *Singing Jailbirds* [by Upton Sinclair, done as the first production of the third season] * and I think that Emjo Basshe is likely to develop still further when he gets the chance. The play itself seems to me to be a masterpiece.

The Belt was a success all along the line. It was a play that had something to say very much in the spirit of American workers; it said it simply and recklessly and the audience understood.

The Centuries was an experiment with multiple stages carried out with great difficulty on account of the small size of the theatre. There were moments when the production came off. Anyway it was probably the first attempt in America to put an ethnological document on the stage, to move the audience with a slice of history of a race [sic] instead of with episodes in the lives of individual puppets.

The International, I feel, was the most interesting experiment we made. Many people disagree with me I know. The form of farce-melodrama it seems to me is one of the best for transmitting large-scale ideas to an audience. The enormous popularity of this form in Russia at present more or less proves that. In Lawson's play it was combined with a series of direct lyrical outbursts like those of the choruses of Greek tragedy. In the production all the conventions of the picture frame stage were dropped and an attempt was made to introduce the audience to a set of conventions much nearer those of the ballet or operatic pageant. You couldn't show 'em a thing. People of all shades of political opinion united in damning it. I think in many cases it was the successful scenes [which] annoyed people most. It was obvious that there were many weaknesses in the last act of the play and that much of the acting was poor and a large part of the production rather sketched in than accomplished. But I think the reason why the abuse was so universal was that in *The International* a new type of theatre was taken for granted. And everybody was trying to see it in terms of a three-act problem play by Pinero.

Hoboken Blues was more or less a failure, due partly to what Mrs. Eddy used to call the malicious animal magnetism that by that time surrounded the theatre, and partly to the fact that nobody would take for granted the rather childish but unpretentious blackface minstrel show method of presentation.

Singing Jailbirds was the best example presented of the method where a director treats the play as if it were a musical score. I think it

*Piscator staged Sinclair's *Singing Jailbirds* a month before the NPT production opened in 1928 (by this time Basshe had taken over the theatre).
—Ed.

28

got over so easily to the audience because it did not depart too far from the methods of expressionism with which they were already familiar.

About my own play [*Airways, Inc.*] I can only say that, in spite of much adverse criticism, from my own point of view the production was very successful: the best acting we ever had and a method of setting and direction that made the audience accept the elimination of the proscenium and the curtain without batting an eyelash.

It may seem silly to many people, my continued harping on abolishing the pictureframe stage where the audience lets itself be tricked into imagining that it is *really* seeing a slice of life. I think it is very important. That form and content in the theatre are indissolubly linked is a sort of axiom that needs no argument. The revolutionary theatre will aim to justify the ways of politics (mass action) to the individual-in-the-mass much the way the Greek theatre justified the ways of priestinterpreted gods to the citizens of the city republic. The whole scale and category of ideas is entirely different from that of the bourgeois theatre which aimed to make the lives of wealthy or hope to be wealthy people interesting, exciting, tragic or funny to them for a couple of hours after dinner. The first step toward realizing a revolutionary theatre seems to me to be to work with new tools. This, neither radicals nor reactionaries are willing to grant, [n]or the fact that the first attempts with new tools are sure to be clumsy.

Einstein said last summer that Meyerhold had carried the theatre as far as it was possible to take it in every possible direction and that the theatre was dead in the modern world. I don't agree with him, though I think it fairly obvious that all that function of the theatre which came to be more economically and successfully taken over by the talkies is damned. It seems to me that the theatre still has enough vitality even in America to carve out an empire for itself if it can show enough flexibility to use the tools that are being discarded by dying circuses and vaudeville shows. It's nip and tuck and the theatre director must have the means to use each living instrument at hand and discard everything that shows the slightest taint of death and decay.

I think the New Playwrights Theatre failed, in the first place because authors are largely too preoccupied with their own works to make good producers, and secondly because the problems involved were not seen clearly enough in the beginning. But the fact that it existed makes the next attempt in the same direction that much easier. One thing is certain: the time for halfway measures in ideas or methods is gone, if indeed it ever was.

WORKERS THEATRE

What, then can propaganda do? It can, in general, express the proletarian's own instincts in a new, more definite and more apt form. It can sometimes precipitate and facilitate the awakening consciousness of the masses themselves. It can make them conscious of what they are, of what they feel, and of what they instinctively wish; but never can propaganda make them what they are not, nor awaken in their hearts passions which are foreign to their own history.

Michael Bakunin

The Depression affected the US theatre more deeply than any other event ever has—it was an actual, insufferable and nearly complete explosion of the Amerikan Dream. Its first significant theatrical consequence—as unemployment rose to four million in 1930, eight million in 1931 and peaked at thirteen million in 1933—was to justify in the public imagination the existence of voices that offered alternatives to catastrophic capitalism. In the twenties most people thought of the Bolshevik Revolution as a disreputable and godless threat. Now there was widespread interest in the Marxism that inspired it. By 1931 it was common knowledge that the Soviet Union was successfully completing its first Five Year Plan and was on the way to becoming an important industrial power. Most impressive: there was virtually no unemployment in the USSR.

The first people to respond to the Depression with an emotion more substantial than strained disbelief were the foreign born and radical workers in the ghettos. The twenties hadn't been so great for them: unemployment was already about two million, wages were low, unions were weak and without bargaining power. On March 6, 1930, barely five months after the stock market crash, the Communist Party organized demonstrations in major cities around the world protesting unemployment and wage slashing. The *New York Times* for the following day was filled with reports of police violence. In Paris 20,000 police massed to prevent any demonstration. In New York when 35,000 workers decided to march from Union Square to City Hall to confront Mayor Wagner they were charged by 1,000 police "supported by scores of detectives, motorcyclemen and emergency service crews." In Detroit mounted police charged a crowd of 75,000; in Cleveland twenty persons were injured during clashes with police. In Washington, D.C., police caused a riot by tossing tear gas into the crowd just as government office workers were pouring into the streets for lunch. Earlier they had pulled the demonstration leader from the base of the White House fence where he was attempting to speak and beat him. President Hoover, however, was "not disturbed." A Boston march on the State House was broken up by police. Demonstrations in Philadelphia, Chicago, and San Francisco were peaceful.

Already during 1928 and '29 perhaps a dozen workers' theatres were springing in and out of existence, performing militant labor plays written or adapted by their own members at radical union meetings. Most of these groups were foreign language speaking. They had all been inspired by the agitational theatres of the Soviet Union which they knew were disseminating revolutionary axioms in factories and fields, and by the agitation-propaganda theatres of the workers movement in Germany. Such theatres made sense in Communist Russia and in economically depleted and politically chaotic Germany. In the US, in the prosperous, self-satisfied twenties, they attracted little attention outside radical circles. But once the stock market crashed, these agitprop theatres did not even have to camouflage their Communist bias. All they had to do was to take their explanation of the economic crisis out of the union hall and into the streets. It could not help but be more convincing than the official government explanation that persisted throughout 1931.

The Hoover Administration said that the stock market

crash was only a temporary interruption in the upward trend of securities. It comforted the country with assurances that jobs would be restored and prosperity regained. It urged them to look backwards, to remember the good old days and to meet the crisis with the same passivity that the government displayed. Hoover was willing to give federal money to keep banks and railroads solvent but he adamantly opposed any "dole" for the jobless and destitute. He thought relief was economically unsound and regarded it as morally offensive because it would discourage initiative among the working class.

Certainly the street play *Vote Communist*, which told its audience:

> The Communist Party leads the workers in their fight against starvation. The Communist Party leads the workers in their fight for unemployment relief and social insurance . . . .

had at least as much appeal in 1931 as Hoover's assurances that the workers weren't really hungry (government studies of hospital death lists showed no one was *dying* of starvation) and that private charities were adequate to care for the few who were temporarily "idle."

It is curious to remember the content and title of this play in light of charges made in the forties and fifties by the House Committee on Un-Amerikan Activities that the Communist Party sought to overthrow the government of the United States by violence. The fact is that as soon as economic conditions in this country began to foment general unrest, the Communist Party began to urge the establishment of socialism through legal and electoral means.

An Election Play for Street Performances

VOTE COMMUNIST*

Performed by the first agit-prop Street Group in New York in 1931. Revised for the next election campaign.

Note: Plays for street performances should always have some kind of a prelude to attract .the workers to give them time to

------
Workers Theatre, June-July, 1932.

gather around the platform. The content of the play, therefore, should begin a few minutes after the performances started. The slogans of the capitalist and the workers at the first page of this play are to be considered at the prelude.

Characters:

CAPITALIST (representing at the same time the three capitalist parties: Republican, Democratic, and Socialist Party)

NEUTRAL PERSON (willing to get rich; later one of the workers)

3 WORKERS with megaphones; mingle with audience

COMMUNIST (first in audience)

I.

CAP: (on platform) (Top hat and big $ sign) Prosperity! Prosperity is just around the corner!

1st. W: —————We are starving!

CAP: We will give you wine and beer!

COMM: —————We cannot pay our rent!

CAP: Donate to block-aid!

2nd W: —————We have no clothing!

CAP: Keep your money in circulation!

3rd W: —————12 million unemployed!

CAP: America first!

2nd W: —————Thousands of workers committing suicide!

CAP: We have given 500 million dollars to stabilize our banks!

1st W: —————Workers get police clubs and bullets instead of relief!

CAP: Make the world safe for democracy!

2nd W: —————Thousands of workers arrested!

1st W: —————Deportation of the Foreign Born!

3rd W: —————Discrimination against Negroes!

CAP: RIGHT OR WRONG—MY COUNTRY!

WORK: —————1. Wage-cuts, 2. Speed-up, C. Lay-offs, 3. Child labor, N.P. Evictions, 2. Suicides, 1. Depression, C. Crisis.

CAP: (After every word CAP. says "Keep smiling.") Then: NO DEPRESSION FOR ME . . . .

N.P.: Why is there no depression for you?

CAP: Because I learned the trick of making money.

N.P.: I would like to make money, too. How about teaching me your trick?

CAP: Well, that's a very big order. I'll do it—on one condition . . . .

N.P.: And that is?

CAP: You have to be a good boy! First lesson: You can't get rich working. The only way to get rich is to make others work for you. And remember, the longer the hours you make them work, the more money you make for yourself. The more you speed them up, the more money you make for yourself. The less you pay them, the more money you make for yourself. The more you exploit them, the

33

quicker you get rich like me. You get me?

N.P.: Yes, but you are only 1% of the population. How is it that the other 99%—the workers—stand for it? How is it that so many millions of workers let themselves be exploited by a handful of bosses?

CAP: Easy! Second lesson: Give money to the schools and the teachers will teach the children to die defending your interest. Give money to the press and the newspapers will print any lies you want.—Money will do the trick!

N.P.: But suppose, there is **only one** worker who gets wise to you? He'll explain these lies to the other workers and they, of course, will rise and overthrow the whole system.

CAP: In this case, my dear fellow, you have the police and the army. Such workers are clubbed, put into jail, framed up and given the electric chair.—Get rid of any rebellious workers! No matter how!—You get me?

N.P.: Yes,—but—we are going to have elections. Every worker has a vote. All these workers will get together and vote against me. How can I keep these workers from voting?

CAP: On the contrary. You have to **insist that they vote.** But you have to teach them **how** to vote. You can appear before them in various forms and make them **vote for you.** Now, watch me, I'll show you how to do it.

Puts on Sign: Republican

CAP. R: My dear workers! The Republican Party is always trying to better the conditions of the workers. We believe that rugged individualism is the backbone of our prosperity.

2nd W: The rugged individualism of Rockefeller to massacre miners!

1st W: The rugged individualism of Ford to fire on starving workers!

3rd W: Rugged individualism is the backbone of capitalist exploitation!

CO: Rugged individualism is the right of the bosses to step on the workers!

CAP. R: The Republican Party has always had the interest of the workers at heart.

CO: That's a lie! Here, I'll show you what he has at heart! (*Tears down sign: Republican, money bag and big $ sign is seen*)

CAP: (*Puts on sign "Democrat"*) My beloved workers! Do you really believe that the Republican Party is interested in the workers? Who backs that grand old party anyway? The Big Bankers!

2nd W: And who backs the Democratic Party?

1st W: The bosses!

N.P.: What is the difference between the bankers and bosses?

3rd W: None!

N.P.: And what is the difference between the Republican Party and the Democratic Party?

3rd W: None!

CAP. D: The Democratic Party has always had the interest of the workers at heart!

CO: That's a lie! That's what he has at heart!

Tears down sign "Democrat", $ sign is seen again)

CAP: *(Puts on sign "Socialist")* Ladies and Gentlemen! Fellow workers! The Socialist Party does not agree with the existing system. But that does not mean that we have to overthrow it by violence. The Socialist Party does not believe in violence.

CO: In all countries the socialists voted for war appropriations during the world war.

2nd W: —because the Socialist Party does not believe in violence!

1st W: The German Socialists under Noske and Ebert shot down thousands of workers!

2nd W: —because the Socialist Party doesn't believe in violence!

3rd W: Socialist Mayors in Reading and Milwaukee had workers clubbed and arrested!

2nd W: —because the Socialist Party doesn't believe in violence!

CAP. S: Ladies and Gentlemen! Fellow workers! These are minor shortcomings. Theoretically we are for a straight, but sensible Socialism which is to be built up thru cooperation of all classes.

1st W: Cooperation between bosses and workers?!

3rd W: Cooperation between parasites and producers?!

CO: Cooperation between exploiters and exploited?!

CAP. S: Don't you realize the point? The bosses have the money, the bosses have the jobs, the bosses have the goods, the bosses have the food, and the bosses have the police. Therefore, when you want money, jobs, goods, and food, then you have to cooperate with the bosses who will provide you with . . . .

CO: POLICE!

CAP. S: You—are—a Communist!

CO: Yes, **I am a Communist!** And you are *(tears down sign)* a **Capitalist.** *(pointing to the sign)* That's what is behind the Republican Party, what is behind the Democratic Party, and what is behind the Socialist Party: Three different masks to hide **one** enemy: the Capitalist Class.

CAP: Workers, I am not your enemy at all. Cooperate with me, and you will get what you want—as far as your demands are reasonable.

1st W: The 12 Million Unemployed demanded jobs or relief. What did they get?

2nd W: Machine guns and tear-gas from the police. Flop-houses, breadlines, slop apples for sale . . . .

1st W: The bosses wont give anything to the unemployed unless we force them thru militant struggle.

CO: The Communist Party leads the workers in their fight against starvation. The Communist Party leads the workers in their fight for unemployment relief and social insurance at the expense of the state

35

and the bosses. Therefore Vote Communist!

ALL: Vote Communist!

CAP: Workers, vote republican, vote democrat, vote socialist, no matter which of them, but vote for me. I give you the jobs. I pay you the wages . . . .

1st W: You cut our wages

2nd W: 10%

3rd W: 20%

1st W: 50%

2nd W: No Factory

3rd W: No shop

1st W: No store

2nd W: —without wage-cuts.

CO: The Communist Party fights against the Hoover wage-cutting policy. The Communist Party and the Trade Union Unity League leads the workers in their fight for higher pay and better working conditions. Therefore—Vote Communist!

ALL: Vote Communist!

CO: The Communist Party fights against the deportation and persecution of foreign born workers. The Communist Party fights for all exploited workers, regardless of sex, age, race, or nationality. Therefore—Vote Communist!

ALL: Vote Communist!!

COM: The Communist Party fights lynching and discrimination against Negro workers. The Communist Party demands equal rights for the Negroes and self-determination for the Black Belt. Vote Communist!

ALL: For the unity of negro and white workers! Vote Communist!

COM: The Communist Party fights against bosses and for the defense of the Chinese people and the Soviet Union.

1st W: Workers! Organize and fight!

2nd W: Against the Hunger and war offensive of the Capitalists!

3rd W: For the Unity of the working class!

COM: Vote for the Communist Candidates!

1st & 2nd: Vote Communist!

1st, 2nd, 3rd: Vote Communist!!

ALL: VOTE COMMUNIST!!!

In April 1931, Workers Theatre League, an organization of Communist working class theatres around the country, founded a monthly magazine. In *Workers Theatre* they printed scripts, notices of performances and activities, articles about the aesthetics of agitprop. No one argued whether or not the workers' sketches were responsible for a new aesthetic. It was apparent they possessed artistic virtues completely absent from the bourgeois stage. The workers were poor and they played for free (perhaps this is the most radical gesture a theatre in Amerika has ever been able to make: abolish money). They were amateurs and to be at all effective they had to emphasize the group's ability over that of individual members. So their organization and their production methods became reflections of their communal class consciousness. Their theatre was decentralized and it was non-competitive. They were mobile troupes playing in union halls or on the streets and they could not rely upon sets. They expected their work to be useful to the class struggle instead of conforming to preconceived notions about the art of the theatre. Facts and ideas were more important than emotions. Rather than reproduce the social struggle on stage, they presented it with symbols and gestures—like the dollar-sign vest or the capitalist's silk hat and his strut. These were simple devices but they, like Brecht's *Gestus*, made the social experience of each character immediately clear. The workers' agitprop plays began to turn the theatre back into a public place. You didn't have to peek through a keyhole to become involved. You were already involved by virtue of being alive in industrial Amerika. The problem on stage wasn't *like* your problem, it *was* your problem.

In November 1931, Hallie Flanagan, director of the Experimental Theatre at Vassar College and later head of the Federal Theatre, introduced the workers' movement to the establishment with an article in *Theatre Arts* called "A Theatre Is Born." She wrote:

If the [workers'] theatre can throw all these things [of the commercial theatre] into the discard it may perhaps become, as it has been at certain great moments of its history, a place where an idea is so ardently enacted that it becomes the belief of actors and audience alike.*

John E. Bonn was the editor of *Workers Theatre* and the most vocal theorist in the movement. For the May 1932 issue he wrote a long article in which he noted the substantial growth of the new movement and discussed its evolving form and function.

---

*Later in the decade members of Congress who wanted to abolish the WPA Arts Projects would quote this article as evidence of the subversive sympathies of Federal Theatre's director.

John E. Bonn

DRAM BURO REPORT*

COMRADES:

Two weeks ago the Agitprop Department of the Communist Party called upon the workers theatres in New York for active participation in the coming election campaign. A week ago the Unemployed Council of the Harlem Section New York asked for an Agitprop group to give regularly street performances at open air meetings. Yesterday's Spartakiade in which 14 workers theatres of New York, Newark, Philadelphia, and Chicago participated proved that the political and artistic quality of our groups stands well in comparison with the best workers theatres of other countries.

The simultaneity of all these events shows that it is not just an accident that this conference takes place at this time. This conference was necessary at this moment, in order to conclude a certain period in our development and to begin a new phase in the history of the workers theatres of this country. This is the moment when the "splendid isolation" of the workers theatres of this country, from each other, from the masses, and from the political events, has been definitely canceled, when the American workers theatres finally abandoned that "minority complex" willingness to be a second hand means of amateur entertainment by and for workers, when we are conscious of our political task and responsibility toward the working class. And this is the moment, when the workers and the working class organizations, instead of ignoring us or smiling at our attempts as they used to do, recognize us as an important factor in the revolutionary movement of the working class.

THE POLITICAL BACKGROUND

This turn in the history of the workers theatre movement of the U. S. A. coincides with a most important event in world history: the crisis of the capitalist system and the rise of Soviet System, the transition of the political and crisis of the capitalist system and the rise of the economic dictatorship from the capitalists to the workers. While in one sixth of the world the rule of the proletariat has been established, in the other part of the world the capitalists are still strong enough to defend their lost position—at the expense of the toiling masses. And we, the workers of this country of prosperity, feel this burden no less than our brothers in the other capitalist countries.

THE BOURGEOIS THEATRE

All the culture is determined by and is the expression of the

*Workers Theatre, May 1932. Edited version KMT.

bourgeois theatre. The bourgeois theatre is also a weapon in the class struggle—on the side of the bosses.

On the other hand, the bourgeois theatre reacts passively, as a victim of the capitalist crisis. More and more theatres are forced to close. The economic situation. The capitalist decay must find its reaction in the capitalist, i.e. bourgeois theatre.

The bourgeois theatre takes an active part in the class struggle on the side of the capitalists. It broadcasts the bourgeois-capitalist ideology. It covers the facts of capitalist decay. Just think of all the plays and movies demonstrating, explicitly or implicitly, that money does not make happy homes, that every worker in this country has a chance to become a millionaire when he starts as an obedient wage slave and rises to exploit others, that millionaires are often unhappy and always charitable, that we have to defend and to die for "our country" etc., etc. The erroneous conception of many of us that the bourgeois theatre is a matter of "art for art's sake" while the workers theatre is a weapon in the class struggle, must be revised. The slogan, "art for art's sake", is nothing but a cover for the political reactionary character of the remaining theatres reduce the wages of the employed actors, directors, and workers to a minimum. The number of the unemployed theatre artists and workers is growing from day to day. The artistically highest form of the bourgeois theatre, the "Little Theatre", has practically disappeared. And even the cinema and the most popular American form, the "vaudeville", are in the same critical situation.

OUR ATTITUDE TOWARD THE BOURGEOIS THEATRE

Our attitude toward the bourgeois theatre was up to now incorrect. I in particular had taken a wrong leftist standpoint in my report at the Workers Cultural Conference on June 14, 1931, when I stated that there is no relation between bourgeois theatre and workers theatre, as the bourgeois theatre approaches the rich while the workers theatre approaches the workers. This attitude led to a dangerous neglect of the bourgeois theatre. But after a closer study and wider experience I now agree fully with my critics who urged a more active attitude toward the bourgeois theatre. The bourgeois theatre, as an instrument of our class enemy, must be fought by exposing its class character to the workers, by replacing it by a qualified workers theatre art. As a victim of capitalist decay the bourgeois theatre must be attacked by approaching those who are affected by the crisis, in order to win them over into the ranks of the class conscious militant workers.

THE AIMS OF THE WORKERS THEATRE

In contrast to the bourgeois theatre, the workers theatre shows openly its political character: it is the theatre of the revolution, it is a weapon for the workers in the class struggle. We expose the whole capitalist system with all its tools. We expose the class character of the bourgeois press, of the police, of the army, of the courts, of the church, of the schools, and of all capitalist institutions. We must propagandize the campaigns for Unemployment Insurance, for liberation of political prisoners, for strike relief. We must report and analyze the day-to-day events. We must prove that the revolution is the only way out. And we have to broadcast the truth about the Soviet Union, and the necessity for all workers to defend their only fatherland.

But it is not enough to propagandize and to dramatize the class struggle. The workers theatre must take an active part in the class struggle. We must support and build up the revolutionary mass organizations by raising money and by winning over the workers. We must help the revolutionary press by collecting money, by winning new readers and subscribers. The workers theatre must stand in the front of the class struggle, reflecting it and carrying it out.

METHOD OF WORK

As agitation and propaganda groups, we have to convince the masses of workers of the necessity of the class struggle and to arouse them to action. But how can we propagandize the class struggle if we are not clear about it ourselves? How can we inspire our fellow-workers to action if the spirit of action is not in ourselves? That means: the basic prerequisite for a successful work is

Political Training

of each member and political orientation of our entire work. Not before each group considers itself as a shock brigade and each group member feels as a soldier in the class struggle can we expect to fulfill the other prerequisite of our work:

Proletarian Discipline

I do not have to explain here why workers theatres have to expect more discipline and more responsibility from each individual member than other organizations. Everyone of us is convinced of this necessity. However, for many of us the question is still open, how to accomplish the necessary group discipline. One thing we know by experience: we cannot and will not enforce this discipline. It must be a voluntary discipline, which can only be the result of political education. A group member who does not understand the political importance of his group cannot keep a strict proletarian discipline. A group member who is convinced of the political necessity of our work cannot act undisciplined and irresponsible.

Collective Method

based on political education and on voluntary discipline guarantees the best results.

THE PROBLEM OF FORM

What should the Workers Theatre look like? Which is the proper form for our plays, for our staging, for our acting? When we compare *Workers Theatre* with the Workers Theatre magazines of other countries we find that we in this country are more concerned with these problems than our comrades elsewhere. Again and again we meet articles, speeches, discussions, letters dealing with the following problems: Shall we learn from the bourgeois theatre or not? Do we need a stationary theatre or an Agitprop Theatre? Shall we write and perform naturalistic or symbolistic plays? Shall we use scenery, costumes, and make-up or not? The way these questions are put shows that most of us have a purely formalistic therefore wrong approach toward the problem of form. We understand the aims, working conditions, players, directors, writers, audience of the workers theatre are different from those of the bourgeois theatre, and at the same time, we try to find the appropriate form for our theatre among the forms existing in the bourgeois theatre! This is an obvious contradiction.

We cannot wait or look for a ready made style for our new theatre; we have to develop the style of the workers theatre by bringing it in conformity with its tasks and its means of expression.

MOBILITY

Our task is to bring the message of the class struggle to as many workers as possible. When we want to reach the masses it is not enough to wait until they come to us or call for us. We have to go there where the masses are: in meetings, in workers affairs, on the streets, at factory gates, in parades, at picnics, in workingclass neighborhoods. That means we must be mobile.

Our organizational structure, our plays, the term of our production must be such that we are able to travel with our production from one place to another, that we are able to give the same effective performance on a stage, on a bare platform, on the streets.

PROPAGANDA AND ENTERTAINMENT

It is not enough to bring our message to the masses. It is necessary that the masses accept our message. Our production must be such that the workers like them. We have to consider the expectations of the audience. And a theatre audience expects in the first place entertainment. A production with the best political content is worthless if this content is not presented in a form which is interesting for a workers audience. But we do not achieve this entertainment value by adding certain entertaining elements—like a dance, a song, a special stage effect—to the political content. The form in which we express our propaganda must contain the entertainment value. Both elements—propaganda and entertainment must be interwoven in a workers theatre performance.

41

SIMPLICITY AND ART

The organizers, players, writers, and directors of workers theatres are workers, the audiences are workers. Both are not prepared by a long literary and cultural education, which is only available to the members of the bourgeois class who have the leisure and the money for it. Worker players are not able to express, and worker audiences are not able to understand, complicated structures of ideas and refined intellectual language. The workers theatre plays must be simple, so that workers can produce them and workers can understand them. Simplicity, however, does not mean crudity, does not mean absence of art. On the contrary: the more artistic our productions are, the more effective they are, and the more efficient is the political education and propaganda we carry. The art of workers theatre will be an art using the simplest elements, according to creative elements at our disposal, according to our economic situation and according to our audience.

In 1928 several German-speaking radicals, led by Bonn and Anne Howe, had formed the *Prolet-Buhne*. The group developed a rhythmic choral delivery style and they continued the mass chant form Gold had employed in *Strike!* in 1926, which was used by poets like Langston Hughes (*Angelo Herndon Jones*) and Alfred Kremborg (*America, America!*) throughout the thirties. Mass chants are another manifestation of the notion implicit in the New Playwrights work: that an external rhythm might determine an emotional response that will then lead to a radical action. In *The International*, office workers mime the constricted movements of stenography until the noise from the uprising in the streets liberates their muscles—making them dance—and turns their mechanistic responses into affirmative ones. In the chants, performers being united first by an artificial means—an imposed rhythm—find as they allow themselves to follow that rhythm that the individuality separating them from their neighbors is less than they expected. They are united. Even if just tenuously enough to be able to speak and move together, it is still more securely than they had previously believed. In this way the symbol turns into the reality; the new rhythms become, temporarily, at least, the new life style. The audience becomes involved when it joins the performers at the end of the chant in a united action—usually the singing of "The Internationale."

The Prolet-Buhne's *Scottsboro*, first performed in 1931, is the earliest mass chant of this group to have been published (in the January 16, 1932, issue of the Harlem edition of the *Daily Worker*, called *The Liberator*). *Workers Theatre* reported a performance on June 18, 1932, in West Haven, Connecticut, at a rally in support of the Scottsboro defendants.

A Play for Workers

SCOTTSBORO

THIS PLAY CAN HELP
FREE THE INNOCENT
SCOTTSBORO BOYS

The play printed on this page has met with great success when produced by the worker-actors of the German Proletarian Theatre in New York City. It is a simple play, easily learned, easily produced, which can be used to bring home vividly to new thousands of Negro and white workers the murder now planned by the bosses of Alabama against nine innocent Negro boys.

To produce this play requires no stage apparatus other than a table and a couple of chairs. Get a group of eight workers together—seven workers and a leader to drill them. If at all possible, both Negro and white workers should be in the group. None of the players need have had any previous experience in acting. The lines are easy to learn. They must, however, be spoken slowly and distinctly. Probably the most difficult part will be to speak in unison those sentences said by All. The leader must drill until the effect of unison has been achieved.

The play can be produced at street corners, at demonstrations, at indoor mass meetings, as part of an evening entertainment.

Set up a table large enough to hold two workers. In front of the table, two chairs. In front of the chairs, leave space enough for 3 workers to stand. The players run from the back of the audience shouting "Attention! Attention!" until they are in their positions. The workers stand as follows:

1 and 2 on table
3 and 4 on chairs
5, 6 and 7 on the ground.

The players pause a second, then start. If there is no drum, use a gong or a hammer on a pot lid to give the desired effect.

ALL: Attention! Attention! (*the drum beats*)
  1: Attention! Workers!
  2: Friends!
  4: Fellow-workers!
  3: Comrades!
  5, 6, 7: Attention!
  5, 6, 7, 3, 4: Attention!

ALL: Attention!
1: Hear the story of the nine
   Negro boys in Scottsboro,
   Alabama!
(*The drum beats*)
ALL: (*Bending slightly forward, speaking in low, threatening voices*):
   In Scottsboro, in Scottsboro
   Murder is being done.
   In Scottsboro, in Scottsboro
   Death is threatening.
1: Glee in Scottsboro!
4: Thousands are crowding around.
2: Calling out and laughing and questioning and singing.
3: Upon the market-place in Scottsboro.
1: And the sun gleams
4: Upon the gay Sunday clothes
6: Of the wives and children
7: Of the factory owners, of the store keepers,
   Of the town officials and the bankers.
5: Everyone is here
3: Upon the market-place in Scottsboro!
2: The children with flags,
3: And the men with guns,
4: And the badges of the sheriffs gleam in the sun.
3: And the brass band plays
6: The Star-Spangled Banner!
2: And everyone is singing
4: And everyone is screaming
ALL: "Lynch! Lynch! Lynch!"
ALL: Glee in Scottsboro!
ALL (*Bending slightly forward speaking in low, theatening voices*):
   In Scottsboro, in Scottsboro
   Murder is being done!
   In Scottsboro, in Scottsboro
   Death is threatening.
4: On the market-place in Scottsboro
1: Stands the court house.
2: In it are nine Negro boys!
5: Nine Negro boys have been arrested
4: For a deed they never committed!
2: Nine Negro boys stand before the court.
4: No proof of their innocence is wanted here!
1: Nine Negro boys are accused
4: And await a sentence long decided!
1: And the prosecutor on the bench
   Hears the voices from the market-place:

44

ALL: "Lynch! Lynch! Lynch!"
  4: He does not want to lose his job.
  6: And the judge on the bench
    Hears the voices from the market-place:
ALL: "Lynch! Lynch! Lynch!"
  4: He does not want to lose favor with the electors.
  5: And the boys' attorney
    Hears the voices from the market-place:
ALL: "Lynch! Lynch! Lynch!"
  4: He does not want to lose his clients.
  2: And the jurymen—storekeepers, merchants, employers
    Hear the voices from the market-place:
ALL: "Lynch! Lynch! Lynch!"
  4: They do not want to lose their customers.
  1: In the court house at Scottsboro, Alabama, stand nine Negro
    boys—alone!
    (*Pause*)
ALL: In Scottsboro, in Scottsboro
Murder is being done!
In Scottsboro, in Scottsboro
Death is theatening!
  1: In the courthouse at Scottsboro, on April 9, 1931,
    Sentence is pronounced against the nine Negro boys.
  3: (*Steps forward in front of 6 and 7 and reads, as if pronouncing the
    sentences in a court house*):
    Eugene Williams, 13 years old, death;
    Ozie Powell, 14 years old, death;
    Willie Roberson, 17 years old, death;
    Haywood Patterson, 17 years old, death;
    Olen Montgomery, 17 years old, death;
    Andy Wright, 18 years old, death;
    Clarence Norris, 19 years old, death;
    Charlie Weems, 20 years old, death;
    Roy Wright, 14 years old, mistrial.
    This sentence is pronounced in
    Scottsboro, Alabama.
    (*Goes back to his former place*)
      (*Pause*)
ALL: In Scottsboro, in Scottsboro
Murder is being done!
In Scottsboro, in Scottsboro
Death is threatening!
  7: In Scottsboro nine Negro boys are sentenced
  5: For the rape of two white prostitutes
  6: Whom they never saw,
    Never spoke to,

Never knew.
4: Why?
ALL: Why?
1: Because twelve million Negroes
must be kept in slavery
By fear,
By lack of rights,
By violence.
2: For the landlords, bosses and bankers
3: Squeeze profits from these twelve million Negroes
4: By long hours,
Speed-up
Cheap labor.
5: If twelve million Negroes work long hours,
3: White workers also must work long hours
6: If twelve million Negroes speed up their work
3: White workers also must speed up their work.
7: If twelve million Negroes work cheap,
3: White workers also must work cheap.
(*The next lines very slowly and clearly*)
4: Negro workers,
3: White workers,
5: The same exploitation!
6: The same fate.
7: The same class!
4: Negro workers.
3: White workers,
2: The same power,
4: The same might.
1: The same sure victory
5, 6, 7: If you unite
2, 3, 4: If you organize.
ALL: If you fight!
(*Pause*)
3: In Scottsboro murder is being done!
4: In Scottsboro death is threatening!
ALL: Your death!
5: Will you let them murder the young Negroes in Scottsboro?
6: Will you deliver up your class brothers to the capitalist murderers?
7: No! No! No!
3: Organize!
2: Demonstrate!
1: Protest!
4: Raise your voices!
3: Raise your fists!
5: Call your comrades out of the factories!

46

6: Call the housewives out of their homes!
7: Call the children out of the schools!
3: Shout into the ears of your exploiters:
   MURDERERS!
4: Scream in the faces of the class judges:
   STOP!
ALL: STOP! STOP! STOP!
1: The fight for the freedom of the Negro boys
2: Is part of the class struggle
6: Led by the workers of all countries.
4: Against the bosses of all countries.
ALL: Workers!
Unite!
And fight!
(*The players and audience join in singing "The International."*)
THE END

Next to demands for relief for the unemployed, the Scottsboro case was the most urgent radical cause of the early thirties. The International Labor Defense (ILD), the legal aid branch of the Communist Party, took over the defense for the eight black young men (the ninth had been acquitted on a mistrial) after quick trials during which Southern whites convicted them of rape and sentenced them to die. Rallies and demonstrations succeeded in creating a great deal of public indignation about the obviously trumped-up charges. ILD lawyers won new trials at which they got one of the women to testify that she lied about having been raped. The NAACP also joined defense efforts, and in 1937 a deal was made with the Southern authorities. The charge of rape was dropped, three of the defendents were freed while five remained in prison on lesser charges.

The three theatre works that propagandized in behalf of the Scottsboro victims all took the Communist point of view. *They Shall Not Die*, a full-length play, contrasted the subservient liberal lawyers employed by the NAACP with the strong defense prepared by the Communists. (The NAACP charged the Communists with using the case for their own purposes; the Communists charged the liberal organization with being willing to make a deal with the Alabama courts.) The Prolet-Buhne's *Scottsboro*, along with *Scottsboro Limited*, an agitprop in verse by Langston Hughes, showed how the case called for unity between black and white workers against their common oppressors.

47

Scottsboro Limited was first published in *New Masses* and then issued along with four of Hughes' poems about the case in a slender volume by Golden Stair Press. Despite its thumping lines and certain linguistic idiosyncrasies ("Too long have my brains been dumb/ Now out of the Darkness/ the new Red Negro will come") that typify the radical expectations of the early thirties, the play retains its vitality and innovativeness.

Hughes retold the Scottsboro events and projected their possible victorious conclusion in a manner that placed the major confrontation between the events on stage and the people in the audience, instead of between characters in a story. By planting in the auditorium voices of Southern reaction and voices proclaiming unity with the defendants, he surrounded his audience and forced them to move, at least psychically, toward one side or the other.

The play begins as:

Eight Black Boys, chained by the right foot, one to the other, walk slowly down the center aisle from the back of the auditorium. As they approach the middle of the house, there is loud commotion and a White Man rises in the audience.

Hughes made no attempt to differentiate the boys' personalities, except to make the Eighth Boy the militant spur of the group, nor did he have any desire to give the White Man a character. The same actor plays all the white roles; he is variously the sheriff, the judge, the preacher, the man on the street. His color indicates his only important trait: he is always against the Scottsboro boys. What Richard Schechner pointed out in the preface to Megan Terry's *Viet Rock* (1966) is also true of *Scottsboro Limited*: disruption of the usual one-to-one actor/character relationship redirects attention from personality onto the activities of the actors and, specifically, onto the similar social consequences of their activities.

In *Viet Rock* actors change parts and locations by the technique of transformations, as first described by Viola Spolin in *Improvisation for the Theatre** and most fully developed by Open Theatre actors. (Paul Sills, Spolin's son, has also developed the technique with his Second City and

*Evanston, Ill., 1963.

48

Story Theatre actors but not for radical political purposes.) Though Spolin's work did not become generally known until her book was published in the sixties, it is worth mentioning here because its theoretical roots are clearly in the Marxism of the thirties. The connection is obvious in her transference of objective materialism to the center of her acting system. She actually accomplished for acting what many of the creators of early people's theatre were trying to accomplish through their scripts: the visualization of a Marxist world view that located the source of our oppression and the key to our liberation in objective reality. "Being objective is basic to improvisational theatre," she writes in her introduction. "Objective reality" is "that which can be seen and used between players; a means of sharing our humanness; a changing theatre reality that springs from group agreement." In contrast, "subjectivity" is "self-involved; inability to contact the environment and let it show itself." The key to improvisational acting is physicalization, which she defines as "a physical manifestation of a communication; a physical expression of an attitude; *using self to put an object in motion*; a visible means of making a subjective communication." Transformations occur when "creation momentarily breaks through isolation, and the actors and audience alike receive (ahh!) *the appearance of a new reality*." [ital. added]

Hughes called for transformations in *Scottsboro Limited* for two reasons: to advance his story quickly (by skipping logical connectives) and (more interestingly and tentatively) to show how the function of things in the material world can be altered. Thus he provided a theatrical conceit for the Marxian dialectic (which is very similar to Spolin's) in which the object (a prop or place) plus its variable use by the actor equals a new reality. The stage directions illustrate both points:

> The chains break away, and the Boys find themselves on a moving freight train. They sit down in a haphazard line on the stage, as though they were seated on top of box cars, rocking back and forth as the train moves.

To begin the trial:

> The Man parades sternly up to the raised chair. He is the

49

judge now and as he mounts the legal bench, he puts on a black gown that had been lying there . . . . The trial is conducted in jazz tempo: the white voices staccato, high and shrill; the black voices deep as the rumble of drums.

After the trial:

> The Boys divide up into groups of two's now, in a row across the stage, in the cell of the death house some of them sitting down, some of them weeping, some of them pushing against the bars with their hands.

The Boys' terror mounts until several white voices are heard in the audience. "We'll fight for you boys. We'll fight for you." The Eighth Boy walks to the raised chair and sits; it has changed from judge's bench to electric chair. As the voices grow louder, the boy gathers strength from them (another example of psychological change being effected by external rhythms), he breaks the straps holding him to the chair and stands on its raised platform to shout:

> All the world, listen!
> Beneath the wide sky
> In all the black lands
> Will echo this cry:
> *I will not die.*

The chair is the emotional center of the agitprop. As it is used differently its changing functions reflect the boys' changing relationship to the world. It has been judge's bench and electric chair, now it is the platform from which the cry for freedom is heard. The agitprop ends once the Scottsboro boys turn the intensity of their experience as victims into the strength for their new role as revolutionaries:

EIGHTH BOY: The hands of the red world
  Are our hands, too.
RED VOICES (*from audience*): The hands of the red world *are* you!

In this way the situations established by oppressive society generate the energy that will defeat it.

The Workers Laboratory Theatre (in 1935 renamed the Theatre of Action), founded in 1928, was along with the

50

Prolet-Buhne and Artef, the Yiddish-language group, the most influential of workers' theatres. In 1933 at a New Theatre Night they presented *Newsboy*, their most innovative work and one of the most acclaimed agitprops of the thirties. In a pamphlet that explained their organization and aims, WLT offered a definition of workers theatre:

> Will the culture of that system which offers them starvation—the Hollywood movies, the radio, the musical comedies, the newspapers—will this present-day culture make the workers conscious of their power, of their ability to better their living conditions? Hardly! This culture either provides for the workers a meri [sic] dream world of escape from the problems of life or actually dupes and misleads them through subtle propaganda of a fascist and jingoistic nature.

> Because of this, then, the workers and students—members of the Workers Laboratory Theatre—conscious of their class position in the society of today, are building a socially conscious theatre which dramatizes the life and struggle of the workers, a theatre which serves not as a means of escape but as an aid in making them conscious of their strength and of the need for action. A theatre that fits these needs is a Workers Theatre.

In *Newsboy* Alfred Saxe, director of WLT, worked consciously with transformation techniques—he called them "transitions." Saxe's transitions created a dramatic structure expansive enough to include any material that was thematically useful. (*Newsboy*, based on a poem by V. J. Jerome, incorporated short scenes from *1931-*, by Paul and Claire Sifton, and *Merry-Go-Round*, by George Sklar and Albert Maltz.) Transitions allowed for activity to be decided on the basis of what—according to a Marxist analysis—needs to be done, instead of what seems psychologically probable. Emotional recall, the way in which an actor brings subjective responses into the play according to the Stanislavsky system, is a regressive tendency not especially suited to radical theatre because it limits the actor to situations he has already lived through. Spolin defines recall as "dead . . . confused by many with acting; to use past experience deliberately evolved for a present-time problem is clinical and can be destructive

51

to the theatre reality." Transitions (or transformations), because they break remembered connections, free the actor from recall by letting him come to the circumstances of each dramatic segment without preconceptions, and by working through them to create a new situation.

By adapting a game schema to improvisational acting, Spolin established a system that surpassed Saxe's imposed Marxist analysis of content: "When players are working on a problem and solving it, the spontaneous changes that appear are seemingly endless." In other words, Spolin made sure that even when the content is not about a revolutionary synthesis, the structure of the activity definitely is. Transformations reflect a world in flux and a world view that supposes people can change their lives.

Alfred Saxe

NEWSBOY—FROM SCRIPT TO PERFORMANCE*

There has been much discussion pro and con about form in the workers theatre. Which is the real revolutionary form? Is it satire, realism, symbolism, etc? Must we laugh in the revolutionary theatre or shall solemnity rule the day? In the Workers' Laboratory Theatre we have been producing various forms for the last four years. Patiently, diligently we have gone about dissecting the elements of various theatrical *isms* looking for forms which will best solve the problems of the theatres of action—namely, to present a story dynamically, clearly in terms of dramatic images within a time space of not more than forty minutes . . . .

Four years' work then have helped in the attempt at mastery of the old forms and, further, have already assisted in the development of a new form which to date shows great possibility for use in the Workers' theatre. One of the most pliable, dynamic theatre of action forms which has yet appeared is the technique utilized in *Newsboy*.

What essentially makes *Newsboy* dynamic? It is the intensity, speed and conflict of present day industrialized America. Nothing more. Here we must look for our answer to form such as *Newsboy*. The more deeply we go into the processes responsible for the growth of society and all its mainsprings; the more thoroughly we study the conflicts in today's and tomorrow's events, the more capable we become of producing such dynamic material. Conflict is the first and primary factor. Conflict never leaves *Newsboy*. An analysis of any part of the script finds this clash—everywhere. In the opening scene, for example, playing time of sixty seconds, the following conflicts take place:

New theatre, August 1934. Edited version KMT.

Newsboys fighting. Clash—Competition under capitalism.

Young man tries to "pick up" girl. Clash—Conflict of sexes.

Blind woman begs from newsboy. Clash—he doubts her blindness.

Charitable gent gives blind woman penny. Clash—between smile and penny.

Within the space of sixty seconds four completely separate conflicts take place. We will find consistent conflict through the entire play. *Newsboy* is built around a series of conflicting images to the ideology of the newsboy and the attempt to draw him to a higher level of understanding. Every scene drips with this clash. The scene from "1931" is built on conflict. The third degree scene is one of tightening tense conflict between the Negro and his torturers. Every available inch of space and time is taken up with the clash of two forces—the dialectical method is the manner of conceiving the things and beings of the universe as in the process of becoming through the struggle of contradictory elements and their resolution. Thus with a thorough grasp of dialectics and its application, directors of the Workers' Theatre will be able to produce dramatic dynamic realities.

Under capitalist society we are educated to believe that incidents take place without rhyme or reason—that chaos bestrides the world like a colossus; that luck, opportunity, good fortune, chance and the roulette wheel make or break not only kings, queens and presidents but also, alack-a-day, the poor masses. The Marxist approach smashes this theory to bits. The Marxist interpretation of history clarifies and shows scientifically the relationship of the smallest details and incidents in every part of the world. The clash between the two dominating classes (Historical Materialism), the growth of this struggle leads today to a terrific heightening and quickening of the process of struggle throughout the world—and increase in the pitch acceleration and rapidity with which the above events happen. *Newsboy* as a form is particularly suitable to throw into relief, to bring out the relationship of these incidents. Here is not the conventional two or three-act production which requires an organic and intricate development of plot—a psychological analysis of characters—a growth of character to character and act to act. There is no plot, no relationship as we are acquainted with it in the ordinary theatre. Instead we take as our plot the line of Marxist thought of a particular poem, a short story, etc. Around this thread we are at liberty to choose any scene at random . . . .

ECONOMY—TRANSITION—TIMING. To carry through successfully such a form requires not alone the thorough study and application of dialectics and historical materialism—but, it goes without saying, theatrical knowledge; of problems of the theatre conquering of all its forms (for such a form as *Newsboy* which is a composite and makes use of several forms in one—where the characters are at times symbols then real—where they jump from newsboy to thug to minister) and mastery of technique is essential. In *Newsboy* as in other plays of a similar character there are several outstanding technical problems which face director and actor. I choose at the present stage of theoretical development to touch on three elements. Economy—transition—timing. Here it is necessary to state that none of these elements are clear cut. Each overlaps into the other, each molds and affects the other . . . .

I have seen many potentially good plays ruined because there was a lack of recognition of that essential element—economy of words and movement—no growth to new ideas but a constant repetition of the old ideas hiding in different words—prolonging a scene and dragging in ideas which are not important and in keeping with the sum total of the content. *To assist in achieving economy in production a clear and thoroughly planned script, step by step, from idea to idea, is highly important, with constant revision from rehearsal to rehearsal.*

Economy is closely tied up with the element of timing. Timing is a problem of every Workers' Theatre production. In such a script as *Newsboy* timing becomes even more a part of the whole than in the conventional drama. Here we depend on speed and precision, one scene must dovetail into the next without a second's loss. A cross-section of events takes place—a bread-line—a street—a torture cell—never for a moment is the stage empty—as one actor leaves the other enters. How are we to know the proper moment when actions should begin—stop—? What is the basis for an understanding of the timing problems? Here we must understand the value and relationship of rhythm to the theatre. We find everything in life is rhythmic. The earth spins a rotating rhythm on its axis. The seasons come and go in rhythmic succession. All nature is rhythmically arranged. Our bodies work, play, walk in rhythm. Timing is the concrete application of these rhythms to the theatre . . . . The director, let us say, is faced with the problem of bringing out competition under capitalism. He is given Capitalist A representing one trust, and B the other. The action is worked out as follows—at no time do A and B sit or stand together. When A sits—B is standing fully erect. And when B hits the chair we find A standing. If the scene is to be effective it depends on exact timing. *At exactly the point when A hits the clair B is standing* . . . . *Newsboy* is filled with a series of subtle rhythms. The timing, the exact beat when one scene gives way to the next, one character enters, does his bit and makes way for a new character—a new scene—is what helps build the intense speed and excitement of the production.

Perhaps the most difficult task in evolving *Newsboy* and one which is still far from clarified in its actual technical process of growth is what we term *Transitions*—changes from scene to scene. In a series of unrelated incidents as in *Newsboy* the task is that of bridging the gap from realism to symbolism, from street scene to home scene to breadline and yet allowing your audience to understand to believe with the character in the illusion of this change. Here the change will be dictated by the material—at times soft, at times smooth, flowing easily into the next scene itself. Timing plays an important role. Mechanically again let us do our transition by means of beat. In three beats we shall change from a street scene into a breadline. As the street scene ends—Beat One—the actors freeze—not a soul moves. *First movement*—preparation for the transition.

Beat Two—the actors make one movement which relates itself to hungry men on the breadline, for example—hunching over—turning up collar, etc. Here the softness or strength of the movement is dictated by the content, *i.e.*, if the content is weak the transition movement will be weak and *vice versa*. *Second movement*—transition half accomplished.

Beat Three—all actors turn on the third beat and to an increased rhythm fall one behind the other to a steady hunger pace—*third movement*—simple mechanical transition accomplished. Some times these transitions are violent. In *Newsboy* for example—a line of the poem:

Two hundred white men take a black man for a ride and string him up a tree and shoot his body full of holes because a white woman said he smiled at her.

Action—Negro breaks from group back stage and runs forward to audience. The position of the figures on the stage all grouped at the back—the figure of the Negro worker at the front of the stage makes it · very difficult to change to the next scene which is from *Merry Go Round*. Four of the figures must leave the stage—four others who are at the moment class-conscious workers must become thugs. The position of Negro and white workers must be completely reversed. The scene is a third degree. Very well. We will make our transition violent. While the Negro worker has been speaking, those not in the scene shuffle quietly and quickly off. At the same time, the white men turn their back to the audience, and as the Negro finishes a white man grabs him and hurls him back. Crash—the Negro finds thimself thrown to the floor into a frame-up scene—the backs of the white men loom ominously and obviously tell the story of the change. There are hundreds of transition methods. Many of them have not been touched at all—the actors' problem, of thought, imagery, concentration, etc., is a book in itself. I have merely attempted to open new avenues of thought and have tried to give a picture of the thorough study and concentration necessary to solving the vastness and scope of our problems. These problems will develop and grow with the development of Workers' Theatre.

NEWSBOY*

An adaptation for the American League Against War and Fascism by

*Though this unpublished version of *Newsboy* has no date, the American League Against War and Fascism was not founded until 1935.

Gregory Novikov from the poem by V. J. Jerome, as co-ordinated by the Workers Laboratory Theatre.

The Scene: The entire action takes place on the stage which has been draped in black so that we cannot distinguish its limitations. Before the black back-drop there are three two-feet platforms, which serve as elevations for certain scenes and certain characters. However, these too must be covered with a black fabric, so that they are not seen by the audience. A street lamp is optional.

When the curtain rises the stage is dark but the shuffling of many feet are heard. Slowly a light is thrown along the street surface which lights up only the feet of the passersby. We see all types of feet, well-shod, and poorly-shod, walking, strolling, and running back and forth. In the center stands the Newsboy, in the dark.

NEWSBOY: Extry, read all about it! Love nest raided on Park Avenue, Extry! Marlene Deitrich insures legs for fifty thousand dollars! Extry! Mrs. Vanderbilt calls Mrs. Whitney a liar! Read all about it! Babe Ruth joins Boston Braves... Extry... College Student murders his professor's mistress. Get your papers. American, News and Mirror. Morning papers!

Slowly a spotlight creeps over the Newsboy's face and spreads until it covers the entire stage with a sickly amber glow. Now we see the crowd in full, passing back and forth in front of the newsboy. Occasionally someone stops to buy a newspaper. We see the following episodes as the newsboy continues his shouts

1. An attractive girl, evidently a stenographer, walks across the stage, followed by a well-dressed man. She stops to buy a paper which the man pays for. They go off together.
2. A blind woman comes tap, tap, tapping across the stage, wailing: "Alms for the poor blind .... Ain't no one goin' to help the blind .... Alms for the blind!" A pompous man with a mustache drops a coin in her cup, and then stops to enter an item in his budget book.
3. Two shabbily dressed radicals cross the stage talking earnestly.
4. A nice young girl walks tearfully across the stage followed by a pleading young man.

The murmuring of the crowd grows louder. The strollers now appear like some mad ballet, forming various patterns behind the newsboy, as they buy their papers. The headlines of the newspapers scream out the words, MURDER, SUICIDE, and DIVORCE. A piano has joined the medly of voices and the effect is of a discordant babble. Above it all we hear the newsboy.

NEWSBOY: Read all about it! Murder ... Rape ... Scandal ... All the latest sports events ... morning papers ....
The crowd is chanting Murder, Rape, Scandal, Suicide. The sym-

phony of sound reaches a climax when suddenly we hear the boom-
ing voice of the Black Man, as yet off-stage. At the first sound of his
voice the murmur begins to die.

BLACK MAN: Hey, there, Newsboy, how long you goin' ter stand
there under the "L", yellin' yer guts out? How long yer goin' to keep
yellin' that workers should be murdered and strikes outlawed?
(crowd continues soft chant)

BLACK MAN: Because somewheres in a hotel room in Frisco a Follies
girl shot the brains out of the old rip that kept her? Don't you ever
get tired, Newsie, shoutin' about hold-ups, and murders, and raids on
Love Nests? Come into the light, Newsboy, Come into the light! . . . .
As he speaks he advances into the sphere of light. The crowd pays no
attention to him but the newsboy watches him carefully out of the
corner of his eye, as if he senses a menace.

NEWSBOY: JAPAN WANTS WAR WITH THE UNITED STATES . . .
SOVIET RUSSIA INSULTS UNITED STATES CONSUL . . .
GERMAN OFFICIALS ATTACK AMERICAN GIRLS . . . .

CROWD: *(as the chant changes in nature, their attitudes change from*
apathy to hatred) Japan wants war . . . Soviet wants war . . .
Germany wants war . . . Down with the Soviet . . . Down with the
Soviet . . . .

NEWSBOY: Eight thousand boys join C.C.C. camps . . . Make Profes-
sors swear loyalty to government . . . Bill passed in Congress to
outlaw strikes . . . Japan prepares war . . . Germany arms 100,000
men . . . Italy masses troops on her border . . . attack on Abyssin-
ia . . . Mrs. Vanderbilt calls Mrs. Whitney a liar . . . Mary Pickford
granted her final decree . . . read all about it!

BLACK MAN: Why don't yer stop kiddin' yerself, Newboy? Don't yer
see yer drunk with the poison gin of lies? All this talk of C.C.C.
Camps and Boy Scout parades and International insults . . . you've
got poison in yer bellies and its eatin' yer guts and rottin' away yer
minds. Yer linin' up fer war . . . that's what! Yer gettin' ready to
fight again and kill again, and slaughter again . . . .

CROWD: We need another war—War will end depression—We need
another war—

BLACK MAN: They're gettin' yuh ready to be killed, I tell yuh,—just
like I seen 'em do at the dog pound—first they give 'em chloroform
so's they don't realize what's goin' ter happen to 'em—

CROWD: *(growing louder)* We need another war. War brings out the
best in men. We need another war. War is natural. We need another
war—

BLACK MAN: They're chloroforming yuh with lies, I tell yuh. Lies!
The noise grows again to a crescendo as the crowd repeats the last
speech and as the BLACK MAN keeps shouting "Lies." The scene
fades off. A corner of the stage is brightened with a white spotlight,
slightly above the level of the crowd. In the spotlight we see a man at

57

a telephone. Behind him on the wall are the title streamers of the New York American, Mirror, *and* Journal. *It is William Randolph Hearst.*

HEARST: (*into phone*) Rush through the following scare heads. Very boldest type. "Six Million Starve to Death in Soviet Russia." "Communism Must Go." "Down With American Reds". "U.S.A. Spends One Billion Dollars on Armaments to be Vested as Airplane Bombers, Cannon, Gas Bombs . . . ."

The voice fades with the spotlight. A light fades in on the other side of the stage. We see a man making a speech before a mob of people. Behind him is draped the bunting of Red, white, and blue. It is Huey Long.

LONG: Every man is a king. That's my motto. Share the wealth. Everyman is entitled to his rights, but no man should make over a million dollars. Every man a king, that's the motto of the Kingfish. A war wouldn't be such a bad thing. Boys, ha, ha, ha—every man a king . . . .

The lights and voice fade. A light on center of stage shows a man behind a microphone, in priests' clothes. It is Father Coughlin.

COUGHLIN: . . . But our country, right or wrong. Of course, I am not a militarist . . .(*sweetly*) No man of Jesus can be a militarist . . . Our Lord Jesus Christ teaches humility and pacifism . . . BUT on the other hand, if our nation is in danger of an attack by a foreign nation who is after our gold—or, more particularly, our greatest asset, our silver supply . . . it is the God-ordained duty of every American Citizen to fight and die for its protection. Our government will be only as safe from without her borders as she is from within. Let us stamp out this ugly stain of Communism with its militant peace policies. I can only repeat the words of that other great American, Chauncey Depew—"Our Country, right or wrong . . . ."

The light and voice fade out, and again we see William Randolph Hearst speaking.

HEARST: Our country right or wrong. Japan insults U.S. envoy. Russia plans to attack the U.S.A. U.S. Steel up 40 points. Anaconda copper up 23 points. Du Pont powder works rises 82 points . . . Soviet Union plans to attack . . . .

Voice dies away and spot fades. Murmuring of the crowd has begun again and grows louder. Sound of drums and martial music is heard in the distance, growing louder. As the lights reveal them, the people in the crowd line up in army formation, with rolled newspapers carried like rifles. They march back and forth and finally march straight front, and unroll their papers, revealing War Scare Headlines. The BLACK MAN runs up and down the line trying trying to make them listen to him. They pay no attention; the BLACK MAN is shouting over the music.

BLACK MAN: Come into the light, comrades, come into the light. You're being chloroformed. Your heads are full of lies, and you're

58

gettin' ready to be killed. Caint you see they're fixin' you for the slaughter. Caint you see . . . .

They pay no attention. Black Man goes over and sits on the curb, his head in his arms. An unemployed man in ragged clothes comes in and stops a well-dressed man.

UNEMPLOYED MAN: How about a nickel for a cup of coffee, buddy?

WELL-DRESSED MAN: Why don't you get a job?

UNEMPLOYED MAN: Why don't I get a job? Ha, ha. That's rich. Why don't you get a job? Where do you suggest I look for one—in the White House?

WELL-DRESSED MAN: Why don't you go to a C.C.C. Camp?

UNEMPLOYED MAN: Thanks, buddy, but I can starve here just as well as there. (*The well-dressed man goes on, and the unemplcyed man approaches a dignified Old Man.*) Can you spare a nickel for a cup of coffee, sir. I've got to eat.

OLD GENTLEMAN: I don't believe in it.

UNEMPLOYED MAN: I don't get you.

OLD GENTLEMAN: I don't believe in charity. Why don't you join the army? It would make a new man of you. (*Feels his muscles.*) A man with a body like yours should be in the service. It would build up your morale.

UNEMPLOYED MAN: I want to hang on to my arms and legs for a while, thanks. I'm not anxious to have them blown off in a war.

(*Old Gentleman goes on. Unemployed man accosts a KINDLY OLD LADY.*)

UNEMPLOYED MAN: Lady, can you spare a nickel for. a cup of coffee?

KINDLY OLD LADY: (*opening her purse*) Here you are, my good man. Always glad to help the unfortunate. But why don't you join the army? That would keep you off the streets.

UNEMPLOYED MAN: (*throwing nickel back at her*) Thanks for the charity.

KINDLY OLD LADY: It was only a suggestion.

OLD GENTLEMAN: A good suggestion. Why don't you join the army?

UNEMPLOYED MAN: And get blown to bits!

WELL-DRESSED MAN: (*coming back to him*) Or why don't you join the C.C.C. camps?

UNEMPLOYED MAN: And starve!

The cry of Why Don't you join the army? and the answer: And get blown to bits, and the other cry of Why don't you join the C.C.C. camps? And starve, are taken up by the crowd. They surge forward, and the chant becomes rhythmic. The BLACK MAN jumps to his feet. The left entrance of the stage lights up. From off stage left is heard the voice of a SECOND NEWSBOY, quieting the other sounds.

SECOND NEWSBOY: Fight against War and Fascism. Learn the truth about the munitions racket. (*He enters with a magazine bag at his side. He is holding aloft a handful of papers, spread fanwise, so we cannot see their title.*) Fight against War and Fascism. Fight NOW against that Racket of the death manufacturers. The C.C.C. camps are preparing men for war! Learn the truth!

The FIRST NEWSBOY belligerently steps forward to bar his way, but the BLACK MAN and the UNEMPLOYED MAN place themselves before the SECOND NEWSBOY as a shield. They hoist him to the top of a box stage center, and he gives them a stack of papers, which they distribute to the crowd. The FIRST NEWSBOY slinks away. The crowd reads.

MAN IN CROWD: (*as he reads*) Think of it. Eight and a half million men killed in the last war.

GIRL IN CROWD: (*as she reads*) Ten million will probably die in the next war.

ANOTHER MAN IN CROWD: (*as he reads*) Eight and a half million men killed for the profits of the munition makers.

CROWD: (*taking up cry*) Eight and a half million men. Eight and a half million men. Killed—wounded—shell-shocked—millions more. Eight and a half million men murdered in war—murdered in war.

The crowd is huddled in the center, near the second newsboy, with their backs to the audience, continuing this chant. The FIRST NEWSBOY runs on the stage, shouting his slogans, and wheeling each person of the crowd around so they face the audience. He is faced by a solid wall of "Fights" (the paper of the American League Against War and Fascism), displayed to the audience. Above the wall, like a banner, the SECOND NEWSBOY waves his copy of "Fight". The FIRST NEWSBOY runs up and down the line, shouting his slogans, but gets no response.

FIRST NEWSBOY: Japan insults the U.S.A.—Germany insults the U.S.A.—Soviet Russia insults the U.S.A.—William Randolph Hearst says—Marlene Dietrich insures her legs—Soviet Russia wants war with U.S.A.

He runs angrily off the stage, having gotten no response. The crowd is still chanting "Eight and a half million men" and so on. The tableau is something like the following:

NEWSBOY

Fight

Fight Fight Fight Fight Fight Fight Fight

Black Man   Unemployed Man

BLACK MAN: (*exultantly*) Get yourself a trumpet, buddy, a big red trumpet, and climb to the top of the Empire State building, and blare out the news ... Now is the time to fight war and fascism. (*Comes center and speaks to audience*) Black men, white men, field men, shop men.—It's time to fight war. It's time to fight fascism .... Get yourself a trumpet, buddy, a big red trumpet ... and blare it out ... time to fight war ... time to fight fascism ....

CURTAIN

DEPRESSION DOCUMENTARIES

Art is not a mirror, but a hammer. It does not reflect. It shapes.

Trotsky

After the stock market crash professional writers and theatre artists turned Left almost for self-preservation: the ruling class had only retrogressive policies to offer; life was going on most vitally in the union halls, on the street corners, among the thousands of veterans in Washington for the 1932 Bonus March. If artists, by documenting the poverty and the perseverance of people during the Depression, could help the masses recognize their power, they would be assured of a large audience for their work. It was not a mercenary impulse—no one ever thought of the left-wing theatre as a get rich quick scheme—but they did think of it as ending their artistic isolation by making them contributors to a social order rather than only its freakish depreciators, as they were under capitalism.

The first two non-workers' theatre plays agitating for an end to Depression misery were *1931-*, by Claire and Paul Sifton, produced on Broadway in December of that year by the new Group Theatre and *Can You Hear Their Voices?*, by Hallie Flanagan and Margaret Ellen Clifford, produced first by the Experimental Theatre at Vassar College and subsequently by Artef and numerous other workers and college theatres.

The Group actors performed *1931-* for nine days to a packed and cheering audience in the balcony—which proved there was an audience for radical plays, but one that would have to be sought off-Broadway, at ticket prices it could afford. *1931-* is not a very good play; the Sifton's had no ear for language that seemed true in the theatre, a failing they shared with some other radical writers. But it is saved in the same way as *The Belt* is saved—by the pertinence of its sociological observations. It is a boarder drama, crossing from the militant, but un-immediate protests of the New Playwrights to an era when strikes, bonus marches, bread lines, and police brutality would be dramatized on stage practically as they were unfolding in the streets.

The play begins in the spirit of the twenties: Adam, a healthy young worker, gets sick of being driven like a mule and talked to like a robot. He rebels joyously, laughing in his boss's face, certain he can get another job at any time. He storms out of the warehouse and into a Depression that starves his body and destroys his confidence. The play ends with the dominant themes of the early thirties: desperation and revolution. The first was *the* fact of the Depression. The second was what might become of it once every man, torn from his family and from his sense of self, deprived of the possessions he had spent a decade accumulating, realized his fate was inseparable from the fate of his class. The Siftons recognized two simultaneous and mutually dependent progressions: that of the individual toward defeat and that of the mass toward triumph.

Their play is a broader drama stylistically, too. It leans on the experimentalism of the twenties by alternating dream-like interludes depicting the growing solidarity of the masses with mainly realistic scenes of Adam's suffering. The two modes come together when the mob marches past the restaurant where Adam has finally found a foul job, and he smashes through a window to join them. An authors' note explains this scheme:

> *1931-* is concerned with an individual in the tidal movement of a people caught in a situation which they can neither explain, escape nor exorcise. As the play develops, the contrapuntal design of the ten interludes suggests a ground swell that is bearing Adam, his group, and the audience itself, on to revolution of one sort or another. The fourteen scenes comprise one line of action, the drama of Adam; the ten interludes, occurring as flashes between the scenes, comprise the drama of the

group to which he belongs. The two lines converge, slowly at first, then more rapidly, as Adam is beaten down and down while the group grows, stiffens, rises, welded together by the blood, heartbreak, blind hatred, despair and desperation of its million atoms. The alternating rhythm of the scenes and interludes is progressively accelerated, as a wave seems to race when it nears the crest, then curls and breaks.

The interludes are a working out of the radical possibility. The scenes are still-poignant remembrances of the Depression years. When Adam tries to learn to beg (the scene used in Newsboy); when he has to accept, along with the slop house coffee and stale bread of a private charity, the moral superiority of the rich who fund it; when he works all day shoveling snow for the city without boots or gloves or the strength to finish; when he travels to an out-of-the-way corner to get the want ads as soon as they hit the street and finds a dozen men ahead of him; when he meets his girl and cannot think about her because he is starving—these were real humiliations that could be documented by the thousands in every city across the US. Putting them in a Broadway play that also said they would end in revolution was an astounding act. (The reason that this "bad play stunned an audience so completely," as Brooks Atkinson wrote.)

Can You Hear Their Voices? gets its strength, too, from the accuracy of its Depression scenes. On the train from New York to Poughkeepsie, Hallie Flanagan read Whittaker Chambers' story in the *New Masses* about an armed uprising of farmers in England, Arkansas. Depression conditions were aggravated in the South Western states by a serious drought, ruining crops and putting farmers at the mercy of the Red Cross. When that charity was unable to provide sufficient food, five hundred farmers and their wives took shotguns and invaded the town. They asked for more food at the Red Cross office and then marched on stores and took what they needed.

Can You Hear Their Voices? was researched and written in ten days. Each of its scenes was based on an episode documented in newspaper, magazine and *Congressional Record* accounts. At Vassar it was staged on a platformed and pillored set. "By this simplification realism is discarded

63

and reality gained," read a stage direction. At intervals slides were projected that provided the factual background to the story. Three slides in between the second and third scenes related the hideously ironic story of pre-New Deal attempts at farm relief:

> The Senate insisted that since the money was a loan to farmers it should be used when necessary to keep them alive. The President, backed by a majority in the House, maintained that the money should not be used for food because this would constitute a dole. The farmers said, "millions for mules but not a cent for humans."

In the most moving scene in the play, Hilda, a young wife and mother, smothers her baby because she can not stand to watch the sickly infant starve to death. It was poverty that finally proved strong enough to shatter sentimental myths like those about Amerikan motherhood; the same situation (taken from another actual case) would reappear in the living newspaper *1935*.

Scenes depicting the farmers' growing solidarity (a corollary to the increasing desperateness of their situation) alternated with scenes from the life of a wealthy senator who is actively opposing any sort of government "dole." His daughter Harriet links the farmers' situation directly to the Vassar audience; she uses her privileged position to agitate for relief. The play ends with a projected slide calling upon the "educated minority" to hear the farmers and help them.

Radical theatre understandably objected to this interpretation (which was influenced, as Flanagan continued to be, by strong faith in New Deal-like reforms). In the Artef production the senator/daughter scenes were de-emphasized and the play ended with preparation for the coming battle between farmers and National Guard.

Hallie Flanagan had been working on a study of European staging techniques. She knew Meyerhold's experiments first-hand and adopted some of his innovations in this play. That she still chose to fashion the individual scenes from the conversational fabric of Broadway realism, indicates that the urgency of this project (people *were* starving in Arkansas) forbade the luxury experiment.

John Wexley, a radical journalist/playwright, had had two of his plays produced on Broadway in the first years of the

64

thirties: *The Last Mile*, an indictment of capital punishment, and *Steel*, which exposed working conditions in the mills. In 1933 the Theatre Guild optioned *They Shall Not Die*, about the International Labor Defense's fight to have the death sentences of the eight Scottsboro victims commuted. Haywood Patterson ("Parsons" in the play), the most articulate of the defendants, had become the focus of public attention. Eventually he was tried four times in Alabama, receiving the death sentence three times and then a 75-year prison term. Late in the forties he escaped from a Southern prison farm and co-authored with Earl Conrad the story of his life, *Scottsboro Boy* (New York, 1950).

Because his play ends with Patterson's second trial, Wexley was anxious for it to be produced in New York while ILD lawyers were appealing for and engaged in Patterson's third trial. Guild managers, however, considered delaying it indefinitely.

It was felt that this play should not be produced until after the current trial, because if the Negroes were acquitted the play would not be so vital, whereas *if they were convicted or lynched the play would be of tremendous interest.* *

[ital. added]

Why Wexley let this Broadway outfit option his play at all is curious. Perhaps he had no other interested producer; more likely, he was happy that a well-known organization like the Guild wanted to do his play. Ben Blake described the results in *New Theatre* (April, 1934):

The Guild gave a revolutionary play the same kind of treatment stylistically that it gives to a drawing room comedy or a "Strange Interlude." Realism, the production board, with Phillip Moeller directing, decided. And to them realism means literal faithfulness in the representation of characters, locale, tempo and so forth.

Mordecai Gorelik had done several design studies for the play, published in *New Theatre* and *Theatre Arts* magazine in

*Roy S. Waldau, *Vintage Years of the Theatre Guild 1928-1939*, Cleveland, 1972, p. 177.

65

February. He wanted to project slides on the back wall of the courtroom (possibly of the mass Scottsboro defense demonstrations then being held across the country), and his stylized setting for the third act which included an ominously oversized judge's bench was meant to show that a fair trial was impossible here. But Lee Simonson, the Guild's regular designer, saw the play realistically. His courtroom set prefigures one from a TV crime show, though Blake did observe that he made the "poor-white home" of one of the witnesses into "a high walled, spacious place where the directions called for a small cramped shack."

Wexley's script is itself a mixture of powerful documentation and less effective realistic playwriting. It was not that

the Guild completely misinterpreted his work; they just emphasized its weakest elements. It was Wexley who felt that certain scenes, for which there were no transcripts, had to be created as if they were part of a realistic play. The second act scenes, in which he reveals through her evolving love affair Ruby Bates' (Lucy Wells in the play) guilt at having given false testimony, not only make tiresome reading, but tended, in production, to discredit his first act. The play opens in the local jail where the Scottsboro victims were forced to sign "confessions" in 1931. And if presented with a kind of single-minded attention to oppression, Act I could have been a convincing indictment of prison brutality. Instead the Guild chose to emphasize the psychological truth of the proceedings, causing Edith Isaacs to remark in her *Theatre Arts* review (May, 1934) that she just could not believe all Southern whites connected with the prosecution were villains, and that the play seemed more like "yellow journalism" than "social tragedy." It is a too-often repeated paradox (especially by groups like the Guild) that realistic treatment of a radical play discredits the notion of propaganda in the theatre instead of highlighting the bourgeois bias of realism.

villains, and that the play seemed more like "yellow journalism" than "social tragedy." It is a too-often repeated paradox (especially by groups like the Guild) that realistic treatment of a radical play discredits the notion of propaganda in the theatre instead of highlighting the bourgeois bias of realism.

It was not until the third act for which Wexley had

condensed days of trial record that the play's convictions overcame its production:

No we're not finished. We're only beginning . . . . If I do nothing else in my life, I'll make the fair name of this state stink to high heaven with its lynch justice . . . these boys, they shall not die! (*Laughter from the jury room dies down and the court audience stares at him with eyes and mouths agape.*)

THE THEATRE UNION

Here i am at strike head 1/4 an' its plenty hot. These here bosses we got in town keep yellin' in the papers that communism and paying 54 1/2¢ an hr is one an' the same thing. Well, if that's what it is I gues i'm a communist an' I expect most every one in the world except a small bunch of pot bellyd titefisted bosses must be to.

> Union newspaper during Team-
> sters strike in Minneapolis

Late in 1932, when organized labor's role in the Great Depression was still unknown, Charles Rumford Walker, his wife Adelaide, Michael Blankfort, Albert Maltz, George Sklar and Paul Peters began to organize a professional theatre that would dramatize the struggles of the working class.* They were motivated, Walker says, by two ideas: "1. We were playwrights and we wanted our own plays—which were leftist—produced. 2. *We believed deeply that the trade-unions were the rock bottom base for any kind of future society.*" [ital. added]

---

*Sylvia Feningston, formerly of the Group Theatre and NPT, and later director of the TU's acting workship; her husband, Manuel Gomez; Victor Wolfson and Joseph Freeman were also active in the theatre's planning stages. Margaret Larkin, who would marry Albert Maltz, became executive secretary and the TU's laison with the press. It took a year to raise the first $1,000, from $5 and $10 contributions; then John Hammond, Jr. donated $2,000 and with a $3,000 loan the TU began production.

When the Theatre Union opened at the Civic Repertory Theatre on Fourteenth Street on November 29, 1933, the first and most desperate phase of the Depression was over. The people had elected a President who promised to work things out and Congress had given him more power over the banks, trade, the military and the states than any chief executive had ever had. The Hundred Days of the New Deal began almost immediately after the inauguration with the institution in March, 1933, of the National Recovery Act. Section 7-a of the NRA gave employees "the right to organize and bargain collectively," and with this sanction the trade-union movement began to revive. (Union membership had been declining since the twenties, after every important strike between 1920 and 1924 was broken.) Trucks moved among workers with signs reading "the President wants *you* to organize." Trade unions appealed to hundreds of thousands of non-radical workers because they offered specific and immediate remedies for local conditions and a way out of the lethargy of the early Depression years.

But once having legalized collective bargaining, the NRA board was lackadaisical about its enforcement; in the courts Section 7-a was being interpreted as sanctioning company unions. Taking advantage of the NRA's timidity, industries activated blacklists, hired goons and enlisted the help of local law enforcement agencies to forcibly break strikes. Anti-labor Citizens' Commitees for Law and Order appeared and armed themselves. Paid informers infiltrated plants, reporting any worker who seemed sympathetic to a union. Violence against union members was commonplace; police, National Guard and hired goons worked hand and club.

By the winter of 1933-34, when the economic situation of the country had hardly improved despite the promise of the New Deal, it became clear that labor would have to win its right to organize. At once workers and radicals had something definite to unite and fight for and they had an obvious enemy whose tactics were often as illegal as they were immoral. The year 1934, labor historian Irving Bernstein writes, was a time of "strikes and social upheavals of extraordinary importance, drama and violence which ripped the cloak of civilized decorum from society, leaving exposed naked class conflict."*

*Turbulent Years, Boston, 1970, p. 217.

69

The Theatre Union existed from 1933 to the spring of 1937, throughout the period of greatest strike activity. They produced seven plays; four of them dramatized the labor struggle then in progress in the US: *Peace on Earth* by Maltz and Sklar, *Stevedore* by Sklar and Peters, *Black Pit* by Maltz, *Marching Song* by Lawson. Three plays—*Mother* by Bertolt Brecht, adapted by Peters; *The Sailors of Cattaro* by Friedrich Wolf, adapted by Blankfort; and *Bitter Stream* * by Victor Wolfson, TU production manager—depicted the fight of workers against repression in pre-revolutionary Russia, the Austro-Hungarian Empire and fascist Italy.

Sklar says:

The TU was unique in the fiercely political climate of the time. There was much talk of a united front on the political scene but it was rarely realized. The TU did encompass in its Board a grouping of various political attitudes. There were independent liberals and trade unionists, Norman Thomas socialists, CP fellow travelers, Trotskyite radicals. Somehow they managed to function without the usual internecine infighting so common among groups of the Left. They were united in their devotion to a viable professional theatre which would make social plays of substance available to audiences unable to pay Broadway admission prices. I don't know of any other group on the Left which operated with such dedication. Only at the end, when the theatre was no longer viable, did the individual differences begin to surface—with as much sorrow as anger.

The audience for the 1,100 seat theatre consisted of trade union members, who ensured a six-week run for nearly every production by purchasing blocks of tickets in advance; unemployed people, to whom the TU gave free tickets; and working and middle-class radicals, who paid between 30 cents and $1.50 for a seat. Actors, directors, designers, administrators, stage hands received a standard salary of $40 per week for senior members, $25 per week for junior members.

From the start the Theatre Union founders recognized that

---

*This script is not available and it will not be discussed here.

a radical coalition in the midst of liberalized government policies was precarious, because the New Deal could provide the means for realizing some of labor's demands without upsetting the basic inequities of the capitalist system. They instituted collective working methods to ensure the clarity of each play's message. From the time a script was selected until opening night, a three-man production committee, the Executive Board, actors, and stagehands, were all in active consultation with the author and/or adaptor. Often a play was read by workers especially familiar with its material. Black and white longshoremen gave judgments about *Stevedore*; several Italian immigrants commented on *Bitter Stream*. The Amerikan plays dramatized the most impoverished conditions and the most reactionary bosses. They discounted government programs as tokenism and emphasized that working class unity was the only means of survival in a hostile, capitalist environment. Yet none of the plays ignored or exaggerated history. Rather they selected the historical situations which most demanded radical solutions. Even such an atypical occurrence as the union of black and white longshoremen in *Stevedore* had actual precedents. In 1919, in Bogalusa, Louisiana, for example, a white organizer named Lum Williams was killed for defending Sol Dacus, leader of the Negroes.

Inseparable from the labor history of the thirties, these strike plays (and others produced independently) also meant to shape it. The consciousness they developed in their characters and brought to their audience was a prerequisite for action that would ultimately go beyond the Union hall; the strikes that climaxed them prefigured a working-class revolution—of the kind that was made to seem increasingly preposterous once the Communist Party instituted the United Front Against War and Fascism in 1935, and Roosevelt's National Labor Relations Board began in the same year to effectively mediate strike disputes.

Michael Blankfort says: "We hoped to make radicals out of the audience and, further than that, we hoped to make communist sympathizers out of the radicals. The socialists on the board hoped the same for the Socialist Party."

Peace on Earth is an anti-war play set around the campus of a prestigious Eastern university (Yale was the one Maltz and Sklar attended). Its central character, Peter Owens, a

71

liberal professor, becomes sympathetic to the striking dock workers' refusal to load munitions shipments. He is arrested at a strike support rally for reading the Declaration of Independence without a permit, and a few days later his best friend, a radical journalist, is murdered by hired gunmen after he throws boxes of munitions into the harbor. Owens interrupts a dance for honorary degree candidates at the university and accuses John Anderson, a trustee and a shipping company owner of war profiteering, hiring gunmen and instituting a reign of terror in the town. At graduation exercises the next day Owens leads a protest that is turned into a brawl by right-wing alumni. A man is shot to death; Owens is framed and sentenced to die, after his liberal colleagues refuse to endanger their reputations by aiding his defense.

Both *Peace on Earth* and the TU's next production, *The Sailors of Cattaro,* are about the betrayal of the radical objective. But while Maltz's and Sklar's play blames the natural timorousness of bourgeois liberals, *Cattaro*, the more radical work, blames members of the working class for being so unsure of their own goals that they accept the anti-revolutionary plans of a "humanitarian" captain.

Franz Rasch (the name is historically accurate as are the events in the play) leads a successful revolt of 6,000 sailors in the Austrian Navy. The rank and file, however, desperately want to get home to their families. They refuse to listen to Rasch's advice to storm out of the harbor and unite with the sailors at Pola. Rasch refuses to undermine the Sailors' Council by giving the tactically correct order to sail. The council wastes valuable days until all insurrectionary forces have been brought back under military control and are ready to fire on the revolutionary command ship Sankt Georg. At the crucial moment the sailors of the council, led by the revisionist Kuddel, succumb to the ship's captain, who believes in using "psychology" to keep the men in line. The wish to get back to home and family has been driving the conspirators in this strike for peace. When the captain sets about getting the men to surrender, his trump card is responsibility to one's family:

When a man is single he can toss life around lightly, as if it were an apple. But a married man—I don't know

72

whether any of you have wives and children at home—a married man takes life much more seriously.

Franz Rasch has no family. In the midst of the crisis he asks a friend to recount the story of an old romance and remarks, "You see I never had anything romantic—really wild . . . like that." The working-class family—constructed under economic oppression as a unit of suffering—provides a constant anti-revolutionary pull in strike plays. The working-class hero is always without family ties, without a stake in the bourgeois order.

STEVEDORE

Now, the *fellah,* the unemployed man, the starving native do not lay a claim to the truth; they do not *say* that they represent the truth, for they *are* the truth.

Frantz Fanon

Stevedore, which opened at the Theatre Union on April 18, 1934, began as *Warf Nigger*, a series of loosely connected vignettes based upon Paul Peters' experiences in the South. He had been a publicity director of the ILD and worked for a time on the New Orleans docks. George Sklar rewrote the play with Peters, bringing its episodes into a three-act frame and adding the character of a white union organizer.

The play's general popularity with working class audiences and newspaper reviewers, in spite of its militant indictment of white supremacy, was remarkable. Also remarkable is *Stevedore's* combination of the epic and the three-act structures; Sklar and Peters had found a form able to keep its audience enthralled while it related the sprawling story of a community in upheaval.

Stevedore opens in the back yard of a middle-class white neighborhood in New Orleans. A married woman has just been beaten by her ex-lóver. Surrounded by neighbors she bitterly sobs a story about "a nigger" jumping her from the bushes as she was taking out the garbage. Immediately a dragnet of black neighborhoods is begun; an amplified voice from a police radio calls for a pick up of "all suspicious Negroes." Lights come up on stage exposing a room in police headquarters where Mrs. Florrie Reynolds is viewing for the

73

fourth day a line-up of "suspicious Negroes." The sergeant, angry at her inability to identify the attacker, tells each man to say the words he supposedly spoke: "Don't scream or I'll kill you." Lonnie Thompson refuses to say the sentence explaining:

> You know none of us ever touch dat woman. She say she don't recognize nobody. What you holding us here fo? Why don't you let us go?

The sergeant urges Mrs. Reynolds to identify Lonnie and when she bursts into tears he disgustedly sends the line-up out, warning Lonnie to "keep your face shut."

Lonnie returns to Binnie's lunch room (in scene three) but he is unable to accept the comfort of his girl friend, Ruby, and her father, Sam Oxley, who have been anxiously waiting for him. Sam is concerned about Lonnie's restlessness, and also about his new friendship with union organizer Lem Morris:

> You tell me you want to marry and settle down, Well, you ain't gwine settle down this way, boy.

Lonnie's fellow workers from the wharf enter. After their initial surprise at seeing him free and unharmed they resume complaining about a short pay envelope. Lonnie is outraged about his wharf gang being gypped of two hour's pay and he convinces the men to follow him to the company superintendent's office.

In scene four Lonnie confronts Jeff Walcott, superintendent of the Oceanic Stevedore Company. With great magnanimity, a cover, one suspects, for his fear of the determined blacks, Walcott gives the men their money. But he quarrels with Lonnie, punching him in the nose after he has dismissed the others. Walcott is strongly affected by the incident; he feels his control over the men slipping away and so seizes the first possible excuse to terrorize them:

> That god damn shine's been hanging around with Reds, that's where he gets those notions! Organizing! Equality! Christ, those coons are just running riot! This country won't be fit to live in any more. Look at all the rapes they've been pulling in this town. Look at what

they did to that Reynolds woman. And did they catch anybody for it? No! Where the hell are the cops? . . . If they don't do something about it, I'll organize a posse and go after them myself. It's high time those niggers were put in their place.

Scene five opens with an amplified radio call urging a renewed search for the Reynolds case assailant. It is noon on the wharf. The men are lounging around and singing after lunch when Lonnie enters, bruised and cut. He has been beaten by a white gang patrolling union headquarters. Lonnie grabs a crowbar and asks the men to help him go after the gang:

Lawd, when de black man gwine stand up? When he gwine stand up proud like a man?

Just as the men begin to pick up tools and clubs the wharf whistle blows, pulling them back to their work. Walcott and two detectives enter. They seize Lonnie, mumbling some words about the Reynolds case, and drag him off. The men make one lurch in Lonnie's direction, but reading the order in Walcott's stare, they shrink back to work.

The five scenes in Act I have shown the black man discriminated against by the dealers in law and commerce, used as a scapegoat by the white woman, and denied individuality even by his own people who urge upon him the role of "good nigger." The relations between these various means of repression have also been revealed: Florrie's lie gives police and newspapers the chance to bolster egos and circulation by becoming the defenders of the white man's home, the white woman's chastity. Lonnie's belligerence gives Walcott an excuse to incite the police once more and also to involve a lawless gang in the pursuit of "justice." And the sped-up terrorization forces most of the blacks to become still more submissive to the "bosses'" will.

Early in the act Lonnie is derisively dubbed "Black Jesus" by one of the stevedores. At the end of Act I he is dragged off stage to be lynched. When he returns to the wharf, bloody and exhausted, but miraculously free of tormentors (in Act II, scene two), he has accepted the role of "Black Jesus." He has been through the valley of death and has emerged carrying the whole burden of the black race:

I don't know how I get away. We come to dat bridge, de
mob getting bigger and bigger, and I can't stand it no
mo'. Somehow I break loose and jump right in de water.
Dey shoot after me, Sam . . . . No, dey didn't hit me.
Bullet don't get de nigger. You go to lynch de nigger,
burn him, burn him alive. Oh, Sam, every black man dat
was ever lynched, I know how he feel, I know how he
feel.

Lonnie has begun to make sense of his suffering, he understands that it is necessary for the survival of white capitalistic
society. And he is beginning to grasp the kind of actions that
will allow him to stand up from under the white man's heel.
The integrated union, his violent will to take that piece of life
which belongs to him—the twin revolutionary precepts of
solidarity with all the oppressed and certainty of the righ-
teousness of the cause will turn his private pain into communal hope.

Act II opens in union headquarters. Lem Morris attempts
to win support for Lonnie and fights with one union member
who refuses to pass out leaflets condemning the arrest of a
"rape nigger."

In scene two Lem joins Lonnie on the wharf and Lonnie,
ignoring Ruby's and Sam's fears, agrees to hide in the white
man's house. After Lem leaves to borrow a car Mitch, the
leader of the white gang, appears with one of his henchmen.
They find Lonnie in the shadows, but after a fight he manages to escape with Ruby, Sam and Joe Crump. At Binnie's
lunch room (scene three) the other wharf hands are sullenly
eating, complaining about the white boys waiting in the
shadows for them. News of the fight at the docks has been
broadcast over the radio and when Lonnie arrives he is
bawled out for picking a fight with white men when racial
tensions are running high. When Lem Morris arrives the
Negroes are even more upset, with good reason. Soon after
Mitch's gang and a policeman force their way into the lunch
room. Unwilling to let Lonnie be captured, Binnie has the
lights put out and the blacks run. Lonnie has time to escape
but Sam is shot. The act ends with Ruby mourning her
father.

Act III has only two scenes. The first is a wake for Sam
Oxley. The preacher, Mose Venable, urges perseverance for

his scared and miserable flock. Only Ruby Oxley refuses to join in the spirituals. Lonnie arrives with news of a planned attack by Mitch's gang on the black neighborhood. He demands the blacks stand and fight, telling them they have no place to run, conditions will be the same all over. The preacher is silenced by Blacksnake Johnson:

> Put dat Bible on de shelf, preacher. We got something mo' important to think about. We worrying about our necks.

The blacks surge into the courtyard to begin constructing a barricade out of household junk. They arm themselves with lumps of coal, bricks, and rabbit guns. Lonnie builds their courage:

> ...We hyar to show 'em we men and we gwine be treated like men. And remember we ain't only fighting fo' ourselves. Dar black folks all over de country looking at us right now: dey counting on us, crying to us: "Stand yo' ground. You fighting fo'us. You fighting fo' all of us." Now how many of you gwine stand hyar and fight? How many of you gwine stand hyar and never move if it's de last place on earth you ever stand? Raise your hands. Show me! Raise your hands.

Mitch fires the first bullet and Lonnie falls. For a moment the blacks cower in the corners of the yard, but anger suddenly gets the better of fear and they rush the barricade throwing bricks and rocks. At this moment they are reinforced by Lem Morris and a group of union men. Binnie takes aim and shoots Mitch. The white gang flees. The curtain falls on a tableau like the Pieta: Ruby holds Lonnie's lifeless body in her lap.

Each act of *Stevedore* ends with a moment of pathos: Lonnie is dragged away, Sam Oxley is shot, Lonnie is murdered. Yet the crux of each act, the moment of conflict which determines in which direction the future action will go, occurs as the black community confronts its white oppressors. In Act I they meet Walcott's stare and shrink back to work; in Act II they resist Lonnie's arrest by throwing off the lights and running; in Act III they stand at the barricades and fight. Each act moves toward a moment of communal

77

decision. The defeat and deaths of individuals provide three emotional endings. Yet this focus on the family group (Lonnie, Sam, and Ruby) and on the conventional relationships of domestic tragedy is undercut by an epic movement which is all the time attempting to include a world in flux, a nation struggling to be born. *Stevedore* was politically radical because it called for the militant union of black and white workers (it even revitalized the standard "cavalry-to-the-rescue" scene, making it into a show of working-class solidarity). For the Theatre Union the play was dramatically radical because it admitted the shortcomings in the three act well-made play and compensated for them with an epic movement that expressed the desires of an entire population.

The TU's first total departure from the well-made play, the production of Bertolt Brecht's *Mother* in November 1935, was a financial, critical, and artistic disaster. Ironically, the group's most ill-fated production is also its best known. Brecht has written of it, so has Mordecai Gorelik.* Critic Lee Baxandall has pieced together the whole story in a long article, "Brecht in America,"** in which he writes that the Theatre Union, anxious to produce what they thought would be a moving adaptation of Maxim Gorki's realistic novel, was totally unprepared for the job Brecht expected them to accomplish: introduction of his epic theatre to US audiences.

One afternoon in the rehearsal hall convinced Brecht that "someone had turned *Mother* not only into English but into suspenseful, saccharine trash." To keep the play's performance time at two hours, supposedly the limit of audience stamina, the Theatre Union cut what Brecht felt to be the main scene in the third act. If a group of workers had been consulted, he wrote in his essay on the production, they would have demanded the anti-war scene be put back, because its exclusion meant:

> . . . having a scene which shows how the Bolshevik programme was rejected by the great bulk of the proletariat in 1914, then having the 1917 Revolution follow immediately on it like a passively-awaited gift from

---

*Bertolt Brecht, *Brecht on Theatre*, trans. John Willet, New York, 1966, pp. 81-84; Mordecai Gorelik, "I am the Einstein of the New Stage Form," *Theatre Arts*, March 1957, pp. 72-73.
**Brecht*, ed. Erika Munk, New York, 1972, pp. 33-60.

heaven . . . Arguing thus they would incidentally have saved the aesthetic structure of the third act, which was wrecked by the ill-conceived cutting of its main scene.

Brecht rejected Paul Peters' first adaptation which, among other deviations from the original, had brought Pavel's murder on stage in an emotional and suspenseful scene. Peters did another version, used in the playing. Though it still lacked the anti-war propaganda scene it is much closer in tone to Brecht's intentions.

After several meetings with Brecht, Mordecai Gorelik became a convert to the author's epic theories and redesigned the production to suit them. Gorelik's enthusiasm for epic theatre is probably the most positive result of the Theatre Union's *Mother* production. Certainly his book *New Theatres for Old* (New York, 1940) is inspired by it. The article he wrote for the summer 1937 issue of *Theatre Workshop* is the first to present a cogent theory of epic theatre to a left wing audience that had been turned off by the disaster on stage.

Gorelik's setting for *Mother* was anti-illusionistic and skeletal. Slides which commented upon the action were projected overhead. However, the costumes by Fania Mindell and the lighting by Charles Friedman remained picturesque. The direction by Victor Wolfson and musical arrangements by Jerome Moross (original music was by Hans Eisler) aimed at the very illusion Brecht despised.

Mother ran for 36 performances. Only pre-booked theatre parties kept it going that long; there was almost no walk-up business. Critical reaction to the second production of a Brecht play in Amerika (*Three Penny Opera* had been unsuccessfully produced earlier in the decade) was generally unkind and uncomprehending. Richard Lockridge complained in the *New York Sun*:

Certainly *Mother* has nothing whatever to do with the American theatre, from which the Theatre Union seems at this point to have seceded.

In the *Times* Brooks Atkinson declared, "What *Mother* lacks is cumulative power." On the Left an intelligent and basically favorable review by Stanley Burnshaw appeared in the December 13, 1934, edition of *New Masses*, but in the *Daily*

Worker Michael Gold asked the Theatre Union to stick to Amerikan scripts since "they are not yet equipped to interpret Europe to us." And John Gassner, writing in *New Theatre*, revealed the fundamental inconsistency of critics and theatre people on the Left; he seized the heart of the matter and then proceeded to operate on it with bourgeois tools.

There is a certain diffuseness in the text which the slides and the chanting fail to overcome and sometimes even accentuate.

Mordecai Gorelik

EPIC REALISM:

*Brecht's Notes on the
Three-Penny Opera**

We in the United States have only a vague knowledge of the experimental work carried on in the German theatre between 1919-1932, although three plays of the "epic" theatre of Brecht and Piscator have been presented in New York in recent years. *The Three-Penny Opera* was produced by Gifford Cochran and Jerrold Krimsky, April, 1933. *Mother* was put on by the Theatre Union in December, 1935, and *The Case of Clyde Griffiths*, taken from the script by Piscator originally entitled *An American Tragedy*, was produced by the Group Theatre and the Shuberts in April, 1936. But even when the New York examples of epic productions were before us, we were not able to see clearly the functioning and purpose of the epic form. As is pointed out in the following notes, the existing institution and methods of the commercial stage are perfectly capable of putting on epic works in such a way that practically nothing remains of their creative value. The show-business is not in the least perturbed by any new dramatic idea, even when this "novelty" contradicts everything that the show-business stands for.

In Germany the epic form dominated many of the productions of two Berlin playhouses: the Theater am Nollendorfplatz, under the direction of Erwin Piscator and the Theater am Schiffbauerdamm, directed by Bertolt Brecht. The latter theatre had this form as the

---

*Theatre Workshop, April-July 1937. Edited version KMT. Full translations of Brecht's *Threepenny Opera* notes have been made by Desmond Vesey in Brecht: *Plays I* (London, 1950), and Eric Bentley in *From the Modern Repertoire I* (Bloomington, Ind., 1949).

specific object of its research. In scale alone the dramatic experiment conducted by these two playhouses was the greatest in our day. Brecht has estimated that the combined cost of their productions totalled half a million dollars.

Productions specifically epic in character, which astounded Europe at the time they were put on, and which have since had an ever-growing influence on the world stage, usually failed to achieve even moderate runs. The epic theatre developed in the face of almost continuous box-office defeat and open hostility. But there were two notable exceptions to the rule: *The Good Soldier Schweik* at Piscator's theatre, and *The Three-Penny Opera* (text and direction by Brecht, music by Weill, settings by Neher), at the Schiffbauerdamm Theatre. The success of the *Opera* was as unprecedented as the failures of the other plays at this theatre: it ran for 400 performances—a Berlin record for a serious play—and was re-staged throughout Germany and Europe.

The excerpts here given from Brecht's notes on *The Three Three-Penny Opera** will help to define the term *epic theatre*.

Neither Brecht nor Piscator claims to have invented the epic form: on the contrary, they insist on its antiquity. They merely recognized it and put it to new uses. Its discovery, they say, was forced upon them when they tried to put classic works of the drama on in a way which would have meaning for a new theatre audience—primarily, in their case, an audience of the Berlin proletariat. Existing theatre-forms, which were focused on individual stage characters, did not permit of a clear view of the necessary historical and social background of these characters; and even the characters themselves remained vague, no matter how centrally they might be placed in the stage picture. The Brecht-Piscator attempt to overcome this difficulty resulted in drastic innovations in the theatre. (This development was coincidental with, but independent of, the discoveries made by the proletarian theatre of the Soviet Union working under directors like Meyerhold and Vakhtangov.)

Epic theatre is the name given to the sum of the new theory and practice. Two main lines of demarcation separate it from the practice of the conventional theatre: the epic style does not accept the principle of the emotional "carrying-away" of the spectator, nor does it accept the principle (as advocated by Wagner, Craig, Appia, etc.) of the fusion of theatrical arts in production. In his theories Brecht is even more drastic. He places the epic form in contrast to the Aristotelian theatre as defined by the use of intensification, climax and catharsis. For this

---

*From *Versuche*, by Bertolt Brecht, Vol. III, Gustav Kiepenheuer Verlag, Berlin, 1931. Brecht's collected works, under this title will shortly be reissued by Malik Verlag, London and Prague.

Footnote in original.

81

reason he has been accused of championing a purely intellectual theatre in which there is no place for human feelings. This, however, is a misconception.

The epic style in itself does not banish the emotional element. The epic dramatist believes in taking sides for or against his characters; he may even take sides more openly and vehemently than the more conventional dramatist; but for this very reason he is the more careful not to let his partisanship run away with him. He is as merciless in his criticism of his favored characters as he is of the characters whom he hates. There must be room in the theatre for the mind as well as the passions. The theatre has too long been decapitated. The question of the exact place of emotion in drama is a serious one; it has occupied much of Brecht's studies and, as will be seen, it has led him to some very definite conclusions.

With his innovations Brecht combines an appreciation of non-climactic theatre forms such as that of the Chinese theatre, from which he derives much of his own practice. These researches far afield have served to emphasize his quality of thought, which, to borrow some nationalistic phrases, is deeply German and Lutheran in its dogged, workmanlike skepticism. Even so, his work and that of Piscator, is so uncongenial to the present German Nationalist regime that both these men are in exile. Nevertheless Brecht is not forgotten in his native Germany where the "underground" demand for his literary work is so great that the books of his plays are said to receive the highest prices paid for illegal literature.

Brecht's notes disclose the advent into the theatre of a scientific temperament—a mind which systematically questions every accepted opinion. It cannot be said that he sets about this scientific task in scientific fashion: his approach, like that of many other pioneers, is polemical. It may be debated whether the epic theatre is outside the framework of the Aristotelian theatre as Brecht maintains. But there can hardly be any question as to the stimulating quality of the notes, or the penetrating observation of their author.

In translating the notes I have, with the author's approval, freely altered the text. Acting and dramaturgy are discussed in these excerpts but the epic theory of the stage setting deserves an additional study.

BRECHT'S NOTES ON *THE THREE-PENNY OPERA*

We witness today the ascendancy of the theatre over dramatic literature. The priority of the institutionalized theatre and its stage apparatus represents the priority of the means of production over the production itself. The established method of the theatre resists any adaptation to new uses. On coming in contact with a new dramaturgy it at once assimilates this new dramaturgy, eating away from ít everything but the most indigestible elements, which appear in performance to be mere eccentricities.

Genuine adaptation to new uses would seem to be an inexorable
law of the theatre but the institutionalized theatre manages to get
around this law—it turns everything into show-business. [Brecht]

The tendency of an already established theatrical form to "eat away"
a new dramaturgy was illustrated during the inception of the naturalistic theatre. Plays written in the new style were destroyed by romanti-
cist productions. After three naturalistic plays had failed in the established theatres of that period, Antoine, founder of the naturalistic
Theatre Libre, wrote to the dramatic critic, Sarcey: "Well, the very
simple reason for this three-fold happening in which the actors, as a rule
excellent, were judged mediocre for one evening (and for this time
only) is that not one of the three works was produced and played
according to its true meaning. The fact is that this new (or renewed)
drama requires interpreters who are new or renewed . . . . What do you
expect will be the fate of a play drawing its effect from life when it is
presented in a falsified atmosphere?"
The opposite situation, the "eating away" of older dramaturgy by
newer but incompetent methods of production, is an even more common phenomenon. Consider the average modern production of Shakespeare.

The new dramaturgy rejects the principle of the tightly-knit play
which attempts to subordinate everything to a single idea. It
rejects the mania for entraining the spectator on the path of a
single, overpowering emotion—an emotion which actually sup-
plants the issues of the play and which allows the spectator to
look neither to the right nor the left, neither up nor down. Room
must be found for the footnote and the reference page, even in
dramaturgy. [Brecht]

The commercial drama, it is contended, has little power or inclina-
tion to teach anything. Its method today is to focus on human behavior, claiming that thereby it can describe the laws of human environment. The epic drama claims the contrary: to teach dramatically, one
must unfold a logical analysis of the laws of human environment as
they bear upon human behavior. For instance, in depicting the effect of
the conveyor-system on workers in an automobile factory the method
of conventional drama is to build up a tense emotional relationship
among certain workers, employers, etc., who are intended to typify
various sociological aspects of the conveyor-system. The epic drama
puts into the foreground, not these emotionalized symbolic figures but
the conveyor system itself, of which human figures, in all their complexity, are only a part. This may seem more complicated than before.
Actually it is much simpler. It is far more direct and truthful to
describe the conveyor-system bodily in this way than to describe it by
indirection and in terms of psychology.

The conventional dramatist "solves" the problems of environment either by turning the environment into local color, or by ignoring it altogether. The laws of human environment are objective, complex, and, in their operation in modern times, often technologically conditioned. Conventional dramaturgy makes little effort to cope with such a formidable problem. In place of necessary scientific thought it substitutes a pattern of emotion, hurrying the spectator from one incident to the next, exciting him and leaving him finally with an idle sensory adventure but with no practical experience gained. From this point of view, the present-day forms of drama are guilty of vulgarization, and the more thorough-going the emotional stimulation, the more reprehensible they are.

Today, when the human being must be grasped as "the sum total of social relationships" (Marx) only the epic form can enable the dramatist to find a comprehensive image of the world. The individual, precisely the flesh-and-blood individual, can be understood only by way of the processes wherein and whereby he exists. The new dramaturgy must acquire a form which will not make use of throbbing suspense, but will have a suspense in the relationship of its scenes, which will charge each other with tension. (This form will therefore be anything but a stringing-together of scenes such as we find in revues.) [Brecht]

Brecht offers a choice between the old drama (which uses fervent intensity and hypnotic identification with the stage characters for the purpose of "carrying away" the spectator in a dream), and the new, which is to take the form of conscious laboratory examination of human experience. Brecht proposes the use of the epic form as against the Aristotelian. Instead of a series of scenes of fervor, each depending on the last, and rising to a climax, he proposes independent scenes in each of which one phase of a social process (of which the situation and characters are a part) is examined and solved. In the epic form these scenes, while independent of each other, form together a thorough investigation of some particular social process. The discoveries of one scene (anywhere in the play) have a bearing on other scenes (anywhere in the play). Theoretically it is possible to start playing an epic drama with any one of its scenes, and to play the rest in any order one cares to, just as any phase of a laboratory experiment can be undertaken apart from other phases. Epic construction is therefore not closely knit; it is not built for the purpose of conducting an ever-rising tide of emotion. On the other hand, it is evident that the epic form is anything but a revue form: it does not string together an assortment of unrelated scenes. In the revue, the problems of timing, variety and music are entirely superficial.

84

Why two arrests of *Macheath* and not one? From the point of view of the German Pseudo-classic (Goethe, Schiller, Lessing, Freytag), it is redundant to show two prison scenes: such repetition slows up the action. From our point of view these scenes are an example of primitive epic form. Climactic dramaturgy, intent on subordinating everything to one idea, tries to give the spectator the sense of a relentless approach to a goal (in this case the execution of the hero, *Macheath*). It provokes in the spectator an ever greater emotional *demand* for a *supply* of emotional release. It has to use causation in a straight line in order to ensure a large emotional investment on the part of the spectator. Its causation must be simple and foreknown because emotions will risk passage only across fully assured terrain; emotions cannot bear disappointment . . . . Epic dramaturgy, with its basis in objective fact instead of subjective emotions, has little interest in providing an emotional investment for its audience. It knows no dramatic goal except a logical conclusion; and it is aware of a different sort of causation, whose direction is not in a straight line, but in curves, even in jumps. [Brecht]

A caustic evaluation of the "well-made play" in terms of its manufacture for the market! According to Brecht, this type of drama is compounded largely of idle sensation. The commercial dramatist proceeds to arouse in his audience the utmost degree of emotional craving, to which he supplies a corresponding emotional release. The greater the craving, the greater the release, and the greater the box-office returns Q.E.D.

Unfortunately for the outlook for serious drama this practice is not confined to the commercial playwrights. It is copied even by the socially-minded dramatists who disagree with the commercial playwrights as to content, but accept the conventional form without too much examination. Albert Bein in *Let Freedom Ring*, John Howard Lawson in *Marching Song*, Clifford Odets in *Awake and Sing*, Albert Maltz in *Black Pit*, Leopold Atlas in *But for the Grace of God*—in fact, the entire progressive movement in American dramaturgy—attempts to convince an audience, not with the logic of documented events, but with the machinery of intensification. The build-up of emotion becomes the central objective, while the sociological process becomes not much more than "atmosphere" in its final effect.

It is necessary to see that a new form is indispensable to a new content. In a far less critical period of history Ibsen required a new scenic form (the fourth-wall stage) and a new dramatic form (the well-made play perfected by Scribe and Sardou) in order to convey his message. Our social dramatists might well learn from this.

Emotional drama is idealistic in its philosophy: that is, it is based

85

upon ideal conceptions of justice and ethics. Its special province is the individual character. But it is worth noting that when this dramaturgy began its course (with the Elizabethans) it was far more radical than the German Pseudo-classic two hundred years later. The Pseudo-classic separated the process of stage production from the purpose of production itself, and moulded its individuals to suit ideal conceptions . . . . As for the epigones of the epigones—the little Goethes and third-rate Schillers of today—the individual is not to be found in their work at all. By now even the dynamic of production has been turned into a sly handful of effects, "good ideas." At the same time the individual, in full process of disintegration, is transformed into a "role" . . . . Even the middleclass novel has been less backward: it has attempted to analyze the individual psychologically (Thomas Mann, Hauptmann, Proust). Unfortunately this attempt is too late—the individual has long since fallen apart. [Brecht]

Here the fight is carried to middleclass drama on its own ground, that of the individual personality. It is contended that this drama has dealt less and less capably with the individual. At the same time the significant middleclass individual has himself faded away until there is no longer any material left to deal with. It is Brecht's idea that the *average* Elizabethan burgher was a far stronger and more dynamic personality than the *average* middleclass citizen today . . . .

The titles projected on to a screen are a primitive beginning of the "literarization" of the theatre. Such literarization will continue to develop, not only in the theatre, but throughout public activities, and on the widest scale. [Brecht]

The epic theatre's use of titles (like movie subtitles or chapter headings) projected on a screen from a stereopticon, has aroused much discussion, and even resentment. To the charge that such titles slow up the dramatic action, the reply is that they are used precisely to slow up the heedless emotional impetus of the spectator. Precise thought is possible only in writing; the spectator may compare his own opinion with that of the dramatist whose printed words place themselves on record as the play unrolls . . . . Brecht insists that this kind of literate relationship already exists to a large degree in our daily life. Not only do books, magazines and newspapers accompany our daily activities, but we are conditioned at every moment by printed matter—shop signs, street signs, billboards, mathematical and other symbols. At present this relationship is a chaotic one in the theatre and outside it. We are confronted with the problem of turning it into an orderly creative process . . . .

What is the "emotionalism" on which Brecht has concentrated so much fire? It is not the emotional capacity of the audience or the dramatist: this he finds normal and constructive. What he opposes is the inflated development of emotion at the expense of the teaching function of the drama . . . . Not only does Brecht isolate the misuse of emotion as a main symptom of decayed drama, but he believes that *the fusion of theatrical elements into one emotional system is the technical means whereby this unhealthy process is carried into production.* * New dramatists who have a serious message should critically approach the technique already in use in the established theatres for this technique will insidiously destroy them.

BLACK PIT

Revolutionary societies have been tragic societies at a depth and on a scale that go beyond ordinary pity and fear.

Raymond Williams

The Theatre Union's inability to relate to Brecht's epic theatre, despite its instinctual adoption of a few of its tenets in *Stevedore*, becomes more understandable once we recall the highly conservative nature of most criticism at the time. It was not that US radicals were waving the flag for Stalin's favored socialist realism—Michael Gold was almost the only one who did that, and since he really couldn't explain the Russian theory he couldn't press his point too far. But they were never able to formalize a theory of people's theatre that could be forcefully opposed to notions of psychological realism. (In part, too, they were stunned into silence by the Group Theatre's success with Stanislavsky's system.) The absence of suggested alternatives led some playwrights toward a theatre in which the recurrent conservative criti-

*"In his monograph, *How's Your Second Act?* [Arthur] Hopkins sets for the director the task of capturing the unconscious mind of the audience, the deep, subliminal self whose exploration by Freud and Jung has made over modern psychological science. Like the hypnotist, Hopkins would 'still the conscious mind.' This can be accomplished in the theatre through simplification of background and through confining the actor to the most unobtrusive and natural expression of his emotion, 'by giving the audience no reason to think about it, by presenting every phrase so unobtrusively, so free from confusing gesture, movement and emphasis, that all passing action seems inevitable, so that we are never challenged or asked consciously why. This whole treatment begins first with the manuscript, continues through the designing of the settings, and follows carefully every actor's movement and inflection. If, throughout, this attitude of easy flow can be maintained, the complete illusionment of the audience is inevitable.'" —Kenneth MacGowan: *The Theatre of Tomorrow.*

Footnote in original.

87

cism—that characters in "propaganda plays" lacked depth—was taken seriously.

In February 1935, the Theatre Union issued a press release explaining their fourth production, Albert Maltz's *Black Pit*:

> The dramatic conflict does not coincide with the physical conflict of the picket line, but takes place in one man's mind. In other words, the play is a human, personal drama, built around characters, as opposed to the more schematic *Peace on Earth* and *Sailors of Cattaro*. [*Mother* would not be produced until the following fall.]

Maltz called *Black Pit* a "psychological play" and hoped that he could make its stool pigeon subject "understandable in human terms and yet increase the horror of the audience at his act."

Black Pit opens with a prologue. Iola Prescott and Joe Kovarsky are being married. Immediately after the service Joe is handcuffed and led to prison to begin serving a three-year term for his part in a recent strike of West Virginia coal miners.

In Act I, three years later, Iola waits for Joe's return with his sister and brother-in-law, Tony and Mary Lakavich. During Joe's imprisonment Tony was crippled by a fall of slate in the mine. Three adults and two children have been living on his weekly compensation of $10.50. Joe Kovarsky enters and awkwardly greets his wife. After finding her still faithful the goodness of the moment overcomes him. He tells her: "We got be happy now, Iola, we got have lil' bit sun now."

During this reunion scene the night noises of the mine camp are heard: "An automobile starting, a woman calling her child, a girl's laughter, a boy playing a mouth organ." The profusion of sound effects, here and throughout the play, recalls Stanislavsky's more earnest attempts at stage realism. But here the sounds are meant to distract, rather than intensify the mood of the scene. They keep the audience aware of the swarming humanity which surrounds even the most intimate moment.

The summer before he wrote *Black Pit* Maltz had travelled to the country's mines, farms, and factories in order to familiarize himself with the details of each poverty. He was

Scene two takes place six months after Joe's homecoming. Blacklisted in West Virginia, he has finally found work under an assumed name at the Munson Mine in Pennsylvania. It is Saturday night, Joe is writing to his pregnant wife. A moment later the mine overseer enters the room and tells Joe to get out of the patch, his strike record has caught up with him. Several months pass before scene three. Joe has been determined to present the culture of his subjects as well as their economic grievances. Iola reads to Mary Lakovich from a True Story Magazine or cuts out fashion pictures for Anna, the little girl. Vincey, Tony's son, constantly teases and swats his sister. Tony and his neighbors play a quick Italian betting game. At a picnic they folk dance to Hungarian tunes played on an accordion. The play's language is a compound of dialects ranging from Iola's lilting mountain speech to Tony and Joe's nearly incomprehensible Slovak-accented English. trying to get relief. He returns home after having walked seventeen miles to town in a futile effort to secure the money a local official has promised, but not delivered. Tony says:

I tol' you, Joe. You go by self—get noddings. You go wit' whole bunch—lot feller—mak' holler—you get rah-lief.

But Joe has no faith in solidarity. He sacrificed three years of his life for the union only to find that conditions among the miners have steadily worsened and that the bosses refuse to believe his debt to them has been paid. Iola, afraid to deliver her baby without the company doctor, has gone to her cousin, mine superintendent Prescott, to ask for a job for Joe. Prescott comes to the house that night and offers Joe his old job back on condition that he "be friendly" with the company, informing the managers of any union organizing in the mine.

Joe and Iola decide he should take the job, convincing themselves that he need not tell Prescott anything of consequence. Joe explains:

Sure! Sure, I fool heem. Take'm job, Get dohctor. Make lil' bit mohney. After awhile—say g'bye, go away—sure. Man got live lak man, Iola. Man no can live in hole, lak animal!

Joe's movement to company stool pigeon parallels the course of Iola's pregnancy. As her delivery draws near, the pressure on Joe to prove himself financially capable increases. Iola's labor pains begin two days after Joe has spoken out against strike plans at a card game, lying about the safety of one area of the mine. Prescott comes to the house to find out the name of the union organizer. As Iola cries out in pain from the next room, Joe spits out the name "McCulloh." Then he turns toward the room where his wife waits and says: "Yah, Iola . . . I call him. We gone get Dohctor now awright."

Black Pit is made of two separate actions, one personal and one communal. Joe goes from trusted union man and beloved husband to stool pigeon and outlaw. Conversely, the community climbs out of the depths of poverty toward solidarity and the industrious hopefulness of a strike. The sounds, which in Act I called our attention to the life outside Joe's house, are heard in the following acts to have come from actual characters. Mrs. Floyd, constantly dipping snuff and clowning with the neighborhood children, pot-bellied Lyster, vain Pauline Anetsky, blind and half-crazed Jimmie, are specific reminders of the community Joe is betraying. In Act II these characters intrude into the story until Joe is trapped by scenes alternating between their aspirations and the demands of Prescott. The play has become a series of confrontations which Joe tries to avoid.

By Act III, the community is dominant on stage; its will controls Joe's destiny. With part of his ten dollar fee for betraying Hansy McCulloh, Joe has purchased a keg of beer and invited his neighbors to a picnic honoring his new son. For the first time he appears other than as a timid, hunted creature:

Joe (is swaggering, expansive, happy. He jumps up on the porch): Hey you, everybuddy come drink'm beer! Free beer! Dis my peecnic for Tony Kovarsky! I pay for beer. Drink'm opp 'fore she get hot.

Joe's happiness has been paid for by the community. The previous night, company goons dragged Hansy McCulloh from the patch and beat him. During the picnic another explosion occurs in the mine and Tom Floyd, whose wife has

90

been drinking Joe's "free" beer, is killed. In front of the guests, Barolla calls Joe a stool pigeon. Joe storms into the house as the other men go off to form the picket lines. Tony follows him and forces a confession. Finally Joe understands what has happened:

> Christus, why I do dis? I no wan' do .... Listen everybuddy, I be good feller. Why I got mak' lie out myself get piece bread eat? Why I got cut heart out have wooman? Goddam cohmpany, I gone smash cohmpany.

But his error is not so easily retractable. No miner will be able to trust him now. He must leave the patch, deserting wife and child.

As Joe goes out the door, the mine whistle blows signalling the men to strike. Iola stands weeping, the baby in her arms. Tony turns to her:

> Nevair min', Iola . . . nevair min'! . . . Leely feller gone grow oop . . . he no got crawl on belly get piece bread eat . . . outside miner be fight . . . By God, miner gone raise head oop in sun . . . Holler out loud 'Jesus Chris' miner got blow whistle . . . not boss blow . . . miner blow' . . . Jesus Chris' I nevair gone die . . . I gone sit here wait for dat time!

Joe Kovarsky hardly exists as a tragic character: his actions are too predictable; his intellect is too weak—he accepts Tony's sentence without comprehending the thought process behind it. But as a pawn in a power play he takes on special significance. *Black Pit* is a study of two societies in conflict (the one in capitalistic decay, the other in revolutionary turmoil) which will not let the Joe Kovarskys live.

Joe's tragedy is that of the neutral in a world which is being polarized. After three years of prison he: "Wan' have some lil' bit good tings—wan' have house . . . He accepts a job from the superintendent hoping to fool him. He plays cards with the union organizers but uses Iola's pregnancy as an excuse for not delivering their leaflets.

Joe desperately wants to provide a few of the "good things in life" for his family. The society he lives in demands that he be a good provider before it calls him a man, yet it refuses

91

him the economic opportunities necessary to do so. Joe's quest for manhood ironically unites him with the female characters in the play. Iola urges him to accept Prescott's offer. Iola and Mary Lakavich, Tony's wife, both know of the super's ten dollar "baby gift" and both promise not to tell Tony. Tony, who as a cripple is no longer capable of earning a living, is the real man because he is committed to destroying a system which constantly puts him down. Tony understands that a domestic existence is impossible in a time of revolution; hence, his indifference over the break-up of Joe's family, and his utter lack of concern about how his own family will survive once the strike stops his company compensation payments. The wish for a family, a home, a few leisure-time pleasures, which was allowed to pathetically linger in a society which offered slight hope for its attainment, must in revolutionary times be forsaken.

No Theatre Union production caused more controversy than *Black Pit**. Intermission arguments on Fourteenth were loud and zealous. Some people felt "the production of *Black Pit* by the Theatre Union was a scandal and a disgrace," and the audience should have been made to despise Joe instead of pity him. Other observers "argued that the play was good propaganda because it proved the rottenness of economic conditions by showing how Joe "got that way." The argument was carried over into the left-wing press where Joseph North stated in *New Masses*:

> It seems to me the selection of the emphasis—the stool pigeon story—undoubtedly derives from Maltz's relatively recent initiation into proletarian environment. Else, this spectacular, this unhealthy and atypical aspect of the labor movement, would not have caught his dramatist's eye.

Herbert Kline countered in *New Theatre* with the suggestion that Maltz had written "our first revolutionary tragedy":

---

*Maltz, whose radical sentiments strike one as sincere and honorable and those of a committed liberal, had a way of arousing the ire of the most dogmatic. Later in the decade he wrote an article regretting the limitations radical politics impose on a writer. It caused such a bitter controversy he decided to publically repudiate it, thereby proving his point.

The tragedy . . . is told with such understanding artistry that only a few sectarians, missing the point completely, mistake the human portrait of a man who is crushed by the system and by his own weakness for what they foolishly call "the glorification of the stool pigeon."

Black Pit provided the deepest excursion back into Naturalism of any Theatre Union drama. Maltz focused on one of society's victims at a point before the victim knew (or when he had momentarily forgotten) why he was being victimized. So the Joe-Iola segments of the story point toward social change indirectly; something must be done, but just how that something is to be accomplished is left, as it was in the Naturalistic plays of the nineteenth century, to the mind of the beholder. In this sense the play is not revolutionary, and criticism like Joseph North's becomes understandable, though not agreeable.

The play's concession to revolutionary certainty is Tony's final speech where he predicts the union's ultimate victory. But the speech serves a strange dramatic purpose: it makes the ending of *Black Pit* bitter instead of tragic. At the final moment, the community and Joe have slipped from view. Iola and the child remain, and with this background Tony's speech brings home the exorbitant price revolution exacts from the innocents whose lives it forms. The strength of this bitterness nearly overshadows the facts of Joe's personal tragedy. For Joe the ultimate physical and moral degradation is being forced to "live in hole, lak animal!" not being a stool pigeon. An actor would have this spectre—of a man hunted, clinging to cave walls—to help him haunt the character he created. If he succeeded in visualizing Joe's horror of this fate, he might also succeed in pointing out a basic tragic irony: what Joe feared most and sought most desperately to avoid is precisely the homeless, outlawed life his actions have led him to.

There is still another, more subtle, tragic proportion to the play, one which grows clearer with the passage of time. It is the failure of the revolutionary dream. Tony Lakavich's prediction has not come true. Miners do not "blow [the] whistle"; they still must work in unsafe mines, and they are so estranged from their union that the bravest of them are slaughtered for opposing it.

93

Working conditions in the new factories, on GM's own description, are such that discontent and "balkiness" are rational, not exceptional reactions.

Emma Rothschild

Marching Song, John Howard Lawson's play about the unionization of the automobile industry, opened as the final production of the Theatre Union just six days after Governor Frank Murphy announced settlement of the historic sit-down strike by members of the United Automobile Workers in Flint, Michigan. The strike halted General Motor's production and effectively cracked the company's anti-union facade. Before the strike, Irving Bernstein writes, "Flint and its more than 150,000 people belonged to General Motors . . . GM dominated the only daily newspaper, the radio station, the pulpit, relief and the schools. Its spies covered the town like a blanket." Though there was some bloodshed, the UAW's victory was won without large-scale violence. Lawson's mythical Brimmer Company was actually modeled on the Ford Motor Company and the reactionary policies of its patriarch. Henry Ford's most trusted employee, Harry Bennett, staffed the Ford Service Department with "a large number of professional boxers and wrestlers and underworld types," according to Bernstein. Ford employees, terrorized at work by the Servicemen, were afraid to talk or smile, drive Chevrolet cars, smoke, sit down or lean against a post. On May 26, 1937, the servicemen attacked and brutally beat a group of UAW organizers, the late Walter Reuther among them, who were attempting to pass out leaflets. It was not until 1940 that the company was unionized.

Except for frequent but brief letters to editors defending his favorite causes, Lawson had been strangely silent during the Theatre Union's existence. He was busy formulating his revolt against "the sickness and emotional hypocrisy" of the Broadway stage. The attack, when launched, was in two stages. A critical work, *Theory and Technique of Playwriting*, was published in 1936. A year later, on February 17, 1937, the Theatre Union produced *Marching Song*, the dramatic application of the book's insights.

Lawson was the US playwright most continually occupied with finding a dramatic form uniquely suited to the expression of radical ideas. The Marxian dialectic provided his outline. His thesis was the existing bourgeois penchant for psychological realism; his antithesis was the notion that a character's personality could be immediately altered through contact with revolutionary events. A new and dynamic drama, capable of showing men in their shifting relationships to society, instead of lost in an emotional void, was to be his synthesis.

Like *Stevedore* and *Black Pit, Marching Song*'s scenes alternate between the pathetic experiences of a family group and the awakening revolutionary energies of a community. But the Lawson play, certainly the most complex production ever undertaken by the Theatre Union, denies itself the strength of a linear plot progression and chooses instead a series of short episodes, seemingly unconnected except by place, as the truest way to picture the dawning of a radical consciousness. Forty-seven actors were employed for the production, twenty-four of them had substantial parts. The setting throughout was an abandoned factory, beautifully designed by Howard Bay as a study of industry's steel, glass, dynamos, and switches fallen into massive decay. The set's walkways, ramps, and ladders amply provided for the fluid movement demanded by the script. Following his description of the setting in the acting edition of the play, Lawson had drawn a map of Brimmerton, USA, the industrial city where the action takes place. The factory is bounded on two sides by a garbage dump and a swamp. The river which runs along behind the swamp, separating the industrial section of town from the business district, is called the Jordan. Also along the course of the river, but separated from it by a railroad track, are the two large plants belonging to the Brimmer Automobile Company. The patents and good will for the objects manufactured in the abandoned factory have been sold to Brimmer; the land and building were retained by Warren Winkle, owner of the now defunct Winkle Company. A group of transients, several of whom worked in the old factory, have made the decrepit building into a temporary hostel. Pop Fergus, ex-time keeper at the Winkle Company, says of his residence in the building: "It seemed natural to come back here. Seemed like a natural place to come to."

Many of Winkle's former employees have gone to work in the Brimmer plant. They found conditions in the mammoth company intolerable, joined the struggling Automobile Workers' Union, and went out on a strike which was busted by black laborers brought in from St. Louis and forced to do scab work in the factory. Many strikers, including Pete Russell, were blacklisted and have been unable to find work for several months. Without warning the bank forecloses on Pete's mortgage, evicting him, his wife, Jenny, their baby, and Jenny's sister Rose Graham from their small home. The Russells' eviction, presumably at the order of the Brimmer Company, becomes a rallying point for the weakened union Gradually all working class Brimmerton, fed up with the policies of this company town, become involved in strike action. They surround the Brimmer plants, protecting the sit-down strikers inside from hired gangsters who have been ordered to break the strike.

As the play opens Jenny Russell is seated on a concrete stoop in the factory, singing to her baby in a broken, absent-minded voice. She has come to the factory to escape the gossip of her neighbors. While she had a home, Jenny, like the rest of the neighborhood women, had carefully avoided walking close to the decaying factory:

> We used to be afraid. I mean, we'd pass at night, see a fire burning, or a lantern or a candle. We'd walk on the other side of the street, walk fast, afraid of shadows coming out asking for bread or pennies . . . . Sometimes they'd come to the back door. You can't tell about hungry men, that's what we'd say. We'd say that sitting at home, lock the door, hide in the kitchen, fire in the stove, bread in the oven, smell the warm bread, keep warm by the stove.

Now that she is suddenly homeless, the factory seems the most hospitable place around; but while she rests there she tries to maintain herself apart from the transients. Frantically she explains to Fergus:

> I tell you it's all right, we're going away, we don't need to worry. We always had a home. A few hours or a day or two, it's nothing.

As Jenny speaks, the transient tenants appear from their

various corners of the factory. They watch Jenny suspiciously, fearful of any newcomer, especially a woman whose presence might bring them to the attention of the law. Jenny's sister Rose and her neighbor, Mary McGillicuddy, enter, followed by the rest of the neighborhood women. The transients stand in the shadows, the housewives are silhouetted at the doorway by the morning sun. "As the scene proceeds, the sense of latent hostility between the two groups increases." Jenny, separated from her neighbors by a wall of pity, finds herself unwillingly drawn closer to the homeless men. When Mary tells her she can't stay in the factory alone, she answers: "I'm not alone." When Mary finally convinces her to bring the baby to her house, Lucky, one of the blacks brought into town by Brimmer as scab labor and fired as soon as the strike was over, picks up Jenny's baby basket and carries it out with the women.

When your whole adult life has been occupied with maintaining a home, being suddenly homeless is terrifying. Jenny is so distracted that she cannot remember the words to the lullaby she sings. Her conversation with Fergus and Lucky has an hysterical urgency about it: her emotions are uncontrolled, they seem potentially destructive. Lucky intensifies her fears by explaining the hostile behavior of the men:

> We most all got what you call transient trouble. Ain't no help for bein' a transient. You want to pray to God that peanut in your arms don't turn out to be a transient. Can't get away, 'cause it follow you wherever you go: that's what they write when you ask for relief . . . . Transient! That's what the sheriff write in the book o' the Law, that's what the parson write in the book o' God . . . . You think every road got an ending, but the road they call transient go from sun-up to nowheres, gotta walk that road in the heat an' cold, starshine an' sunburn, sweat an' frost . . . .

Besides establishing the anguish of the dispossessed, this scene begins to employ the recurrent structural pattern of the play and in doing so it also begins to explain the process of radical change. The principle of thesis, antithesis, synthesis could be aptly applied to the arrangement of characters on the stage and to the tensions between characters in specific

97

scenes and throughout the play. In the first scene, the thesis is the presence of the housewives, suggesting the normal bourgeois family unit. The antithesis is the group of transients, representatives of economic and social collapse. Jenny Russell, caught halfway between the two groups, will be the agency of their synthesis. Her loss becomes the community's cause; it in fact gives the community its definition. The new order is not reached in this scene, but the movement toward it is graphically begun. As Lucky, the migrant black, walks off stage with the housewives, and as Jenny feels herself drawn toward the transients, traditionally discordant forces have begun to merge.

Lawson was working consciously with character types in this play. The opposition of recognizable American personalities to hostile social forces would cause a new man to emerge. Pete and Jenny Russell and Rose Graham are brought by the social forces around them to the point where they overcome personal problems and simultaneously become capable of revolutionary action. Characters who begin the play already fully committed to destroying Brimmer's control over the town find their actions leading them to an ever more comprehensive understanding of their own personalities. Bill Anderson, the union organizer, Mary McGillicuddy, Lucky, and in a final symbolic scene, the entire workingclass population, become representatives of humanity, instead of stereotypes of a specific occupation, sex or color.

The only static characters are those who support the old order: Inspector Feiler of the Red Squad, the other policemen, the gangsters employed by Brimmer to break the strike, and even the kindly employer, Warren Winkle. Their every action is anti-revolutionary since it is meant to reinforce the boundaries between people, rather than to tear them down. Yet collision with their values often provides a greater stimulus for radical activity than all the speeches of Bill Anderson, the working class hero.

Rose Graham is described as "moody, undisciplined, trusting implicitly in her own instincts." She recalls the "new woman" of the twenties whose heart was full of craving, fingers tense with daring. This willful, desirable woman is a favorite character in Lawson's earlier plays, as in the plays of Clifford Odets. In *Marching Song* she undergoes a transformation. Rose has been watching the break-up of Pete's and Jenny's marriage. She has seen her sister lose one child and bring another sickly one into the world. Her boyfriend, Joe—"a pallid, goodlooking boy of weak character"— personifies the escapist urge, so rampant in the establishment art of the thirties, which has been ignored by all the Theatre Union plays thus far. He dares her:

Where's your nerve? The bravest thing we could do is walk down a road . . . an' never look back!

But Rose is beginning to distrust his grandiose dreams. She is hungry and poor and painfully aware of all the things she does not have:

All I got in my head is like fingers reaching for things, like a baby reaching—Gimme love, gimme what it takes, gimme ride, gimme money, gimme hot chocolate with heavy whipped cream, and a smiling baby and a sweepstakes ticket and a Cadillac and a permanent and a facial and a diamond ring . . . .

And she is beginning to be sick and tired of wishing for them.

Joe and Rose speak of the scow out in the swamp. They used to sit there and pretend they were on an ocean voyage. Suddenly Woody Rosenbloom, a sprite-like tramp known as Rosy, enters covered with mud, carrying, under his arm, pieces of wood from the old scow. Rosy has travelled all over the Depression-laden country. He has no illusions left. A transient without money is welcome nowhere; he has a body full of scars to prove it. This factory seems like a fine place to Rosy. People leave you alone; you can patch up the holes in the wall and be assured of a warm place for the winter, the season that was most dreaded by the nation's homeless. Rosy's advice makes Joe sullen and hostile, but it has the opposite effect on Rose:

Joe . . . see how it is? This is our scow. We sat there, dreamed it was going fast, moving through the free water, engines shaking with speed, plowing blue water to a place that never was. But it didn't move an inch . . . . If you tried to push it you'd sink over your eyes in mud. But he's *building* something with it. It's

99

rotten wood, but he's using it. It's no time to dream, got to build with what you got . . . See what I mean Joe? Can't you see what I mean?

Rose's transformation is sudden and complete. When the sit-down strike begins at the Brimmer plants, she is one of its first and most dedicated supporters. Her energy and youth make her a perfect match for union organizer Bill Anderson. Normally we would expect a romance between them: when the author takes the trouble to make the ingenue grow up it is usually to suit her for a mature lover. But romance is suddenly far from Rose's mind; taking notes and mimeographing leaflets seem more necessary.

Mary McGillicuddy also transcends her traditional role—as housewife and unquestioning helpmate. Though she has loyally supported her husband's union activity she has been unaware that a militant worker's wife can find her own revolutionary role. In Act III she watches Maria Malucci, a widowed mother of eight, being deported for supporting the strike. Guiseppa Malucci also watches the police drag her mother away. Then she calmly paints her thirteen-year-old face with rouge and lipstick, breaks through Mary's motherly arms, and goes off to earn support for her seven younger brothers and sisters. Mary turns to the neighborhood women who have gathered at the factory entrance. Guiseppa Malucci's actions suddenly are understandable:

She's using her rights, she's free! I found out about them girls: the men pay a quarter, the girls get a dime, and fifteen cents goes to the house. On a big night Giuseppa can make two dollars. That's big pay for a thirteen-year-old . . . She's a woman, born of a woman. You think you're different, but you're selling your bodies and souls dirt cheap. Woman, born of woman, how long you gonna walk like a slave with chains on you? . . . Go out, go to every street and every house. Tell 'em to come out tonight, to form the picket line again, to make a wall of people around the plant, so the men inside will be safe.

Bourgeois prejudices must be overcome before a new world can be born. If prostitution is the only weapon a thirteen-year-old girl has to use against the system, then prostitution becomes inevitable.

For Pete and Jenny Russell the transformation to radicalism is a long time coming. Too many personal problems are in the way. Pete Russell is described as "slow-minded, suspicious of new ideas, clinging tenaciously to his opinions and prejudices. He is a kindly man, but given to occasional violent outbursts under the influence of liquor." He returned from the war a hero, married a pretty young girl, went to work on the assembly line, bought a house, acquired a mortgage, got a few appliances on time payments. If the crash had never happened his life might still be intact. He would never have had to question his ability to support a family. He tells Hank McGillicuddy that money he borrowed for baby medicine was spent on a fast drunk and a two bit whore. The girl was Giuseppa Malucci. Her young naked body on the bed made Pete afraid of his own daughter's future:

> I came home blind, tried to kill my kid—lift her in one hand, smash her brains out. Jenny tore the kid away from me and ran out of the house. I fell down in the garden, went to sleep with my face in the mud.

Because he desperately needs to feel superior to someone, Pete clings to his learned prejudices. He meets Lucky in the factory and begins a bitter argument threatening to "burn out the whole o' darktown." Bill Anderson enters with a hand full of leaflets. He has gathered a crowd in front of the Russells' house and wants to bring them into the factory for a meeting. Pete wants no part of a union meeting, but when questioned by the police a few minutes later he denies having seen Bill Anderson, so as not to give Bill away. As storm clouds gather in the sky outside, Hank and Mary come into the factory leading a crowd which is carrying the Russells' household belongings. Jenny runs from chair to lamp, straightening and protecting. These inexpensive items are the last proof of her claim on a home.

Bill Anderson asks the crowd to raise their hands if they will follow him to the bank to demand return of the Russells' home. Pete and Jenny stand silently apart from their neighbors and each other. Jenny watches her husband as his hand goes up slowly. She raises her hand to meet it. The act ends with this image of fledgling determination.

101

By Act II, Pete and Jenny have arranged their furniture to make a living room in the factory. Yesterday's march was a failure, but it stirred up the automobile workers enough to begin a sit-down strike on the Brimmer plant. Pete, who tried to kill his child because he could not stand not being able to afford to care for her, condemns the strike because of the violence it may lead to. Bill Anderson tells Pete:

> It's like you got a spotlight on you, whether you want it or not. The way people see you, you're bigger than yourself like a man makes a big shadow.

But Pete remains hostile to the strike effort until events, instead of rhetoric, lead him to take part in it. He remains in the factory where he meets Warren Winkle, who has been summoned by Inspector Feiler to inspect his property. Winkle, remembering Pete's ten years of service on the assembly line, gives him a Havana Perfecto cigar and goes to telephone his friends at the bank to have Pete's mortgage extended.

Meanwhile Bill Anderson has been shot in the arm. Rosy brings him back to the factory and helps him hide in the furnace room. Winkle is jubilant about restoring the house to Pete and Jenny. He comes back to the factory to tell them the good news and finds Pete being questioned about Bill Anderson by Feiler. If Pete won't cooperate with the law, Winkle cannot accept responsibility for the mortgage. Pete is torn between his duty to Jenny and his allegiance to the workers. At the crucial moment he asks for Jenny's advice and she releases him: "You got to do what you know is right, Pete."

Bill Anderson has been temporarily saved, the Russells' house has been lost, and the line between workers and bosses is drawn a little sharper. Isolated acts of charity like the one Warren Winkle sought to perform are gratuitous at best because they obscure the real causes and consequences of the economic rift. Jenny and Pete have become liberated by refusing Winkle's offer. An idea, unity with each other and with the town's workers, becomes more important than a possession. So Jenny transcends her bitterness and Pete overcomes his fear at not being able to provide. Act II ends with their embrace.

Marching Song combines lyricism and near-documentary events with an epic form. Yet it has traces of the Broadway brand of realism—where every character has to be "believable," a system which leads to a feast of palatable half-truths. The Pete-and-Jenny scenes especially recall the sentimental aspects of Broadway drama, rather than oppose them. Lawson's use of the dialectic was precariously close to the standardized sentimental reconciliation, except that in all other episodes his radicalism led him to startling syntheses.

Two characters in *Marching Song* are not made braver by the events of the strike. Sellers, a transient inhabitant of the factory, hires himself out to the anti-strike "Citizen's Committee for Law and Order" because: "If a man's got a clean collar, they don't ask questions." He is present when the town's hoodlums invade the factory dragging Pete with them, hoping to terrorize him into giving information. Pete manages to escape, but not before he had heard enough of their talk to become disgusted with the law and order they supposedly represent. He hurls his World War I medal at their feet:

That's what you want now, kill again, kill for the white race, kill the hungry men . . . I don't know where I stand, walking in a fog; but I ain't with you—not me.

Later, when the workers leave the factory to form picket lines around the Brimmer plants, Pete falls in step with Lucky. Both men have overcome the artificial boundary created by color.

Rose's old boy friend, Joe, has been hiding in the factory. Feiler and the gangsters discover him and threaten to kill him if he won't tell where Bill Anderson is hiding. Joe resists their threats, but when they offer him money he gives in. Though Anderson manages to escape this time, Joe was ready to sell a man's life for a ten dollar bill. When he does see the organizer's mangled body, Joe cries: "It's for money, they do it for money, his heart and his brain destroyed for money . . . ."

Jenny Russell's baby has died; the workers are determined that the Brimmer strike not be crushed. The gangsters are desperate for information about the strike's leaders. Bill names a dead child and infuriates them; they plunge their hot pokers down on his back and legs. But with each new wound Bill Anderson's will becomes stronger. As his life is burned away, slowly and with hideous accuracy before the audience, he becomes the symbol of an idea which will not die: "Me? . . . Big? . . . Yeah, I'm big. There's a hundred million of me!"

The final conversion in the play happens immediately after Bill's death and concerns the entire community. Police have fired tear gas and bullets into the crowd. The pickets stream into the factory for protection. Beaten, frightened bodies fill the stage; sounds of street fighting and terrified screams fill the air. Suddenly the factory is blacked out. Workers across town have cut off the electricity. The guns have been stilled. Lucky, visible in the moonlight coming in through a window, begins to speak:

No light but the moon shining from here to nowheres. But there's people, more'n you could count if you never quit counting. Streets full of quiet people. We stopped the power 'cause it's us that made it! . . . We put a saddle on the lightning like you saddle a mule! We strung them wires . . . We built them motors. You hear me, you multitude, power is people!

[As he speaks, the people who fill the darkened stage have risen from their broken and despairing positions. The action of the crowd, slowly rising to their feet, is completed as the curtain descends on Lucky's final words.]

The synthesis is complete. A strong new people, leaders of a new and equitable world, have risen from the dust.

NEW THEATRE LEAGUE

The experience of the mass of humanity today is such that social and political themes are more interesting, more significant, more 'normal' than the personal themes of other eras. Social themes today correspond to the general experience of men.

Joseph Freeman

In 1935, as one of the name changes that took place during the United Front years, the League of Workers Theatres became the New Theatre League, taking the name of the magazine it had been publishing since 1934. In *New Masses* Ben Blake explained the goal of the League: "A mass development of the American Theatre to its highest artistic and social levels; for a theatre dedicated to the struggle against war, fascism and censorship."

In New York City, full-length radical plays were being produced by the Theatre Union (1933-37), Artef (1927-37, '39, '41), the Federal Theatre (1935-39), the Theatre Collective (1933-36) and the Actors Repertory Theatre (1934-37). Across the country between three and four hundred theatres were affiliated with the New Theatre League: the Contemporary Theatre in Los Angeles, the Civic Players in Milwaukee, a San Francisco Theatre Union, the Theatre Collective in Newark, and New Theatres in Pittsburgh, Philadelphia and Boston.

The League ran a school in New York to train people from the regional theatres, dispensed scripts, and tried, not very successfully, to collect royalties. The monthly magazine *New*

Theatre, edited first by Ben Blake and later by Herbert Kline, ran reviews of current productions, articles of interest to new theatres and reports of their activities. Short plays like *Waiting for Lefty* and *I Can't Sleep* by Clifford Odets, and *Dimetrioff* by Art Smith and Elia Kazan, also members of the Group Theatre, were published there. *New Masses* published mass chants like *Free Thaelman*, by Ernst Toller, and *Lynchtown*, which was originally part of Paul Peter's and George Sklar's left-wing review *Parade*. Written for the Theatre Union but rejected by them, *Parade* was produced by the Theatre Guild on Broadway in May 1935. The Guild, however, found many of its sketches too radical and cut *Lynchtown* and other scenes. *Newsboy* was temporarily in as the revue's finale. "It was in opening night in the Boston try-out; it was yanked out after Governor Fuller (who had been a judge on the Sacco-Vanzetti case) walked out when the case was mentioned, followed by 35 other Brahmins," George Sklar says.

Peters, Sklar, and the Guild solicited sketches from other writers, some of which were published in *New Theatre* along with the comment:

> As we go to press, the critics are "taking it out" on the Theatre Guild's first revue . . . This much of their criticism is true . . . *Parade* is something of a hodge-podge. This is due, not to the weakness of the original *Parade*, but to the failure of the Guild to really let the revue go on as originally written—as a left review.

Alan Baxter and Harold Johnsrud

THE DEAD COW*

A sketch from *Parade*

Scene: A simple house. Unfurnished except for a gnawed plain table, and an ungnawed antique what-not. Father, Mother and their two young sons [sic] are clad only in copies of The New York Journal. One copy of the Journal is in Father's hands. Otherwise there is absolutely nothing but the three walls.
At Rise: MOTHER sits chewing the tabletop. JOHNNIE and MARY sit

---

New Theatre, June 1935.

106

*against the back wall. FATHER sits reading his copy of the JOUR-
NAL.*

FATHER: *(Looking up jovially)* Hey, now Mother, just you save some
of that there table-top for me. I ain't et yet.

MOTHER: You got a fine right to complain. I'm savin' a whole leg for
you, ain't even been touched.

FATHER: Never mind—you know durn well the top's the best part.
The legs is maple. You lived with me long enough to realize I'm
partial to white pine.

MOTHER: *(Sitting back on the floor.)* All rightie. There's a nice piece
left around the nail . . . You know, Henry sometimes I sorta wish we
had somethin' else to eat outside of the papers and this here table.
Not that I'm complainin'—we been better off the last four years than
most.

FATHER: Yer durn right we been. You oughta be glad we're livin in
the good old U.S.A. Looka these here pitchers in the *New York
Journal*—looka this one—a Rooshian fambly. Looka them starvin'
Rooshian kids standin' by that dead pig. My gosh, ain't that terrible?

MOTHER: Yes, sir, Henry, it sure is awful. But I can't help wishin' we
had a pig like that.

FATHER: What for, Maw?

MOTHER: For eatin', Henry, for eatin'.

FATHER: Durned if ya ain't right. Ya can eat 'em cantcha? I plumb
forgot.

MOTHER: They taste good if they're cooked.

FATHER: Well now, I dunno. Speakin' of eatin', today's the day the
Government Relief Man promised to send us a butchered cow.

MOTHER: Oh, Henry! Honest?

FATHER: Sure, I spoke to him last year about this time, an' he said
he'd send one this year on April Fool's Day—that's today.

MOTHER: Why, that's wonderful, Henry. Makes me wish we had that
old stove we hocked two years ago.

FATHER: Gosh, these here *(on his side)* are swell pitchers of Rooshia. I
wonder how they got 'em? It must be awful dangerous takin'
pitchers in Rooshia. Mr. Hearst is sure got a lotta guts to live over
there and be takin' snapshots.

MOTHER: You're a good provider, Henry. I don't know what we'd do
without that there subscription to the *Journal*. It was a right smart
thing to do with yer savin's. With th' *Journal* comin' in every day fer
three years, we ain't got nothin' to worry about. We can burn 'em to
keep warm, wear 'em fer clothes, an' them comics an' pitcher
sections makes right flavorsome eatin'.

FATHER: Eatin? *Readin'!* Looka here, what them durned *Communists*
done to these here Rooshian kids.

MOTHER: I seen it.

FATHER: No, ya ain't. This is a diff'rent one. In thissun there's *three*

107

starvin' kids, and they're a-settin on a dead *hoss* . . . Looka this, Jimmie—get some edjication. Ain't it awful?

JIMMIE: *(Looking)* I'll say. It's sure funny how Mr. Hearst c'n get them pitchers without bein' killed by them Communists.

MARY: Paw, I'm cold!

FATHER: Waddaya mean, cold? Don't be a sissy. How many times I got to ast ya to remember ya spran from a long line o' dauntless pioneer forebears? If ya was livin' in Rooshia, now, ya'd have somethin' to kick about. At least, we got a roof over our heads. *(A section of the roof falls through.)* Well, that there plaster'll make good eatin' . . . especially if th' relief man don't bring that there cow like he promised.

Mother begins gathering plaster.

JOHNNY: Hey, maw, look at Mary. *(Mary has lighted a match, is about to apply it to Father's newspaper suit, from behind.)*

MOTHER: *(Rushing over, knocking match from Mary's hand)* Mary, what on earth do ya think yer doin?

MARY: Well gee maw, I'm cold!

MOTHER: Well that ain't no reason you should set fire to yer paw!

FATHER: That's the last straw! Bring me that table, maw. Time fer dinner.

Mother drags table over to Father, who begins munching it, then takes plaster she has gathered and goes out. Father looks up, notices Johnnie chewing at the what-not.

FATHER: Hey, Johnnie—what in tucket are ya at? Durn ya, how many times I got to tell ya to stop chawin' on that there what-not?

JOHNNIE: It tastes good.

FATHER: I don't care how it tastes. That there what-not belonged to yer maw's grandpaw, what fit in the Civil war an' it's gonna be th' last thing to go.

Mother rushes in.

MOTHER: Henry—the relief man's here! He just driv up, in a big truck, an' he's got two men carryin' up a butchered cow—jest like he said!

FATHER: *(To the kids)* There ya are—wh'd I tell ya? Now if you was livin' in one o' these heathen furrin' countries you see in th' pitchers would ya get service like that?

They compose themselves happily and wait. Enter men with cow and a camera.

MAN: Here we are folks!

108

They pose the family and take a flashlight picture.

CAMERA MAN: All right. Take it out.

Cow is removed.

FATHER: Wait a minute. Leave that for us to eat!
MAN: Hell, no.
FATHER: Ain't you the Relief?
MAN: We're from the *Journal*. We're out for a picture of a starving
   Russian family!
   BLACKOUT

Paul Peters and George Sklar

LYNCHTOWN—A MASS CHANT*

*Two Theatre Union playwrights recount
an incident of life in the Deep South*

> *The light begins to fade as the music builds to a terrific climax.
> There is a clash of cymbals, followed by the low muffled beat of
> a drum. A dim pool of light comes up, revealing a group of black
> and white workers who stand facing the audience.*

ALL: *(Low to the beat of the drum)* Fire swept this cabin
   Fire blazed in the night
   Here twelve people lived and breathed and
      stood their ground and fought to live.
   And were consumed by fire.
FIRST NEGRO: And ten charred bodies lay in the embers
   And two lay quiet in a pool of blood.
VOICES: The nickelodeon tinkled at Jerry's place
   And the boys were lined up at the bar.
   The billiard balls clicked at the Starlight Casino
   And Joe chalked his cue and watched;
   And the radio was going in the barber shop,
   And in the back room the gang was shooting crap,
   And the boys hung around the corner with not a thing to do.
   At eight o'clock John T. McGuire, sheriff of Blue Earth County,
      State of Mississippi,
   Strode down the street with his holster bulging on his hip:
   That Lewis nigger—down by the woods—slugged the colonel.
   That Lewis nigger—

New Masses, December 1936.

109

Slugged the colonel.
Nigger bastard
Slugged the colonel.
And the boys piled out of Jerry's place,
Out of the casino,
Out of the barber shop.
And from out of stores
And out of houses
People came running to the corner.
The street became alive,
Excitement swept the crowd
And they buzzed and laughed and yelled.
And from mouth to mouth it spread:
    That Lewis nigger (in whisper) nigger
Slugged the colonel
Slugged the colonel
Slugged the colonel
Nigger bastard—bastard
Slugged the colonel
Slugged the colonel.
Brakes squaled
Cars drew up,
White hoods appeared.
A shout from the crowd:
"Here they are, boys!
Where's that rope?
Get that torch!
Where's that can of gasoline!"
And frenzied anger seized them
And they surged forward!
And a roar went up from the street:
"Get that nigger,
String him up.
Lynch that nigger,
Lynch him. Lynch him, lynch him!"

Down the main street,
Over the Red Creek bridge
And out the Mobile Road they went,
The cars in the lead,
The men behind.
Trudging in a cloud of dust.
And as they marched
Their spirits grew higher and higher
And they laughed and sang and cheered.
And somebody started up:

"There'll be a hot time in the old town tonight."
And other voices picked it up.

A sudden silence gripped them
As they hit the old swamp road;
And all you could hear was the tread of feet,
The slow, grim tread of many feet
Marching in the night.
An owl hooted
And a frog croaked in the swamp.
And all was silent again,
Silent except for the slow grim tread of many feet.

And inside the cabin twelve Negroes waited,
Waited with guns in their hands.
Silence: then slow drum beat.
Their bodies stiffened and their fingers tightened on their triggers
Drum beat grows faster.
As they heard the tread of feet
Marching in the night.
And the twelve Negroes in the cabin heard the hushed voices of
   the mob
And they remembered that they had sworn an oath to stand their
   ground!
*Silence: the drum beat continues and out of it comes a voice
singing.*
"Oh, Mr. Sheriff, we giving you warning,
You better turn round and go back;
'Cause if you come anywhere near that doorway,
We going to shoot you down in your tracks"
Drum beat builds and is terminated abruptly by a gun shot.
And guns roared
And pistols blazed in the night,
Men cursed and fell and women shrieked.
Suddenly a torch flared and hurtled through the darkness
And landed on the roof
And flames licked at the shingles
And the mob went wild and laughed and yelled.
And inside the cabin twelve Negroes who had sworn an oath
Stood with their guns in their hands
And held the mob at bay.
And now one of them cried out: "It's burning! It's burning!"
And confusion seized them
And some of them were struck with terror

111

And dropped their guns and rushed to the door
And threw it open:
*There is a quickly mounting drum roll, which culminates in the
hoarse scream of a man and woman.*
And on the ground, with the warm blood flowing from their
  bodies lay
Asa Potter, Negro, 19,
Eula Roberts, Negro, 13,
Struck dead by bullets from the guns of the mob.
The rest drew back into the cabin and barred the door
And stood their ground in the thickening smoke
And answered shot for shot.

And from the trees at the edge of the clearing.
Guns roared and pistols blazed in the night
And a red glow fell on the faces of the mob
As they watched the doorway and waited for the Negroes to
  emerge.
And as the flames shot higher and higher
They ceased their shooting
And a silence settled on them
And their eyes were glued on the doorway.
And they watched with wonder and awe.

And suddenly they saw a burst of flame
And heard the timbers crack
And the roof caved in with a thundrous roar;
And from the cabin came shrieks of human agony
And a figure enveloped in flame
Streaked across the clearing and fell burning to the ground.

And over the old swamp road and the Red Creek bridge
The men trudged back to town.
An awful silence seized them and their eyes were on the ground.
An owl hooted
And a frog croaked in the swamp.
Someone stumbled and swore under his breath.
And all you could hear was the tread of feet
The slow grim tread of many feet
Marching in the night.

Fire swept this cabin
Fire blazed in the night,
Here twelve people lived and breathed and stood their ground—
And were consumed by fire.

And ten charred bodies lay in the embers
And two lay quiet in a pool of blood.

New Masses published a scene from Peters' and Charles Walker's documentary account of the Bonus March, *The Third Parade*, produced in Yiddish by Artef. (The first parade was when the troops marched off to World War I waving flags and laughing; the second was when they came home wounded and disillusioned; the third was their march on Washington in the summer of 1932 to demand full payment of the bonus the government had promised by 1945. Sklar and Peters went to Washington and interviewed the marchers at their camp. Subsequently the veterans were driven violently from the capital by federal troops led by General MacArthur.)

Many short plays and dance pieces were premiered at New Theatre Nights held at the Theatre Union's Civic Repertory Theatre. *Newsboy* was introduced there and so was *Waiting for Lefty*, two years later. The Sunday evening festivals got a reputation for being exciting, and most of the people's theatre workers looked forward to them. They were social events for the movement, helping it cohere and giving the people in it a sense of their accomplishments.

Alfred Kremborg contributed a mass chant, *America, America!*, to the new theatre movement. Archibald MacLeisch wrote *Panic*, a verse play about capitalism's collapse. It was directed for a limited run by John Houseman and starred the 19 year-old Orson Welles. Langston Hughes wrote *Angelo Herndon Jones*, a chant for a black worker who faced life on a southern chain gang because he had agitated for better working conditions, and in 1938 *Don't You Want to Be Free?*, a poetry play with blues tracing black history. The same year Hughes founded the Harlem Suitcase Theatre, which performed the play several hundred times in halls and meeting places around Harlem. It was published in *One Act Play* magazine (October 1938):

There is no curtain, so a Young Man simply comes forward and begins to speak.

Listen folks! I'm one of the members of the group, and I want to tell you about our theatre. This is it right here! We haven't got any scenery, or painted curtains,

113

because we haven't got any money to buy them. But we've got something you can't buy with money, anyway. We've got faith in ourselves. And in you. So we're going to put on a show. Maybe you'll like it because it's about you, and about us. This show is for you. And you can act in it, too, if you want to. This is your show, as well as ours.

Now I'll tell you what this show is about. It's about me, except that it's not just about me now standing here talking to you—but it's about me yesterday, and about me tomorrow. I'm colored! I guess you can see that. Well, this show is about what it means to be colored in America.

In 1934 the Workers Laboratory Theatre formed a separate puppet department, headed by Louis Bunin. Bunin, with Meyer Levin, had run a repertory marionette theatre in Chicago during the twenties, where they produced George Kaiser's *From Morn to Midnight*. In *New Theatre*, November 1934, Bunin described the reaction to a street corner puppet play:

On Tuesday, October 2nd, President Roosevelt, Madame [Frances] Perkins [head of the National Labor Relations Board] and Bill Green [AFL president] addressed the workers on the corner of Tenth Street and Second Avenue, New York City. The Blue Eagle was there, too, perched on F. D.'s shoulder. But they were not received with patriotic approval as shown in the newsreels. In fact, they were enthusiastically booed, hissed and laughed at by a large and growing crowd. A puzzled cop stood by rubbing his thick neck in bewilderment . . . "Jesus," the cop probably thought, "if they were four feet taller I'd call out the riot squad." The fact that these nationally known figures were only two feet tall was not the only difference between them and their human counterparts; their hypocrisy and demagogy were removed and the people in the streets saw them and the "raw deal" as they really are.

New scripts were constantly needed and the League ran periodic contests to find them. Some of the regional theatres produced original plays and chants: *Eight Men Speak* documented a Canadian labor dispute, and Alice Ware's *Mighty Wind a Blowin* was premiered in New Haven at the Theatre Progressive. But most of the theatres relied upon scripts coming out of New York. It was for performance by new theatres around the country that Odets wrote *Lefty* and Albert Maltz wrote *Private Hicks*. Irwin Shaw's anti-war play, *Bury the Dead*, and Ben Bengal's strike play, *Plant in the Sun*, were also performed by many new theatres outside New York.

Though New York was the organizational and publishing center of the League, it had branch offices in various other cities and it organized numerous projects to fit the specific needs of local communities. Ben Golden spent the summer of 1935 working with an integrated troupe of miners' children in West Virginia who toured a play demanding free text books. Morris Watson, who was in charge of the living newspaper unit of Federal Theatre, directed 80 automobile workers and their wives in a documentary account of their strike; it was performed at Union Hall on the eve of the victory celebration. Chicago's branch of the Workers Laboratory Theatre documented local struggles and, like other theatres, did frequent picket-line duty to encourage participants in near-by strikes.

Alice Evans

THE LIVING THEATRE*

IT'S not help we're asking. It's fighting together for the same things—homes and families. Irish or Negroes—it don't make any difference. If we're apart, we're licked—if we're together, we win. Are you with us?"

"Am Oi crazy, or is he talkin' good sense?"

With these words the Irish woman decides to help her Negro neighbors resist the eviction notice served them. She shouts across the back stairs. When her friends arrive with rolling pins, we know that the struggle is as good as won.

The Workers Laboratory Theatre is presenting *Eviction* at a community meeting in a settlement house across the street from the home of Herbert Newton, Negro Communist, and his wife, who have received an eviction notice for daring to live in an all-white building in the heart of Chicago's black belt. The audience is composed largely of Socialist

New Theatre, March 1935.

115

members of the neighborhood Workers Committee on Unemployment. Many of them have agreed with the Irish woman that the problems of Negroes are "none of moi worry!" until they see her confronted by an eviction notice herself, tell the landlord:

"Oi'm only two months behoind in me rent. An' me auld man can't help it if he's out of a job. An' moi kids are goin' to have a roof over their heads—see!"

The lesson sinks home. The audience pledges to fight the Newton case, and makes a mental note to find the rolling pin.

The test comes two days later. A collection of shabby furniture is out on the street. A baby's crib—a washing machine—books and papers. The Newtons have been evicted. Although the white tenants in the building have signed a petition demanding that this Negro family stay, the landlord's greed for preserving property values persists.

Up and down the street go members of the Workers Laboratory Theatre. They knock from door to door, telling the neighbors. Soon sixty Negro and white workers are in front of the building. Four of the huskiest are chosen to break through the door—four others to carry in the washing machine. As dusk gathers, a silent procession, each carrying one piece of furniture, files carefully through the door. In five minutes the Newton family is at home.

Two weeks later, we are in the courtroom next to the largest jail in Chicago. At the trial of Herbert Newton, charged with disorderly conduct. Two hundred workers sit in the courtroom for two days—they do not talk, they scarcely move. They sit there—sullen and defiant and powerful. The judge knows they are there. The jury knows they are there. When the landlord, his face red, his voice tremolo, sputters: "This man is a Commoonist!" the courtroom breaks into spontaneous laughter. The judge pounds with his gavel. He cannot stop the laughter—it is contagious, it is triumphant. It runs its course before proceedings can continue.

On the evening of the last day, Newton is defending himself. He stands before the jury, his broad shoulders contrasting strangely with his thin face. He has been charged with profanity and disorderly conduct towards a policeman. He begins quietly in his low clear voice, with the clipped definite speech of a Harvard graduate. His emotion rises and you hear it thundering behind the clipped tones, the quiet manner:

"I have the greatest contempt for policemen," he says. "I have had too much contact with their prevarication and cowardice to have anything for them but contempt. But I have sufficient words in my vocabulary, I believe, to express this contempt without resorting to profanity."

The jury sits up and looks startled. What is this? But some of them hate cops too. Some of them are impressed by the strangely-quiet nobility, the finely-tempered strength of this Negro Communist. In spite of the State Attorney's rabid speech, calling on the ancient hackneyed prejudices, in spite of all the legal traps, in spite of the howl of press, red squad, landlord and prosecutor for the maximum penalty—two hundred and costs, or four months in jail—the jury argues for three hours and brings forth a ten dollar fine. The case is appealed, and Newton is free.

Throughout the entire proceedings sits a young girl who is writing a play about this Newton case. The courtroom scene will be her third act. She is former vice-president of the University of Chicago Dramatic Association, now working in the Repertory Department of the New Theatre League. Writing into her play the sullen power of two hundred workers sitting in a courtroom for two days—the drama of class struggle ruthlessly outlined before the judge's bench—the excitement of personalities confronting each other over fundamental human values. Could there be a better school for playwrights than such a courtroom?

A CROWDED, smoky hall in the dingy end of Chicago's downtown. Cold, tired workers just returned from picketing the Evans Fur Company on State Street, nervously pacing the floor, joining in staccato conversation with their fellow members of the Fur Workers Industrial Union. A sudden burst of applause, as the door opens and twenty-five workers file in. They are just released from jail—arrested that morning on the picket line. The cops are picking them up as soon as they get in front of the shop—fifteen yesterday, twenty-five today. Last night two girl strikers were beaten up by members of the rival A. F. L. union at whose instigation the Evans Fur Company broke their contract with the industrial union. The chairman raps on the desk and calls the strikers to order.

"While we are waiting for news from the committee that has gone to see the NRA board, we will have some entertainment from the workers' theatres."

A girl in a red sweater takes the floor: "The Chicago Workers Theatre will present *Perkins and Green*. You will meet someone you know in this sketch."

Frances Perkins, wearing a business-like bustle, and Bill Green, with the familiar cigar, enter arm in arm. To the jaunty tune of the Man on the Flying Trapeze, with clever dance steps they introduce themselves:

"Oh I am Bill Green
Of strike-breaking fame
And I'm very clever
At that little game—"

The Fur Workers recognize the enemies they are dealing with even at the moment—as their committee meets the NRA board. Hisses, boos, and delighted laughter accompany the two through the sketch and as they swing off the stage in a final self-righteous fury of motion—"And we lead the strike gently away!"

"In the next play, you will meet someone else you know well—one of the strikers at the Evans Fur Company. The Workers Laboratory Theatre will present *Recruit*. Imagine yourselves in front of a U.S. Army Recruiting station."

A young Negro worker is confronted first by an army officer who tries to make him into a disciplined recruit, then by a girl striker, against whom the officer urges him to use his bayonet. For tense minutes he wavers, then he decides. He turns his gun upon the officer and drives him off the stage, to the delighted howls of the audience. He turns to the girl striker, who tells him:

"The Fur Workers are striking
For a Union of our own—
Down with the breaking of contracts
And the bosses' wage-cut song."

The young recruit is with her now:

"I'll stick with the workers
And fight with you.
I've got a gun in my hands
And I know what to do.
Against bosses' terror
This will come in fine.
So, let's go, people—
To the PICKET LINE!"

The audience is roaring and ready for the picket line itself. The program ends with a song, the audience joining in the chorus. "Write Me Out My Union Card" is begun, the resonant voice of the young Negro worker from the Laboratory Theatre leading the way:

"Oh, come with me
To the picket line
We'll stay there
Till the bosses sign
Time to fight those hunger blues away."

The whole room is singing now. And still singing as the theatre members, carrying their properties with them, quietly leave the hall.

THE tiny office of the New Theatre League that has become somehow a symbol of the creative fury of the young workers' theatre movement in Chicago. Nine people in four square feet of space—all trying to work. One typewriter pounding furiously away. From left to right, we have: A handsome middle-aged actor from the German professional stage who wants to get connected with the workers' theatre; a studious-looking Negro who directs a South Side church group and wants a play—"They're still conservative, but interested in social problems;" a blonde young girl from the YWCA who wants a theatre group to perform for them; a young furniture worker, turned actor, discussing *Waiting For Lefty* with a girl who has tears in her eyes. She has just finished reading the play in NEW THEATRE and is eager to begin producing it. Here is the director of the Russian Dramatic Circle,

118

formerly with the Moscow Art Theatre, with a manuscript under his arm. He has just written a play, *Human Aid Society*, and wants it translated. The organizer of the Fur Workers Union has come in. He wants to know why the theatre groups have stopped performing every day at the strike hall after the first week.

"Don't you have more than six programs in your repertory? What would you do if a strike lasted three months? We need you there to keep up the strikers' spirits, and where are you?"

The organizer of the New Theatre League can only shake her head, and determine that we build our repertory.

Here is a tall young man who reports the formation of a theatre group at the University of Chicago, sponsored jointly by the National Student League and the League for Industrial Democracy. He is a Socialist, a former stock company actor, now writing his master's thesis, on "A Marxian Approach to the Theatre." Next to him is an excited young teacher with a proposal for the New Theatre League. He thinks we can arrange to have our theatre groups perform at the workers' education classes in the city. Thus we would reach the widest possible audience of non-revolutionary workers in every corner of the sprawling metropolis. In our excitement over this proposal, we forget that it is almost midnight and ten hours since we have eaten. We troop downstairs and next door, to our friends in the little Greek restaurant. We swap two NEW THEATRE magazines for two cups of coffee and four doughnuts and begin serious discussion of the Chicago theatre front.

Ben Golden

CHILDREN'S THEATRE ON TOUR*

Slowly the little red truck winds its way up the hollow, carrying its cargo of young actors, who are about to give their first performance after three weeks of intensive training and rehearsal.

We are on our way to the little mining town of Black Hawk, West Virginia. When we arrive, we find some of the audience already waiting for us, while others are coming. A space has been cleared and staked off on the side of a hill. This is to be our stage; the audience is to sit below the hill on a level plot of grass. Gradually the large space is filled with men, women and children, Negro and white. As they find places to sit, one of our group goes up to collect the five cents admission that is used to pay our travelling expenses.

The sun falls behind the hill on which we are to perform, and darkness envelops the entire hollow. We have no spots, nor any other light for that matter, but the miners help us out by lending us some carbide lamps. Two of us station ourselves on each side of this natural

New Theatre, October 1935. Edited version KMT.

119

stage and focus the lights on the actors.

In the distance we can see miners going to and from work, the carbide lamps stuck in front of their caps glimmering like tiny stars in the darkness.

The anti-war mass recitation is the first thing on the program. The audience is tense as the narrator tells of the horror of war, and actually thrills, when it hears the mass of young people in front of the narrator beginning to whisper at first, and then gradually becoming louder, to shout, "Black and white, unite to fight."

The audience feels that here is something real, that these boys and girls are telling them the truth, that this *is* what war means, "maimed," "crippled." "hunger," "misery," "death," "despair." They wait tensely to the last line, when the actors point their fingers at them and say, with raised fists at the last word, "But the world shall be Ours!" Then the audience rises to its feet, cheering and applauding.

This was the first of nineteen scheduled performances in as many mining towns. These performances had been arranged for by Pioneer Youth, a non-partisan organization that works among the miners, chiefly the youth, of West Virginia, organizing them on a class struggle basis. Realizing the importance of dramatic work, Pioneer Youth had requested New Theatre League to assign one of its members to work on their staff this summer.

Immediately upon arrival, we had been confronted with the Negro question. The problem of course was to get a mixed group of children, Negro and white, to take part in the dramatic work. At first, we were unable to find any white kids who were willing to be in the same group with Negroes; where the children were willing, the parents objected. However, Pioneer Youth was determined that there would be no discrimination, and after a week of going from town to town, and speaking to children and parents, we were able to assemble a group of ten boys and girls, six white and four Negro, ranging from fourteen to eighteen. . . .

The white members of the group soon realized for themselves that working with the Negroes did them no harm. More, they saw that they could learn a great deal from the Negroes, who were much better actors, and who excelled in imaginative interpretation and character-ization.

Throughout my work with the group, I tried to get them to tell me what should be done, instead of my telling them what to do. We talked over a long time what kind of plays we should do. Since they were to write the plays themselves, each of them presented what he or she thought would be a good subject. Gaylord, a white boy, told of a large family he knew who were getting only $2.50 a week, and who lived on corn bread, mostly, and berries that they gathered on the hillside. "We ought to make up a play about that," he said, "and maybe show them how to fight for more relief." Roy Lee, a Negro boy, thought that the

120

burning of the tipple at the Eskadale mine would be swell for a play. "We could show what it means to the miners to be thrown out of work through no fault of their own." Louise, white, whose father was crippled for life by a slate fall and who has had to fight constantly for his compensation, wanted to dramatize a compensation case, and show how the company tried to cheat the miners out of what was rightfully theirs.

Out of all the suggestions two were chosen which dealt with the most urgent problems confronting the youth of West Virginia: a play against war, and a play showing how to organize a struggle for free text-books. The latter question is a heated issue in the state: it is almost impossible for miners who are working only one or two days a week to buy school books for their children. This means that many children have been dropping out of school before their work is nearly completed.

For the anti-war play we used a mass recitation, arranged by the group, with my help, from a chant by Ernst Toller that had appeared in the New Masses last winter, an anti-war poem written by a member of the Paterson New Theatre League group and published in Printer's Voice, a trade union paper.

The school book play we built through improvisation, memorizing only the statistical material, such as figures on taxes and the cost of providing books for all the children in the state. Working through improvisations proved very fruitful for its training value, and kept the performance fresh and lively—we had many variations in the first few showings.

Our dress rehearsal was shown to an audience of farmers from the surrounding country—the ones from whom we bought our vegetables and supplies. About twenty-five came, some of them walking miles through the woods to get there. It was dark before they arrived to take their places on the benches we had made (planks across logs). The school book play went over big. Here was something the farmers knew and understood. When the scene of the Pioneer Youth was played, with the plans being made for organizing children and parents into a demonstration and going down to Charleston to demand free books from the Governor, the farmers applauded enthusiastically. During this scene the group draws up a petition and elects a committee to go out among the audience and collect signatures. This was done at every performance, and each time met with an eager response.

During the anti-war play comments were constant: "That's right," "You bet," and one young man, "The only war I'll ever fight in is when the poor fight against the rich!"

After the performance we spoke to the audience about our work, explaining why we had a mixed group, and pointing out the necessity of uniting Negro and white workers and farmers. We tried to involve the audience in this discussion, but none of them would talk. Some of the youngsters in the group took part, however, and told their experiences

121

at camp in a mixed group.

Gaylord said, "In this fight for free text-books we need the Negro children, because if we went to Charleston without them, they would say, 'The Negro kids aren't asking for books, why should you?' and the same if the Negroes went down there alone." Others showed how the Negroes like other workers were threatened by war, and how unity was needed in the fight against the bosses, that all this prejudice was a trick to keep them from fighting together for their needs.

After this performance we left camp, to begin our nineteen scheduled performances. Many interesting things happened during our travels. There was the town of Galaghar, where we were supposed to get the little Negro school for our performance. At the last minute, those in charge, without giving any explanation, wouldn't open the school. All they said was, "We are not allowed to open the school." Where the pressure (if any) came from, we were unable to find out.

But undaunted, we led the audience into a Negro family's back yard and gave our performance there. This Negro town cooperated one hundred percent, many people bringing chairs and other furniture for the audience to sit on.

That night also we spoke to the audience, telling them why we gave a play against war, pointing to Italy's attack on Ethiopia, and foretelling what war would mean to the miners and their families. The audience applauded the plays and players, and many told of the need for such plays.

From these sketchy notes, it can readily be seen what a field there is for theatre work among miners, steel workers, etc. Not only can the theatre provide entertainment for these people who, through poverty are denied almost every form of amusement and pleasure, but it can be a powerful force for organizing them to struggle for their own immediate needs.

Morris Watson

SITDOWN THEATRE*

THE loudspeaker said: "Who are you?"
The worker replied: "I'm an automobile worker."
The loudspeaker said: "What have you got there?"
The worker held up a soap box labeled "JOB".
"It's my job," said the worker.
"What are you going to do with it?"
The worker placed it on the floor and squatted on it.
"I'm gonna sit on it!"

Two thousand automobile workers, their wives and children in Union Hall, the Penngelly building, at Flint on the night of their victory in the

---

*New Theatre and Film, April 1937. Edited version KMT.

122

General Motors strike settlement roared at every line of this colloquy.
"You ever heard of property rights?" asked the loudspeaker.
"You ever heard of human rights?" asked the worker.
"But the court said—"
"I don't care what the court said," replied the worker. "This is my job. I own it, and I'm a gonna sit on it and nobody's gonna take it away from me!"

When I arrived in Flint to lecture for the League for Industrial Democracy on the Monday before the General Motors strike settlement I found Mary Heaton Vorse and Josephine Herbst industriously preparing a Living Newspaper script on the strike. They called it *Strike Marches On*—The Living Newspaper. They asked me to direct it. I had to speak the next night at Lansing and there were only two free days after that. It was with some misgivings that I undertook the job. *Two days to whip up a show with a cast of 80 amateurs!*

The misgivings were unnecessary. The show shaped itself like plaster in a mold and I think the experience was amazing to everybody except the workers who did it. The result was a folk play.

The script was without dialogue. It consisted of a paragraph by paragraph explanation of scenes. Nothing more. Jo Herbst explained it to the workers in Union Hall (Union Hall usually was full, day and night) and asked them to participate. There was no response. I whispered to her to tell them they wouldn't have to act, they would merely be telling the story of their strike. The response was immediate and enthusiastic.

At the outset, each one of the workers in the cast of eighty had his own ideas as to how the play should be directed. I carefully explained that inasmuch as we had only two days in which to stage the play I would have to have strict discipline. I told them there would be only one director and that no matter how painful the scenes seemed to them not one of them was to say a word to me in correction until the end of each rehearsal. They respected the request and maintained admirable discipline.

The first scene called for an assembly line to illustrate the work in an automobile factory. I explained to them that a Loudspeaker was to be used. A worker stepped up and said he would like to try out for the part. Each worker on the assembly line did in pantomime what he had actually done on the job.

The man on the Loudspeaker said:

"1928—notice how leisurely the boys work. See the foreman exchanging a chew of tobacco with one of the boys." A slight note of excitement entered his voice. "1930" he said, "Notice the slight speed-up"—and then, "1932—here began the era of industrial progress in America." (His own words). "Now look at the foreman pulling a man out of the line—too slow—the others must do his work—see how fast they go."

123

Accompanying these words of the Loudspeaker, the workers and the foreman, and a superintendent thrown in for good measure, acted out the scene with improvisation of their own invention. The scene moved with more verve and imagination than any outside script writer or director possibly could have furnished.

The Loudspeaker said:

"1936—now look at them. Tails between their legs."

The foreman jerked out several workers and laid them off. He whipped the others into a frenzy of activity. He grabbed a worker wearing a large button.

"What's that thing?" he asked.

"What's it look like? You know God damn well what it is," the worker replied.

"It's a union button."

"Well, you got eyes."

The foreman and the superintendent, quickly flanked by a couple of company cops roughly pulled the worker from the assembly line and shoved him off the platform. "We don't want no damn union here," shouted the foreman.

It must be remembered here that these lines were not given to the workers. Nor was direction necessary. The only thing I told them was where to stand on the stage. I was bowled over by the fact that a group of workers placed upon a stage and told to tell their story could and did tell it with vigor and directness.

The next scene called for a stool pigeon. Nobody wanted to be a stool pigeon. I had to use powers of persuasiveness to convince a prospective stool pigeon that the representation of such a low creature was in this particular instance an important, a very important strike duty. In the hall, and in the cast was the woman who a few days before the sitdown pointed out a stool pigeon. She played her own part with the same feeling of sincerity (I feel sure) that was exhibited upon the original occasion. It gave the play a thrilling reality.

The Women's Emergency Brigade came on to picket "Chevy-9." Workers carrying their lunch boxes came on to go into the "plant." The women grabbed them: "Don't be a scab!" There was a crash and a scream and the women began to stagger. One of them shouted "Gas" and several of them rushed up to the windows and began breaking them. "They're gassing our boys." The Loudspeaker said: "Please keep order. Please keep order." The Loudspeaker was playing the part of the sound truck. "Everybody to 'Chevy-4.'" The women stumbled off, rubbing their eyes as people do under the influence of tear gas. The Loudspeaker explained the attempts at strike settlements, the dodges of General Motors.

For the finale the women ran on and circled a small platform which rose above the larger platform on which most of the action

124

took place. They locked hands. Five policemen ran from either side of the hall. The policemen were striking bus drivers in their uniform with large tin badges pinned on their breasts. The audience hissed loudly. Swinging their clubs with a vigor that frightened many of us for fear that some of the cast would be hurt, they attempted to crash through the Women's Emergency Brigade. The locked hands held fast and the women sang the Women's Auxiliary theme song: "We shall not be moved." A worker leaped up on a window which was in the back of the union hall behind the women and shouted "Brothers and sisters, we have decided to die in the plant rather than on the picket line if this is the way General Motors is going to treat us." The women turned toward the worker, locked hands again and sang: "You shall not be moved. We are behind you, you shall not be moved." The frustrated policemen fell back toward the corners of the platform and there remained until the Loudspeaker announced settlement of the strike. Then they moved dejectedly off to the accompaniment of hisses.

The women sang the chorus of "Solidarity" and were joined by the men.

The Loudspeaker asked, "Detroit, have you heard of our victory?" From the audience came "Detroit has heard of your victory." This was repeated through "Cadillac," "Ford," on up to France and Spain and the World—and the entire audience roared, "The world has heard of your victory."

The night of the performance was the victory night. The women in the cast all had husbands coming out of the plants. The union hall with its bottle-necked staircase was crowded to capacity and two hours before the beginning of the performance no one could get in or out. A few missing members of the cast managed to fight their way up at the last moment. Two of them never made it and I had to press into service two spectators. There were many speeches to be made on victory night and the cast of *Strike Marches On* waited nearly two hours to get on. The women who hadn't seen their husbands in forty-four days were all for bolting. Never have I had to speak with such persuasiveness!

There were audiences at rehearsal as well as at the performance. Union Hall was always filled—to my mind a valuable rehearsal asset. The workers building their own parts were continually stimulated by the applause received from these rehearsal audiences. To most of the workers both in and out of the cast the meaning of the labor struggle was vague. Unionization was new to them. The play served to clarify their minds, to reduce to simple and understandable terms the purpose of the struggle of which they were a part. It stimulated them to inquiry and it fired them with new enthusiasm. I am convinced that a workers' theatre, of and by the workers, must become an important department of the trade union movement.

125

THE GROUP THEATRE

What makes them representatives of the petty bourgeoisie is the fact that in their minds they do not go
beyond the limits which the latter do not go beyond in
life . . . This is in general the relationship of the political
and literary representatives of a class to the class that
they represent.

Karl Marx

The Group Theatre solved the problem of an establishment
approach to social questions. They took what was most
potent (and commercially attractive, as it is today) from the
radical theatre—moral outrage—and grafted it onto a drama
structured by the belief that neither human nature nor
society can be fundamentally changed. They did this with an
acting method that limits the actor to the portrayal of his
own emotional past.

The plays that fulfill the formula most brilliantly are by
Clifford Odets, and with them the Group achieved what none
of the people's theatres was able to do: their playwright's
world view became an amplification of their approach to
acting; Odets' and the actors' styles were reciprocal creations,
and both became imaginative representations of their Group's
economic relation to society.

Early in 1935 *Waiting for Lefty* was premiered at a New
Theatre Night, where it caused the greatest sensation since
Newsboy. Odets' first play, *Awake and Sing!*, was staged in
February by the Group on Broadway. In March a hastily
written anti-Nazi play, *Till the Day I Die*, completed a double

bill with *Lefty* which the Group produced on Broadway. By the end of the season Odets was considered the most exciting new Broadway writer and the most brilliant hope of the revolutionary stage; the Left and commercial theatres seemed strangely to agree.

Odets began the next season with *Paradise Lost*, his most symbolic play and probably the most difficult play of his to act. It is a dream-like extension of the social concerns in *Lefty* and *Awake*, playing on their contradiction between middle class desires and Depression realities and concluding with their characteristic fire.

Harold Clurman was just back from the Soviet Union when he began directing *Paradise Lost*. "The deepest impression I carried away . . . was the sense of a sane people . . . . Above all there seemed no conflict between the ideal and the real, between what their hearts dreamed and what their hands were doing." he wrote in *The Fervent Years* (New York, 1967). In contrast, the US, in the summer of 1935, "all seemed a bit mad," and *Paradise Lost* presented itself as the perfect emblem of that madness. In a *New Theatre* article (January 1936) Clurman explained the "propagandist slant" he gave the play:

> There is no enemy in the middle class world except an intangible "fate"; there is no fight except with one's own contradictions—and real life . . . enters upon the scene like a fierce, unexplained intruder.

The disintegration of the Gordon family and friends (ranging from small businessmen to petty gangsters) occupies the play's three acts. Julie, the eldest son who had hoped for a place on Wall Street, is the literal victim of the sleeping sickness that affects the other characters figuratively. Ben, the most likely to succeed, marries a callous and materialistic girl. A heart murmer ends his athletic career and he is killed by police bullets after committing a robbery he is too demoralized to run from. Leo Gordon's business fails after his partner, Sam Katz, embezzles money from it. The Gordons lose the house they mortgaged to support the business. The daughter, Pearl, loses her piano to creditors, her boyfriend to the search for work in another city, and her dreams of becoming a concert pianist to an economic situation that cannot support artists.

127

Of all the characters in *Paradise Lost*, only Clara, Leo's wife, does not seem, as Clurman put it, "a trifle touched." She buys the food, straightens the house, offers the cure-all piece of fruit. As long as the domestic tasks have to be performed her activities continue to correspond to the middle class notions that have failed the other characters, and her mind retains its stability. (The same tasks that keep Clara "sane" also keep her from being an important figure in the play; they repress her potential as a character. This is true of bourgeois drama in general. Women characters who are significant are those who are unhinged, like Blanche DuBois in *Streetcar* or Mrs. Tyrone in *Long Day's Journey*. Their "failure" as women which, paradoxically, makes them "successes" as characters, is manifested by their inability to keep house or to satisfy a husband.)

Paradise Lost is a series of unrealized desires which are described through a succession of abortive confrontations. Leo Gordon tells his wife to get rid of their German parakeet. His only aggressive action in the play, it is supposed to mark him as politically sensitive but comically ineffectual. When a delegation of workers from his shop comes to demand better conditions, Leo is deeply moved. "My brain has been sleeping . . . . Tomorrow I mean to start fresh." But Sam Katz tells him there is no money for raises and he forgets his promise.

When Pearl's boyfriend says he is leaving town, she just walks away. When Julie enters a room in time to hear he is dying of sleeping sickness, he walks out, returning only to ask that his mother not be told he knows. Ben forces a confession from Kewpie, the best friend who is having an affair with his wife, then he starts to walk out the door. He picks up a gun, but does not use it. Julie walks around the house in evening clothes with nowhere to go but to sleep. Pearl says, "I'm homesick all the time. For what?" Leo simply doesn't answer when Sam tells him he has stolen the company's money. Pike, the furnace man, tops his revolutionary speech with the announcement that he wants to kill himself. Sam Katz, "a man like an ox," has been impotent for seven years.

Until the final moment of the play, not one of the possible confrontations is realized. Characters slip away from each other like life is slipping away from each of them and, by implication, like power is slipping away from the middle class. When the house is gone, Ben is dead and Julie is nearly dead, Leo Gordon tries to give some money to two transients. They refuse, pointing out that his situation is just as bad as theirs and asking: "Who the hell do you think you are?"

For the first time in the play Leo responds directly; he confronts the gravity of the situation and poses an alternative to it. The verbal motif changes simultaneously from images of sleep and decay to those of birth and community:

> Everywhere now men are rising from their sleep. Men, men are understanding the bitter black total of their lives ... Heartbreak and terror are not the heritage of mankind! The world is beautiful. No fruit tree wears a lock and key. Men will sing at their work, men will love. Ohhh, darling [to his wife], the world is beautiful and *no man fights alone!*

The curtain falls on this affirmation, an echo of the strike call in *Lefty*: "Hello America! ... We're stormbirds of the working class ... We'll die for what is right, put fruit trees where our ashes are!" and of Ralph's big speech in *Awake:* "I swear to God, I'm one week old. I want the whole city to hear it—fresh blood, arms. We got 'em. We're glad we're living."

If the activity in the strike plays of the decade seemed disproportionate to the depth of the emotions leading to it, Odets' plays were just the reverse. Here was wonderfully articulated sentiment freed from the slightest organic possibility of action.* Yet, *Paradise Lost* is not dishonest. Finally, its last speech is not even an anachronism. Rather, it completes Odets' symbolization of the middle class by showing its deep-seated need to give itself emotionally to current ideas (an aspect of consumerism, as the middle class gives itself physically to current clothes) without enduring the changed life-style that such ideas demand. Strangely predictable from this play is Odets' appearance in 1952 as a friendly witness before HUAC, and his subsequent belief that his conciliatory testimony had defied the Committee because they didn't thank him as they thanked other witnesses that day.

Paradise Lost was not financially successful. Most of the uptown reviewers did not like it; it was too diffuse for them.

---

*The static structures of *Lefty* and *Awake* have been analyzed by John Howard Lawson in *Theory and Techinque of Playwriting*, New York, 1960, pp. 249-54.

On the Left, Robert Forsythe in *New Masses* and John Gassner in *New Theatre* wrote appreciative articles about the play. The group took ads stating their faith in it and cut salaries. With financial help from Odets, who had gone to Hollywood, they managed to keep it running for nine weeks. (The production had been financed originally with $17,000 from Metro-Goldwyn-Mayer, for reasons, Clurman records in *The Fervent Years*, that were completely "mysterious to me.")

The Group's next production was *The Case of Clyde Griffiths*, a Marxist adaptation by Erwin Piscator of Theodore Dreiser's *An American Tragedy*. Clurman, who usually had more influence in play selection than the other two Group directors, Cheryl Crawford and Lee Strasberg, "did not care for this play":

It was schematic in a cold way that to my mind definitely went against the American grain . . . In other words a play of instruction to demonstrate a thesis.*

The production, directed by Strasberg, was abstract and vague—another disservice to the theories of epic theatre—but it confirmed the impression of uptown reviewers that the Group was a left-wing theatre. It was an impression that the directors, constantly faced with gathering thousands of dollars necessary to produce on Broadway, no longer wanted to enforce. Clurman wrote a letter to newspaper editors signed by Cheryl Crawford announcing that the Group did not necessarily agree with the views of the playwrights it presented. His other letter, addressed to play agents, was reprinted in the *New York Herald-Tribune* of February 16, 1936, and quoted in *New Theatre* in July:

. . . the impression has arisen that the Group Theatre is primarily interested in the production of so-called "propaganda" plays. This is false. The Group is essentially interested in plays that make for exciting and intelligent theatre . . . .

I might say that any of the following plays would have been considered by us as possible Group material: *Journey's End, First Lady, Russet Mantle, Winterset,*

Fervent Years p. 163.

Petrified Forest, Road to Rome, Pride and Prejudice, Children's Hour, The Jest and *Dinner at Eight.*

Around this time members of the Dramatists Guild were trying to secure a stronger contract for scripts that were optioned commercially and might turn into films, and they were facing a great deal of hostility from motion picture producers and commercial theatre managers (who, like the Group, often depended on Hollywood financing). The Group acting company, which consistently voiced more radical opinions than those of the three directors, voted to support the writers. The directors, however, delayed signing the agreement until an amended version was accepted by the League of New York Theatres. Thus, Norman Sterns wrote in *New Theatre* (July, 1936), the Group "tacitly capitulated to motion picture producers who were attempting to break trade unionism among writers." Following ratification of the contract, Clurman would peevishly remark in *Fervent Years*, "Movie money was almost impossible to get now that the new Dramatists' Guild contract had caused a revolt among picture executives."

Left critics were annoyed by the Group's capitulation to commercial interests, but they were unwilling to give the Group up; it was too potentially perfect an emblem of the united front. Stevens wrote:

> The Group's audience function lies in developing and coordinating an audience of a preeminently middle class character . . . The Group has a magnificent task to perform. It is possible that the richest art of our time may be developed out of the conflicts of middle class life.

In the same article he considered the basic contradiction of the Group's organization:

> The end to which the Group's work is dedicated is artistic integrity and independence. The *means* are audience support, critical approval, financial backing.

About *Paradise Lost* he wrote:

> Odets has shown the middle class reaching social aware-

131

ness only through its own annihilation. This constitutes on the one hand an evasion of social issues, and on the other a romantic gesture of "leftism" which covers the evasion.

In the summer of 1936, Clurman rejected two plays for the Group. One was *Marching Song*, which struck him as "cold, artificial, a creature of the author's will—lacking in spontaneity."* The other was Odets' unpublished and never finished strike play, *The Silent Partner*, which got as far as beginning rehearsals. When he visited Odets in Hollywood Clurman thought he was uneasy with his role as "revolutionary" playwright and that he wished instead to be "at the very center of standard playwrights of quality."** The play he was working on, however, was his most radical, politically and theatrically. It focused on a working class community and the effects of decaying capitalism on them. And it was a departure from the usual Odets format in which inaction leads to revolutionary rhetoric. In *Partner* militant strike action results in .sobriety and an increased understanding of radical responsibility.

Odets had one scene of his new play published in *New Theatre*. The wives of the strikers are gathered at a bakery to wait for a milk delivery from sympathetic farmers. The milk arrives and so do company thugs who dump it in the gutter. After publication, Odets penciled three alterations into his own copy of the script. They were meant to clarify how a minor character, Mrs. Finch, is changed by this confrontation from outspoken opponent of the strike to one of its most volatile supporters.† This is the only scene in which the Odets script approaches the radical conversions that provide the greatest strength and the stiffness (when cast in domestic form) of *Marching Song*. But the entire design of the play is evidence that his mind was working in a new way, challenging the efficacy of revolutionary rhetoric that was separate from an active and expansive structure.

Clurman's reaction is interesting:

Fervent Years, pp. 174-5.
**ibid.*, p. 170.

†He gives her two additional lines and lengthens one from *"Your Town!"* to *"Your town! Yours?!"*

132

No play of Odets had a wider scope, a greater variety of characters, or more exciting scenes. But the play, intuitively sound in its basic perceptions, was very weak in all its central characters and situations. The maturity that the Italian baker was supposed to possess was exactly the quality that Odets himself lacked.*

Like his criticism of *Marching Song,* which ignored the fact that every play is "a creature of the author's will," his criticism of *Silent Partner* does not seem exactly to the point. Certainly playwrights do not have to possess every quality they write about. Odets had written about Nazis and gangsters, but no one supposed he was either one. Considering the needs of the Group, however, Clurman's rejections were sound. 1937 was the year of the great CIO sit-ins; both plays were as timely then as *1931-* had been at the beginning of the decade. But the strike play had seldom been popular with uptown reviewers, and the Group was still dependent on box office receipts. Both plays, like *Clyde Griffiths* but in a much more symbolist way, were concerned with how social forces determine the development of a community. But the Method,** with its emphasis on individual passions was far removed from this. Method acting allows each actor to understand the situation of the play only as it is reflected in the emotional response of his own character. The audience is similarly limited, it can perceive the situation only as it is reflected by actors who are each concerned with separate aspects of it. In this way it is possible to see how individuals react to events but not how events are determined by the activities of individuals.

The Group did one more production during its left-wing period, *Johnny Johnson,* a musical play with an anti-war theme adapted by Paul Green from *The Good Soldier Schweik.* Then, financially exhausted, it disbanded, and Clurman and many of the actors left for Hollywood. In April 1937, Lee Strasberg and Cheryl Crawford resigned as co-directors. In August Clurman returned to New York and the Group began rehearsing their most financially successful

op. cit., p. 174.
**". . . the thing that most of the actors of the Group still call the Method is in reality Lee's [Strasberg's] own method of work," the Group actors wrote in an appraisal of their directors in 1936.

production, *Golden Boy*, by Odets. In this play and in *Rocket to the Moon, Night Music* and *Clash by Night* which followed, Odets had wholly individualized his themes.* The struggle now is always between a happiness that would only be possible if the character could be completely freed of social obligations and his or her need to maintain financial or domestic stability. The revolutionary fire that had once existed was subsumed by speeches in which a character passionately projected the state of mind he would achieve if he was ever emotionally fulfilled (and emotional fulfillment is often equated with illicit love).

Paradise had in fact been lost; but it was not one synonymous with the middle class garden—that was beginning to revive and was even being courted by the Group; it was the revolutionary promise which could not be tended amid the economic imperatives of the Broadway stage and the theatrical limitations of the Method.

V. Zakhava

CAN WE USE STANISLAVSKY'S METHOD?**

(V. Zakhava makes this Marxian analysis of the Stanislavsky system on the basis of his experience as Director of the Vakhtangov Theatre in Moscow. The founder, E. B. Vakhtangov, ranked with Meyerhold as Stanislavsky's most talented and original pupil. His artistically and socially revolutionary productions with the Habima players were staged during the trying first years of the revolution. His early death in 1922 removed one of the three outstanding Soviet directors and cut off his work, described in this article, of adapting the Moscow Art Theatre methods to the uses of the new socialist theatre. For a full exposition of the Stanislavsky system readers are referred to NEW THEATRE of December 1934 and February 1935. The following article was translated by Mark Schmidt for the Group Theatre, with whose permission it appears here. It has been edited and condensed by Molly Day Thacher.)

The roots of the creative method of the Vakhtangov Theatre are deeply imbedded in K. C. Stanislavsky's system. At the same time, after the influence of the October Revolution, Vakhtangov subjected the artistic principles in which he had been trained to a searching criticism

---

*He did write one more leftist play, *Flight Over Taos*, about a Cuban revolutionary. It was never published or produced.

**New Theatre*, August 1935. Edited version KMT.

and a radical revision. In certain respects he assumed an artistic position opposed to Stanislavsky's. The latter had arrived at the formula, "The audience should forget that it is in the theatre." "This led him to a blind, to a tragic blind," Vakhtangov said, "The audience should not forget for one single instant that it is in a theatre."

Yet Vakhtangov, notwithstanding the seemingly diametrical opposition between his position and Stanislavsky's, still continued in his creative work and in his teaching to make use of Stanislavsky's methods. What is this? Inconsistency? Discrepancy between pronouncement and practice? No. Because Vakhtangov's negation of his teacher's creative position is not barren and skeptical; his work establishes a bond with the tradition behind it and aims to retain the positive aspects of the latter. In other words, this is a dialectic negation, carried out with realistic appreciation of the circumstances.

A creative method of art takes shape according to two factors: the social orientation and intention of the artist (which leads to his choice of content and his attitude towards it) and the medium that is the working material of the art. What are the philosophic roots of Stanislavsky's school [until 1920] and what are its social orientations?

As is known, Stanislavsky's theatre concentrated all its attention and art upon the inner life of the acting characters, upon the psychologic, subjective, side of their behaviour. The soul of the hero, his inner world, his psyche, his "inner experiences," his "spiritual essence"—that is what absorbed the actors and directors of that theatre. In revealing this "inner experience" to an audience of many thousands lay the joy of the theatrical artist, the joy of the actor. "And if," said Dantchenko, co-director of the Art Theatre, "the actors have talent, that is, the ability to infect the audience with his experiences, then we shall have the triumph of art."

The actor in such a theatre is indifferent as to the occasions which employ his feelings: the playwright provides the situation, but feelings are brought forth by the actor who uses his "affective recollections." From the point of view of the inner technique of his art, it does not matter to the actor whom he impersonates—a sincere monarchist or a sincere revolutionist, for the feelings of both are the same (universally human), the difference being only in the occasion. One is joyful when the other is desperate, and vice versa—each being right from his own point of view. What concerns the actor are "joy" and "woe" in themselves, the subjective essence of the soul of the created character, and not his objective links with the outer world.

This actor of the natural-psychological theatre also proceeds in an identical way, whether he is acting in a tragedy or a farce. The feelings are the same in both—the difference is in what occasions them. His business is to become sincerely horrified or to break out in sobs. This has to be done in a vaudeville act as well as in tragedy, only in the farce the reason for the character's sobbing is trivial, and this lack of

135

proportion between the paltry occasion and the real woe will be funny. But the "comic effect" is a result which has nothing to do with the actor.

We see hardly any thought is given here to the idea that vaudeville and tragedy demand various manners of acting, radically different methods of craftsmanship. The evaluation of the portrayed object on the part of the theatre is altogether lacking. To evaluate, to show an attitude to the reality that is portrayed—this the naturalistic theatre would leave to the audience.

The business of the theatre is to evoke sympathy toward each character, to draw the audience into a sympathetic experience and thus to bring the character close to the spectator. The "characters" are the same kind of people who sit in the auditorium. The audience comes to the theatre and finds upon the stage its friends, close acquaintances, relatives. Stanislavsky rejoiced that the audience came to the Moscow Art Theatre not as to a theatre at all, but as if invited to the homes of the Prosorov or Voynitzky families. *(Three Sisters, Uncle Vanya.)* The characters together with the audience talk about the affairs and needs, the hopes and sorrows, of the Russian intelligensia. There are no just, no guilty, people—each is right in his own way . . . all are human . . . .

An idealistic individualism which views the human psyche as an insulated and self-sufficient value. A "universally human" morality as the ethical base. out of which character is built. An objective, "beyond class"—and consequently passive—attitude towards actuality. An utterly apolitical character. These are the most characteristic qualities of the social and philosophical outlook of the psychological naturalistic artists. (And, obviously, the outlook is class conditioned.)

[Stanislavsky] sees the meaning of art in revealing the subjective side of personality. But his experience leads him to a formula: "To work upon a role is to seek for a relation." From this follows the objectively correct view of a character as a complex of its relations to its environment. And thus he came very close to the recognition that the essential in a character is not the subjective aspect of its life, but its objective connections and relations. The subjective side of a character's experiences is the signalizing service with the help of which the (biologically expeditious) function of adapting the organism to the environment is carried out. Another step, and the stress will go from the subjective to the objective moment. But this step was not made by Stanislavsky, and so he remains imprisoned by contradictions. They can be resolved only when one understands the dialectic unity of the subjective and the objective, of the inner and the outer.

Stanislavsky becomes convinced, practically, that feeling will not come of itself; that the more an actor orders or pleads with himself to cry, the less chance there is of his doing it. "Feeling has to be enticed." The decoy for feeling, he finds, is thought, and the trap is action. "Don't wait for feeling, act at once." Feeling will come in the process of acting, in the clashes with environment. If you ask for something, and you do it with an awareness that you really need it, and then you are turned down—the feeling of offense and vexation will come to you spontaneously. Don't worry about feeling—forget it. Remember only your own action (in this case, to ask for something). A counsel of genius. A discovery worthy of genius.

But we see that action is regarded by Stanislavsky only as a means of arriving at feeling as the aim of the creative process. Yet the creative practice of the theatre artist convinces him at every step that action is the essence of the theatre. What matters in the theatre is that I am begging for something while he refuses, and *not* what I feel because of it. Feeling is a subjective moment. It is necessary, but only insofar as it becomes an impulse to a new action.

The contradiction between the inner and the outer technique—that is the most painful moment in Stanislavsky's creative life. When he concentrates upon the inner technique, which he elaborated so lovingly, he feels that along the line of external expressiveness (especially when the playwright's material makes definite demands in this field) there appear yawning gaps. The feeling, already elicited, does not find any means of expressing itself. But when he concentrates upon physical expression, then feeling is not even born, and the demands of inner technique remain ungratified. The trouble here again lies in the dualistic notion of human nature, in the false separation between subjective and objective, the failure to understand that anything external is at the same time in the nature of an internal process, and vice versa.

CAN the Stanislavsky system—the system of the naturalist-psychological theatre whose philosophical root is idealistic individualism—be taken over bodily into the proletarian theatre? Of course not. In Stanislavsky's system the elementary A. B. C. is colored by a definite world view. Unless we use it in a very discriminating way, we run the danger of accepting not only his scientific, but also his idealistic influence. The task is to force out of his system the philosophy with which it is permeated, and to saturate it with a different socio-philosophical meaning.

I myself erred many times in public statements about the system—maintaining that it was universal, and the only basis upon which any theatre, of any tendency, could be built. My statements were countered by those who maintained that a method invariably entails a content, and will finally entail its own philosophy. My opponents were of course right. The mitigating circumstance in my favor was that my opponents usually went on to advocate the breaking up and abandoning of the entire Stanislavsky system. The complete taking over of the method is wrong—but it would have been even more false and destructive to have deprived the nascent proletarian theatres of the vast riches that are contained in Stanislavsky's system. The method contains a number of elements and laws which can and should be used. After criticizing the

137

system as a whole, the values should be selected so that we can begin applying them in a manner different from that used by Stanislavsky.

For instance, we pointed out above Stanislavsky's assumption that a character is a complex of relations, and that to work on a role is to seek for relations. That is correct. But how shall we determine and analyze those relations? These relations are the thing which will show one's social viewpoint. It is true that in any theatre an actor should know before coming onto the stage why he comes there, what he is to do there (not in terms of feelings, but of actions). But the basis for the planning of the actions will be different in different theatres.

Even such an elementary demand as concentration of one's attention upon the stage has its own biology and sociology. The fact that the actor must have an object for concentration at every minute—that is A. B. C. But what he chooses as the object of attention, that is already the interpretation of the role, and involves the philosophy of the production.

Thus if we subject Stanislavsky's system to a thorough criticism, using the methods of dialectic materialism; if we examine it attentively in the light of modern scientific data; if we force out of it the idealistic world view which creates contradictions within the system itself; if we select whatever is necessary and sound in it (which, essentially, is the materialistic parts), and translate it from the language of idealistic philosophy and subjective psychology into modern scientific terms—we shall then have the A. B. C. of the actor's art. It will be rooted in the biologic bases of the actor's creative work. We will then apply this alphabet for other purposes, and in a different manner.

We can be sure that Stanislavsky will be revered in the history of the theatre as the greatest performer of theatric art, as the genius who created the alphabet of the actor's art, its first primer, and so brought the teaching of that art from the stage of medieval barbarism into that of scientific and cultural development.

ARTEF

Artef (a Yiddish abreviation for Workers Theatrical Alliance) was founded by young Jewish workers in 1927 as a studio for production of agitprop sketches and for studies in the arts of the theatre. By 1935 the acting company occupied a small theatre on Broadway, and was being praised extravagently by the Left and by uptown critics for its Yiddish productions of Maxim Gorki's *Dostigayev* and *Yegor Bulitchev,* and Sholem Aleichem's *Recruits* and *200,000.*

Artef sponsored six acting studios that taught 120 students and resulted in a permanent company of 29 people. These actors performed in the major productions, built and painted scenery, continued their political activities and, in most cases, held, full-time jobs as office or factory workers.

Late in the twenties, Nathaniel Buchwald, a founding member of the Artef board and theatre critic for the *Freiheit* the Yiddish radical newspaper, met Benno Schneider at a party and asked him to give a class in make-up at the Artef studio. Schneider was earning his living painting batik in a factory, but he had just come from Russia where he had studied under Stanislavsky and Vakhtangov, and acted with the Habima. He found the Artef actors following the ornate, declamatory acting style of the popular Yiddish theatre on Second Avenue, and he began to impose on them a selective, theatricalized realism learned from Vakhtangov.

"I was a complete dictator while I was with Artef. They were all amateur actors and I would say they were wonderful material in the hands of someone with good taste. A few of the actors grew up very well, but I think that Artef was created through my knowledge of Vakhtangov's directing techniques," Schneider says.

Schneider says he was "completely unpolitical" when he was with Artef, though "all the actors were working people and they used to be out on the picket lines all the time." They urged him to join the Party but he refused, saying that he could contribute nothing to it. The Artef directors' disinterest in left-wing politics was kept curiously well-hidden during the thirties. Buchwald, the group's public spokesman, was a Communist. Whatever ideological distance existed between Schneider and the actors was bridged by his ability to supply a style that allowed them to exist as a singular acting company.

The sight of their collective acting was what turned many people on to the excellence of Artef. Productions were nearly choreographed. A distinct rhythm was discovered for each scene and each actor responded to it with a set of carefully selected and executed movements and gestures. Because this approach gave the crowd a lot of visual weight in plays by Sholem Aleichem, the Artef is said to have found a style that glorified the mass as a hero. But this sort of communistic accomplishment was never duplicated in productions of Amerikan radical authors. Schneider found these scripts distinctly inferior to the Russian classics, and he was not in sympathy with their authors' wish to create a revolutionary theatre in the US. So no real interchange between young playwrights and an acting company ever materialized, though a situation seemingly existed where one could flourish. Artef's picturesque approach remained applicable only to Russian plays. Though the Artef mobile troops continued to present mass chants and agitprops, they never made the potentially beneficial connection between these performance styles and the demands of the full-length radical plays. Consequently, *The Roar of the Machines* by P. Tchernev, *Haunch, Paunch and Jowl* from the novel by Samuel Ornitz, and *The Third Parade* by Peters and Walker and an adaptation of *Can You Hear Their Voices?* were all uncuccessful when produced by Artef.

Brecht, propagandizing for the A-effect, described a performance of *Haunch, Paunch and Jowl*:

In the New York Yiddish Theatre, a highly progressive theatre, I saw a play by S. Ornitz showing the rise of an East Side boy to be a big crooked attorney. The theatre

140

could not perform the play. And yet there were scenes like this in it: the young attorney sits in the street outside his house giving cheap legal advice. A young woman arrives and complains that her leg has been hurt in a traffic accident. But the case has been bungled and her compensation has not been paid. In desperation she points to her leg and says: "It's started to heal up." Working without the A-effect, the theatre was unable to make use of this exceptional scene to show the horror of a bloody epoch. Few people in the audience noticed it; hardly anyone who reads this will remember that cry. The actress spoke the cry as if it were something perfectly natural. But it' is exactly this—the fact that this poor creature finds such a complaint natural—that she should have reported the public like a horrified messenger returning from the lowest of hells. To that end she would of course have needed a special technique which would have allowed her to underline the historical aspect of a specific social condition.*

In 1939 Artef presented a well-received production of *Clinton Street* by Ornitz, using a narrator to emphasize its social comment. The company disbanded the next season; its final production in 1941 was a series of review sketches. In the late forties and early fifties the most dedicated members of Artef attempted to revive the theatre, without Schneider who was working in Hollywood. The Ensemble Group gave five productions in halls around New York, including *Hard to Be a Jew* by Sholem Aleichem; the anti-Nazi play by Tchivjanovsky, *Family Sonnenbruch;* and J. B. Priestly's utopian drama, *They Came to a City.* In 1953 Morris Carnovsky directed their final effort, *The Devil in Boston.*

Nathaniel Buchwald

THE ARTEF ON BROADWAY**

A WELL-KNOWN theatrical producer and the owner of one of the biggest "hits" on Broadway, who may be embarrassed if his name is

---

Brecht on Theatre, p. 98.
**New Theatre*, February 1935. Edited version KMT.

mentioned in this connection, happened to stumble upon the Artef, attended the premiere of *Recruits* and—has never got over it . . . To him, and the scores of professionals he has induced to see *Recruits*, the Artef is a thrilling discovery. It has become that to thousands of playgoers who at a dollar top have seen and thrilled to one of the most captivating shows in the theatre.

Yet the Artef has been in the theatre field now for six years and has gained a high standing as the most accomplished group in the revolutionary theatre. The language of its productions, Yiddish, and the fact that its scene of operations has been a long distance away from the amusement mart, account for the tardiness of the Broadway denizens and visitors in discovering this most stimulating and close-knit aggregation of acting talent, producing enterprise and revolutionary zeal. Away from Broadway where lights are dim and fire-traps plentiful, where Jewish workers gather in their clubs and neighborhood folk seek amusement in their own idiom, the Artef and the individual *Artefniks*, as members of the group are fondly nicknamed, are known and liked by many, many thousands. For the Artef has been producing not only "regular shows" at regular playhouses and at modest admissions, but has made good theatre available to workers in their own neighborhoods, performing sometimes upon bare platforms, sometimes upon improvised stages and always to admiring audiences. Even in the revolutionary theatre field it is not generally known that the Artef has to its credit a score of short plays and skits of the *mobile* type and that neighborhood bookings of Artef groups and individual concert performers have been more numerous than its performances of full-length plays. When the Workers Laboratory Theatre was still in its formative period, the Artef was already known as a vigorous and creative *mobile* theatre as well as a producer of full-length plays in the "orthodox" manner.

Nor does Artef's pioneering end here. As a revolutionary theatre it blazed the way to audience organization. The Theatre Union has built its system of "benefits" and organization bookings essentially along the lines developed by the Artef. Indeed, the very name of Artef (an abbreviation of *Arbeiter Theatre Ferband*, meaning "Workers Theatrical Alliance") reflects its close tie-up with organized bodies of workers. Structurally, the management of the Artef is nothing but an executive committee deriving its authority from a kind of theatre-lovers' association in which are represented upward of one hundred trade-union, educational and fraternal organizations. It is to them that the Artef belongs and it is from among their midst that the Artef Players were mobilized. Structurally, then, every fraternal branch, workers' club, Women's Council and parents' group in the left-wing labor movement is a *constituent member of the Artef*. As organizations, these are also the potential and actual clients of the Artef Theatre, and it is from its own organization membership that the Artef derives most of its benefit

142

bookings.

Added to this, there is a body of individual subscribers numbering about three thousand and steadily growing. Organization bookings and subscriptions account for the bulk of the Artef audience. Even now, with its large and ever-increasing box-office clientele, bookings and subscriptions take up about sixty per cent of the capacity of the Artef Theatre.

So much for the organizational side. On the artistic side the Artef has the advantage of a well-trained acting *collective*, unified by long association and bound together by a common idea: to use the theatre as a weapon in the fight for a better world. The advantage of a permanent company plus an animating social purpose lift the Artef artistically above all other so-called Art Theatres in this country. The qualitative growth of the Artef collective has been amazing. Both individually and as a group they increase in stature with each new production. It is only a year ago that Artef produced *Yegor Bulichev*, the first drama of Gorki's revolutionary trilogy. In every department, acting, staging and setting, it was a production of high merit, acclaimed as such by critics and audiences alike. Yet the second Gorki play, *Dostigayev*, now current at the Artef, is so much superior in the consummate acting of a number of performers . . . that one wonders when they had time to develop to such a remarkable degree.

A goodly portion of the credit for the excellence of the Artef Players is due their art director and regisseur Beno [sic] Schneider, a pupil of the great Vakhtangov and a talented and imaginative master in his own right. He is not merely a director who drills his actors and puts them through their paces, he is a teacher and patient maker of actors. Under his tutelage the Artef Players have learned much and unlearned even more . . . .

The Artef production of *Dostigayev* is superb in its portrayal of solid, three-dimensional character. Goldstein's portrait of Vasily Dostigayev is nothing short of a masterpiece of "socialist realism." While making the industrialist thoroughly real and individualized, Goldstein at the same time makes him marvelously clear as a symbol of opportunism and compromise. Ready to climb on the band wagon in the event of Bolshevist victory, Dostigayev is ever preoccupied with the idea of "placing a stumbling block on their difficult and untried path." It is in the sense of the greatest menace to the revolution and not in the sense of the chief dramatic role that Dostigayev is the central character of the play. In the Kerensky epoch Gorki quite properly put the accent on the opportunist and compromiser. It is to the honor of the Artef that this figure emerges also artistically as the most impressive of the whole array of competently portrayed and socially significant *characters*.

There is not space to dwell at length on other admirable performances in *Dostigayev*. The direction of the play is as subtle in its overtones as it is clear in its design. Schneider had the good taste and

143

the fine artistic sense to forego fetching stage effects and dazzling theatricals, something he likes doing and is very clever at. He concentrated entirely on character and on spinning out of mood and thought a dramatic texture of all-pervading "spirit of the times," with all of its ominous social forces at play, with the impending revolution as the dominant, hopeful note in a welter of agony and confusion. Zolotaroff's sets furnish a fitting frame and background for this penetrating play of social character and *stimmung*.

One wishes one had more space to dwell on the shortcomings and the handicaps of the Artef; its deplorable tendency, of late, to neglect the work of the *mobile* type and the danger of its attaining a state of "splendid isolation" and tearing itself loose organizationally from its mass basis; the lack of worth-while American plays in its repertory and the discouraging prospect of continuing to subsist on foreign plays alone: the lack of cooperation between the Artef and the revolutionary Jewish Writers organization, the Proletpen, which is in some measure, at least, responsible for the lack of adequate scripts by local revolutionary writers; the handicap of operating on a part-time schedule with an acting company on a volunteer basis and the difficulties and dangers attending the projected transition to a professional, full-time theatre. These and many more difficulties besetting the Artef make the life of this splendid organization not as easy and romantic as might seem from a distance.

LIVING NEWSPAPER

Don't be afraid when people tell you this is a play of protest. Of course it's protest, protest against dirt, disease, Human misery. If, in giving great plays of the past as greatly as we can give them, and if, in making people laugh which we certainly want to do, we can't also protest against the evils of this country of ours, then we do not deserve the chance put into our hands.

Hallie Flanagan*

In 1935 the Works Progress Administration authorized funds for a Federal Theatre that would remove artists from relief roles and put them back to work in the profession for which they had been trained. Hallie Flanagan would direct the project from Washington, aided by regional directors around the country. The plan for a government-supported national theatre, staffed mainly with people who could not find work in the professional theatre, met at first with hostile disbelief from the commercial producers, but it was enthusiastically supported by the Left, which recognized what its nation-wide organization and its personnel and economic resources could mean to the foundation of a real people's theatre in the US. (Of course they considered the possibility of government censorship and they determined to fight it when it happened. But this possibility was no reason to refuse the great opportunity the theatre presented.)

---

*Address to members of the Federal Theatre summer workshop, 1937.

Federal Theatre might accomplish what none of the financially strained radical theatres could even dream of doing: it would create a mass audience by integrating popular forms like circus, vaudeville, melodrama, and marionette shows, which the people already loved and would come to see, with plays of protest, which the people would learn to come to see and respond to when they realized their Federal Theatre was worth supporting. And the attributes of the popular theatre—the physical dexterity of its performers, its spectacle and humor—could not help but combine with the serious but ultimately joyful purposes of the protest plays into a form that would rouse the people, because it was made out of festivities they naturally found exhilerating.

The living newspaper is the form indigenous to Federal Theatre and the one that began to acheive this union of popular entertainments with people's theatre. It had roots in the people's hunger for news, being currently demonstrated by the crowds at March of Time newsreels; their admiration for the buffoon who conquers; their love of large casts, music, magical effects (the electrically projected waterfall in *Power*, for example); and their ability to believe in the unreality of the vaudeville sketch.

Hallie Flanagan had been trying to convince Elmer Rice to take over the New York Federal Theatre project. They went together to see *The Night of January 16th*, by Ayn Rand (!), a Broadway play with an unusually large cast. Leaving the theatre, Rice told her that the play had convinced him not to accept the Federal Theatre post. He was not bothered by the standard doubts of professionals: that people on relief would have no talent and that production budgets would be hopelessly small. But he didn't see how it would be possible to keep all the actors busy: "We'd have to have twenty plays with thirty in each cast, and then how could we get the sets built?"

Flanagan improvised: "'We wouldn't use them all for plays—we could do living newspapers. We could dramatize the news without expensive scenery—just living actors, light, music, movement.' Elmer seized upon the idea, accepted the directorship for New York, secured the sponsorship of the Newspaper Guild and appointed Morris Watson to head the living newspaper."*

---

*Hallie Flanagan, *Arena*, New York,1940, pp. 64-5.

146

The living newspaper grew out of the necessity to use as many as possible of Federal Theatre's greatest asset: unemployed people. It was a gigantic experiment in communal play creation and the results are still impressive. At least 100 reporters and playwrights were on the living newspaper staff, which was set-up like a city daily. Arthur Arent was managing editor. A playwright and satirist, he and Harold J. Rome had just finished writing the sketches that would become *Pins and Needles*, the musical review produced by the International Ladies Garment Workers Union (ILGWU), one of the unions that took labor's involvement in theatre most seriously. Watson assigned the topics; the reporters researched them, going through quantities of newspapers, magazines, and books, and regularly to the *Congressional Record* (all the scripts include extensive footnotes). Arent and his staff sifted the facts and put them into scenes.

Because the demand for living newspapers was constant—a full production unit of actors, stagehands and pit musicians was always waiting—the writers had to keep turning them out; and under the pressure of instant production each script represented an advance in concept and form. "If left to myself, I might have written one play during this period," Arent said. Yet during this conversation one year before he died in May 1972, Arent was reluctant to admit that he had had any help in the creation of *Power* or *One Third of a Nation*, the two best living newspapers. He was indeed their principle author; but without the living newspaper staff this form so suited to his writing talents would never have been devised. Isn't this the real purpose of communal writing efforts—to create a situation conducive to the best work of the community's most talented member.

The first living newspaper, *Ethiopia*, documented the defiance of Mussolini by Haile Selassie. Before it could open, government officials issued a directive forbidding representation of foreign heads of state on a Federal stage. Emer Rice arranged a private press showing of the production where he explained that he would not remain "the servant of a government which plays the shabby game of partisan politics at the expense of freedom and the principles of democracy." The immediate consequence of *Ethiopia's* repression was that all subsequent living newspapers were restricted to domestic concerns, making them even more fearsome to the reaction-

147

aries who were finally able to kill Federal Theatre four years later.

When the project ended, *Triple—A Plowed Under*, about farm relief, *1935*, and *Injunction Granted*, a labor history, had been produced by the living newspaper unit in New York. *Power*, urging public ownership of utilities, and *One Third of a Nation*, a history of slum housing and land speculation, were created by Arent and the New York staff, and played all over the country, adapted to local conditions. The Iowa project wrote a living newspaper, *Dirt*; Oregon did *Flax*; Newark presented a history of black people in the US; Cincinnati documented flood control; California did *Clown's Progress*, a history of vaudeville; Chicago produced *Spirochette*, about syphilis. After Federal Theatre ended *Medicine Show*, a living newspaper about health care was presented briefly on Broadway, and after the war Hallie Flanagan's script demanding public control of atomic energy received a workshop production by the Experimental Theatre. But without the people of Federal Theatre there was little chance of continuing the form: it was too expensive and too explosive for private production.

The challenge of the living newspaper was to find theatrical analogs to contemporary social problems; its purpose was to educate the public. This was shared knowledge among the project's creators, as the following excerpts from articles by Watson and Arent show. The living newspaper came in the middle of the thirties, after agitprop, New Playwrights (whose *Centuries'* factory fire is an antecendent to *One Third of a Nation's* tenement fire) and the strike plays had begun to explore the documentary implications of theatre, and after the work of Piscator and Brecht had begun to be known in the US. It was created with an astonishing amount of conscious theorizing for the Amerikan theatre (which is usually lacking here) and this made for the widest possible use of the living newspaper's inherent virtues: its muckraking ability; its elasticity; its focus on theme instead of plot, on situation instead of character. This last is crucial because the exposing of personalities will never lead to radical change, and that is why it is tolerated so benignly in this country. Get rid of Nixon or Rockefeller, and any one of a hundred thousand petty bureaucrats will be eager to do their jobs.

The people of the thirties were in the midst of economic

collapse and facing the rise of fascism. They met both catastrophies with a kind of guileless amazement and unstudied perseverance. The escapist genres of the period, which have recently regained vogue as homosexual camp, exploited the reverse of these qualities, turning amazement into sentimental fantasizing and perseverance into blind acceptance. But the people's theatre, especially the living newspaper, turned these qualities into a stumbling, naive, but hopeful mass march to power.

In the thirties, certain character types appear in all sorts of plays from the most frivolous to the most visionary: the fat, rich lady, the whore with a heart of gold, the hard-as-nails society girl, the gruff financier. The living newspapers first presented these characters so that the audience would recognize these stereotypes as their own; then they bombarded the audience with facts until the audience realized how these stereotypes could be upset once the conditions that created them were changed.

In *Power*, the Consumer, personified by a character named Angus K. Buttonkooper "walks across the stage timidly, looking around to see if he's in the right place." He has come to protest the amount of his electricity bill, but is cowed when the company owner gives him a cigar, a smile and some facile explanations.

CONSUMER: Thank you, thank you . . . .
CARMICHAEL: Good day, Mr. Buttondropper, Mr. Buttondripper, Mr. . . . . (*Consumer starts to exit, but comes back and returns cigar to Carmichael*)

As the play progresses, the Consumer/Investor realizes he has been tricked into putting up all the money (four million dollars worth of common stock) for a corporation that Samuel J. Insull controls, though the latter has not invested "one red cent" in it. In time Buttonkooper blows his top:

Instead of his normal, timid self, he has become a roaring lion. He crosses, full of determination, his shoulders high . . . .
I'm sick and tired of all this kicken' around. Every time they want to take a sock at somebody, I'm the guy that

149

gets it. First it was the rate raise, then it was the holding company . . . I say to hell with 'em! I'm going to fight!

Morris Watson

THE LIVING NEWSPAPER*

The current edition of the Living Newspaper at the Biltmore Theatre, *1935*, recounts various happenings of the year for which it is named and represents a deliberate experiment in the matter of presenting news visually.

The Living Newspaper's first offering, *Triple-A Plowed Under*, took a single theme and developed it along news lines and actually was more pamphlet than newspaper. In *1935* unrelated items are presented on the same program, and the temper of the year, rather than the history, is stressed.

The edition opens its story at 11:58 p.m. of the last day of 1934 with a crowd of merrymakers at Times Square. The commentator asks if they remember Hindenburg, John L. McGraw and Marie Curie who died in 1934. And do they remember the assassination of King Alexander and the burning of the Morro Castle? Midnight comes with a blast of noise.

"Make news!" the commentator pleads. Twelve representatives of the Great American public get into a box to judge the events and the Voice of the Living Newspaper quickly announces January 2, the opening of the trail of Bruno Richard Hauptmann for the kidnaping and murder of Baby Charles A. Lindbergh, Jr. A Flemington, N.J., ballyhoo man proudly conducts a crowd of curious through the courtroom and tells them where Gloria Vanderbilt, Big Nick Cavarro and other celebrities parked themselves for the trial. The trial goes on with the crowd rushing for seats, with reporters quarreling over the purchase of exclusive stories from the principals. Betty Gow is called. "I couldn't hear the baby breathe," Miss Gow testifies. As she speaks the courtroom blacks out, a spot comes up on a stylized witness stand in the center. The stand becomes a crib. She feels over the covers. Her expression becomes one of horror. She hesitates an instant. Then she screams: "Colonel Lindbergh! Colonel Lindbergh!" and rushes off. "Jafsie" Condon comes on to testify. But he does not testify. He acts out what he has to say and the mysterious "John" of Van Cortlandt Park and the cemetery helps him. The spotlight turns to an eerie green. Leaves rustle. "John" sits with the elderly Bronx pedagogue and asks: "Would I burn if the baby is dead?"

Thus the technique of reporting a trial visually without merely reproducing it on the stage in a word-for-word manner.

New Theatre, June 1936. Edited version KMT.

Next comes a scene that violates all the rules of dramatic writing. But the Living Newspaper is a combination of newspaper and topical revue. It is reporting the passage of the Wagner-Connery labor disputes bill in the terms of an actual case. A young lady appears to testify before an examiner for the board. Her words become reality. "They shut off the power and made us all go to a big room," she starts. She is talking about the Somerset Manufacturing Company of Sommerville, N. J. The curtain opens on a bunch of scared young girls and reveals the lengths to which small New Jersey towns will go to keep America safe for the exploited open shop. The episode ends with another piece of testimony acted out. One of the young ladies finds her pay is short. She goes to the office girl. She's right. Her pay is short. But wait—that's the book for the NRA code inspector. According to the book she gets *paid* by, the miserable wage she got is all she had coming. No climax. The critics call it anti-climax. The boys of the fourth estate who edit the Living Newspaper are just telling a story for what it is worth. The scene may lack the customary punch expected at the end of a dramatic sketch. Anyone viewing it, though, should be able to see why labor needs some legal protection.

That the scene should have a "wallop" at the end may be a valid criticism. I'm not saying that it isn't. The usual news story is written with the punch at the top. We newspapermen are newly wedded to the theatre. We have a lot to learn about each other. A dozen more editions should put us in step. The stride may surprise us.

A sop to humor follows the labor problem in *1935*. Bugsy Goldstein is sore as hell. Officials have re-rated the public enemies—and he's only No. 6. Just a flash. The Great American Public plays a Giants-Dodgers ball game from its bunting-bedecked jury box. The scene means nothing to me because I never saw the Dodgers play. I can't take sides here. The fans laugh like hell, and that makes it a good item for the Living Newspaper's sports page.

Barbara Hutton gets married. This time to a count. The Living Newspaper falls back on the manner in which Miss Ruth McKenny handled the story for the New York Post: the manager of a Woolworth five-and-ten would be glad to let the Post photograph one of its workers who also was to be a bride that day—only, Miss Hutton might not like it!

The next scene makes its own comment on the human race. William Deboe is hanged at Smithland, Ky. Folks turn out early to get good seats. Deboe was convicted of rape. He points to his accuser and says: "If I had five hundred dollars I wouldn't be here, she'd a taken it." What a thing to say! "Not if you offered me a thousand," she comes back. A preacher intones the Lord's Prayer. "Peanuts, Popcorn, Crackerjack," yells the candy butcher. So far as we could determine, the scene is staged exactly as it happened. Two minutes before the curtain went up on opening night the actor who plays the preacher

151

became convinced the Living Newspaper was poking fun at the Lord's Prayer. He said he wouldn't go on! We had to explain the idea.

Under the general heading of "Trivia" comes the case of the prisoner who was forgotten, who served eighteen years of a five year sentence, and the man who advertised that he found a lady's purse in the backseat of his automobile. He was willing to pay for the ad himself if the owner would explain the matter to his wife who couldn't imagine how the purse got there. A laugh.

The Voice of the Living Newspaper sweeps through the mention of several other headlines of 1935 and then Dutch Schultz comes on the scene—to beat the law, to die at the hands of the mob. The Great American Public discusses matters, not too relevantly. Then, Huey Long manipulates his legislators like puppets and swaggers on to his assassination. The legislative scene is stylized. It becomes a living cartoon and through it the Living Newspaper learns that it can pack potency into its editorial page.

The Great American Public convenes again—to disagree on whether the assassination of Huey Long was a national crisis, and winds up by being indifferent to the whole matter.

In 1935 Jeremiah T. Mahoney and Avery Brundage argued about American participation in the Olympic games at Berlin. "Sport must confine itself to the affairs of sport and no other," says Brundage. The Living Newspaper reports the incident, and illustrates sport as it is practised in the land of the Nazis. The best tennis player is removed from his team because he is a Jew. A Polish-Jewish soccer player is killed. A Catholic swimmer is stoned. The Living Newspaper doesn't say anything is right or wrong. The audience does pretty well in making its own decision on the matter. I know of no way to censor hisses.

John L. Lewis makes a plea for industrial unionism. President William Green of the American Federation of Labor is adequately quoted. The Living Newspaper tries to illustrate the argument. No kick there.

The China Clipper flies from Asia to America in 62 hours for the sake of commerce. A thriller, and another experiment. The Living Newspaper is feeling its way.

Angelo Herndon in jail with a "mercy" sentence of 18 to 20 years on the chain gang.

"That's sho' death," says another prisoner who spent six months on a Georgia chain gang. Here a test of visual reporting. The prisoner stands in the cell and describes the horrors of Georgia torture. The lights on him dim. The curtains open slowly and the audience gets a vivid glimpse of what he is saying. Silhouettes against a red light wield picks on a road. Over them hover the ominous, 20-foot high shadows of guards, rifles and whips held in position of "ready."

"Ef yo' can't stand it no mo' and drop in yo' tracks that ol' whip come crackin' down agin and somp'n make yo' get up and raise a pick

152

and drop a pick agin," the prisoner says. The silhouetted whip cracks.

The crowd is in Times Square again. Horns are tooting. Bells are ringing.

Happy New Year! Welcome 1936.

It is difficult to compare this kaleidoscopic report of the year's events which lent themselves to staging with the Living Newspaper's first edition, *Triple-A Plowed Under* which tied the plight of the farmer to the plight of the city man and disturbed the mental processes of those who saw it. In other words, it made people think. *1935* hasn't as much of that virtue, and it is open to a great deal more criticism. Each of its scenes is likely to be judged from a purely theatrical standpoint. They cannot, as did the scenes of *Triple-A Plowed Under*, flow into each other.

Whatever the idea behind the Living Newspaper in the beginning, circumstance and influences of one kind and another have modified it. A literally rough estimate of it at the moment would be: "Combine the newspaper and the theatre and to hell with the traditions of both."

Elmer Rice lent a vigor to the Living Newspaper which still is apparent. In the beginning we thought we would dramatize current news, it never occurring to us at the moment that the current news at hand was likely to be very weak stuff. The Living Newspaper staff of dramatists began culling the papers and writing for all they were worth on such items as "Tart Shoots Lover," and "Robber Seizes Jewels of Movie Queen." Rice's criticisms resulted in a complete reorganization of my own news sense. Rice said things were going on in the world and he thought we ought to talk about them. I agreed. He thought of things that affected peoples' lives and happiness and he didn't care if we stepped on a few toes and made somebody mad.

Armed with this moral backing, we decided to dramatize that part of the news which was controversial, hence current when we reached the stage with it. In part this decision was based upon our disillusionment over the length of time it took the government to purchase equipment for the theatre, since it became apparent that any news item which had the value only of timeliness would be valueless by the time we could get it to the audience.

We lost no time in changing our direction. We launched into *Ethiopia*. Here unadorned fact became so powerful that federal officials were alarmed. Sympathies were bound to be with Ethiopia . . . .

"Science" was suggested as a good, safe subject for the next show. It was quickly rejected. We had ready a script on the "Southern Situation." It dealt with lynching, share-croppers and the several social struggles now going on in the south. Rightly or wrongly we compromised. We offered to do the Agricultural situation. With little in the way of facts to go on, several of the executive staff of the Living Newspaper literally wrote like hell on a Sunday to have a script ready on the following day so that the acting company could be immediately put to work. We wrote and rewrote *Triple-A Plowed Under* up to the day of its opening. The last scene, for instance, already revised five or six times, was completely rewritten the day before opening.

There were many predictions and few of them favorable for *Triple-A Plowed Under*. One director connected with the Living Newspaper declared it was "breakfast food" and quit his job rather than be connected with it. Some theatre people said it violated all the rules. An official from Washington saw a dress rehearsal and said it was "dull." It was my own opinion, that there exists a large potential audience of the theatre composed of people who are thinking, and who want to think more of the vital social changes which are going on in the world, and that *Triple-A Plowed Under*, with all its inadequacies as a theatrical production, came nearer to satisfying this need than any fictional play I have seen.

From time to time in the preparation of scripts many interesting and controversial elements arise, elements which would occur neither in the writing of a newspaper story nor in the preparation of a straight sketch or one-acter for the commercial theatre. Since the medium of the Living Newspaper is a combination of both, the predominance of one force over the other is frequently a moot matter which finds dramatist ranged against reporter on the question of which is more important and what leeway can be taken to make a yarn sustained on the stage. For instance, in the sketch about Huey Long in *1935* which is divided into three lightning scenes, it was felt that nothing could top the second, the puppet sequence, in which Huey conducts the legislature on strings. Yet the newspaper boys felt and insisted that the assassination was *the* news. The dramatists insisted that on the stage it was anti-climax. Both were right .

Inevitably, the Living Newspaper's technique is compared to that of the *March of Time* movie and radio programs. The difference between the two is essentially the point of view. *March of Time* is put out by a rich magazine and a rich advertiser. The Living Newspaper is written, edited, staged and acted by people who struggle for their living. It is bound to catch the flavor of that struggle. What it puts on the stage is the combined effort of a group trying its best to compose its differences and march in one direction. So far, there are no stars. I hope there will be none.

Arthur Arent

THE TECHNIQUE OF THE LIVING NEWSPAPER*

Ethiopia decided for all time the question of Living Newspaper content. It was also noteworthy because it introduced the Loudspeaker

---

*Theatre Arts, November 1938. Edited version KMT.

as a commentator—a kind of non-participating dateline which introduced the various scenes. It is interesting to note that the original idea was to use a teletype across the top of the proscenium arch, giving an effect somewhat similar to that on the Times Building. This proved impracticable, since it necessitated a constant shifting of the eyes and head from the scene on stage to the moving ribbon of light above. A loudspeaker was hurriedly requisitioned and it remains in use to the present. Another thing of interest about the production was the rigid adherence to the use of the direct quote. With the exception of the finale, *Ethiopia* consisted of nothing but speeches artfully juxtaposed to build a dramatic situation. In considering the script in the light of what has come after, one thing stands out boldly: with all its unreality and stiffness, the line of cause and effect (the motif of every subsequent Living Newspaper) stands out clear and firm and could well serve as a model even today.

With *Triple-A Plowed Under*, the type of creative scene just mentioned was introduced. Characters labeled FIRST FARMER and FIRST CITY MAN appeared to leaven the succession of speeches by Secretary Wallace, Al Smith, Hugh Johnson, Milo Reno, and so forth. Here, too, the adroit manipulation of quotes was first used. It implies a pardonable skulduggery on the dramatist's part in which a direct quote was broken into many speeches, all given in response to questions which had no existence in fact but were conceived by the dramatist the better to bring out the factual testimony. One of these scenes dealt with Dorothy Sherwood who had just gone on trial for drowning her infant son. Her statement, as published in the *Daily News*, was as follows:

> She (Mrs. Sherwood) walked into the Police Court with the baby in her arms and said, *'He's dead, I just drowned my son because I couldn't feed him and I couldn't bear to see him hungry . . . . I let him wade in the creek until he got tired. Then I led him out into the middle and held him there until he stopped moving. I had only five cents and he was hungry . . . . I just thought it had to be done, that's all.'*

That was the quote. And this is what the scene looked like on the stage of the Biltmore Theatre:

LOUDSPEAKER: Newburgh, New York, August 20th, 1935 . . . . Mrs. Dorothy Sherwood . . .
(Overhead spot picks out police desk, down right. Behind it, a LIEUTENANT. Enter, MRS. SHERWOOD, left, with dead infant in her arms. She walks to desk, follow spot on her.)
MRS. SHERWOOD: *(Stops at desk.)* He's dead, I drowned him.
LIEUTENANT: You *what?*
MRS. SHERWOOD: I just drowned my son, I couldn't feed him and I couldn't bear to see him hungry . . . . I let him wade in the creek

155

until he got tired. Then I led him out into the middle and held him there until he stopped moving.

LIEUTENANT: *(Calling, not too loudly)* John! (POLICEMAN *enters lighted areas.*) Take the body. Book this woman for murder.

(Blackout everything; music; a solitary spot picks out MRS. SHERWOOD, *centre, facing out.)*

OFFSTAGE VOICE: *(Amplified)* Why did you do it?

MRS. SHERWOOD: I couldn't feed him. I only had five cents.

VOICE: Your own child! Did you think you were doing the right thing?

MRS. SHERWOOD: I just thought it had to be done, that's all.

VOICE: How could a mother kill her own child?

MRS. SHERWOOD: He was hungry, I tell you. Hungry, hungry, hungry!

(As her voice mounts, it is blended with that of another, the first in a progression of twelve voices crying, 'Guilty!' These, amplified and varying in color, increase in fervor until—)

DIM-OUT

.Compare these two ways of presenting the speech and you'll see what I mean: the build of dramatic emphasis, the repetition and the splitting of the testimony into two parts—the first part set in a Police Station, the second in a Court Room.

Triple-A was also noteworthy for the use of projection which was attempted on a small scale, not too effectively, as well as for the very successful results obtained from the shadowgraph device. In the latter, the members of the Supreme Court were seen in shadow, their voices amplified. Larger figures—of historical and contemporary characters— were superimposed on the shadows, presenting a striking effect. On the unlighted apron before the glass curtain, dark figures crossed from right to left and off, commenting on the decisions. The device was spectacular and successful and served as another way of dressing up quotes.

In *Injunction Granted!* a unit set was used, an abstraction. This production brings out one point which is of the utmost importance and should be gone into here. It is the use of the montage. From my point of view, the dramatist has two avenues of attack: the montage and the episode—or episodic. The first act of *Injunction* was pure montage. The scenes were skeletonized and flowed into one another without pause, building up to the act curtain. The act as a result was dull and repetitious, with about twice as many scenes as the first act of *Power* or *'One Third of a Nation'*, both of which had approximately the same running time. Most writers attacking the problem of a Living News- paper for the first time tend to fall into this method. I do not like it and I believe it is too much to ask of an audience. The episodic approach is altogether different, the fewer scenes being self-contained and having each three primary functions: 1, to say what has to be said; 2, to build to the scene's own natural climax; and 3, to build to the climax of the act curtain and the resolution of the play. The smaller number of scenes also permits of roundness. One aspect of the problem should be explained or dramatized fully and completely in one scene and then forgotten, with the next scene going on to another point. A single idea spread over two or three scenes becomes diffused and lacks wallop. The episodic type of construction is patterned closely on the revue, with the same kind of spotting: the flash scene, full stage; the down in one scene; the factual, the comic and the realistic sketch. The musical interlude between scenes in the episodic method is of great help, giving the audience a chance to catch its breath before chewing on the next morsel. As examples of making a point once and for all, clearly and dramatically, I may cite the opening sequence in *Power*, which explains what would happen if our supply of electricity were cut off; the Carmichael scene, in which a utilities magnate makes a deal with himself across a table, being the head of both holding companies involved; and the Grass Carpet scene in *'One Third of a Nation'*, showing the growth of land values.

Going further along in the series, we find two important developments which appeared in *Power*. First and foremost, the Loudspeaker or Voice of the Living Newspaper ceased to be merely an annotator or dateline and began to take on individuality and coloration. It spoke lines, it editorialized, it became a definite character, but never the same one for long. It was at various times in the same play ignorant, thirsting for information and a veritable Britannica of esoteric facts and statistics; it became helpful and sympathetic at one moment, bellicose, disdainful and sly at others. In short, it was all things to all men, and particularly to the dramatist.

The second innovation was the use of projection as background. Lantern slides, some hand-drawn, others photographs—a tree, a door, a lamppost—were thrown on a scrim and replaced the usual flats. The acting area, downstage, was necessarily restricted to avoid wash, but the experiment worked.

It was the intention to continue these projections as a definite part of all future productions, but here again the element of content entered. The next show was about housing. It dealt with people, not abstractions. And so it was decided that a real tenement was required to illustrate the problem.

The projections in *'One Third of a Nation'* are not backgrounds, not static. They are functional, a part of the action itself. Thus, two characters go for a stroll around New York in 1850. We project stills of that period. The characters observe them, talk about them. In the second act, another trip around New York—in 1938. This time, motion pictures, more in keeping with the period. Again the projections are discussed and the changes in the city's appearance noted.

157

And so it goes, each production bringing forth change in content and stagecraft and, most of all, change in the technique of dramatizing an abstraction which is the essence of the Living Newspaper—*the business of unrolling ten feet of grass carpet on a stage and saying 'This is five acres of land'—and what's more, making your audience believe it.*

FEDERAL THEATRE

> The ten thousand anonymous men and women—the et
> ceteras and the and-so-forths who did the work, the
> nobodies who were everybody, the somebodies who
> believed it—their dreams and deeds were not the end.
> They were the beginning of a people's theatre in a
> country whose greatest plays are still to come.
>
> Hallie Flanagan

I keep going back to the last chapter of *Arena*, her history
of the project, where Hallie Flanagan describes, with that
mixture of WASPish determination and authority that was
her response to the Depression era, the murder of Federal
Theatre by the House Committee to Investigate Un-Amerikan
Activities (Chairman Martin Dies) and the sub-committee of
the House Committee on Appropriations (Chairman Clifton
A. Woodrum). Her outrage is still pertinent. A handful of old
men, on the basis of hearsay and prejudice, effectively
stopped, what 33 years later looks to be forever, the growth
of a national theatre, which was bringing employment to
thousands, and plays, circuses and vaudeville to hundreds of
thousands of people.

Consider what our theatre would be like today if it could
offer a livelihood (I don't mean merely money) to everyone
who wanted to work in it: if actors did not have to spend
their time herding like cattle from one audition to the next;
if, tired of one ensemble, they could easily move on to
another, instead of back into the commercial situation; if
playwrights had many ongoing theatres for which to develop

159

plays, and did not have to follow the caprice of critics or producers or cater to the few directors who today are working collectively; if each region in the country had been involved over the decades with developing its own native forms of theatre to deal with local conditions and problems; if reviews and financial considerations had only minimal effect on both what was produced and how long it ran.

Even more infuriating, consider the impact this theatre would have on the lives of people: if there were a mass cultural alternative to the rot of television and road shows; if plays were free or very cheap; if they were as accessible as the library or the post office; if the living newspapers had continued to urge all of us to take power over our lives.

Federal Theatre was dangerous and that is why it was eliminated.

Federal Theatre was abolished June 30, 1939, by act of Congress. Four years earlier the WPA had created a place where most of the dissident voices in the US theatre could consolidate their efforts. "The Theatre Union disbanded because Federal Theatre really took over," Michael Blankfort writes. George Sklar's episodic play, *Life and Death of an American*, first scheduled by the Theatre Union, was being performed by Federal Theatre when the project ended; *Stevedore* had been revived by several regional projects. Artef, unable to overcome money problems, lost many of its members to Federal Theatre. In 1938, New Theatre League, which had gone from several hundred to 25 affiliated theatres, linked its decline to "the fruitful field of the Federal Theatre." John Bonn, Lem Ward, Joe Losey, Morris Watson, Howard Da Silva, John Howard Lawson—the list of radical theatre people who worked in Federal Theatre goes on and on. To get rid of it was to silence them.

Federal Theatre was meat for the reactionaries and it satisfied them enough so that they allowed the other WPA projects to continue for awhile. The fight to save it was led by Flanagan, members of the project, critics, actors, directors, designers, audiences from all over the country; not by WPA officials who had decided to offer this tiny part of their domain as an hors d'oeuvre to cannibalistic congressmen. The end of Federal Theatre was the first substantial sign that the Congress was in the grip of reactionaries, that the liberal coalition which had controlled domestic policies for much of the thirties would soon be powerless.

Hallie Flanagan

WHAT WAS FEDERAL THEATRE*

The question asked me most frequently since the Federal Theatre ended is "What will become of the people?" and that is the question with which those of us who have been engaged in the project are most vitally concerned. For the Federal Theatre was set up for people. It was not set up because the government wanted to go into show business or intended to make money by so doing, though ironically enough a number of irate gentlemen on the floor of Congress during June shook their fists at the Federal Theatre, demanding to know why it hadn't made more money.

As a matter of fact, there was no provision in the beginning for the Federal Theatre to take in any money whatsoever. Its job was to employ theatrically trained people from the relief rolls in socially useful ways. This was always considered its chief job, and consequently 65 percent of its productions were free for people who needed entertainment but couldn't afford to pay for it—free to children in orphan asylums and hospitals, free to the aged in institutions, free to the unfortunate in insane asylums and prisons, in all of which places it was increasingly regarded as a valuable therapeutic, social and educational agency.

However, the directors of the project disliked the idea of everything going out and nothing coming in. We believed that certain experiments the Federal Theatre was making would be, in the opinion of the public at large, worth paying for. Therefore we asked permission to charge admission in certain cases, with the hope that we could pay for other than labor costs—that is, scenery, costumes, properties, theatre rentals, royalties to playwrights, transportation and advertising—many of which expenses were difficult to pay for out of government funds. We spent weeks in consultation with WPA financial and Treasury officials and finally worked out a plan whereby admissions could be taken in by a bonded agent cashier and deposited in a national bank, to be available for certain project uses under United States Treasury regulations. Considering the stringency of our Treasury rulings, the insinuations made by members of the Woodrum Committee are too fantastic even for indignation. (May 1, Mr. Taber of New York: "Did you get any idea of what they, Federal Theatre employees, were doing with the money they took in, as to whether they were putting it into the Treasury, or putting it into their pockets?")

---

*Originally in *The New Republic*, October 1939. Reprinted by American Council on Public Affairs, 1721 Eye St., Washington, D.C.

161

In spite of the fact that admissions were charged in only a fraction of Federal Theatre productions, and that these admissions were small, ranging from five and ten cents for circuses and marionette shows to a quarter, and from 50 cents to $1.65 for major metropolitan productions, the amount taken in at the time of the closing of the project was approximately two million dollars. Expressed in another way, that means that in the early months of the project operation the government paid 100 percent of the other than labor costs mentioned above; by the end of the second year the project itself was paying 33½ percent of its other than labor costs; by the end of the third year it was paying 50 percent for its other than labor costs; and by June 30, 1939, when Congress ended it, those productions which charged admissions approximated 100 percent—or *all* other than labor costs.

The project was becoming cheaper, because of the fact that the initial expenses necessary to setting up theatres had already been made; box-office receipts, because of the increasing excellence of shows and many long runs of from three to twelve months, were increasing. It was probable that the project would move on to partial liquidation of labor costs also.

However, the irate gentlemen of the Woodrum Committee and their standard bearers in the House and Senate refused to read anything as simple as these facts and figures, all of which had been presented to them. They thundered indignant demands as to why the Federal Theatre had not made more millions and, at the same time, as to why the Federal Theatre had done plays which were so successful that they "competed with private industry."

All this money talk was just dust thrown in the eyes of Congress, which, if it had been informed of the facts by its so-called "fact-finding committee," would most certainly have voted (as its better informed members did vote) to continue the Federal Theatre. For the closing of the Federal Theatre did not save the taxpayers a cent of money. In fact, it cost them money, since, quite aside from the human values we are discussing, it threw into the discard a theatre plant which, through extensive gifts as well as careful buying over a four-year period, was unique and irreplaceable.

No, the reasons motivating the Woodrum Committee were not financial, but political, and as such worth analysis. This article, however, does not propose to discuss those reasons, for we are concerned here not with the cause of the Committe's action, but with its result. The result of closing the Federal Theatre is that 7,900 people, with an average of three dependents each, are now without jobs and will quite probably have to turn to their communities for help.

Ironically enough, these people were thrown out of their jobs in spite of the fact that they had, in the opinion of critics in their own field, members of their own profession and the public in general, done for the most part an excellent job.

162

I sat in the gallery of the Senate on June 28 and heard Senator Reynolds say, "The difficulty about the Theatre Project is that real actors are not employed." By virtue of being a Senator the gentleman from North Carolina can make any charge, however libelous, with impunity. The men and women he maligned have no recourse. At the moment the Senator made that assertion he had in his possession statements not only from the director of the Federal Theatre, but from the president of the Four A's and from Actors' Equity, saying that the old-line theatrical unions claimed jurisdiction over 85 percent of the Federal Theatre employees. He had statements endorsing the work of Federal Theatre employees from such theatrical authorities as Helen Hayes, Brooks Atkinson, Herman Shumlin, Otis Ferguson, John Gassner, Eugene O'Neill, Robert Benchley, Orson Welles, Frank Gillmore, Lee Shubert, Sam H. Harris, George S. Kaufman, Moss Hart, Eddie Dowling, Victor Moore, Burns Mantle, Raymond Massey and many others. Yet he ignored all of this evidence, as did Congressman Woodrum and his biased committee.

Who are these people? Are they, as Congressman Woodrum alleged on May 1, "fish peddlers, garment workers . . ."? Certainly there is nothing wrong in giving employment to fish peddlers and garment workers, but it was not the job of the Federal Theatre to employ them. It was our job to employ men and women of the theatre profession and that is what we did. Mr. Frank Gillmore, president of the Associated Actors and Artistes of America, testifying before the Senate Subcommittee on Appropriations, said: "I can speak for all of the actors and artistes of America, as I happen to be the accredited head of their organization . . . . The Federal Theatre has been a godsend to my people."

These are the people.

James Brennan, international vice-president of the International Alliance of Theatrical and Stage Employees, testifying before the same committee, said, "I want to talk for the 2,000 stagehands on the Federal Theatre lists . . . ."

These are the people.

The Circus Fans of America, writing to the Senate Committee, said: "The Federal Theatre circus performers are 100 percent tried-and-true circus performers from the big top."

These are the people.

So impressive was the array of vaudeville talent on the Federal Theatre that in "Two-a-Day," the revue giving the history of vaudeville, written and produced and running for seven months in Los Angeles, many famous headliners were played by themselves.

These are the people.

About 50 percent of the men and women thrown out of work by the ending of the project were performers—actors, singers, pit musicians, dancers. The rest were technicians, stage hands, stage carpenters and electricians, ushers, box-office men, maintenance workers, accountants and all the staff necessary to run a theatre under government auspices.

Not all of our artists were to be found on the stage. Every day for four years people entering the New York project offices signed in at the desk of a woman who had once been a famous star. She gradually built up the morale of theatrical people who in the early days used to come to collect their pay checks with veils over their faces, so ashamed were they of being connected with a relief enterprise. I have seen her during the difficult days when at recurrent intervals our office was besieged by desperate men and women who, because of cuts in appropriation, were being thrown off the project. No role she ever acted on Broadway—and she acted many—required more versatility and power. Certainly none was more humanly useful.

These are examples out of hundreds illustrating the professionalism of Federal Theatre workers. It is true that an organization set up necessarily almost overnight to take care of acute human distress also contained some people of inferior talent, some who were lazy, some who were stupid and some who seemed bent, with apparently suicidal intent, upon fomenting trouble. However, any person who made an unbiased study of our project throughout the country would testify to the fact that people in the above categories were the exception rather than the rule, and also to the fact that every effort was being made to retain only such people as were entitled and able to work on a theatre project.

It is true also, that because of the destination from which many of our people came, some of them were ill, discouraged and in need of special direction. In Los Angeles I listened to a rehearsal of one of our orchestras in an original score being composed on the project for Shaw's "Caesar and Cleopatra." "I'm interested in the flute motif," I said to the conductor. "It is so fleeting that one always wants more." The conductor-composer smiled. "My flutist has a tremor of the lips and can only sustain for a bar at a time. I had to compose with that in mind." It was the job of those of us directing the project so to compose our plans and our plays that they would make assets and not liabilities out of the tremors developed through years of unemployment and despair.

Probably the best evidence of the caliber of Federal Theatre employees and their tremendous gain in health, stamina and talent under government sponsorship, lies in a record of what they actually accomplished. In four years they produced over twelve hundred plays, including an extensive classical cycle, an extensive religious cycle, Americana, modern plays, "Living Newspapers" and dance drama, vaudeville, musical comedy, marionette plays, pageants and circuses. They gave an opportunity to a hundred hitherto-unknown young dramatists, and the list of dramatists whose plays they performed includes almost every American playwright of note from Bronson Howard and Clyde Fitch to Sidney Howard, Thornton Wilder, Clifford Odets and Eugene O'Neill. They built, equipped and manned stages in tents, on trucks, on showboats, on platforms in parks, schools, and playgrounds, on overturned tables in remote CCC camps and in the wake of flood and disaster; they reclaimed, literally through their own labor, working long hours without watching the time clock, magnificent old theatres, which, before the government entered the picture, had fallen into disuse and often into decay: the Walnut Street in Philadelphia, the Baker in Denver, the Blackstone and Great Northern in Chicago, the Rialto in Tampa, the Alcazar in San Francisco.

They traveled by truck through the rural areas, in Illinois, Michigan, Maine, New York, Oklahoma. In Florida they covered the turpentine circuit and people came in by ox cart, carrying lanterns, came in barefoot to see Shakespeare.

These people turned out designs, working drawings and blueprints for every conceivable type of play, from marionette shows with scenery which could be carried in a suitcase to a children's hospital, to vast constructions such as the one on which practically the entire state of Arkansas took part in the Federal Theatre production, "Arkansas Sings." They designed, built and painted scenery of every type, from flats and wood wings for plays of an earlier period to the newest type of impressionistic and surrealistic objects. Out of inexpensive material, which their skill made look expensive, they designed and built every type of costume demanded by our extensive repertory, including tailored suits, boots and shoes. They ran electrical shops, turning out and assembling a great deal of our equipment. They ran property shops, making period furniture, drapes and every type of object, from the witch masks for "Macbeth" to the whale in "Pinocchio." They ran print shops for turning out programs, posters and throw-aways. They ran dry-cleaning establishments and laundries for taking care of the thousands of costumes. I shall not soon forget the absorption of a group of older actresses on our Los Angeles project who, no longer able because of physical infirmity to appear on the stage, had developed a jewelry project on which they made out of wax, beads, paste and paint jewelry for all of our projects west of the Mississippi. The crown was for the Red Queen—"Alice in Wonderland" in Seattle; the jeweled robes were for our big Los Angeles production of "Volpone"; San Francisco got the barbaric witch jewels for the forest scene in "Run, Little Children"; and the sparklers were for a Christmas pantomine in Denver.

These Federal Theatre workers set up, developed and ran a service bureau in New York City which read and recommended scripts, typed them and sent them to the field, negotiated with authors and agents, handled royalties. They engaged in extensive theatre research on the origin, history and development of American folk lore, folk music and drama in the various regions of our country, research so important that it was sponsored by various state universities and requested for Congressional Library. This bureau received and answered about five thousand inquiries a week. It compiled records, written and photographic, of all FTP activity, running into thousands of volumes.

What is to become of these people? Can they be absorbed by private industry? Before the project closed, 2,660 had been so absorbed. This was because they had, through the Federal Theatre, an opportunity to show commercial managers what they could do. With the closing of the project there is little likelihood of such return to private industry. Over half the plays on Broadway last year employed people from the Federal Theatre. Many others went to jobs in cinema, radio and kindred fields. Some received scholarships for distinguished work in the theatre. Private enterprise bought up "The Swing Mikado," but that is the only instance where a whole company was taken over, because no matter how interested commercial producers are in our shows, such shows are usually too large as to cast (due to our necessity to employ many people) to make our plays practicable commercial ventures.

Can our people be employed in the many fields in which the Federal Theatre has been trying to discover new uses for dramatic talent? That is, can schools, hospitals, social settlements, reform schools, prisons, police departments pay for the theatre services which they have been receiving for several years from Federal Theatre companies? The answer is that they were gradually beginning to do so, but that the experiment was cut short midway.

For example, Federal Theatre marionette companies in Buffalo were so valuable in teaching health to children that the Board of Health paid all their other than labor costs and gave them a place to work. However, it is doubtful whether, much as they wish to do so, they can pay the labor expense involved. In the same way hospitals, prisons and reform schools which at first received our companies very dubiously, have in the past two years come to regard this work as such a therapeutic and morale-building agency, that they pay other than labor costs. However, they cannot as yet pay wages to the people involved. In the same way Boards of Education in Florida, Michigan, Ohio, New York and elsewhere have for several years paid transportation and other costs for our companies touring the schools with classics which they themselves chose. But obviously they cannot, at least as yet, pay wages.

All of these services are valuable and are surely part of the work any government-sponsored theatre should do. It is not, however, a form of work that can become immediately self-supporting.

Can Federal Theatre workers be employed on other government agencies? I had hoped so, but I now know better. During the month of July, in the thirty days in which our small staff in Washington was ordered to liquidate a project involving 7,900 people operating in twenty states, a plant worth, roughly speaking, a million dollars, and some ten thousand volumes of records of the first government-

166

sponsored theatre in the United States, this problem of the reemployment of the people was the paramount issue. I quote from my final report to Colonel Harrington on this point:

> Plans are under way for transfer of an as yet undetermined number of Federal Theatre personnel to the Historical Record project. The plan includes the immediate setting up of one project to handle the material in Washington; one small project in each state where we have operated; with possible further projects, after the records are set in order, to carry on historical theatre research started by the Federal Theatre.
>
> The Recreation Project intends to absorb, eventually, as high as 25 percent of our personnel, not, of course, in theatre work, but in visual education, recreation and leisure-time activity.
>
> Other personnel we hope will be employed by the National Youth Administration.

It would be pleasant to record that at least part of this plan has been carried out. It has not been carried out. Instead, our Federal Theatre workers are being informed by the Youth Administration, the Recreation Administration and other branches of the FWA that "orders from Washington do not encourage the employment of former Federal Theatre employees and soft-pedal any work in drama whatsoever."

To the question often asked, "why cannot the workers in the art fields turn to jobs on heavy construction," the answer is that they can and do—when they get the chance. However, they are not trained for these jobs, and furthermore the heavy-construction projects have been so seriously cut that they neither need nor want to fill their vacancies with white-collar workers.

No, as citizens we cannot comfort ourselves by the idea that the professional men and women thrown out of their own kind of work by the discriminatory action of Congress can get any kind of work, manual or otherwise, elsewhere. They need work as much as they needed it when the project started. They did their work and, in the opinion of critics in their own field, they did it well. Suddenly, through no fault of their own, because of political maneuvering in which they had no part, they were thrown out of work under circumstances which make it almost impossible for them to be re-employed.

Let us hope that not only people who care about the theatre in America, but people who care about justice in America, will see to it that when Congress reconvenes, the wrong done to 7,900 American citizens is righted.

167

MERCURY THEATRE, THEATRE ARTS
COMMITTEE, JOHN LENTHIER TROUPE

No event forshadowed the government's changing attitude toward Federal Theatre more clearly than the censorship, in 1937, of Marc Blitzstein's labor opera, *The Cradle Will Rock*.

A whore (Moll) and a union organizer (Larry Foreman) end up in jail along with members of the town's Liberty Committee. Mr. Mister, the businessman, arrives to bail out his flunkies on the committee. As they appear before the judge, scenes materialize illustrating Larry's explanation to Moll about how the anti-labor Liberty Committee members—a college president, the editor of the paper, the doctor, an artist, a druggist—have sold themselves to Mr. Mister. Outside the jail house a strike continues, until, after mock justice frees the terrorist committee's members, the stage is liberated by a band of strikers singing of a new day. *Cradle*'s broad characterizations, multiple scenes and integration of music and theatre recall the early aims of New Playwrights. But the opera would not have existed without the strike play, whose familiar content it abstracted into musical form, or without knowledge of Brecht's *Threepenny Opera* and that author's suggestion that Blitzstein write about prostitution in each of its forms.

Rumors circulating Washington said that the opera was dangerous, but an official sent up to a preview told Flanagan it was "magnificent." Several days before the first night, Washington issued a directive "mysteriously" forbidding any new Federal Theatre production to open before July 1. Orson Welles, director of *Cradle*, flew to Washington to try and get a reversal of the decision. He and John Houseman, producer, had been with Federal Theatre since its start and had created two of the project's most significant productions—a black *Macbeth* and a mad-cap Amerikan version of a Labiche farce: *Horse Eats Hat*.

Welles and Houseman determined to produce the opera privately despite the fact that the government had confiscated all their scenery, costumes, lights and every musical score but the single one they managed to smuggle out. The audience was already gathered outside the darkened theatre when Houseman announced the show would open without government auspices at the newly hired Venice Theatre twenty blocks away. Archibald MacLeish describes the performance in his foreward to the script:

> In an unaired theatre, on a stage illuminated by a couple of dusty spots, with a cast scattered through the audience (where a ruling of Equity kept it), and to the music of an upright piano manipulated by the composer in his shirt sleeves, there occurred a miracle. From the first voice of the first singer the thing was evident: There was no audience. There was instead a room full of men and women as eagerly in the play as any actor . . . that evening made it very evident that the monstrous beast which devours plays and playwrights is a creature of the theatrical illusion which can be killed if the illusion can be killed . . . . To destroy this exceptionally shopworn illusion and set up a play for what it is—a play—means self respect and association with life.

For a moment *Cradle Will Rock* indicated the rebirth of the independent people's theatre movement. To the *Daily Worker* the production signified that "the day for sloganizing was over." It's success, along with the end of their association with Federal Theatre and the cancellation of other plans, led Welles and Houseman to form their own repertory theatre the following fall. The Mercury Theatre, Houseman announced in the September 18, 1937, *Worker*, was "another step towards a real People's Theatre in America." The Mercury produced a modern dress *Julius Caesar* to parallel the rise of fascism, *Shoemakers Holiday*, and *Danton's Death*. But despite the talent of its individual members and its interest in low-priced repertory, it cannot be remembered as a people's

169

theatre. Houseman explains why in his memoir *Run-through* (New York, 1972):

> In the grandiose and reckless scheme of our lives, the Mercury had fulfilled its purpose. It had brought us success and fame; it had put Welles on the cover of *Time* and our radio show [Mercury Theatre of the Air] on the front page of every newspaper in the country. Inevitably, any day now, the offers from Hollywood would start arriving. It was too late to turn back and we did not really want to.

Theatre Workshop, a quarterly similar in concept to *The Drama Review* in the sixties, was begun by the New Theatre League in 1937. The April 1938 issue contained a debate, "Scenery or No Scenery," motivated by a memo Flanagan had sent to Federal Theatre producers urging the artistic and budgetary advantages of minimal scenery. The editors commented:

> The best application of the scenery-less technique serves to implement the flight from a stereotyped and shop worn naturalism . . . . In America, the New Playwrights Theatre and, later, the new theatre movement, abandoned the boxed-in proscenium and sought to embody the new social drama in a framework which was more or less scenery-less. From *Scottsboro, Scottsboro*, through *Newsboy* and on to *Waiting for Lefty* the trend can be clearly traced.

Of the participants (Flanagan, Blitzstein, Howard Bay, Mordecai Gorelik, Norris Houghton, Lee Strasberg, Charles Asheim) John Gassner was in most complete disagreement:

> As a matter of fact, labor audiences identified themselves more completely with such realistic plays as *Stevedore* and *Let Freedom Ring* than with such nonrealistic dramas as the Theatre Union's *Mother* and the Group Theatre's *The Case of Clyde Griffiths*, which found their greatest response among the intellectuals.

In the same issue of *Theatre Workshop* appeared an article

170

by Ben Irwin, national secretary of the New Theatre League, called "Resurgence of the New Theatre." Irwin argued that censorship of *The Cradle Will Rock* caused many left-wing "turn to work with the new theatres again. Enriched artistically by their project experience Lem Ward, Brett Warren, Maurice Clark, Al Saxe, are all actively engaged in production work in new theatres in New York and Philadelphia."

The Spanish Civil War was taking its toll of the new theatre movement in two ways. Theatre people were being lost to battle: John Lenthier, of the Boston New Theatre and an actor in *Newsboy* and many other agitprops, was killed in Spain at the age of twenty-two. William Titus, author of *Tilly the Toiler, or Virtue Rewarded*, which was toured by the Brookwood Labor Players from A. J. Muste's labor college, was also killed. Bob Stech, *New Theatre*; Mike Webb, Nat Weisberg, Mario Noble, Detroit Contemporary Theatre; Jack Jordan, Joe Hamberger, Chicago Repertory Group; Peter Frye, New York Theatre of Action were among the theatre workers who fought with the Abraham Lincoln Brigade for the defeat of fascism in Spain. (The CIA did not remove the brigade name from its subversive organizations list until December 1971, the first time they up-dated that social register in fifteen years.)

In New York, Theatre Arts Committee for Democracy was producing Cabaret TAC to raise money for the Spanish Republican Army, and as Harold Clurman put it in *Fervent Years*, "lending the New York night scene a fillip of fresh zest." The skits done there were lively and confident, but they had the political vagueness characteristic of a united front organization (the fight in Spain was so clear-cut that Republican forces seemed just to everyone whose politics were only slightly Left of the US government's foreign policy) and the theatrical shallowness of nightclub reviews, with titles like "One Third of a Mitten" and "The Chamberlain Crawl." These TAC sketches meant to move left-wing theatre toward a less illusionistic style but they never did more than substitute revue satire for Broadway realism. TAC also published a magazine carrying news of theatre people's work for Spain.

New Theater magazine ceased publication in 1937. Its final issue, April 1937, was titled *New Theatre and Film*. Increasing numbers of playwrights and actors were going to Hollywood, not always because they could make more money there than they had ever made (though that was often true) but because they no longer could earn even subsistence wages in the (by now mostly disbanded) people's theatres. So they tried to convince themselves that they could have the same "progressive" influence on Hollywood films that they had had on the theatre.*

News of the approximately 25 workers' theatres still affiliated with the League was carried in the mimeographed *New Theatre News*, which published bi-monthly into 1940; significant work on a small scale continued until then. In Oklahoma City the Red Dust Players presented *Bury the Dead*, Irwin Shaw's anti-war play about six corpses who stand up in their graves refusing to be buried, are wept over, then forgotten:

> We had a packed house . . . about 300. Several car loads of faculty members drove in from Normal and the Worker's Alliance, which was supposed to meet that night, adjourned its meeting and marched over to the play . . . . There were two criticisms which I prize above all others; one woman from the silk stocking district said the play made her sick at her stomack; another woman, who is supporting herself and three kids on $1.66 (a month) this state allows for relief, said she would have given $1.50 to see that show.

The Actors Repertory Theatre, composed of people who had played in Albert Bein's *Let Freedom Ring* on Broadway, where it was financed by labor unions, and at the Theatre Union, formed a mobile company, The John Lenthier Troupe, that continued to tour after productions of *Bury the Dead, 200 Were Chosen* and *Washington Jitters* failed to sustain them in New York. They presented *Middleman* in the summer of 1939. Unlike the TAC skits, *Middleman* is a direct descendent of early agitprop; it means to radicalize the

---

*The story of people's theatre workers in Hollywood, which culminates with the blacklisting of most of them is not a happy one. Their work in movies is nowhere as impressive as the work they did in the theatre. Aside from some union organizing, the radicals' ability to transform Hollywood's exploitive structure was miniscule; finally they were the victims of the industry's reactionary nature.

farmers instead of satirize current events, and it takes its nonillusionistic form from that goal.

THE JOHN LENTHIER TROUPE ON TOUR*

Playing for the assembled farmers and miners of Bucks County, Pa. in an apple-booking shed, the John Lenthier Troupe, which is the mobile unit of the *Let Freedom Ring Company*, opened its fifth summer tour on April 25, 1939. Our members, Janet Burns, Charles Gordon, Horta Ware, Will Geer and Burl Ives planned to tour the country with a program of ballads, skits and short plays especially suited to farmers' audiences. Before beginning our penetration of the rural areas, which have been neglected as much by our new theatres as by other cultural agencies, we repeated this program in Philadelphia on May Day, and in Chicago at the Chicago Repertory Theatre, where other actors from the Pare Lorontz picture being filmed were drawn in.

The troupe's real work began when we reunited in California in July, and made our first West Coast appearance on Olive Hill in Hollywood. Here we were joined by Woody [Guthrie] the famous California Ballador, who is carrying on the Joe Hill tradition in terms of today. During the summer months, we played week-ends in the Imperial Valley in San Francisco, San Joaquin Valley and Kern County. During October we set out to play the government migratory workers' camps throughout California.

Like most new theatres, the troupe needed material, particularly suitable for the agricultural groups we were reaching. So we ran our own play contest, with Albert Bein, Bill Robson and Will Geer as judges. The prize play, *Middleman*, was selected by actual performance rather than by a judgement on reading it; it was played at a *Grapes of Wrath* party in Bekersfield, Cal.

The troupe's first regular performance of our prize play *Middleman* and a new group of ballads, together with a ballad contest was given in Indio, Cal., in the heart of the date country. Brawley and Callopatua were also towns played in Imperial County—center of reaction, below the Salton Sea, which Mr. Dies has called "the most patriotic valley in America". In Kern County, during October (famous for its banning of Steinbeck's *Grapes of Wrath*, for it is the novel's main locale) we found ourselves in the midst of a cotton strike. New ballads came into being: Forty cent cotton, eighty cent wheat, How in hell can a poor man eat?

The troupe would like to call attention to the fact that there was little interest in the Cabaret TAC material. However excellent its skits and songs may be for New York and other metropolitan centers, its satire was too sophisticated and out of the experience of the agricultural workers and farmers. Songs and ballads and parodies of popular

New Theatre, December 1939.

173

airs written with great simplicity and directness were the favorites everywhere.

With the need for this kind of material in mind, we are presenting the script *Middleman*, our prize play. At first reading it may seem impossibly naive to groups conditioned to "Broadway sophistications with social significance", which is unfortunately too often the fare they offer trade unionists and other working class audiences in their towns. But with sufficient precision and deftness in performance, this slight sketch can be tremendously effective, even for more experienced audiences. But for a vast number of farmers and workers, most of whom have never seen a play before, and some of whom have not even seen a movie, this is what we need. The John Lenthier Troupe hopes that one result of its touring work, which it intends to continue every summer, will be to bring this realization of audience needs to New Theatre League groups throughout the country.

MIDDLEMAN

A million years ago, long before there were any books about anything, our kinfolks were trying to get enough to eat and to wear and a place to live, just the way we are today.

They had to kill wild animals in the struggle, and many times the animals killed them. Then somebody invented a bow and arrow, and the fight became a little easier. Somebody learned to move heavier weights than before by using a stick as a lever. They found out by cutting slices from logs for wheels they could make carts to carry heavy loads and make the work easier.

Thousands of years went by and always our kinfolks kept inventing things to make the work less hard. Finally, a few hundred years ago, labor saving machinery began to develop, with one man turning out enormous amounts of things, much more than he could possibly use.

In the whole history of the world there never was a time when there was enough food to go around. Someone had to be poor. Now—for the first time in history—we can produce much more than we need. No one has to be poor any longer. All of these tractors, reapers, shoe machines—food canning machines—weaving machines—all of them, had to borrow the ideas of our ancestors to be built. The most important parts of every machine today are the wheels and the levers.

What is it? Who is it, that keeps all of us from enjoying the good things that these millions of years planning and work could give us? What happens to the surplus we produce, but don't get? Think it over, it doesn't seem fair to me. Here's a little song we made up that sort of fits the idea. We'll try to act it out for you, too.

Well .... Here's a tailor sewing one pair of pants. He can't afford a machine, he's too poor, but even by doing the work by hand, we can make a lot of pants. He's very skillful with his needle, isn't he? Yes, and

174

he's very proud of his work. He looks a little thin to me. He should eat a little more, don't you think?

FARMER ON HANDS AND KNEES

What's this over here? Why it's a farmer, isn't it? Yes, he must be a farmer . . . look at the potatoes. He's raised a good crop. What's he going to do with them? There's twice as many as he needs himself. *Two sacks. FARMER PUTS SPUDS IN BASKET AND RISES. HE HAS NO PANTS.*

Oh, heavens. The farmer hasn't any pants. The poor fellow! He must feel terrible. How would you like to go around without any pants? It isn't funny to him. Why, I believe he's cold! Just look at the poor farmer shivering, and hear the wind howl between his knees. But don't laugh now! You'll embarrass the poor farmer, and it's bad enough to have no pants and to freeze without being made to blush with shame also. At that . . . I'll bet some of you fellows out there don't have such very good pants yourself.

But say! Wait a minute . . . . Pants! Why, yes. Remember the poor thin tailor. He's making a pair of pants. There he is just finishing them. They're dandies, too! And he already has one pair on so he doesn't need them. Isn't he thin, though. Why he's hungry, too. Look at him hunting for food. (repeat) Nothing there, empty. Say, I'll bet he'd like those extra potatoes that the farmer can't use. And . . . why of course! The farmer needs a pair of pants. Perfect! See they've noticed each other. It won't be long now till all their troubles are over!

THEY FACE EACH OTHER ON OPPOSITE SIDES OF A RIVER

But wait a minute! There's a river between them. They can't get across! Oh, yes, they can too, for wherever there's a river there must be a bridge, thanks to the W.P.A. They're going to cross the bridge.

MIDDLEMAN STOPS THEM

Hold on! They've been stopped! Whose this? Why, I'll be doggoned! It's the middleman. That's a nice name for him. There's other things you men call him, but I'm a lady. I'll have to call him middleman. He won't let them across the bridge. The tailor has more pants than he needs and he's hungry and the farmer has more food than he needs and he's cold. The sensible thing to do is for the two to get together. What do you think, isn't that right? Is there anything Un-American about that? Is there anything Thomas Jefferson, or George Washington, or Abraham Lincoln wouldn't like about that? Look what's happening now! The middleman tells the farmer that he'll have to have all of his potatoes—both sacks—in exchange for a pair of pants. Middleman says pants are high now! Potatoes are cheap, there's lots of potatoes. They're a drug on the market! Farmer doesn't like that.

Will he give in? He's so cold though. Ah, he's decided he'll just have to wear pants. He's going to have to give all his potatoes for the pants. The middleman tells the poor farmer man he'll have to wait. Now the

175

tailor gets his turn. Tailor is proud of those pants. Just look how beautiful they are.

Middleman thinks they're ugly! He thinks they're made of poor material! He tells the tailor . . . Pants are cheap, now. A drug on the market! I can't give you any potatoes. Potatoes are big, now. They're hard to get. Go away! I don't want your pants. Tailor is hungry, though. He pleads with middleman. Middleman finally gives in a little. Well . . . give me the pants, he says. But wait! Lord Bless you he wants the pants the tailor is wearing, too. Will the tailor give up his own personal pants! Gracious, he can't do that, he'll freeze. And anyhow, who ever heard of a tailor without pants! But tailor is hungry. He just can't resist those potatoes. He's going to do it. Is his face red?
WHISTLE

Six o'clock . . . dinner time. What's the matter with the farmer? He's hungry He's looking for his potatoes, but he's given them all to the middleman. And look at the tailor. He's shivering and shaking in the wintry blast. He looks angry. No! He is angry. Farmer's angry, too! Why, they're motioning to each other across the river. Now, they're starting for the bridge. What are they going to do? What would you do! I thought so. They're going to do it too.
BUSINESS

They did it.

Concluding Chorus

1. Uncle Sam started him a union,
   Uncle Sam started him a union,
   Uncle Sam started him a union,
   Most of the 48 states joined up.

2. They all made on big union,
   They all made on big union,
   They all made on big union,
   Called it the U.S.A.

3. The bankers they started them a union,
   The bankers they started them a union,
   The bankers they started them a union,
   Most of the robbers joined up.

4. The oil men started them a union,
   The oil men started them a union,
   The oil men started them a union,
   John D. Rockefeller joined em.

5. The merchants they started them a union,
   The merchants they started them a union,

176

The merchants they started them a union,
Made a hell of a prof-fit.

6. The Assoc. Farmers started them a union,
The Assoc. Farmers started them a union,
The Assoc. Farmers started them a union,
Most of the farmers joined up.

7. The cottonpickers started them a union,
The cottonpickers started them a union,
The cottonpickers started them a union,
Asked for decent pay ($1.25).

8. You'd better go down and join the union
You'd better go down and join the union
You'd better go down and join the union,
Everybody else is joinin!

You'd better go down and join a cooperative,
You'd better go down and join a cooperative,
You'd better go down and join a cooperative,
Get rid of the middleman.

177

ENDING ILLUSION

In a decaying society, art, if it is truthful must also reflect decay. And unless it wants to break faith with its social function, art must show the world as changeable. And help change it.

Ernst Fischer

After all, it wasn't realism *per se* that people's theatre workers admired so much as the various insights and allusions realism allowed. Their own theatre was much more literal than they desired. Yet this literalness—which was such a source of exasperation to them, especially when critics tried to justify it by rejoicing in how politically accurate it allowed the plays' messages to be*—does contain a positive advance over bourgeois realism.

---

*They did themselves in here by attracting historians to their movement who were more dogmatic in their liberalism than the most near-sighted thirties critics had been in their Communism. Michael Gold always managed to be forceful and humorous, especially when writing about capitalist art. For contrast, check out Morgan Himelstein's *Drama Was a Weapon*. His thesis: the radical plays of the thirties failed to create the revolution the Communists desired; therefore they failed as theatre; therefore theatre is useless as a political weapon. Or check Harvey Swados' hysterical introduction to *The American Writer and the Great Depression*. For a second generation view, milder, but still without sympathy for radical theatre, see Gerald Rabkin's *Drama and Commitment*. All these books reveal more about the rigidity of virulent anti-radicalism than they do about the tumultuous theatre of the thirties.

The mass chants, agitprops, living newspapers have this in common: in each of them the actor is supposed to focus on an external, objective goal; i.e., speaking in unison or completing necessary transitions from segment to segment in the chants and agitprops, presenting relationships which visualize the economics of land speculation (the Grass Mat scene in *One Third of a Nation*) or holding companies (a scene in *Power* where the actor playing a utilities magnate jumps back and forth from a seat behind a big desk to the chair at its side while he makes a contract with himself). How much these examples are like Viola Spolin's techniques—even not quite understandable without knowledge of them! In each case the participant must follow the "rules of the game" until an objectively verifiable task has been accomplished. At no time is the actor supposed to reveal his subjective life, which is simply not relevant to the task at hand.

Two situations necessary to people's theatre result: 1. Participation in the event is open to anyone, whether a child (Spolin's exercises), a worker (the agitprops) or an actor (living newspapers). And because everyone is welcome and able to play, this theatre is noncompetitive (as Spolin stresses again and again). 2. There is no separation between what the will desires and what the body is able to accomplish. This is so because the participants' desires have been limited—by an already agreed upon theatrical frame—to only those which can be satisfactorily realized through externally motivated physical activity.

This union of will with action forcibly negates the very idea most essential to the bourgeoisie, because it is the idea that justifies their spiritual isolation from the natural world and from its citizens, both of which they must exploit—the idea that a fixed and unsurpassable gap exists between instinctive desires and objective reality. (The bourgeoisie also insists upon a social version of this disparity, existing between an individual's needs, and the needs of the masses, which are supposed to be more coarse and less exultant. Thus they "prove" the ultimate absurdity of united action for a common good—even the words "common" and "good" are contradictory—without ever explaining why the need of a military contractor to get rich is higher than that of the peasants to live.) So the bourgeoisie creates and supports a theatre which for it *is* realistic and in which activity exists as suffering.

179

But their assumptions and the dramatic structures that maintain them are not adequate for a people's theatre. For us activity must exist as choice. We must learn how to close the bourgeois gap. And our theatre must focus on the multiple possibilities that only become apparent at the moment of its closing.

Just how the bourgeois gap can be closed is obscured somewhat in the strike plays because performers have to play roles in them and playwrights did not know exactly how to alter inherited realistic structures in order to support radical content. Yet some sort of objectification of desire was necessary to the playwright's Marxist world view. He must have it. And finally he does have it by reworking the standard upbeat ending to show how an alteration in the economic order results in an end to alienated labor. During these activists endings (the storming of the barricades in *Stevedore*, the demonstrations in *1931-, Marching Song, The Belt,* for examples) the physical activities of the characters exactly match their desires for freedom, dignity and wholeness.

These endings are crucial to the strike plays because they circumvent the debilitating assumption of bourgeois realism. An activist ending closes the gap; it unifies the will with the objective reality and therefore it begins to change the world. In a realistic context this union between desire and activity often occurs as a moment of violence. The violence of the characters and the violence with which the scene strains at the realistic mode are recognitions that the objectification of desire can only take place with utmost disruption amid the unceasing cruelty of capitalism.

Activist endings are among the most exciting, most fulfilling moments in the plays. But they are difficult to sustain and, even more important, difficult to prepare for in a convincing manner. Their occurrence is at odds with the sensible progression of a realistic play, and to get at them at all, that progression must be disrupted.

Scenes of persuasion occupy a large portion of realistic drama, and persuasion seems like a logical structure for a writer who is trying to turn characters and audience into radicals. Yet persuasion is just a polite form of domination; it is trying to get another person to do your will. To employ the structure of a persuasion scene is to diminish the reality of characters' subsequent transformations because such scenes progress according to a series of minor and casually connected alterations in understanding. It is, precisely, the moments of rhetorical persuasion that work least well in these plays, and these are naturally the moments non-radical critics have memorialized as "evidence" that theatre and visionary politics don't mix.

Before a radical transformation can occur a situation must be created which cannot be dealt with by recourse to the established structures of capitalist society and/or realistic drama, a sitaution which allows its participants to act in newly evolved organic ways. Spolin did this with the game schema of her exercises. Emjo Basshe approached it in *The Centuries*, when, instead of past-present-future, a structuring device that creates boundaries, he suggested theme-and-variations, a device that explores the ways in which boundaries break down. Lawson began to do it in *Marching Song* by arranging his characters in dialectical relationships. Irwin Shaw began it, too, in *Bury the Dead*, when he opposed the force of his six corpses' unlimited and non-coercive sense of time to the need of the war machine to get them to lie down in a hurry.

Shaw gets distracted from his initial insight when he writes six persuasion scenes. In each of them a woman related to one corpse tries to get him buried, and therefore puts the corpse in the position of convincing her of the rightness of his actions. To do this, each corpse and each woman has to invoke either the past or the future, or introduce a new piece of information—for these are the elements of persuasion. Yet none of these elements can cause transformation. One cannot invoke, explain, or introduce the revolution. The revolution is powerless unless its insights are lived.

Shaw knows this in the overall design of his play. Having dead men stand up creates a situation for which there are no precedents, one for which a proper response must be sought instinctually. And he begins to let this knowledge affect the structure of his play, too. The force of the revolution is not revealed in individual persuasion scenes, but it does exist in certain stage directions which show what it is like to live liberated:

As the Corpses reach the edge of the grave and take their first step out [the Third General] starts firing,

181

laughing wildly, the gun shaking on his shoulders violently . . . . The Corpses pass on, going off stage, *like men who have leisurely business* that must be attended to in the not-too-distant future . . . . Then, slowly, the Four Soldiers of the burial detail break ranks. Slowly they walk, *exactly as the Corpses have walked* . . . . The last Soldier, as he passes the Third General, deliberately, but without malice, flicks a cigarette butt at him, then follows the other soldiers off the stage.

[ital. added]

The ability to be transformed—which is the ability to take control of your life—has to do with the audacity of your choices. The playwright's task is to seize situations in which audacious choices are not only possible, but *are the most reasonable response*. The economic realities of the thirties created such situations, which playwrights then explored in their strike dramas, arriving at the activist ending and other beginning denials of the bourgeois gap.

COLLAPSE

It was a nonaggression pact. I stress here that it was not a union, bloc, or pact of mutual assistance but a non-aggression pact of the type the USSR had with many other states.

Ivan Maisky

This is the chronology of collapse: In March 1939, Madrid fell to the fascists; in June, Federal Theatre was abolished by the US Congress; in August, after the hostility of Britain and France toward the Soviet Union ended the tripartite negotiations, Stalin signed a non-aggression pact with Hitler. The two happy possibilities that would have come like the harvest at the end of the thirties—a defeat for fascism in Spain and the creation of a people's theatre in the US—were undone by the forces of reaction. In their place was growing repression at home and an international agreement between the great fascist and Communist states. Though Stalin was trying to buy time before the inevitable war, nothing since reports of the Moscow Trials and Trotsky's exile had so shaken the faith of fellow travellers, who viewed it as incontrovertible proof of the Soviet Union's duplicity.

Lem Ward's letter to *New Theatre News* reflects the dilemma of theatre workers in 1939, and one that is still pertinent for us. How should we react when governments' policies change enough so that the repertory of people's theatres can be profitably co-opted to serve them?

A LETTER TO THE EDITOR*

(Editor's Note: We publish this letter from a member of our National Executive Board, Lem Ward, director of "... one third of a nation", and other Living Newspaper shows, because it raises an important problem for all of our theatres to consider and discuss. We would appreciate hearing from our theatres as to their reaction to this letter.

Dear Editor:

I had an experience last night which caused me to think seriously about our NTL repertory today. I went for the second time to see *Confessions of a Nazi Spy.* When I had seen this six months ago, I, along with the rest of the audience, was deeply moved and honestly enthusiastic about this fine anti-fascist movie. But you should have seen the audience last night!

Cheers and jeers, hissing and boos and an atmosphere of pure war hysteria. This was no simple, healthy anti-fascist sentiment clamoring for expression ... this was an audience aroused by the 1939 equivalent of World War propaganda.

And I realized with a start that today simple, honest anti-fascist sentiment could be used by those who seek to involve America in this war. Whatever one thinks of *this* war, (and I personally believe that under the direction of Messrs. Chamberlain, Churchill, Bonnet and Daladier this can be nothing else but a brutal repetition of the bloody tragedy of 1917 for the same profit-making imperialist motives) —whatever one thinks of this war, every intelligent progressive must agree that our chief job is to KEEP AMERICA OUT OF THIS WAR.

Then we must realize that our involvement, if any, will surely be on the side of Chamberlain, and that such involvement is already being prepared by the war profiteers. They will seek to send America's best youth to war again, this time using as a lever for their propaganda machine the *decent anti-Nazi sentiment* which our theatres along with other progressive forces in America have helped to build. And that is why I feel that TODAY, at this *moment*, we must seriously consider that anti-Nazi plays will only stimulate war sentiment. Don't get me wrong—I hate fascism as much as ever, and believe the NTL as a progressive theatre movement must fight it as hard as ever. But the way to fight it today is certainly not by giving any aid or comfort to either side in this bandit war. These plays are just as good artistically as they were six months ago. They haven't changed. But the world has.

Just as one year ago to produce BURY THE DEAD meant to hurt the cause of embattled democracy in Spain but today producing BURY THE DEAD contributes to keeping us out of war and thus helps the cause of democracy through the world, so the reverse holds true with

---

*New Theatre News, November 1939.

184

certain anti-Nazi plays. Any anti-Nazi or anti-fascist play that seeks to make a real contribution to the cause of progress today must attack and expose dramatically more than the mere outward manifestations of fascism, which is the characteristic and fault of most our existing anti-Nazi plays. Real anti-fascist theatre today will be an attack not only on Nazi-ism but on fascism wherever it appears, under Daladier, under Chamberlain or Hitler or here at home in Mr. Dies' chambers.

Let us guard against relinquishing our stages to the war purposes of Wall Street. Certainly no NTL group or any progressive theatre wants to do that.

Sincerely,
Lem Ward.

Once Hitler invaded Russia, US Communists no longer opposed this country's entry into the war because they no longer regarded it mainly as a contest between imperialist powers. Regardless of their Party affiliation, all people's theatre workers found themselves involved in a war they had spent a lot of creative energy trying to avert, working for a government they had hoped to change, writing training films for the armed forces, turning out pure entertainment to keep up morale. Convinced that fascism had to be defeated they were stranded without a radical plan for doing it. They had no choice but to lend their energy to government activities. (It is out of this impasse that the first tentative notions of revolutionary pacifism began to emerge.)

185

NEGRO PLAYWRIGHTS COMPANY

The maturing of our literature reflected the maturing of
the American people as a whole. The process was of
course, in some measure a reciprocal one. The writers
learned from the masses, but in giving artistic expression
to the ideas and moods they were learning, the writers
helped to organize consciousness.

Samuel Sillen

Is it peculiar to revolutionary faiths that in times of
greatest desperation they are reaffirmed with equal simplicity
and joy? In 1940, in the midst of war preparations which
probably doomed the venture from the start, Theodore Ward
founded the Negro Playwrights Company in Harlem. Powell
Lindsay was artistic director; Langston Hughes, Theodore
Brown, Owen Dodson, George Norford were other active
members.

Throughout the thirties the two themes of equal importance to the people's theatre were the rights of the white
working class and the rights of black people to control their
own lives. The two were really inseparable, because, as many
of the plays point out, the power of one group was directly
dependent upon the support of the other: both were victims
of capitalism's need to exploit labor.

The Harlem Suitcase Theatre, *Stevedore, Earth* by Basshe,
Hoboken Blues by Gold, *Mulato* by Hughes, the Scottsboro
plays, and especially the Negro Units of the Federal Theatre,
provided chances for black and white actors and writers to
work together to overcome the nigger stereotypes of the

186

commercial stage (*Porgy and Bess, The Green Pastures, Lula Belle, Mamba's Daughters*). In the four years of the Federal project's life, nine new plays were written for and produced by Negro Units in all major cities. One hundred productions of plays by writers like Geroge Bernard Shaw, Eugene O'Neill, Paul Green, many of them especially adapted by the black companies, were also produced in black neighborhoods, at prices that usually did not exceed 25 cents. New York's Negro Unit, under the administrative direction of John Houseman, followed Frank Wilson's *Walk Together Children* with a West Indian voodoo version of *Macbeth*, directed by Orson Welles and starring Jack Carter and Edna Thomas.

The First Federal Theatre hit in New Jersey was *The Trial of Dr. Beck* by a young black writer on the project, Hughes Allison. The play, about the murder trial of a black doctor, required an integrated cast and was produced despite protests from local WPA officials that New Jersey would never stand for it. Later it was moved into Manhattan for a four-week run.

The first living newspaper, *Ethiopia*, had been possible partly because a troupe of Nigerian performers was stranded in the US. Federal Theatre gave them jobs (they spoke little English) chanting support for Haile Selassie. Later they evolved a communal work under the direction of Momodu Johnson. *Bassa Moona* (The Land I Love) was, Flanagan wrote, "from their own homesick memories of Nigeria. The attack of color, sound, and movement was overpowering and often shocking."*

Theodore Ward's play, *Big White Fog*, about the effects of poverty and prejudice and the hope of Garveyism on a black family, was first produced by Federal Theatre in Chicago. It was restaged by the Negro Playwrights Company as their first production, October 22, 1940. "Although it lasted only sixty-four performances, *Big White Fog* dramatized a black man's frustrated and tragic existence more bitterly and more effectively than any play previously produced professionally in the United States," Darwin Turner writes.** NPC would not outlast this production, but Ward would continue his

---

Arena, p. 186.

**"The Black Playwright in the Professional Theatre," *Black American Writing*, Vol. II, ed. C. W. E. Bigsby, Baltimore, Md., 1969.

work throughout the forties. *Our Lan'*,* a revolutionary epic with music, would have a sensitive production off-Broadway at the Henry Street Playhouse in the spring of 1947, and a more lavish and less effective one on Broadway the following September. In 1950, People's Drama, directed by Al Saxe, produced Ward's *John Brown*.

At a benefit held in September, 1940, for NPC, Morris Carnovsky extended greetings from the New Theatre League, Paul Robeson sang, and Richard Wright read "How Bigger Was Born," a paper about his successful novel, *Native Son*. (Wright's story would be staged on Broadway in 1941, directed by Orson Welles and starring Canada Lee, in an adaptation by Wright and Green. The play did not do justice to the novel.). Then Ward delivered his manifesto for a black people's theatre, the last such document to be issued out of the turmoil and the promise of the thirties.

Theodore Ward

OUR CONCEPTION OF THE THEATRE AND ITS FUNCTION**

I once encountered a statement which had been written by one Julius Bob for one of the encyclopedias and which I believe is quite representative of the Negro Playwrights Company's ideas of the theatre it hopes to build here in Harlem. "Every theatre," he said, "in the true sense of the word is a unity at the core of which is the living community finding some vital part of itself reflected in the creations of dramatist and actor."

Certainly, a moment's reflection on the theatre in its beginnings confirms that idea. Historians tell us that in the early society the theatre was undifferentiated; that is, there was no boundary between the arts. The dance was a group festival to harness man's emotions and efforts in a socially progressive way. It may be that in his undeveloped state, early man felt that his dance and gestures possessed a magic power to control nature. But the dance was a collective ritual descriptive of the real process of securing a livelihood. Just as the work songs and songs of protest of our own people demonstrate the relation between man's ways-of-life, his work and art, so did these early dances; for in them, it is said, the dancers strove to persuade others, with

*For script and an appreciative analysis see Kenneth Thorpe Rowe's *Theatre in Your Head*, New York, 1960.
**Edited version KMT.

rhythmic movements to do, to plant, to hunt—their art thus arising out of the economic needs of the tribe. As a spiritual and cultural award, participation in the dance brought an emotional compensation and inspired and motivated conduct on the part of the individual . . . .

But with the passage of time and the universal emergence of the class order in society, a disparity came to exist between the theatre and the life of the ordinary man. Instead of remaining and developing as an institution for the participation of all the people and the reflection of their ideals, their aspirations, their ways of life; the theatre was transformed and sequestered into the exclusive property of the few. Today, the problem is to restore it to its legitimate heirs, for there can be no doubt but that it is the heritage of many.

This is the core of the meaning of the term people's theatre. It is the crux of the idea of the Negro Playwrights Company, and it is the fundamental, guiding principle in their approach to the task of contributing their share in the magnificent movement which is today seeking throughout the land to make the play the thing for the people . . . .

Perhaps, as among all oppressed peoples, large sections of our group *are* given to looking upon the theatre primarily as a means of escape. But the theatre was not a means of escape in its inception, and it has never been such, so far as we are aware, at any high point in its history. The idea that it was designed to give light amusement is but one of the current falsehoods which have been concocted by those who are contemptuous of the intelligence of the common man, and who would have others believe that he lacks the wit to understand what is serious, or the vision to determine for himself what is entertaining and good. It is the product of those who wish to keep the people in ignorance, so that they may be more easily exploited. It is the lie of those who label everything as propaganda that does not conform to their own interests and opinion. It is but a subtle part of the technique which has culminated in the current attacks upon civil liberties here, and the burnings abroad, of books; the houndings of the Jewish people, the flagrant dissemination of the lies of racism, and the destruction of democracy as in prostrate France . . . .

But we know that plays can be written and produced that artistically reflect reality; that is, reflect life in a manner that is truer than ordinary perception is able to determine in the daily round of human existence. These are, and will be, the plays in which through the process of discovery, selection and dramatic fusion of the various seemingly unrelated phenomena of life are cast in their real order and movingly authentic relationships. The funadmental need is for dramatists who are armed with the outlook that is in consonance with the basic interests of the common people, and that also can serve as a guide enabling them to find their way through the maze of phenomena that constitute life today.

189

We of the Negro Playwrights Company believe that ours is such an outlook. We belong to a great race, and one in which the democracy of Paine, of Jefferson and of Lincoln has taken its deepest roots. We have always been lovers of liberty and truth and defenders of the dignity of human personality. And we know of no better way to continue that tradition than that suggested by our illustrious member, Langston Hughes, in his paper read before the Extraordinary Session of the International Association of Writers in Defense of Culture, meeting in Paris, July 23, 1938.

I quote:

> There may still be those who prefer to use words to make people doubt and wonder, to remain inactive, unsure of the good in life, and afraid to struggle for it. But we who know better, must use words to make people believe in life, to understand and to attempt to make it better. We have no right, as decent members of society, to use words otherwise.

It is thus that you should understand us when we say that we conceive of our mission as a mission of sincerity. Being Negroes ourselves, we are convinced that our people want to be rid of fear, and skepticism, of the gloom and despair encouraged in some quarters as the natural accompaniment of the lot of victims of oppression. We consciously seek the achievement of a theatre that embodies the tradition and spirit of Frederic Douglas, of John Brown, Sojourner Truth, of Denmark Vesey, of Nat Turner and of that mighty paragon of human greatness, Toussain L'Ouverture.

Can anyone doubt that a theatre embodying such a magnificent tradition will win the interest and joyous support of the people of America. We know that Harlem can possess such a theatre that reflects all the grace and the beauty and the truth of our daily life, a theatre that gives voice to the best that men have thought and believed; that boldly and honestly deals with the major problems of the world, and that depends upon the deepest interests and aspirations of the race for its dignity and inspiration. Surely, there can be no drama more compelling, more vital, more exciting, more interesting, more all engrossing than that which manifests a coming to grips with life without evasion and affirms with candor the warm aspirations of a people who have come of age and demand their immediate freedom!

HUAC PRODUCES AMERIKA

Ideological termites have burrowed into many American industries, organizations and societies. Wherever they may be, I say let us dig them out and get rid of them. My brothers and I will be happy to subscribe to a pest removal fund to ship to Russia the people who don't like our American system of government and prefer the communistic system to ours.

Jack L. Warner

I believe America should arm to the teeth. I believe in universal military training. I attended Culver Military Academy during the last war and enlisted as a private. Due to my military training I was soon made an officer and it taught me a great many things. I believe if I was told to swim the Mississippi River I would learn how to swim.

Adolphe Menjou

From 1946 to 1956, the House Committee on Un-Amerikan Activities conducted investigations into alleged Communist infiltration of labor unions, the motion picture, radio and television industries. The HUAC hearings were popular spectacles, coming direct via television into many living rooms. They meant to decreate the experience of the thirties and by doing so help to establish the social paralysis necessary for the carrying out of cold war policies.

In his statement opening the Hollywood portion of the hearings on October 20, 1947, Committeeman J. Parnell

191

Thomas explained HUAC's intention to expose the left-wing propaganda content of popular films. This was generally the line of questioning pursued with the 23 witnesses designated by the Committee as "friendly." But even with the help of accommodating witnesses like writer Richard Macauley, who rattled off the names of 28 colleagues whom he felt "morally certain" were Communists, the actual Communist-inspired content of motion pictures was established as existing in patriotic imaginations, not on the screen. When put to the test, Adolphe Menjou could only speculate that an actor might inject "Communism or un-Americanism or subversion into pictures . . . by a look, by an inflection, by a change in the voice. I have never seen it done, but I think it could be done." Not one actual case of Communist ideological infiltration into motion pictures was cited at any of the Hollywood hearings from 1947 to 1956. In fact, the single point on which uncooperative witnesses, studio bosses, the investigating Committee, and according to the evidence in their testimonies, even the friendly witnesses, might finally be said to concur, was that no such infiltration ever had existed.

This was HUAC's dilemma: it was not against the law for a individual to be a member of the Communist Party (or of the Communist Political Association, as it was known for a time in the forties), and it was clearly contrary to the Bill of Rights for a Congressional committee to investigate any citizen's political affiliation. Therefore HUAC, following in the grand tradition of political inquisitions, could not come directly to its point. In order to undermine the Hollywood "Communists" the Committee needed to incite public opinion against them by suggesting that movie audiences were consuming as routinely as their popcorn an unhealthy amount of Red propaganda. Also in the tradition of political trials, it would finally make no difference whether or not this charge was ever substantiated.

The investigators' intent became clear once the ten men designated by the Committee as "unfriendly" began to take the witness stand. Most of them were denied the opportunity granted to previous witnesses to read a prepared statement. All were dismissed as being in contempt as soon as they refused to give "yes" or "no" answers to the only two pertinent questions: membership in the Screen Writers' Guild (HUAC alleged it was a Communist front) and in the Communist Party. After each witness stepped down, chief HUAC investigator Louis J. Russel, ex-employee of the FBI, was introduced. During the investigation he presented ten lengthy dossiers detailing articles written, public statements made and organizations supported by each of the Hollywood Ten.

When the hearings ended on October 30, John Howard Lawson, Albert Maltz, Dalton Trumbo, Ring Lardner, Jr., Alvah Bessie, Lester Cole, Edward Dmytryk*, Samuel Ornitz, Herbert Biberman, and Adrian Scott had been cited for contempt. HUAC's charge was upheld by a vote of Congress—346 for, 17 against. The Ten were subsequently tried, convicted and sentenced to one year prison terms.

The decision of the Ten to invoke the First Amendment's guarantee of freedom of belief as reason why they would not tell the Committee about their political affiliation has been charged against them as indicating the same lack of "candor"** the Party displayed in the late thirties and the forties. But because they were being tried for their ideas—no crime or even a subversive line from a filmscript was ever cited—their defense of the right to hold ideas does not seem particularly evasive. They could have admitted Communist affiliations, but it is difficult to imagine the effect such forthrightness would have had on the Committee. The Ten felt that once they admitted they were or had been Communists, it would be easier for the Committee to fabricate espionage or other serious charges if that is what they intended to do. Their fears were not based solely on the reactionary temper of the times, though it was sobering enough. During the investigation Russel kept promising he would soon have surprising evidence. What he finally presented was too disconnected even for HUAC to pursue. It was an attempt to link Hollywood radicals with a Soviet Russian agent, and it involved a conversation Haakon Chevalier had allegedly had in a kitchen during a party. In other words, it was similar to "evidence" later successfully used to implicate Julius and Ethel Rosenberg in espionage work.

There was only one problem with the HUAC hearings:

_____

*Dmytryk later "cleared" his name by returning before the Committee in 1951 to testify voluntarily.

**The word is Eric Bentley's in the essay which concludes his collection of testimonies before HUAC, *Thirty Years of Treason*, New York, 1972.

after serving their prison terms, what was to prevent these ten men (and others equally suspect) from returning to their jobs in Hollywood and their active membership in the Screen Writers' Guild and perhaps the Party? Only some sort of an illegal blacklist. Just who would be responsible for such a list had been a topic of muted debate between studio bosses and HUAC Committeemen since the Hollywood investigation was announced. Before the Washington hearings the bosses had assured lawyers for the Ten that they would never institute a blacklist in the film industry. Then they spent their time on the witness stand urging the government to pass a law compelling them to do so: "It is my earnest hope," Louis B. Mayer read from his statement, "that this Committee will perform a public service by recommending to the Congress legislation establishing a national policy regulating employment of Communists in private industry." The Committee could not accept the suggestion. Even if they got such a law through Congress, it would be thrown out by the courts. By publically discrediting the Ten and casting grave doubts on Hollywood's Amerikanism, the Committee hoped to force film bosses into establishing their own private blacklist.

One month after the Thomas hearings ended in Washington, studio executives met in New York to do just that.* They issued the following statement to the press:

We will not knowingly employ a Communist or any member of any part of any group which advocates the overthrow of the Government of the United States by force, or by any illegal or unconstitutional method.

In pursuing this policy, we are not going to be swayed by any hysteria or intimidation from any source . . . .

Nothing subversive or un-American has appeared on the screen, nor can any number of Hollywood investigations obscure the patriotic service of the 30,000 Americans employed in Hollywood who have given our Government invaluable aid in war and in peace . . . .

---

*The story of the appalling growth of this blacklist and of the number of lives it wrecked has been told by John Cogley in *Report on Blacklisting*, 2 vols., Ann Arbor, Mich., 1956.

It was Ed Sullivan who offered the best explanation of the decision in his column soon after:

Reason that Hollywood big shots rushed to New York and barred the ten cited by Congress: Hollywood has been dealt a blow that won't please Wall Street financiers who have millions invested in picture companies. Wall Street jiggled the strings, that's all.

When HUAC resumed its investigation of Hollywood in 1951 a new kind of witness was heard. There were still honorable individuals like writers Lillian Hellman, Dashiell Hammet and Arthur Miller, actors Lionel Stander, Gale Sondergaard, Will Geer, Howard Da Silva and folk singer Pete Seeger who risked (and sometimes served) prison terms rather than serve the Committee. But the blacklist accomplished its aim. In order to clear their own names, people who had in more comfortable days thought of themselves as liberals or even radicals chose to villify friends and acquaintances and to debase themselves.

Sterling Hayden, actor, seaman, soldier, one-time Communist, paused in his name dropping to tell the Committee about a meeting with a "John Stapp," whom he assumed to be an important functionary in the Party: "I think he said he doubted that I would make a good Communist, but I am not sure." Hayden continued:

. . . I would like to say that I appreciate very much, very, very much, the opportunity to appear here today. I think that there is a tremendous service to be rendered, not only to the country at large but to the motion picture industry and also to those individuals who find themselves in a similar position to mine.

I have heard that there are many, many thousands—I have heard there are hundreds of thousands—of ex-Communists [!] who don't know what to do about it. I would like, if it is not presumptuous, to suggest in all humility that perhaps some provision could be made by law to permit people who had had a similar experience to make their position clear, so that they could get this thing off their chest, because, believe me, it is a load to carry around with you.

195

By 1952 several witnesses were making repeat performances before the Committee, at their own, not the Congressmen's request. Edward G. Robinson and Congressman
Donald L. Jackson engaged in the following reparté:

JACKSON: Yes, several unimpeachable persons testified as
witnesses for Alger Hiss.
ROBINSON: It is a question of weeding out those who are
really sinister people and those who are really good Americans.
JACKSON: This committee has said that there is no evidence
that you are or ever have been a member of the Communist Party.
ROBINSON: I am here to be investigated, but may I ask you
a question? Do you believe in your heart that I have been
disloyal to my country?
JACKSON: Let me put it this way: I don't believe that you
have knowingly been disloyal to your country, Mr. Robinson. I think some of your activities have lent aid and
comfort to the Communist Party, perhaps inadvertently on
your part.

The artistic highpoint of the HUAC hearings arrived when
director and former Group Theatre actor Elia Kazan sum-
marized the achievements of his career in theatre and films.
First he named his fellow members of the Group who had
been in his Party "cell" (a rather romantic description then
fashionable among friendly witnesses) and he told what this
cadre was supposed to accomplish:

1. "Educate" ourselves in Marxist and Party doctrine.
2. To help the Party get a foothold in the Actors' Equity
Association. [One of the subversive accomplishments of
these Group Theatre Communists was to win rehearsal
pay for all actors in Equity. Until the mid-thirties producers never thought of paying actors to rehearse.]
3. To support various "front" organizations of the Party.
4. To try to capture the Group Theatre and make it a
Communist mouthpiece.

Then he tried to justify his subsequent work in terms acceptable to HUAC:

The Skin of Our Teeth by Thornton Wilder, 1942: One of the plays I am proudest to have done. It celebrates the endurance of the human race and does so with wit and wisdom and compassion.

A Tree Grows in Brooklyn (my first picture), 1944: A little girl grows up in the slum section of Brooklyn. There is pain in the story, but there is health. It is a typically American story and could only happen here, and a glorification of America not in material terms, but in spiritual ones.

All My Sons by Arthur Miller, 1947: The story of a war veteran who came home to discover that his father, a small manufacturer, had slipped defective plane parts to the armed forces during the war. Some people have searched for hidden propaganda in this one but I believe it to be a deeply moral investigation of problems of conscience and responsibility . . . .

What can be said about former "radicals" who acted as friendly witnesses before HUAC? Even if they now seriously believed their country was threatened by a Communist conspiracy from within (which, if they had any real knowledge of the Communist Party-USA, would be impossible to believe) they also knew that their testimonies would be useless to fight this "conspiracy." They did not have any information that HUAC and FBI investigators did not also have. Their testimonies served no public purpose whatsoever; they were absolutely useless to maintaining the government in power.

So the testimonies were useless to the government and harmful to many individuals who could no longer make their livings in Hollywood. Why then did these respected actors, directors, writers testify? In their eyes (and in their eyes only, because to accept this reasoning is to condone acts of gravest cowardice, acts that our generation may be called upon not to repeat, because between us and another radical witch-hunt there is only our nerve) each confession was an initiation back into the mainstream of US society.

It is bitterly ironic that the red-baiting hysteria, the hypocrisy and the despicable "confessions" HUAC produced between 1951 and 1956 contain the legacy of the most serious shortcoming of the thirties theatre. Exactly where the plays failed, HUAC took over. The process the plays could not explain, HUAC perverted into a grotesque parody of itself. In the thirties, theatre workers knew that people must change, but they could not adequately sense how to accomplish this. They trusted objective conditions that were in themselves radicalizing; the Depression and the fascist threat. They assumed that the people reacting to these events would be turned into masters of them.

HUAC proposed instead that the people had been duped— their flirtation with radical alternatives had made them unwitting agents of a foreign power. (HUAC implied treason just as Richard Nixon, who was at this time a vocal member of the Committee, has recently decried the potentially treasonous results of anti-war protests. We must know this history because we cannot afford to repeat it.) The most logical response to the Depression was, if not radical, at least drastically reformist. During the McCarthy period exactly the opposite was true. Once revoltionary alternatives are no longer apparent in the general drift of the people, they have to be sought at the level of basic instincts—before they are perversely altered at the moment they surface in an authoritarian society. It is Wilhelm Reich, not Marx, who provides this clue.

A single Marxist theatre located in Brooklyn did exist for a while in the early fifties on a program of new Amerikan plays. The integrated company was headed by Michael Gold and was called the New Playwrights' Theatre. They presented *Longitude '49* by Herb Tank, *Candy Story* by Barnard Rubin, and *The Big Deal* by Ossie Davis.

Tank's characters are seamen, a logical choice because the Seaman's Union was one of the few that still contained a number of Communists. But even to bring these socially aware characters to the point of radical action, Tank first had to get them drunk. Doing so, he confirmed his connection to the mainstream drama and the connection of his characters to the general sense of powerlessness of the period. The liquor only intensifies the mood of desperation the seamen hoped it would overcome. When sober they put up with the oppression aboard ship. When drunk they grow either passive or belligerent. The activist scenes of the thirties theatre become contorted into moments of wildness and violence that have no purpose discernible beyond the bleary gaze of their protagonist.*

Drunkenness externalized the inner life, making it seem an intriguing, but finally insubstantial aberration. When dreams and desires surface in this way they become associated with the disruption of life rather than with its transformation. Moments that are often physically violent and psychologically lucid—that is, the most exciting moments—are inserted into the plot just so the remainder of it can be concerned with returning the characters to the relationships and states of mind they had before alcohol was distributed. Lillian Hellman's *The Autumn Garden* is a well-known example; Edward Albee's *Who's Afraid of Virginia Woolf?* is the apotheosis of this approach.

In 1953 Arthur Miller, once a young playwright in Federal Theatre, presented his sixth play to Broadway. *The Crucible* meant to parallel the Salem witch-hunt to the current activities of the HUAC Committee and in it Miller develops two reasons for the Salem trials: land lust on the part of Thomas Putnam and the Salem faction he led and Abigail Williams' desire to see the wife of her (former) lover dead. Unearthing historical evidence to support this second motive was "what made the play conceivable for me," Miller wrote in the program for the play's 1972 revival at Lincoln Center.

But he is derelict to charge history to a moment of desperate intercourse in a barn. In the published text, Miller comments:

These people had no ritual for the washing away of sins. It is another trait we inherited from them, and it has helped to discipline us as well as to breed hypocrisy among us.

In place of a cleansing ritual, the Salemites put a witch-hunt and, the inference is clear, the post-war population put HUAC. This is little more than a silly justification of those who testified.

---

*After a drunken struggle touches off the murder of a black Communist seaman by a racist officer, the sailors do unite and demand punishment for this crime.

In his melodramatic fourth act Miller tries to show how John's and Elizabeth's mutual tolerance of his affair with Abigail frees him to oppose the witch-hunt. But tolerance of a "shady" past is what witnesses like Kazan hoped to achieve; it is hardly the prerequisite for exemplary action. What is needed to make *The Crucible* an actual indictment of witch-hunts is not a method whereby the hunted are socially redeemed, but a challenge to the Puritan idea that sex, sin and the devil are indisputably linked. This is precisely the challenge Miller consistently refuses to attempt, even though he consistently equates sexuality and sin with a radical will. (See *After the Fall*.)

A secretly scurrilous past preceded by a loss of innocence—this is the notion HUAC helped popularize in the forties and fifties and the one that defeats all Miller's characters. It is a post-war rather than simply Amerikan phenomenon. Harold Pinter, the most expertly bourgeois playwright of our time, adheres scrupulously to it. He writes plays with nostalgic titles like *The Homecoming* and *Old Times*, or anti-dramatic titles like *Silence*, concluding not only that we can never know our own history but that we cannot even communicate our fantasies on the subject to someone else.

Just how his characters' supposedly provocative pasts relate to their seemingly frivolous present is the question central to his work. The overall structure of the plays is necessarily reactive and the active segments within them are severely limited. The project of the characters during active segments is foreshortened to the point where it is almost immediately realizable: it is to "get the goat of" some other character on the stage.

Samuel Beckett also excludes hope of a future in order to focus on the present, but he does so in a way much more useful to people's theatre. In his plays subjective reality becomes inseparable from stage activity. For instance, Winnie in *Happy Days* carries on a desperately seductive conversation with her husband while being buried waist and then neck high in sand. Though Beckett insures that stage activity is continually emblematic of subjective functions for him, these activities have no connection to the social world. His characters live their psychoses in a void. Hence his pervasive despair.

As a personality, Jean-Paul Sartre enjoyed considerable vogue in the US immediately following the war. He was a hero of the French Resistance and a bohemian philosopher: good copy for the popular magazines. And existentialism could be interpreted, though this is not how he meant it, as a repudiation of Marxism as well as a justification for the insularity and powerlessness that choked post-war men and women. Sartre said we are no more than we make ourselves to be. In decades when there was no will to unite around A Cause (there were *causes*: the Korean War, the Rosenbergs' execution, HUAC purges), existentialism returned the social being to herself.

But Sartre's great assertion is against passive individuality. Rather than excusing a person from an active role in creating society, existentialism makes an active role inescapable:

Man is nothing else but what he makes of himself. Such is the first principle of existentialism. It is also what is called subjectivity ... existentialism's first move is to make every man aware of what he is and to make the full responsibility of his existence rest on him. Subjectivism means, on the one hand, that an individual chooses and makes himself; and, on the other, that it is impossible for a man to transcend human subjectivity. The second of these is the essential meaning of existentialism. When we say that man chooses his own self, we mean that every one of us does likewise; but we also mean that in making this choice he also chooses all men. In fact, in creating the man that we want to be, there is not a single one of our acts which does not at the same time create an image of man as we think he ought to be ... Therefore, I am responsible for myself and for everyone else. I am creating a certain image of man of my own choosing. In choosing myself, I choose man. *

As you create your idea of yourself—by projecting (or living toward) a state of fulfillment—you *simultaneously* create a new objective situation for yourself and, by implication, for all men and women. Subjective and objective realities are not separate; they are two-halves of the same process. They have the same origin: "In choosing myself, I choose man." They are simultaneous creations. "The subjective

---

*Jean-Paul Sartre, *Existentialism*, trans. Bernard Frechtman, New York, 1947, pp. 18-21.

appears as a necessary moment of the objective process, the objective as a necessary moment of subjectivity."*

Sartre's play *No Exit* was produced on Broadway in 1946, where it managed to run a few weeks. Though his ideology has had a seminal effect on the minds of those who revived people's theatre in the sixties, his plays have been almost completely inapplicable to the problems of production raised by it. A philosopher and a man of letters, Sartre takes the structures pre-existing in the theatre and imposes his thought upon them. The plays are weakened because their structure is not analogous to their world view and Sartre is forced to approach his subject through indirection and inversion. *No Exit* is a drawing-room comedy set in hell, which makes it not too funny, to establish that hell is life on earth for people who insist on living as though they were in a drawing-room comedy. It is an existentialist play about characters who refuse the responsibility of existentialism. For them "hell is other people," because they seek to define themselves through the faces and language of others. This is an impossible task. A person can only transcend his distance from others by choosing himself through action (and simultaneously choosing them) and not by selecting fragments from his past for approval by the others. Defining existentialism by showing what it is not, *No Exit* becomes an unpleasant play whose misanthropy contradicts any revolutionary intentions.

The playwright who held the clue to the new arrangement of subjective and objective reality on the stage was Bertolt Brecht. In exile amid Hollywood and HUAC, where his testimony followed those of the Ten, Brecht had found an audience of sorts, though it was hardly the proletariat. The wave of US Brecht productions began in 1945, when Theatre of All Nations produced *The Private Life of the Master Race*. The production was not successful and the audience reaction was hostile. Berthold Viertel reported in the *Kenyon Review* (autumn, 1945) that an audience led by films and novels to believe that Nazis were beasts, was unwilling to confront the crucial question raised by Brecht: "How people like us, or not in their human make-up entirely different from us, could have become so deeply involved in the theory and the practice of National Socialism."

*R. D. Laing and D. G. Cooper, *Reason and Violence*, New York, 1971, p. 53.

202

In 1947 the Experimental Theatre presented the Charles Laughton translation of *Galileo*, with Laughton in the title role. Brecht had already left the country; after testifying before HUAC he did not wish to remain here even for the opening of one of his greatest plays. Carlton College, in Northfield, Minnesota, presented the US premiere of *The Caucasian Chalk Circle*, and Hamline University in St. Paul produced *The Good Woman of Setzuan* in 1948. Eric Bentley directed *Chalk Circle* at Jasper Deeter's Hedgerow Theatre and Uta Hagen did a staged reading of *The Good Woman* in New York.

But more important than these productions was the increased critical interest in Brecht's theories stimulated by the sudden availability of many of the plays (most of them in translations by Bentley). Bentley knew Brecht in Hollywood and, probably more important, he could read Brecht's theoretical works in German and he had seen the Berliner Ensemble. He knew how Brecht's plays could be staged and he was in possession of a startling perception: the Alienation Effect did not destroy empathy, suspense and pathos, thereby condemning theatre to a cold recitation of facts; "these things were not eliminated but limited—limited by being placed alongside their opposites. The total result is a positive enrichment of the drama, even an enrichment of the emotional content." Bentley provided examples, too:

To the general "alienation" of life which is effected by form Brecht adds many particular "alienating" devices, more or less deliberate. One that must surely be very deliberate occurs in *The Caucasian Chalk Circle*. This is the scene in which Grusha feels the temptation of goodness, the temptation to pick up and save the abandoned baby. Grusha acts the whole scene out in pantomime while the Singer relates what she is doing in the third person and the past tense. In this the Singer is doing for Grusha exactly what Brecht, in his essay "A New Technique of Acting," suggests should be done to help an actor emancipate himself from the Stanislavsky procedure. If an actor hears his role talked about in the third person and his deeds talked about in the past tense, he stands apart from the role and the deed and renders them, not as self-expression, but as history.

203

When he uses the device in *Chalk Circle* Brecht of course is radically "alienating" Grusha's actions so that we do not lose ourselves in our compassion. He uses the third person, the past tense, the art of pantomime, and a refined language as massed alienation effects.*

Brecht described this moment in "A Short Organum for the Theatre": ". . . in *The Caucasian Chalk Circle* the singer, by using a chilly and unemotional way of singing to describe the servant-girl's rescue of the child as it is mimed on stage, makes evident the terror of a period in which motherly instincts can become a suicidal weakness."**

Inner life is the motivating force in realistic drama but it remains separate from the actual events of the play. The actor hints at what his inner life is like through a series of realistic activities. The audience looks at how he walks and talks and we guess how he must feel to act in that way. There is a non-reciprocal order between outer and inner; the outer is the clue to the inner, the two are not in dialectical relationship. Brecht's Alienation Effect snatched dramatic conflict from its place in this bourgeois schema. It made inner and outer realities equally perceivable and therefore the dialectical relationship between them is clear. The actress's mime and the narrator's song are part of the same process: Grusha as she lives her project of motherliness. The tension now exists in the open. It is *between* the two component parts of reality. (And Brecht further plays upon this externalization of the conflict by having the song, or poetic statement, be an objective account while the physical, concrete actions of the mime embody Grusha's subjective response to the child.)

Sartre objects to *The Caucasian Chalk Circle*, because in it Brecht has distinguished different levels of reality. Brecht's use of masks and artificial language for the ruling class while Grusha and the soldier appear without make-up and with a simplicity of manner is the issue here. "To put various realities into perspective indicates an extremely dubious ideological position," Sartre says. "Reality cannot be put

---

*"German Stage Craft Today," *Kenyon Review*, vol. 11, 1949, pp. 141-42.

**Brecht on Theatre*, p. 203.

into perspective because it is not *in* perspective. It *is*, on other levels, but a man is a man, whatever he be, and there are no men who must be conceived more or less fully." Sartre concludes:

> Thus, if you wish, we shall say that if there is a clear insufficiency in the epic theatre, this is due to the fact that Brecht never resolved (and he never had any reason to), in the framework of Marxism, the problem of subjectivity and objectivity. And therefore he was never able to make a meaningful place in his work for subjectivity as it should be.*

Though it seems true that Brecht stressed the economic situation of each character above all else (it is one reason Amerikan actors have such a difficult time with his plays), it is important to realize that the Alienation Effect itself does not dictate that this be so. The prejudice is peculiar to Brecht and his pre-war Marxism, and not to the technique which is first of all a way to visualize simultaneous realities. Sartre makes a mistake, I think, in assuming that the actor/character combination must equal another person, and thus he becomes alarmed when some of Brecht's "other people" (always capitalists) are so much less well-formed than others. The approach would never work if one were writing about a socialist society, Sartre says, because then the playwright would be sympathetic to the social role of all his characters and would have to present them all in equal depth.

But to Brecht the actor/character combination is *not* equal to another person. It *is* a dialectical process, which is a means for perceiving the world. This is the notion existentialism calls for but which Sartre's plays do not develop. It is also crucial to people's theatre. The work of the Living, Open, and Bread and Puppet Theatres would be inconceivable without it.

---

*"Beyond Bourgeois Theatre," trans. Rima Drell Reck, *Tulane Drama Review*, vol. V, no. 3, March 1961, pp. 10-11.

THE LIVING THEATRE

The essential present-day advance-guard is the physical reestablishment of community. This is to solve the crisis of alienation in the simple way: The persons are estranged from themselves, from one another, and from their artist; he takes the initiative precisely by putting his arms around them and drawing them together.

Paul Goodman

There is a resemblance between the lower and the higher. Hence slavery is an image of obedience to God, humiliation an image of humility, physical necessity an image of the irresistible pressure of grace, the saints' self-abandonment from day to day an image of the frittering away of time among criminals, prostitutes, etc.

On this account it is necessary to seek out what is lowest as an image.

May that which is low in us go downwards so that which is high can go upwards. For we are wrong side upward. We are born thus. To re-establish order is to undo the creature in us.

Simone Weil

Here are two texts as introduction to some remarks about the Living Theatre. The first from Goodman. The social scientist turned artist. His advice is practical. He writes about the nitty-gritty: city planning, juvenile delinquency, alienation, sexual gratification (of which his own earthy fault—male chauvinism—was a function). The second. Simone.

Determined to suffer as the world is suffering and to meet God at that moment. I don't know if Julian Beck and Judith Malina are familiar with her *Gravity and Grace* (they knew Goodman well and often worked with him), but they have thought in similar ways about the world and they have been deeply influenced by the great religionists of the revolution, of which Simone is exemplary (more so because she did not, like Ghandi, liberate a nation. How many of us could do that? She worked in a Renault factory. Then in England during the war she limited herself to the rations allowed her compatriots in France. All of us could do that.)

Simone's words are prophetic. Goodman's are prehistory, written in 1949 as a way out of the debilitating isolation and lack of nerve felt by people as they balanced World War memories against cold war experiences. Amidst this general paralysis, two revolutionary possibilities managed a tenuous attraction. They were anarchism and pacifism. But there was a serious problem for anyone drawn to the dual doctrine. United States society bore no relationship whatsoever to its tenets. How could pacifism affect the actions of a nation whose boom economy was supported by defense industry? What was the claim of anarchism on minds to whom the suburbs represented the perfect life style: far enough removed from your neighbors not to feel responsible for them; close enough to conform exactly to everything they did.

Goodman's decision, which became the Becks, too, was not to save a world which refused to admit it was in trouble, but to save yourself by finding an area, however small, where you could operate so that your life style coincided with your beliefs. To do this would cause a still farther separation from the rest of society, but it would hopefully untie you and a few like minds with whom you could begin to plan some sort of sensory attack on your own alienation.

Because society bore no relationship to your needs as a human being, it was logical to assume that the realization of those needs resided somewhere in the unconscious. Then, to surface unconscious desires would be a worthwhile, even strangely political, project for the theatre. Other artists were responding to the same impulse. What is Ginsberg's major poem, "Howl," if not an anguished attempt to speak the unspeakable. And action painting and abstract expressionism and John Cage's music all attested to a similar belief that the perceptions still important to human life were those which had managed to escape being formalized. In the theatre a number of verse plays existed and so did the wish, lingering from the early twenties, for a poetic theatre that through the accumulated beauty of its words would exteriorize unconscious desires.

In 1951 when the Becks opened the Living Theatre at the Cherry Lane (once home of the New Playwrights) they thought their major achievement would be finding a way to produce plays in verse. Their hatred of money and distrust of success were not affectations but prerequisites for artistic survival in an artless decade that idolized both. In place of the two bitch goddesses the Becks offered a passion for experiment and a sexuality that would be important on stage later but which was present from the beginning as a real compensation for the material poverty of their venture. They offered actors something they could not get in the commercial theatre: a home. "I loved them," Warren Finnerty says. "You always had a place to crash."

For one year at the Cherry Lane followed by a two-year hiatus and from 1954 to 1955 in a loft on One Hundredth Street they staged plays by Gertrude Stein, Pablo Picasso, Jean Cocteau, Federico Garcia Lorca, W. H. Auden, Alfred Jarry, Kenneth Rexroth. Judith Malina directed most of them and Beck made sets and costumes out of scraps and pieces of other people's garbage. They did four plays by Goodman, who in 1954 wrote about *The Young Disciples*: "I have tried in this play to lay emphasis on the pre-verbal elements of theatre: outcries and gasping . . . trembling, breathing hard, throwing tantrums and throwing punches." Though they needed a new approach to acting, Goodman's plays are too remote to call one into being. Their verse, biblical settings and metaphorical actions work to restrain actors' invention. The passion present at their writing becomes formalism during their presentation. This is why verse has lost the power to liberate an audience; it stands like a screen between them and the actor's knowledge. Yet the power is there in the scripts so poetry retains constant fascination for theatre workers. But the Becks knew their approach was not really working: "We had our greatest difficulty with verse plays. All kinds of agony," Julian Beck wrote in his introduction to *The Brig*.

After their loft was closed for a supposed building viola-
tion (fire regulations were invoked to get them out of the
Cherry Lane) Eric Bentley, who has never managed much
enthusiasm for the Living Theatre, wrote them: "Your
theatre was more like a bohemian club than anything anyone
could take seriously." The clubbishness, which Goodman
would have called "community," and rightly so, was necessary. The Becks have never been able to give up their position
at the center of a select group whose activities are a deliberate affront to middle class society. This is the sensibility of
the avant-garde, which becomes political once the human
value of its disruptive ability is recognized. In itself, the
"bohemian club" is not enough because, like the poetry plays
they produced during this period, its exclusiveness militated
against unrestrained contact with the current events of the
people.

Judith Malina had studied with Erwin Piscator at the New
School in the forties; most of his work in this country was
non-political, but it was formed by the ideas of epic theatre,
which are essentially political. The Becks knew about Brecht,
had produced his *He Who Says Yes and He Who Says No* in
1951. But Brecht was little more than a fixture of the
avant-garde; it was still years before his Marxian dialectic
would be taken seriously as the real force in his plays.

Between the time their loft was closed and 1959 when
they opened a theatre on Fourteenth Street, in an old building renovated by themselves and their friends, the Becks
spent thirty days in prison for refusing to take part in an air
raid drill. They had also received M. C. Richard's translation
of Artaud's *The Theatre and Its Double*. Artaud's inspired
ravings appealed to them immediately, because just at the
time they were beginning to be punished for their peace
actions, they glimpsed a theatre whose poetry was active and
aggressive and which was the idea of a man locked up in an
insane asylum.

It is here where the life of the prisoner meets the life of
the artist that the history of the Living Theatre as it will
remain important to us began to be determined. Like
Simone, the Becks saw a resemblance between the lower and
the higher, and they sensed that once they looked at the
world in the same way as the victim is forced to look at it,
they would be able to make public the reason the theatre

209

seemed so indispensable to them. The secret was not in verse or in pre-verbal tantrums; all these matters of shaping were secondary to them and would finally be better pursued by Living heirs like the Open Theatre. The secret was *the position of the artist in the world*; their task was to position themselves so that the still unverbalized will of every victim to be free passed through them and into the consciousness of their audience. The oppressed have their oppression in common. To express this is to use the theatre once again for the working out of a collective destiny.

Their prison experiences made them immediately receptive to *The Connection* and *The Brig*, two highly unusual plays by as yet unknown authors. Jack Gelber brought them *The Connection* in 1957; they decided to produce it as soon as their new theatre was ready and it opened on Fourteenth Street in July of 1959. According to the daily press the play was a failure, but the Becks had a successful production of William Carlos Williams' *Many Loves* running, and they managed to keep *The Connection* in repertory until Kenneth Tynan called it "the most important American play since World War II." Gelber's play carried the rest of the repertory for the next two years.

The Connection was the first work that forced the Living Theatre to face the situation in contemporary Amerika. Malina as director dedicated the production to the memory of Thelma Gadsden, an addict she had met in prison. The play asserts that the highly developed subculture of heroin addicts provides a mirror image of the bourgeois world, where people are also hooked—on money and success. Furthermore, the addicts despite their constant paranoia, are more humane and less hypocritical than the representatives of the straight world—an author, a producer and two camera men who expect to make a sensational film about their life. Because an addict's life, composed mainly of private highs and lows, is anything but sensational, the straight character's voyeurism appears as the actual grist for *National Enquirer* tastes.

The Connection implicated the audience in a way that bourgeois drama does not dare to.* Supposedly, a group of

---

*Compare Michael Gazzo's *Hat Full of Rain*, created from workshops at Lee Strasberg's Actors Studio (and included by him in *Famous*

210

street junkies has been gathered in the theatre to improvise around a scenario prepared by Jaybird. Once established, the play-within-a-play device is continually jostled by the addicts to whom the notion of play is alien. They are in desperate need of a fix and have come to Leach's apartment to wait until their connection arrives with the stuff. "You don't think we'd use the real stuff? After all, narcotics are illegal," the "producer," Jim Dunn, explains. There is a knock at the door. "Everyone stiffens."

Here are the three possible realities: an audience watching a play by Jack Gelber acted by the Living Theatre company; an audience watching Jaybird and Jim Dunn film the actions of actual junkies they have brought to the Living Theatre; an audience watching junkies wait for a fix, shoot up and get high. Because none of the actors were well-known and none of them had the gloss of Broadway professionalism, these possibilities were considerably confused. During intermission an actor/junkie panhandled in the audience.

This schema is paralleled by recurring visual and verbal motifs that remind the audience of the moral dangers of non-involvement. During the evening two cameramen hired by Jim Dunn "exchange, piece-by-piece, their clothing and personalities." If you are only watching, it doesn't matter who you are. (But what a wonderful acting task this is. To do it you have to know exactly what you are at every moment.) By the end of the play one photographer and the "author" have been turned on. It is not possible to describe a state of being. It is necessary to enter into it. And who is better off: the photographer who stays straight so he can take pictures or the one who takes heroin to know? *The Connection* asks for an audience commitment, thereby prefiguring the aim of radical plays as they emerge in the sixties. But the commitment (it is not to heroin, but to the notion that experience is the only true reality) is strictly within the beat tradition of the fifties, because like a heroin high it is essentially passive. There is no suggestion that once experience has altered consciousness, consciousness can then alter reality.

American Plays of the 1950s). Gazzo makes the problems of an addict indistinguishable from those of a bourgeois husband. His happy ending: the wife calls the police to turn her husband in. In the midst of his withdrawal symptoms he embraces her and they predict a wonderful future together.

The use of heroin, the most obvious reason an audience would want to see the play, began to predict significant alterations in the actors' approach to their craft. Amerikan dramatists traditionally rely upon liquor to provide a plausible stimulus for feelings that cannot otherwise be externalized within the confines of realism. Gelber's substitution of heroin is neatly ironic. Heroin is illegal and so it implies a protest. "Everything that's illegal is illegal because it makes more money for more people that way," one character says. Heroin is not at all conducive to gainful employment or to consumerism, so it undermines the basic premises of capitalism. There are also essential structural differences arising out of the use of heroin instead of liquor as a motivating force. Liquor induces argument, confrontation and emotionalism. Heroin minimizes the possibility of confrontation and encourages long speeches which are non-aggressive because they seem to work by free association. The long speeches in *The Connection* are the verbal equivalents to the jazz compositions by Freddie Redd that were played intermittently by four musicians on stage. Both contradict a Method approach to the play because instead of being statements of what a character wants, they are expressions of what he is.

Heroin forces each actor beyond a facility with conversation and argument to the point where he must execute motiveless aria-like speeches, improvisations, impersonations, and where his muscles must allow for retimed physical reactions. In *The Connection* an actor's physical activity sometimes assumes a shape that is an actual presentation of his psychological state. For example: Sam "jogging in place" when he talks about being "hooked." Being hooked on top of being in a play-within-a-play forces the actors into a new spontaneity. In one page of dialogue, for instance, one of the actors responds to impulses that have three different origins: he talks out of the window of the set to a woman who is supposedly on the imaginary street below; he sees the audience and greets them sardonically; he goes into a long speech whose free form is dictated by his being stoned, pondering Jaybird's motives for writing the play.

Jaybird's scenario called for conventional rising and falling action. "This part was to be the blood and guts drama," he says, but by the time he says it he has been turned on and is beginning to fall asleep. The play does have the traditional

212

obligatory scene, which one of the "cameramen" filmed in close-up, when Leach shoots up on stage. (And the scene had an effect more potent than usual; during the play's run fifty men in the audience fainted shortly after it.) But the action, instead of coalescing around this event, disperses in several directions. Leach passes out. The musicians split. Leach's condition leads to a discussion of previous overdose cases. Jaybird begins solitary ruminations on the nature of the theatre. The play ends as Harry, the personification of the drug, performs his recurrent activity: he enters, puts on a Charlie Parker record, listens for two minutes and leaves. It is an anti-ritual, meant to recall the one with the belt, the teaspoon and the needle. Both are pitiful because they do not unite the celebrant with a cosmos worth celebrating. They shut him off from a society whose cruelties he is unable to handle.

Gelber's play opened the Living to a new style, not the poetic stylization of the earlier experiments, but a style inseparable from the rhythms and ways of existence in the underworld, among the deviates from and victims of well-made fifties society.

After *The Connection,* the Living explored some improvisatory possibilities. They did *Tonight We Improvise* by Pirandello and *The Marrying Maiden* by Jackson MacLow, billed along with Ezra Pound's *Women of Trachis,* as Theatre of Chance. *In the Jungle of the Cities* opened during the 1960-61 season to become the first critically successful production of a Brecht play in the US. The following summer, the Living Theatre took *The Connection, Many Loves* and *Jungle of the Cities* to Europe, where they began to find an audience that would support them during four years of self-imposed exile. The tour was financed by an auction of donated art, after an application for Federal funds was rejected. A State Department official told Beck: "You ask me to help you get to Europe with one play about fairies, another about junkies and a third by a Commie. Do you think I'm nuts." Around this time, too, application for a Ford Foundation grant (like that which aided the San Francisco Actors Workshop, considered at the time the West Coast counterpart to the Living) was rejected because Ford refused to give money to theatres that did not have the potential to become financially self-sufficient. (Exceptions to this policy seem to have been made in recent years. But it is a general foundation rule and it has gone a long way to ensuring that theatres alien to the capitalist system will be short-lived.)

In 1961 and '62, while President Kennedy was quietly breaking the Geneva Accord in Vietnam, his public showdowns with the Soviet Union were making nuclear war seem an unavoidable result of power politics (unless you believed, as not many people were inclined to then, that the Soviet Union desired peace). The Becks became leaders of the General Strike for Peace. They were being arrested with some frequency and their peace activities began to take more and more time away from the management of the theatre. They had started in the fifties with a terrific sense of isolation from the society and the Broadway theatre it produced. Ten years later they knew that an alternate theatre was possible because they had begun to sense the form that it might take. Yet they were becoming more and more aware that the theatre they envisioned could not exist as long as the current society continued. They were never torn between a commitment to art or to politics. Their dilemma was always how to combine them both. Their experience in the gray world of the forties and fifties was going to make them ardent revolutionaries. For the longest time they had been unable to relate to society in any way whatsoever. Now they sensed that their most valuable contribution to the new radical movement would be to egg it on. (Certainly during the exile their anarchy would intensify as much by pressure to stay ahead of the Left as to confront the right.) To continue as a theatre they had to find a way to crystalize on stage their disgust with US society. If their theatre was not forceful enough, the immediate demands of picketing, marches, and civil disobedience would overcome it. A script of *The Brig* by Kenneth H. Brown arrived around the time of production of *The Apple*, by Gelber, and *Man Is Man*, by Brecht, when this crisis was most acute. Though it is practically inconceivable that any other theatre in the country would have produced it, to Beck "it was as if everything in my life led to the occasion."*

The script is hardly more than a literal transcription of one

_____
*"Storming the Barricades," *The Brig*, New York, 1965, p. 4.

214

day's events in a marine prison camp like the one in which its author had done time. Prisoners are awakened by the crash of metal on metal. They dress, exercise, undress, shower, shave, clean the brig, write a letter, undress, go to bed. Each activity occurs during a bombardment of orders, taunts and blows from the guards, to which the prisoners are allowed only the most mechanistic responses. "Sir, prisoner number __ requests permission to cross the white line, sir," is the closest they get to voicing any sort of desire. There is no escape from this half-life, no way to weld the horrible rigidity of the rules to natural human needs.

Perhaps the Becks' greatest gift is the single-minded ferocity with which they pursue their subject, thereby freeing it from any stagnant notion of what theatre is, so that each of their productions is totally audacious and almost every one, regardless of its final merits, explores new ways as though they were the most immediately accessible avenues in the world. They wanted to make *The Brig* as intolerable to watch as they knew it had been for Kenneth Brown to live through. They wanted to make the audience know the worth of spontaneity in the world by knowing the cost of its removal. (The Becks' vegetarianism is another manifestation of their admirable desire to make known the real—not monetary— cost of things. The taste of roast beef is simply not adequate compensation for the murder it involves.) *The Brig* became theatre of cruelty, defiling repression even as it forced the audience to endure it in as many ways as possible.

For *The Brig* Julian Beck designed a precisely measured steel and concrete replica of the real thing. Then he strung heavy chicken wire between it and the audience, interfering with the view of the actors' bodies just as their mechanistic movements interfered with the audience's need to recognize them as individuals. The sound level was deafening, the white light nearly blinding. Judith Malina had imposed strict rehearsal regulations: penalties for talking, arriving late or being improperly dressed. By the time the production opened, each prisoner understood his helpless terror so well that his movement had lost all natural rhythm. Every step and gesture was performed in definite segments, because it might be stopped at any moment by a blow from the guards, yet quickly because in the midst of traumatizing fear obedience to orders was still a potent motive. A cigarette break becomes a mockery of relaxation. Prisoners at attention in a straight line taking puffs too short for enjoyment; they are afraid to expand their chest muscles enough to let the smoke in.

Above all the repetition unnerves the audience; the guards' repertoire of tortures is so small, yet so constantly active, that even while watching the film of the production an audience experiences physical reactions to it. When a new prisoner is thrown into the brig, and you already know exactly where and with what he will be beaten, it is difficult to keep your own stomach muscles from anticipating the blow.

In the film of the stage version of *The Brig* realism is carried to such an extreme that it finally exposes the fallacy of its own existence. Each muscle that twitches under a club, each frightened stare makes apparent the horror of a system that turns inner reality into furtive signals. The more *The Brig*'s noise and glare and monotony offends the senses of the audience, the more their sensibilities react against repression. The play becomes a "ritual of useless work," in which physical activity is finally isolated from all human needs that could give it meaning. "Teach him not to consider the meaning of the act, but to act out the command," reads the *Guidebook for Marines* which was used as a rehearsal source.

In a prison world the mind is severed from the body. Nothing in the prisoner's surroundings corresponds to his awareness of himself. The self can only be realized through incoherent and desperate acts, as when prisoner number six falls screaming to the floor in an agonized attempt to have his identity confirmed. *The Brig* makes the distance between the inner and outer worlds absolute. Thus it bitterly mocks the bourgeois theatre's assertion that the essential mystery of life is housed in that distance, which is adjustable but uncrossable. *The Brig* destroys the validity of any distance between mind and body. This is what Beck meant when at their subsequent trial he denied having shouted "storm the barricades" to demonstrators who opposed the IRS closing the theatre. But he knew they were words that he or anyone else could have uttered because they were no more than a description of what was being shouted from the stage.

Judith Malina explains in her director's notes how it was possible for the actors to submit to the hatefulness of *The Brig* and how their submission increased their love for the oppressed. *The Brig*'s violence, achieved through attention to

216

the rigidity of its rhythms, confirmed a community of the violated. "Just as we knew where our fellow prisoner was standing and what he was doing without looking at him, so we came to know how he was feeling, if he was in pain, or if he was happy because he clicked in. It was like telepathy. But it wasn't that. It was community," one of the actors told Malina.*

In the rigor of preparing and playing *The Brig* a new, non-Method acting style was glimpsed, one that would begin to explore the intuitive awareness between actors as it was aroused by concentration of the physical proximity of one to the other. It was a style born of the need to counteract oppression. This physical, improvisational, communal approach would be basic to the work of the Living Theatre in exile and would guide the Open Theatre, a part of it that stayed home.

Julian Beck

LETTERS FROM PRISON**

Jan. 28, 1965

DEAR KARL,

Thoughts on the theater from jail. Remember that our two greatest successes, "The Connection" and "The Brig," came out of our jail experience, Judith's and mine. Judith dedicated the production of "The Connection" to "Thelma Gadsden, dead of an overdose of heroin . . . and to all other junkies, dead and alive, in the Women's House of Detention."

She had known Thelma in jail; we both met many addicts there and had come to respect them as individuals. In jail you get very close to your companions in a way that you don't "on the street." There is a candor, an honesty, that prevails in the talk; and the close living breeds understanding and affection. In doing "The Connection" we wanted to show these people not as degenerates, but as individuals worthy of our respect, such as we had felt when we had come to know them.

When you leave jail you don't leave altogether. Anyone who has ever been in is in some ways forever tied to it through a bond of sympathy coupled with the hope that some day everyone will be free. Jail gives you new ideas about freedom. We felt compelled to do "The

---

*"Directing *The Brig*, New York, 1965, p. 103.

**New York Times*, February 21, 1965.

217

Connection," not only because of our great admiration for Jack Gelber's accomplishments, but also because we were still somehow bound to jail and the junkies there and hoped, naively, that a play might help set them free.

The connection between "The Brig" and our jail experience is obvious. When we did "The Brig" we wanted to bring to the production all of the facts, without any faking, as we knew them. That, for instance, is why we made the play so loud. Jail is loud and we wanted the audience to feel the affliction of the noise, the reverberation of sound in steel and concrete buildings. Audiences complained, but we insisted on keeping the sound level, because that's the way it is. And again, by showing facts, we hoped, in our usual naive way, that the theater might bring freedom, at least from the abuses of authoritarian discipline.

It is interesting that in here my chief thoughts about everything, theater and life, revolve around the concepts of freedom and honesty. And when I dream of a theater of the future I dream of a theater that will be honest and free. Now my chief criticism of the contemporary theater is that it is neither honest nor free.

Honesty. I'm not even talking about truth; that's less accessible; the truth is so holy, so related to abstract values, I think, that it would be asking too much to ask for that. I am, however, asking for the simple presentation of things as they are; and I ask this of actors, directors, designers, and producers. Just give us a chance to see what things are really like, then maybe the theater can lead to real understanding.

But the theater, like life today, is so drenched in attitudes and phony concepts; it labors, like life, under the weight of so much propaganda from advertising, newspapers, public agencies like the F.B.I. and the Narcotics Bureau, Senatorial committees, campaign speeches, and classroom information molded by the morals of school boards that we hardly know any longer how to think honestly.

I am not putting down imagination or fantasy or symbolism. The imagination of the poet is not dishonest; it is the real factual statement of his imagining. I do not put down what masquerades as imagination: when writers are only dishing out pre-conceived notions of what's supposed to be imaginative.

I think if we will look at this world as it really is we will find that even what is most ugly has within it the sparks of life, and is therefore moving and worthy of our attention. And I think we go to the theater to glimpse those sparks. That's why we get so excited with anticipation before we go to the theater. It's because we're looking for light in a very dark world.

As I write this I am sitting in a very ugly room in this jail but I find it, strangely, more beautiful than most of the settings I've seen in the past year on the stages of London, Paris, Berlin and New York. (Because stage designers are more concerned with dramatic effects, sentimental lighting, tricks, and imitation of both art and life, rather than with art and life themselves. Life is very dramatic, you don't have to fancy it up. Art does not simply dispose of charm, which seems to be the constant effort of contemporary stage design.)

Life in jail is very real. No one has to fake. I hear real speech all the time, and how I wish I could hear more of this kind of speech in the theater. Actors don't have to speak better than people. Nothing is better than people. We have to get rid of the idea that elocution constitutes good speech; I think elocution and the throaty way even our best actors often speak is related to some kind of respect for royalty, 1965. We ought to be beyond that.

(I want actors to stop posing, I'm talking to Method actors, too, to stop trying to create effects and to break through into the representation of honest life.) It would be thrilling to hear Shakespeare spoken honestly, and Brecht. I think it would be startling. We might be so moved that we might begin to respect ourselves, and, instead of accepting substitutes for life in the theater and "on the street," we might find that what is real surpasses all our foolish notions.

Faithfully,
JULIAN.

January 30, 1965

DEAR KARL,

I got so hung up on honesty in the last letter that I left out freedom, a common fault. Am I overwhelming you with polemic? I'm guilty of that all the time, but jail makes you want to rail and yell. I often think that if the people on the street would realize how the world we live in is a prison, they'd do more yelling and railing, too. The sad, perhaps tragic, thing is that people do not realize they're not free. How thoroughly we have lulled ourselves with our pride into our brand of limited liberty.

There's liberty here, too, within the rules of the institution. There are books, lectures, classes, movies, television, though the programing is table d'hote; pretty good food, air, trees, clean clothes, cleanliness in fact almost to the point of sterilization, much as modern American life upholds cleanliness so much that we have become enslaved to the process of keeping clean. But here we know we're not free.

Outside, people delude themselves because they don't see the bars. I dream of a theatre that is free. What do I mean by that? To begin with, let us recognize the fact that everyone is not free to go to the theatre; it costs too much. And then there are the production costs that are so great that even the plays many people might want to do they are not free to do. But the public is also guilty. We applaud too easily expensive productions, which leads me to believe that we are enchained by the notion that only wealth can give us something worth major attention. In the theater we aren't free to speak freely about sex, or politics, nor

219

are we a free enough thinking public to permit the theater to criticize all but our obvious frailties without becoming irate.

Nor are we free to fail. That's the great fear. We are so much the slaves of the success-pattern idea, that we regard failure as killing. And it is often psychologically killing. Directors and actors aren't even free to work in this so-called free society of ours. You have to plot, scheme, deceive, and dissemble to get a job. Or spend months, or even years, of your life waiting for the opportunity to work. And when, finally, you do work, you are not free to act, you have to be realistic the way, let us say, so much sculpture is realistic. No pubic hair. And when finally you do work, the pressures of time and money are so severe that you are rarely free to see your work through to completion.

What remedy do I suggest? I guess I am recommending complete social restructure. Just changing a few conditions in the theater won't help. That's an illusion. How? No answer. But if enough people start thinking about the state of things we're in, we might find a solution, an action, together. Faithfully,

JULIAN.

Jan. 31, 1965

DEAR KARL,

Will try to make this letter less gloomy than the others. Fortunately you know me, as, at least, occasionally cheerful. A fellow inmate remarked, "You know, there are two kinds of guys in jail, the guys that are hip and the nondescripts." "How do I classify?" I asked. "You? Why, man," he replied, "you're entertainment."

Entertainment. My high-priest act tends to cover the fact that I'm an ardent admirer of entertainment, of the theater of music and dance. I think even the Hasidim regarded the delights of the flesh, and their cultivation, as ways of celebrating the lavish world created by God. But I think entertainment loses its purity and joy when it tries to put itself over as an art and becomes arty.

Genet adores popular songs because of the lush words they put in the mouths of common men who otherwise might never utter such phrases as "I adore you." Bring on dancing girls, pretty boys, music, color. Swing. But too often the true spirit is destroyed by the falsehood of artistic pleasure.

Repertory. Its chief virtue is that it provides a chance for artists to work together on many plays over an extended period of time, and therefore there is the chance to develop the craft of communal work and to develop as men working communally. Repertory theaters will fail when they keep working competitively and will succeed, at least in their work, as they develop communally and as the public develops its admiration for art made by unified groups as opposed to that of lone star individuals only.

The Theater of Cruelty. The only prediction I venture: More and more will be seen and heard and about this kind of theater named by a Frenchman, Antonin Artaud, who envisaged a theater which did not numb us with ideas for the intellect, but stirred us to feeling by stirring up pain. We are a feelingless people (consider all the suffering we permit in this world as we go about our business) and if we could at least feel pain, we might turn towards becoming men again instead of turning more and more into callous automata.

Black Theater. The theater is a mirror of the world. In the West especially in the United States the more it avoids the presence and problems and world of the Negro the more distorted it is. More black writers and actors are only part of the problem; the other part is that the whites, who control most theater, if they want to see the truth will find ways of bringing blacks into the theatre. And to do that we must learn to communicate, black and white, each learning about what goes on in the others' heads and lives. We don't know now. That's part of the work. Love is the measure of the degree of communication. When I love someone I want to be with them.

I look forward to being with you soon.

Faithfully,
JULIAN

While *The Brig* was running, the Internal Revenue Service decided to close the Living Theatre for failure to pay back taxes. The Becks, the cast and an audience staged a play-in at the padlocked theatre, sneaking in through cellar entrances, over roofs and down fire escapes. By the time the performance was over, they had decided not to leave the theatre at all and the IRS men, unfamiliar with arrest procedures, had to call for special officers to carry the protesters down the stairs. Malina and Beck were tried, acting as anarchists in their own defense. They were convicted and sentenced, she to thirty days, he to sixty and then they left the country with 28 members of the company, among them Jenny Hecht, Stephen Ben Israel and Rufus Collins, to keep performance commitments in Europe. Meanwhile *The Brig* had managed a short run in a 42nd Street theatre and, after that closing, Jonas and Adolfas Mekas and the cast sneaked into the theatre to make the existing film of the production. The Becks returned to the US long enough to serve their jail sentences and then rejoined the company in Europe. For four years a constantly changing Living Theatre toured Europe in Volkswagen busses, playing wherever they were wanted, appearing in films to earn extra money. They were featured on European television and in theatre magazines and their productions began to attract a growing number of the European New Left.

Their exile provided space for the breakthrough that was hinted at in *The Connection*, and appeared more persuasively for them in *The Brig*, because now that they had nothing—no theatre, no home, no language or history in common with their audience. The line separating their lives from the cries of the victims that had been echoing through their work became nearly imperceptible. Now they could stop pretending. Characters disappear, they present themselves on stage and they choose more and more to work without authors, developing productions together. Their work in exile reflects a nervous eclecticism that is distracting in the final productions but which is illustrative of their new-found familiarity with every part of themselves that might make theatre. They exercised until, as Lee Baxandall wrote, "their bodies" became "totally accessible to them" and they became a performance group that staged communal spectacles: *Mysteries and Smaller Pieces, Frankenstein, Antigone, Paradise Now.*

The Living is the first people's theatre killed by government supression and lack of popular support that refused to die. And it was during their resistance that they discovered new ways to make theatre; the analogy with the Algerians, the Vietnamese, the Cubans and other people whose modern culture is being forged in struggle is not without meaning. The Becks have often been charged with courting disaster and it has been pointed out that they did not *have* to leave the country. But if they court disaster in their life it is because they realize the necessity of it to their work; there can be no honest creation while the artist is removed from his audience which is in torment. The Becks know their audience is tormented by violence, by money, by subtle and not-so-subtle repression because they themselves are tormented by these things. The circle is complete.

When they returned to the US in 1968, almost directly from the barricades of the general strike in France, they were the publically acknowledged theatrical leaders of the movement that had grown up in their absence, out of the civil rights and peace protests they helped pioneer. It was a curious re-entrance. Their departure had been mourned by authors and actors who knew that they might never find so

222

effective an outlet for their talent again and by a coterie audience that could never supply the money necessary for their support. They returned to a public fanfare and to a press determined to lionize them as celebrities even as it rejected them as artists. *The Brig* and the exile had taught them it was no longer necessary to divide the theatre and life, but it was more apparent than ever that their theatre and their lives were unalterably divided from the commercial adoration that surrounded them. In the US, the media reported them as a freak show so they wouldn't have to deal with the force of their pacifism and sexual liberation. The Living was not entirely blameless, either. They thought to return as gurus to the US contingent of the international New Left, but it was difficult to separate the New Left with what they wanted to communicate from the middle-class culture vultures whom they disliked and wanted to make uncomfortable. By 1968, also, the movement had entered a phase of violence and factionalism that the Living could neither account for nor escape from. While theatre people were running them down for being hostilely aggressive toward their audience, the militants on the West Coast and at the takeover of the Fillmore East, which they helped engineer, were sneering at the futility of their pacifism. In fact, the Living were often hostile as performers and unforceful as sloganizers. The movement was more desperate and less mass-based than they counted on its being, while their productions were less fully realized than they should have been to give their pacifism persuasive force.

George Bartenieff, who acted in *The Brig* but did not go to Europe, remarked that much of the Living's work in exile has been "an acid trip variation of *The Brig*." This is descriptive of the plague segment in *Mysteries* (which is a collection of their exercises), and of *Antigone*, with its attempt through personal references to Malina's banishment, and the assumption of a Texas accent by Beck as Creon, to connect the myth to present day events. But it is more strikingly true of *Frankenstein*, the major work of the four they performed here. *The Brig* was a complete realization of evil as the Becks conceive it—immovable structure. *Frankenstein* set out to answer the agonizing question the prison play raised: Where in men is the source of all this evil? The play was personal to the company in a manner that *Antigone* only approached. Its

223

opening segment serves as an emblem for the Living's relationship to the world. The beginning attempt to levitate a body is a personal commitment to the power of the imagination. Its failure and the ensuing ritual slaughters and torture of the actors by each other becomes a significant record of faith overcome by frustration, or giving matched by acquisitiveness and of the imagination turned sterile by necessity.

The three-tiered set by Julian Beck, with its gigantic light bulb outline of the monster's head, is as close as people's theatre has come to taking over the metal and mechanical spectacle of the industrial West for purposes of cultural revolution. And having actors within that pop-art head act out the creature's changing perceptions of Western civilization was a communal representation of individual consciousness.

The following description of *Frankenstein* was written for the *Village Voice* in 1965 by the late Saul Gottlieb, who worked with the Living Theatre in New York, visited them in Europe and was instrumental in arranging for their 1968 tour. Gottlieb also founded the now-defunct Radical Theatre Repertory (of which Mark Hall Amitin's current Universal Movement Repertory is the ideological child), which in the spring of 1968 held two radical theatre nights and was responsible for booking arrangements for many of the new people's theatres.

Saul Gottlieb

LIVING THEATRE ABROAD: "FRANKENSTEIN"*

The premiere of the Living Theatre's new work, "Frankenstein," early this week marks the beginning of a new era in theatre. "Frankenstein" is a totally different kind of stage presentation from anything that has been done before, and succeeds.

It is that rarest of phenomena in art—a revolutionary masterpiece. Yet it includes every kind of drama from Aeschylus to the absurd, and transcends them all. It is not a play, but a "spectacle"—circus, dance, myth, ritual, magic show—that perhaps only the Living Theatre could create.

From the moment you enter the theatre, "Frankenstein" is full of surprises. It was created by the entire company of 20, under the

---

Village Voice, October 14, 1965.

direction of Judith Malina and Julian Beck, using the Mary Shelley novel and the various Frankenstein movies as source material. It is fantastically inventive and imaginative, superbly constructed, and brilliantly produced. There are flaws, but they are minor, and will undoubtedly be ironed out in the course of further performances—in Berlin in mid-October, where it will also be taped for German network television, in a tour of West Germany and Vienna in November, and in Sweden and Finland in December.

The audience enters the darkened theatre to find 15 actors seated cross-legged onstage engaged in a half hour meditation to levitate one of them—a girl in the center. Behind them looms the set—a huge tubular structure that looks like the framework of a three-story apartment house. The girl fails to levitate and is caught by the others in a huge net and placed in a coffin, which is carried offstage in a funeral procession into the auditorium, to the sound of delicate little bells the actors carry. One actor defects immediately, with a loud "NO!" and runs off. Two others peel off the procession, locate the first with walkie-talkies, and run and grab him in the aisle and drag him screaming onto the structure, where they hang him. Others start defecting, and in a moment the entire theatre, off stage and on, is transformed into a mad killing ground of posses and victims.

Each victim is killed differently—gas chamber, electric chair, rack, garroting, stabbing, firing squad, iron maiden, crucifixion—on the structure, and as each victim is disposed of a member of the posse becomes the next victim, until only two are left.

Collecting Parts

This opening sets the theme, the tone, and the tempo of the spectacle. Now Dr. Frankenstein enters and collects parts of the corpses. The familiar story is used as a mere thread for the show, and even that is handled in a kind of comic-strip pop-art science-fiction manner. This Dr. Frankenstein uses walkie-talkies to communicate with his assistants, modern drugs, an "X-ray cybernetic computer," and electric eyes. He is offered help by Paracelsus, Freud, Norbert Weiner, and the Witch of Endor. The Creature is finally created by a kind of electric-shock therapy of the corpses, who form into a 15-foot giant with two burning coal eyes, swaying in silhouette on the structure.

The second act takes place, for the most part, inside the head of the creature, outlined first by tiny red lights that blink to green and then back to red before flashing weirdly on hands and arms in the darkness. Stage lights reveal a plastic tubular profile of a head mounted on the pipes. Inside the head are actors, each with a Latin sign behind him: Ego, Incognitus. Voluptuas, Aggressio, etc. The coffin of the first act is at the top level of the head, with "Mors" as its sign. At the bottom, a mummy-like figure is unswathed to reveal a man, who haltingly makes his way up through the others. The creature, movingly played by Steven Ben Israel, falls asleep and dreams of a sea storm; the actors transform into sailors and passengers on a ship, making sea-sounds, and in very slow motion which becomes a wonderfully sensuous dance, they are all drowned, "falling" to the stage by means of the pipes. The acrobatics and gymnastics of the whole spectacle are full of vitality and grace, but the movements of the dream sequence are the most lovely.

Painfully, the creature learns to speak as speech is developed in the head by the other actors in a series of grotesque and hideous sounds, and he tells us of his adventure in a monologue that is echoed by the others in the head. The sense of wonder, of being newborn fully adult, of finding joy and pleasure in nature and society, and ugliness and evil, is given fresh emphasis in this speech, taken from the Mary Shelley novel. Frankenstein's hunchback is after him; the creature kills him and becomes a monster, and all the actors in the head become monsters with him, crawling out of the mouth of the head and advancing toward the audience with brutalized, horrific faces and gestures. A soundtrack tells us monsters are at large, but are indistinguishable from ordinary citizens, except for a "false smile", as the actors straighten up and smile at the audience.

An outline of the "scenario" hardly does justice to the rich complexity of the work. It is not merely a "message" play though it says we are all monsters, we are all victims and executioners, and we must put a stop to the endless cycle of dehumanization. More than that, it is an experience, thoroughly felt and intensified. We go through the process of being born, of becoming the monsters that each of us knows in his heart he is, and of finding our humanity again. It is a reminder of how little has been done to change the world, fundamentally, since Ibsen revealed our society to us, and it gives notice that a new kind of theatre is needed to make those changes. This is the second work in which the Living Theatre has utilized the theories and ideas of Antonin Artaud, the French actor-director who invented the "theatre of cruelty" concept. Frankenstein, was developed specifically in accordance with Artaud's notion that a spectacle should be created by a whole company of actors, based on an existing text that they would recreate in modern terms. In this respect, they have succeeded admirably. Whether it will have the effect Artaud envisioned—of actually changing members of the audience, of moving them to action in real life, remains to be seen. Whether or not, "Frankenstein" is a tremendous achievement, and a portent for the immediate future of the theatre.

Paradise Now represented the apotheosis of the Living's rejection by the New York intellectual establishment (whose annual cerebral bachanal, the over-priced and pompus forum Theatre for Ideas, members of the company succeeded in totally disrupting).

226

After four major theatre works devoted to manifestations of evil, it was logical that the Living should try to entangle its audience in a vision of the non-violent anarchist revolution. The apparent accomplishment of *Paradise Now* was that it meant nothing unless you took part, so the boundaries between actor and audience were, if not exactly shattered, at least effectively ignored. The revolutionary problem, however, is not to destroy the distance between art and life (or reflection and action), but to put them back into their proper relationship, which is: the ability to live out through your daily activities the aspirations reflected in your art.

Though in plan it is a definitely structured work—eight steps toward revolution, each one divided into three parts: a physical rite and symbolic image presented by the cast to prepare the audience for an action—in practice this structure all but disappears as soon as audience members refuse to relinquish their involvement long enough to respond to the evolution of the next step. Personal transformations occur (at least in people's theatre) at the moment after an actor reaches a relationship with his environment that is too intense to be sustained and which must resolve itself in a new relationship (instead of subsiding as the bourgeois pattern of climax and denounement suggests). Therefore, *Paradise Now* begins with a deliberate attempt to rouse the audience's hatred. "I cannot travel without a passport," "I am not allowed to take off my clothes," the company moved down the aisles screaming into the faces of individuals. Julian Beck explained:

> Sometimes we feel it necessary to play the role of fascist to make something happen. I come to you with the reality of my bullying so that you will have something real to feel.

But whatever the actual struggle is, these slogans failed to concretize it. They could be answered too handily (by shouting back, "So travel without a passport," or by stripping, as many people did), with precisely the ease that an experience like *The Brig* or *Frankenstein* forbid. Once members of the audience could picture the reality these slogans suggested (and occasionally they did work: I saw a woman break down in tears during the harangue), the Living meant to engage them in an action that would allow their rage to transform itself by a flurry of collective doing. But doing what? Mainly, the idea was to bring members of the audience into physical contact with each other and with the company. The knowledge that sexual liberation is necessary to the creation of a non-violent, non-repressive society is one of the Living's most valuable contributions to people's theatre. *Paradise Now* was supposed to visualize how violent desires could be transformed through sex into a kind of aggressive sensuality, one whose project was to rub up against the world rather than dominate it. But the body pile which was its most common experience was not equal to the idea, which after all attacks Western thought at the level of its essential conceptions. The sexuality of the company, with a lot of help from the press, seemed kooky, an in-group happening available only to those who were willing to come before an assembled audience, exclusive rather than expansive.

People's theatre begins with pre-revolutionary man and is dependent on the bourgeois, avant-garde and popular traditions of his art. So it is not only about his transformation; it is also concerned with the transformation of the familiar structures through which he has been represented. As these structures alter under the impact of revolutionary perceptions the alterations stand out for a moment (which is the current moment) against their tradition. It is this process that contains much of the dialectical richness of people's theatre. *Paradise Now*, though intensely concerned with transformation as subject remained strangely one-dimensional. For paradise to be now, there would have had to have been a revolution yesterday. Revolutionary periods, even the incipient one we are now in, are pretty unparadisaical. The elimination in *Paradise Now* of the requisite distance between the artist and his community—which is the distance that allows for a response to dramatic structure—was an urgent and probably inevitable, yet completely wrongheaded, substitute for the elimination by revolution of this repressive society, which occurrence, we believe, will allow for wholly new ways of perceiving experience.

The ambiance of the 1968 tour was unpleasant and I think no one reacted to this more strongly than the Becks; it

228

caused them to re-examine their entire direction. When the tour ended they returned to Paris. In March 1970 articles were carried in the *Village Voice* and the *New York Times* announcing the split of the company and the Becks' decision to go into factories and fields to reach workers. They went to Brazil, one of the United State's most oppressed quasi-colonies, and worked there until they were arrested in the summer of 1971. There is irony in the arrest story: the Becks were released because they were well-known US artists—thus, the overcoming of bourgeois privilege has a lot to do with the disposition of the authorities, and they are often reluctant to give up their own. At this writing the Becks and the company are back in the US talking through an analysis of Amerikan society.

The Legacy of Cain is a projected series of 150 plays they want to present among the people. *Favela* ("slum") *Project #1: Christmas Cake for the Hot Hole and the Cold Hole*, was translated from the Portuguese by the Becks and published in *Scripts* magazine (vol. 1, no. 1, November 1971). Suddenly the dialectical distances that had escaped them in *Paradise Now* are again clear. The availability of choice, as people begin to move out of the capitalist world and into the socialist one, is nowhere more apparent than in this play. And it seems that in accurate political analysis the Becks have found a currently workable substitute for the autonomous author—whom they abandoned during the exile at the cost of limiting their communication to basically non-verbal methods.

The primary reason for this accomplishment, which is as unassuming in its achievement as *Paradise Now* was excessive in its ordinariness, is that *Christmas Cake* is meant to be played for Brazil's starving population. Julian Beck explains why they worked there:

> I don't feel any chauvinistic guilt: this is my planet and I can move on it wherever I want to move. I also feel that I've given twenty years or more of my unique life working and serving those audiences, those intellectuals, those members of the bourgeois intelligentsia, who are in fact the exploiters of the people I would like to create something for right now.*

---

*"Paradise Later," *Performance*, vol. 1, no. 1, December 1971, p. 94.

Christmas Cake is a voice for the victims—who are now both its subject and its *audience*, which is why an early stage direction reads: "The tempo of the procession is lively. Its dramatic quality is friendly." But it owes its dynamics to *Paradise Now*, the work whose tone it repudiates most completely. It is structured as a serises of thirteen actions: two of these the people do alone (one is a tape of their comments about their lives) and two the performers and the people do together. In each of these actions the involvement of the audience is so natural that it is perfectly understandable. The secret (how simple!) is that the performers put themselves into a situation where it becomes clear that they need the audience's help. The involvement develops from the natural compassion of people, and not from forced exhibitionism or even spontaneous circumstance.

The first nine actions are concerned with the master/slave relationship the state-money-love-property-death-war enter into with the people. The opening procession and the song "What Do the People Want?" lead to six stories about these agents of oppression. Each fable is simple and timeless but the actions that accompany each one—and result in the blindfolding of the entire company—give it concrete political dimension. Actions 4 and 5 occur together: the *favela* speaks on tape—monologues from people who are so tragically resigned—while the actors remove their own blindfolds and look hard at everything that surrounds them. The resignation in the people's voices cannot continue to co-exist alongside the potential for their liberation. The two are posed simultaneously for a moment in awful contradiction: the reality on tape, the new world resonant in the actors' bodies. (It can be objected that untying a blindfold and spinning about is too pale and facile an image of liberation—and a lot depends upon the quality of the staging. But we have to recognize the overwhelming difficulty of our task in order to comprehend our real, if still insufficient, accomplishments. We know so little about what the new world could be like, that every attempt to visualize it is bound to be highly tentative.)

Action 6 is a trance. And here a repetitive chant and spin, which are associated with mysticism, like other activities the Living spent much of its exile in training for, are finally used not as panaceas but to explain the people's mystification to the people. The chant, "My Life is 1 hour for 50 centavos, My life is 2 hours for 1 cruzeiro . . . My life is 40 years for 87,600 cruzeiros," and the spin result in a captive state of mind. Then (action 7) the masters and the slaves from each of the six points of oppression sign a contract and (action 8) they are bound one to the other: "The binding is an act of seduction and compliance, both performers playing out both the pain and the erotic pleasure of the relationship." In action 9 Death reads the contracts between man and money, property, love that enslaves, the state, violence and death.

In a story about the future (action 10) the narrator tells the audience that students have looked at the world and seen everyone tied in knots and they wanted to "go to the people and give them our knowledge that they may learn how to untie us all. But they found that they were gagged. And my question is: How did the people free everyone so that the Treasure Box could be opened so that everyone could eat the Celebration Cake and be merry?" By this time all the actors and any students who have entered the playing circle are bound. They must wait for the audience to untie them; completion of The Rite of Liberation (action 11) depends entirely upon the people. "As the inhabitants of the community untie the actors, the actors begin a chordal sound of joy and liberation. They invite their liberators to join them in making this sound."

Action 12 is the cutting and eating of a giant cake, decorated like paper money. Again this is an unassuming yet accurate, tangible, and therefore completely engaging emblem for a revolutionary situation. Action 13 exacts further commitment from the *actors*, turning them into activists by having them return to the *favela* one week later to continue political discussions with the people.

The first play of *The Legacy of Cain* indicates that this cycle is the leap which, after the 1968 tour, it was hard to think the Becks would make; it is a leap away from spectacle and inverted concern with personal salvation—those twin Amerikan occupations—and toward a serious and consequently artistically convincing revolutionary commitment. Again the Living has put itself alongside the wretched of the earth and again they demonstrate the tremendous adaptability and staying power of the victims—those qualities which

231

should ensure their victory. (But as I type these lines Nixon is dining in Moscow and the Vietnamese people are being bombed more savagely than ever before.)

Judith Malina

JUDITH ON THE REVOLUTION*

MARIO RIOFRANCOS: (Mario Riofrancos was at the time a directing student in the Yale School of Drama.) What I found in *Mysteries* was that it tended to change my instincts. I think that is one of the areas where you can be most useful. Because unless we learn to react in a revolutionary manner through our senses, we will always be sold out, we will always be co-opted, we will always be absorbed. Because anybody can take a factual opposition, that is, an intellectual opposition to the war in Vietnam. The system can take that. That's what they want. They want the war in Vietnam to be discussed peacefully. But what they can't take is people vomiting in the streets at the war in Vietnam. If you can work in that area and people can vomit at this system, that's what's going to do this system under.

MALINA: I agree with you. There seems to be one other side to it, though. Strong enough protest action will shake the system up and make it stop doing those terrible things, and I agree with you that that's a good fifty per cent of what has to happen. But it seems to me that the other fifty per cent is that we have to give the people a faith that there is some kind of constructive alternative, that there is something else to work for than that which makes us vomit. Otherwise they say that we simply have weak stomachs and can't stand reality. We have to build another reality. And I'm not talking about Utopias, about the creation of paradisical ideas, because then we're attacked for that. But if we have an agreed-upon goal, then we can begin to build agreed-upon steps. Otherwise all we can do is fritter away the frenzy in specific protests. We know we need specifics. So we look around and we say, What is there here that is rotten? We have to stand in line too long to get our lunch and they should have two lunch counters instead of one. So we make a protest, because it's a rotten thing and it makes half of us not eat properly. And then all our protest energy goes into a very real concern. But they build the two counters and they say, "You see, now you have the two counters; now be good children. Go and stand on line. You have the two counters, you have everything you wanted." One must protest against immediate abuse. At the same time, rectification of the immediate abuse makes it worse. It's like picketing for better condi-

---

*Yale/Theatre, vol. 2, no. 1, Spring 1969. Edited version KMT.

tions in a prison. (Laughter.) If there are prisons, there must be running water in every cell. And if it isn't in any jail, I'll picket to achieve it. But it's ridiculous to picket for better conditions in jail, and this made you laugh for obvious reasons. But, in a way, that's happening in the schools. And yet it's the only place where this slippery juggernaut can be hung onto. It's this jellyfish quality that wherever you touch it, it smiles at you. (Laughter.) And when you finally touch it where it doesn't smile, it hits you over the head and says, "What could I do?—you touched me here." (Laughter.)

Let us have a program that is concerned not only with the abuses but also with demands on levels which cannot be met by the social structure. We must demand something they cannot give us. And it will be beautiful and good for us from our point of view. Whether they think it good and beautiful doesn't make any difference. If we find something to build on. (Laughter.) But it has to be bad. Now what kind of world can we aim for and build and create that's beautiful and good and useful and strictly illegal?

THE OPEN THEATRE

I went through a personal transformation . . . I was
interested in a very fancy career for myself as an actor. I
thought the opportunity to play this terrific role would
give me all the chance in the world to further this
career . . . But in doing the role every night, I changed
little by little. Like Galy Gay. And I couldn't go back to
those aspirations.

Joseph Chaikin

As Brecht had seen Amerika when he made it the setting
for *In the Jungle of the Cities* and *St. Joan of the Stockyards*,
so Joe Chaikin would see Brecht: not necessarily accurately,
but as if inspired. The Open Theatre began as a workshop
within the Living Theatre to explore techniques for acting in
non-naturalistic plays. Chaikin, cast as Galy Gay in the
Living's production of *Man Is Man*, found that the part
demanded a different set of acting skills than those he had
available as a Method-trained actor. Julian Beck had read
much of Brecht's acting theory to the company, but during a
rigorous rehearsal period an entirely foreign approach could
only be awkwardly assimilated. Furthermore, whatever acting
style was finally developed would have to account for the
Method. To ignore the previous training of Amerikan actors
was impossible because it would shut off access to their
creativity, leaving them only able to ape Amerikan critics'
versions of Brecht's theories.

For Brecht there were always two things: the stage event

234

and the *gestus* ("an attitude or a single aspect of an attitude, expressible in words or actions"*) with which it is presented. The event plus the particular *gestus* produce the Alienation Effect, causing the audience to suddenly see reality in a new way. In order for the A-effect to be achieved the actor must decide on a proper *gestus*. Even before he can do this he must have a frame of reference that he shares with the other actors and through which he can view the play's events because his *gestus* would only be obscuratory if arrived at by whim. The actors in the Chinese theatre (it is in an article on Mei Lan-fang that Brecht first introduces *gestus*) understood every stage event as representing part of a well-known myth and they already had a traditional *gestus*, variable by their genius, with which to present it. The Brechtian actor, lacking this craft tradition (which lack of course meant that he was free to *re*interpret the world) was nevertheless able to look at each event as it corresponded to Marxist class analysis and to select his *gestus* accordingly. By the 1960s, however, Marxism no longer seemed relevant to Amerikan actors. Once they realized the significance of the A-effect, they were left without a plausible way to accomplish it.

What they clung to in the Method and what would keep them from following Brecht whole-heartedly was the belief in the creative value of the individual unconscious; it is the same belief that would keep Amerikan radicals from accepting Soviet Marxism. An acting technique that allowed for physicalization of the unconscious would truly be a signal through the flames. It would give access to the alternate world view that workers in people's theatre had sought since the twenties, because it would concretize, at least on stage, the imagined possibilities of radicalism: that people can initiate internally—and simultaneously win back—a union with their world, and that their needs will finally be reflected in the structure of their society.

The Open Theatre is doing this. And hardly a street theatre, performing group, or the Living Theatre (which incorporated many Open Theatre techniques when OT members visited them during their exile) has failed to benefit from its influence.

But what we think is less than what we know; what we know is less than what we love; what we love is so much

Brecht on Theatre, p. 42.

less than what there is. And to that precise extent we are so much less than what we are.

R. D. Laing

This said, we can begin to form an idea of culture, an idea which is first of all a protest.

Antonin Artaud

While other radical groups take the theatre into the streets to force a confrontation with the people, the Open Theatre sticks to a theatrical space, marks it off—directions to *Terminal* indicate a proscenium stage—reclaims it as a place which the audience must enter, because only there will certain answers become manifest. Since *The Serpent* (1968) they have been building a body of work that is concerned with the essential questions of radicalism, which are, after all, the essential questions about life, re-examined in light of people's actual needs.

The Serpent, words by Jean Claude van Itallie, is a work of profound, almost unrelenting sorrow. Its single image of joy, aside from Eve's momentary ecstasy after having tasted the apple, is formed by the quietly wondrous animals in the garden of Eden, the most striking of which is the stately heron. But the image of mourning is more pervasive; four chorus women *davenn* as though at a funeral throughout much of the ceremony.

The Serpent searches for the beginning of life as we know it, which is also the end of life as it could have been had Eden remained our home. It attempts to discover how the mythical choices made by Adam and Eve and Cain relate to the boundaries of our existence. To this purpose, the assassinations of President John F. Kennedy and Martin Luther King, Jr., have been appropriated into the biblical piece as representing the end of another age of innocence. (Though the duplicity of the President can hardly be compared with the non-violent politicking of the civil rights leader, both men were of a time when fine words covered for non-existent changes.) *The Serpent* ends with a retreat. A sentimental song, "Moonlight Bay," is sung in voices that represent a "slow kind of dying," an "emptying out," and by extension, the Amerikan dream gone sour. More than a definition of origins is needed before the present can be altered. The question asked in *The Serpent* remains unanswered: Given the choices already made (concentration camps, nuclear bombs, power politics—all these are present, though not stated), how can we change our lives?

Terminal (1969-70), words by Susan Yankowitz, co-directed by Chaikin and Roberta Sklar, looks to the end, to death and to dying. It calls upon the spirits of the dead, demanding that they invest the dying with a sense of life. In the original version *Terminal* ends with a scene called "Presence and Absence" in which "the actors stand silently. They are directly present in their bodies, in the space, and in their relationship to the audience." The version re-worked for the new smaller company* ends as the dying live through an image of their judgment. In neither case is the end a retreat. In both it is a confrontation, as though the actors were at the barricades facing the limits of their work, but not charging, just holding the line.

The Mutation Show (1971-72), words by W. E. R. LaFarge and John Stoltenberg, co-directed by Chaikin and Sklar, is a study of change. The Open Theatre's preoccupation with transformation goes far beyond its usefulness as an acting exercise. This is a piece devoted entirely to the possibility of human transformation, as *Terminal* and *The Serpent* are also, but under the guise of death and birth.

If we are to liberate ourselves, we must first break down the institutionalized images of ourselves which we present to the world and which we in turn accept as being accurate. Chief among these is the family. It is the family structure that first gives back the self to us as a socially defined object. So the Open Theatre seizes upon the primary rite of the family and creates a wedding march and dance that moves through the family's complicity with society to become a literal wedding of opposites: "The bride is now dancing with the groom ... The cow is now dancing with the butch-

---

*In the fall of 1970 many long-time members of the Open Theatre left the group. Peter Feldman, co-director, went to teach in Holland. Some of the actors formed a new company which presented a not very satisfactory production of Brecht's *Edward II*, and in the spring of 1972 a work-in-progress called, like their group, *Medicine Show*. Ron Faber and Peter Maloney, two of the finest actors to have been associated with the Open Theatre, created excellent performances off-Broadway in 1971-72 in Fernando Arrabal's *And They Put Handcuffs on the Flowers*. Chaikin reputedly did not oppose the split; he was anxious to work with a smaller company.

er . . . The people are now dancing with the laws." Finally, the activity breaks through satire to celebrate union: two women kiss, the opposites are exploded in a wedding of the self.*

In technique, this scene recalls the "lost on Fourteenth St." segment of the *Interview* play in their first major work,

America Hurrah!, by van Itallie, which was also a performance use of the Phrase exercise:

A phrase is a brief sound and/or movement which the actor repeats in identical form a specified number of times or for a specified period of time as the paradigm of a character. It constitutes the entire characterization thus, although it is naturalistic in form, it is emblematic in function . . . . A scene composed of phrased characterizations takes on a formal rhythm and an abstract composition.**

In mood the scene recalls the group singing of "Wild Mountain Thyme" at the end of benefit performances in 1968, which created an infectious hand-clapping, foot-stomping joy among the audience. Then the Open Theatre repeated over and over again with growing intensity the words to this beautiful song as they passed Mimosa sprigs to the audience. In *The Mutation Show* they repeat a stiff-legged wedding dance until our initial delight at the ferocity of their satire passes into joy at the continuation of the dance and its buoyant rhythm.

So a progression is evident from the sorrow of wrong choices in *The Serpent* to the aggressive joy of *Mutation*. But more important than this notion of "progress" is the connection each of these three works has with the other. They can

---

*Robert Passoli, *A Book on the Open Theatre*, Indianapolis, 1970, p. 94.
**This is a description of the central scene in the then titled *Mutations* as it was presented without costumes at its first open rehearsal at Harvard in May 1971. The piece was still being called a work-in-progress when it won an Obie in 1972; each of the three times I have seen it it has changed rather significantly. The version presented in spring 1972 differs from that of December 1971 chiefly by its more linear organization, and it suffers accordingly.

238

only be approached, finally, as amplifications of one another. We are meant to notice the similar phrases, rhythms, images as they recur within each piece and are lifted from one to the next, and to feel the shock of the familiar. The autopsy at the beginning of *The Serpent* becomes a repeated image in *Terminal*. A visual definition of domination, where the person being carried is distorted as severely as the person doing the carrying, appears fleetingly in *Terminal* and becomes an extended segment in *Mutation*. A tradition, a way of living in the world is being sought, so the echoes are just as significant as the innovations.

How did the Open Theatre come to this notion, which is a complete departure from the plotted drama, in which past determined present and future threatens it? Partly through having worked as a community, a mode that is less suited to linear structure—which demands a group answer to "What comes next?"—than it is to theme and variation, which asks "What else is there?" Partly, too, through their feeling that the theatre has been in complicity with the despised system. The theatre, they knew, would remain powerless no matter what questions it asked as long as the *way* in which it asked them reflected a society based on "the logic of domination." It is the phrase Marcuse uses in *Eros and Civilization* to explain the prevailing rationality of Western civilization.

Radical theatre is nothing if not a search for alternatives to the fundamental assumptions of the "logic of domination." This search led Brecht to embrace the epic, a mode that was already germinal in the historic sweep of German drama. US dramatists began during New Playwright's years to look for impulses that minimized reliance on linear plot. The thirties strike drama brought suspense, causality, rising and falling action back to the foreground; but the playwrights were rebelling against a system that made this structure necessary, and in their rebellion they found transformational possibilities and the need to get rid of the family as the primary dramatic unit. And always in people's theatre the future has been presented in a manner that suggests that men will come into it fulfilled, not at it as an object to be dominated. Such a presentation assumes that the desired future does not exist somewhere ahead of us in time, unknowable and therefore threatening. Rather this future is reachable through a psychic leap, just as it is reachable on stage through an imaginative leap beyond the previous style of the piece. The future of mankind, that is, lies in our ability to delight in our presence within the world, instead of our ever-expanding compulsion to assert ourselves against nations and unborn generations.

If there is an equivalent to Brecht's Marxist outlook in the Open Theatre it is existentialism, especially as it has been applied to psychiatry by R. D. Laing and David Cooper. But it may also be said that the depth and carefulness with which the Open Theatre works (their greatest theatrical strength and also the quality about them which is most infuriating to militant political instincts, their own included) is the result of their basic inability to find in a twentieth century pig-rich and imperialist country—whose privileges they have received directly and which they nevertheless feel ravaged by—a shared and comprehensive radical perspective. They move slowly and seldom in direct confrontation with pressing social problems. They are always searching, through themselves for themselves.

Like Brecht, the Open Theatre had to relocate the dramatic conflict. Brecht did it by forcing the audience to notice that the course of events was not inevitable. Every action involves a choice and he located his tension between those warring alternatives. The Open Theatre makes the personal and still unrealized desires of its actors visible, setting them next to the realistic behavior patterns and objective situations that normally force their supression. Thus they have also externalized the conflict between will and activity. In place of sub-text the Open Theatre has put simultaneous texts. Because the will is no longer hidden, the point of interest is no longer in its ineffectuality, but its stimulus upon and its potential to transform reality. It is here that the Open Theatre is most indebted to the ideas of Laing and Cooper and to other radical thinkers who have challenged the neo-Freudian insistence on the unalterability of human nature. To Laing, mental aberrations are inseparable from social ones. And madness is not an intolerable departure from social order, but a divine suggestion about how it can be overthrown. We might ask why Laing has had such influence with them? Why not Reik or Sartre, to whom many of the original perceptions belong? The answer is that no one tells a better story than Laing and the people who have worked with him

240

at Kingsley Hall and elsewhere. The awareness that "psychosis may be a state of reality cyclic in nature by which the self renews itself" and that "a person may function at several levels of regression at the same time"* are intensely dramatic. They nearly parallel the journey on which the Open Theatre ensemble is embarked. Whether undertaken by "madmen" or by actors the trip demands that same breathtaking audacity which always appears as prerequisite for personal transformation.

The Serpent: A Ceremony is meant to be entered into jointly by actors and audience. A ceremony is distinguished from a play because its parts are equally familiar to all who participate. But here the designation is a theatrical conceit. A ceremony is effective because a certain combination of known actions consistently evokes unknown worlds. To be a real ceremony, *The Serpent* would have to be presented with some frequency, but the split in the Open Theatre makes it unlikely that this work which calls for about eighteen actors will be performed again by the company that originated it.

Simultaneous texts are used throughout *The Serpent* where the technique proves itself by providing for multiple effects and resonances. In the assassination segment near the beginning of the work, four actors mime with studied accuracy the twelve movements made by the Connallys and the Kennedys at the moment of the assassination. Behind them the crowd begins a shout that has been broken down into vowel and consonant sounds. As each group in the crowd adds their part, the words become clear: "I was not involved. I am a small person. I hold no opinion. I stay alive." Words and actions have been separated and assigned to two different configurations of actors. What happened and the guilty withdrawal that accompanied what happened, at a deeper level than the publically proclaimed cries of grief, are presented simultaneously. A new dialectic becomes apparent as the words of one group reverberate off the actions of the other. The activity we comprehend is the sum of these two disparate occurrences. As the scene progresses, the actors in the car repeat the twelve movements, first backward and then in random order. The action, like the actual film of the assassi-

---

*Joseph Berke's acknowledgment of the debt he owes Laing in *Mary Barnes: Two Accounts of a Journey Through Madness*, by Joseph Berke and Mary Barnes, New York, 1972.

nation, can be played back at will, but its cause is not hidden in the sequence of events.

Eve's temptation is one place in *The Serpent* where distinct characters confront each other in a traditional test of will. But the definition of character is extended through simultaneous texts. The serpent is played by five actors intertwined. Each holds an apple. Each speaks a portion of the serpent's argument. Together they form the serpent and the tree. Eve's sentences are repeated immediately by one of the chorus women, only the accent is on different words. The "chorus women look at the audience as if it were the serpent in front of them." They assume Eve's state of mind and share in her choice. The serpent seduces Eve, both with the logic of his argument—logical to Eve because it verbalizes her half-understood desires—and the aliveness of his body. It is not as though the serpent merely feels or acts more alive than Eve. He actually has five times more her life. Toward such vitality she must aspire. And so she eats.

Adam and Eve have eaten and now God curses them. The curses are both a literary recreation of God's rage and an accurate description of our life as we know it now:

Now shall come a separation
Between the dreams inside your head
And those things which you believe
To be outside your head
And the two shall war within you.

Adam and Eve speak to God. They go limp and are held up by another actor as God speaks to them through their own voices, only made "larger and more resonant." Simultaneously we are in awe of God and we know that He comes to us through ourselves.

In what is probably the most remarkable scene in the ceremony, the chorus recites the murder of Abel by Cain just before it is mimed in front of us. Why did Cain kill Abel? Because God had accepted Abel's offering and not Cain's. "Why did he accept your offering/And not mine?" The question is repeated eight times during the chorus narrative. It is a question asked of Abel. But Abel, having no answer, cannot prevent his own death. God has the answer but He refuses to acknowledge the question. Just as He refused to answer the serpent who had asked about Adam and Eve: "Why did they obey me and not you?" Could God have accepted Cain's offering? Could Cain in light of God's rejection have acted otherwise? Can we continue to do good when every good we do is cancelled? The sorrow of *The Serpent* lurks here. If there are no answers to the original questions, where are the answers to the current ones? How can those who have been cast out act with grace? And who does the casting out? Did God mark Cain by refusing his offering or did Cain mark himself by deciding, "There is no judge. There is no law." Cain and Eve have in common that they both hope to escape the consequences of their actions. But the consequence of Eve's decision is Abel's murder. If there were no awareness of separation, there could be no thought of killing.

The first murder is presented as a bungling affair, having none of the grace of an instinctual action. Cain did not know how to kill. He had to learn. He breaks a finger first, then an arm, then Abel's back and finally chops at his brother's throat until the breath is stopped. The minute that Abel is dead, Cain tries to revive him:

> For it occurred to Cain
> To kill his brother
> But it did not occur to Cain
> That killing his brother
> Would cause his brother's death.

The old mystery remains the current one. Every child watching television learns numerous ways to kill. But the mass media, from comic books to the evening news, has effectively separated the act of killing from its consequence, Death. So here the action has been separated from the word; the chorus narrative ends at a crucial point. When Cain kills he also makes the sounds of his brother dying. Simultaneous texts allow for the transfer to Cain of sounds that realistically belong to Abel. The person who kills also dies. The drama is found, as it often is in people's theatre, at the moments when we are seen to be alike.

Similar activities repeated in different scenes take on new associations, but they give witness, also, to what men share. A long scream by the chorus women is repeated twice, in the beginning as the victim of a brain wound stares tensely at the audience, and again as Abel's ghost assumes the same stare and tension. Toward the end of the Curses segment, Adam and Eve begin a "locked action of, respectively, accusing, and of reaching and subsiding." They continue this action throughout the next scene, Statements I. There are two statements sections in the piece. Along with the Kennedy-King assassination and the sentimental song at the end, they provide the contemporary breaks from the biblical story. In Statements I, the verbal motif is the chanted phrase "one lemming." The visual motif is the "locked action" carried over from the previous scene. The actual statements are quite personal to members of the Open Theatre, but they are accurate descriptions of its audience as well:

My home was Cleveland
Then I came to New York
And I didn't have to account to anybody
I smoked: pot, hashish, opium
I slept with a man
I slept with a woman.
I slept with a man and a woman at the same time.
But I'm a gentle person and I collapsed.

The scene ends as the chorus completes the story of the lemming's migration to the sea. It is a story of the abdication of choice. It becomes a vision of the holocaust.

In Statements II, the visual motif begun in the preceding scene is continued; it is blind, exhausted people groping about—a scene from Breughel. The statements are about opposites. Often they are cast like riddles, and in one of them is a partial explanation:

So man created God
What for?
To set limits on himself.

Terminal, their best and most ignored major work, is more difficult for a contemporary audience to respond to than *The Serpent*. Though simultaneous texts continue to give richness to the stage activity, they are not used to extend it to the audience, the consistent function of the chorus narratives in

The Serpent. In *Terminal*, simultaneous texts formalize the activity, distancing it from the audience. *Terminal* has no familiar story, and while its theme is familiar enough people prefer not to dwell on it. That, in fact, is the beginning premise of the piece. Our death which is the culmination of our lives has been institutionalized. It is a job for hospitals and funeral parlors; we are not specialized enough to deal with it. Death has taken on all the reality of a glossy ad for above-ground mausoleums. It has become as personal as the face of Walter Cooke. Surrounded by all the commodities of the affluent society, it becomes comfortable just like life. Death has been turned into the final great evasion.

Terminal wants to rediscover the processes of life which make death possible and it wants to expose the routines that have made both seem remote. Three distinct rhythms alternate throughout the work: (1) biological functions such as seeing, excreting and especially breathing are isolated, presented simply as wondrous; (2) when the spirits of the dead pass into selected actors their bodies and voices are taxed into unrecognizable sounds and movements; (3) in segments representing the Amerikan way of death, the tone is conversational, logical—the audience is addressed as though at a lecture. The techniques for embalming and beautifying the corpse are explained in detail. In the conversational segments, the tone and the actions are familiar and so immediately meaningful. Only the situations are outrageous. Here is an affinity with the theatre of the absurd. In *Endgame*, for instance, Hamm and Clove have rational discussions after the end of civilization. In *Terminal*, applicants are welcomed, stripped, measured, photographed and given beds in a hospital where they have come voluntarily to put their death into someone else's hands.

An altered version of the original script remains in the repertory of the Open Theatre. Several interesting scenes have been cut, the most overtly political among them, presumably because they call for a larger cast than is now available. Yet, the smaller company has given the work an energy that makes its major accomplishment immediately and astoundingly available. At the moments when the dead come through, taking possession of an actor's body, the actor is transformed. He no longer presents activity to the audience, he has become the conductor through which activity

245

passes. His ability becomes necessary to the assembled company because he occupies the position midway between them and the unknown. The actor becomes a shaman. And the line between theatre and ritual actually dissolves. The Open Theatre has arrived at ritual through a theatrical conceit, not, as the prevalent examples go, by grafting ritualistic elements onto their performance. They have developed a reasoning urgent enough to elevate them to a more receptive psychic plane than their audience. They have set themselves apart and given themselves to the frenzy so that the audience can at least see it and hear it. Without the shaman, the mystery is only imagined. With him it becomes tangible. No wonder the shaman was always an indispensable member of the community:

> To be possessed is to make oneself available to the unknown. At the moments when the dead come through, everything is altered—ideas about life, attitudes toward death, rhythms, sounds, movements. The form of the piece itself must stretch to accommodate these unfamiliar energies.

What an amazing stage direction. It says to anyone wishing to present *Terminal* that at this moment magic must occur. Of course, the new sounds, rhythms, and movements were carefully developed by the Open Theatre company during many workshop sessions. But shamans have always been physically expert. Expertise is simply how one becomes available to the unknown.

Terminal is not about death, though its subject is dying. It is about life and that is at once its political strength and its metaphysical weakness. A play can never be about death because an actor can never escape using his body; yet that the body becomes suddenly incommunicative is the one fact of death we know for certain. When the dead come through they speak of this life and of the horrors committed here in the name of inevitability. A soldier "dead because I never knew what the fuck I was saying 'yes' to"; Marie Levau who saw "the killer become policeman/Now he can murder, that's his job." The piece moves toward the moment when the dying imagine their judgment. At that time they are told, "The judgment of your life is your life." As continuous

246

images of men tortured, oppressed, routinized appear before the judge, the verdict is thundered through a bull horn:

There is a space between what was done and what could have been done and you are rooted in that space.

What could have been done, or rather, the kind of intensity and perception with which life could have been lived has been approximated for us during those frenzied moments when the dead possess the actors, transforming them into shamans to give us knowledge of alternate ways of being in this world.

The Mutation Show was still being called a work-in-progress when done in New York in December 1971 and in March 1972, but is much more completely formed than the *Mutations* presented at Harvard the previous spring, and now its joyous connection of alternate life styles with other popularly recognized wonders of the world is apparent, affording such great pleasure from this work. It is, hopefully, a work for beginning the seventies, free from the violence that dominated the movement for much of the previous decade and which manifested itself in the pacifist Open Theatre through the sorrowful concerns of *The Serpent* and *Terminal*.

The Mutation Show is not a utopian work, nor is it idly idealistic. But it knows that something significant has happened to a generation (to several generations; Chaikin is over thirty, yet these perceptions would not seem alien to high school students) separating them forever from the desires of their parents. Brecht understood this about himself also:

The people of my class did not please me
Nor did giving orders and being served
And so I left my class and consorted
With lowly people.

Thus
They bred up a traitor, schooled him
In their arts and he
Betrayed them to the enemy.

At this moment the Open Theatre takes time to celebrate our mutation, which was, perhaps, the significant accomplishment of the sixties (war and racism persist).

247

One of the pleasures of this theatre has always been sensing the personalities of the actors, without knowing them off stage, and watching how they explore the different tasks they have chosen. Now with the smaller company this pleasure is that much greater; there are fewer (only six) people to watch and so you are able to learn more about each of them.

For *The Mutation Show* they have all chosen a sideshow—like deformity (the pun on "freaks" is intended): The Bird Lady (Jo Ann Schmidman), The Man Who Hits Himself (Raymond Barry), The Petrified Man (Paul Zimet), The Thinker (Tina Sheperd), The Man Who Smiles (Tom Lillard). The Barker is Shami Chaikin. The circus motif is new since the first open rehearsal and, like the cuts made in *Terminal*, it suddenly makes the piece cohere. The serious concerns of the segments (domination, liberation, perception) are worked into and out of—and therefore meshed with—the exuberance and skill of popular entertainment. The wedding, which is still the crucial scene, has been made funnier with the addition of a celebration symphony played by the actors on kazoos, a cigar-box fiddle and other uncertain instruments, and accompanied on an accordian by the musician (Ellen Maddow). Music has been integrated completely into the piece. There are only a few lines, most of them delivered as commentary by the musician or the Barker. (Though two writers have contributed, *Mutation* does not really exist as a script.) The actors, lacking the material to make narrative sense for the audience, find their performance instincts freed and the number of pratfalls, sight gags, and slapstick routines has increased accordingly.

In the early *Mutations* a steel box on castors, which looks something like a laundry cart, was used repeatedly as a place for an actor to come out of, to disappear, to be isolated from the others. Now this imagery has been condensed into a segment that provides the most highly serious part of the show. Paul Zimet has been born and raised in a box. "He never saw distance, light, the night sky or another person. One day he was torn from his box and carried to a hill where he was left," Shami Chaikin announces. Raymond Barry rips Paul from the box, puts him on his shoulders and starts to carry him down the road. This is very difficult but Ray does not shirk this burden. He just tries to get it to be as still as possible and not to interfere with his journey. But Paul

248

begins to distinguish objects alongside the road and he wants to get a closer look. He strains his eyes and his neck and finally his whole body leans. He keeps slipping off Ray's shoulders and Ray must spend an increasing amount of energy setting him up there again. The segment continues for awhile: Ray walking, Paul slipping, both struggling with the other. Then the actors separate.

Nothing *happens* in the way of a story (though this and many other segments have been inspired by stories of Kasper Hauser and other wild children). Paul's and Ray's journey is the visual complement to one of the judgments in *Terminal*:

Did you sit on another's head or were you sat upon?
Either way, you will never be free of the one who is above or he who is below.

The Animal Girl segment comes next. Shami chants: "We will namer her/We will straighten her bones/We will give her words/We will caress her ..." Two actresses play two girls raised by an animal pack. Two actors try to capture them. Jo Ann Schmidman is the object of a direct and violent hunt; she is brutally lassoed. Tina Sheperd, however, is wooed by her hunter and succumbs without a struggle. Yet her captivity is as degrading and as horrifying as Jo Ann's. And its accomplishment has been more interesting to watch. Though both actions are played together, the audience cannot help but focus on Tina's capture. Jo Ann's experience seems too obvious, almost melodramatic, dated. Here, simultaneous text is used to clarify the changing nature of our knowledge or our own oppression. Affluence and middle class comfort woo us all; yet Tina is only overcome by her captor after she becomes sensually excited by him.

The final two segments in *Mutation* are the company's attempt to get at the changes they personally have undergone. (Again, as with guilt in *The Serpent* and death in *Terminal*, they do not solve this problem. Alternately, I wish for such a breakthrough, something immediately applicable to take away from the performance; and yet I am alarmed at how this would decrease their stature, even make them complicit with commodity culture they must replace.) The six actors in their circus costumes come forward, each one carrying a poster-size photograph of herself as she was before.

There is Shami Chaikin's publicity shot from her club date days, poufed hair, a chiffon scarf floating from her neck in the manufactured breeze. Tom Lillard is in his army uniform; Tina Sheperd is a school girl with a tight page boy. The actors just stand there while Ellen Maddow reads facts about their life: the army, uncles who are Federal judges, step-sisters, cousins. Nothing alarming, but all of it quite incomprehensible in light of what has been produced, and very funny, especially because anyone in the audience could be standing there with them, holding his high school graduation picture, for instance. In a completely unprofound yet engagingly personal way it is again clear how indispensable these actors are to us, giving form as they do to our own imaginings.

In the final segment the mutants give testimony. Each one in turn sits on a stool and talks about what has happened to him. They communicate in nonsense syllables, short sentences, chordal sounds, spasmodic gestures. Their testimonies are mainly incoherent. But they exist—as confirmation both of our repression and of recent daring attempts through drugs, protests, sex, non-violence to come to ourselves again. Now the actors begin to repeat parts of each other's testimonies; by this activity *Mutation's* theme is reinforced: "I don't know if it happened to me or to somebody else, but I know that it happened."

THE BREAD AND PUPPET THEATRE

Yes, alienation is automatic with puppets. It's not that
our characters are less complete, they are just more
explicit. We want to work directly into and out of the
interior of people. A demonic thing.

                                              Peter Schumann

In the early sixties, when the Bread and Puppet Theatre's
huge puppets and sorrowing masks began appearing in peace
parades, it was apparent that they contained a finer knowledge of the heroic nature of the Vietnamese resistance than
was yet present in many of the marchers. The pale faces, the
gigantic hands in prayer, became emblems for a public morality struggling down Fifth Avenue, the midst of myopic Amerika, to be born. Where had this supraconsciousness come
from? What vision had transformed the Amerikan belief in
sheer size into a towering witness for humanity? The shock
of the puppets—it is always the shock of the Bread and
Puppet Theatre—was in the immediacy of their strangeness.
    A barker stands on Surf Avenue in Brooklyn. He is hus-
tling Bread and Puppets at Coney Island, the amusement park
where our rip-off society is most garishly manifest in the
stuffed animals and cheap china that replace the dreams of
the poor. Peter Schumann, a sculptor, choreographer and
creator of the Bread and Puppet Theatre, came to the US
from Germany in 1961. He had not grown up alienated by

the commercial manipulation of mass tastes. Medieval pageants, public festivals did not seem altogether unreal to him; he knew that what is popular can also be aesthetically excellent. Surrounded by television's stale emotions we think the popular taste is hopelessly corrupt. It is surprising to us to learn that it needn't be scoffed at so much, rather, the honest needs it springs from should be recognized. (Black theatre workers are also aware of the necessity of presenting the beauty in the current popular culture. But this is precisely what middle class radicals find most difficult to do.) No other people's theatre has so closely joined the popular with the artistic imagination. That this can be done offers hope for the future and great delight in the present.

This union of popular tastes with revolutionary perceptions is an important goal for all people's theatres. Schumann recognized it first and has pursued it most insistently; this is his gift to the movement. The Open Theatre's *Mutation Show*, for example, may have been directly influenced by the Bread and Puppets' carnival-like appearance. There are other similarities between these two theatres: their moral concerns, their wish to exteriorize subjective experience, their rejection of realism; though one has made the suppleness of the actor the center of its mystery while the other has located it in the clash of frozen attitudes.

The Bread and Puppet's theatre in the Coney Island section of Brooklyn is a loan from the owners of Nathan's, whose hot dog palace stands across the street. The outside is decorated like a side show: Jenny, the flying lady; the thin man; the fat lady have been painted on its wooden panels. Across the top of the second story a huge clown face and torso with outstretched arms stops passersby. Schumann is perched on a platform outside the second story window playing "When the Saints Come Marching In" on his fiddle. On the street below a performer dressed in tails announces through a megaphonee the performance of *The Bird Catcher in Hell*, a free puppet play, in just five minutes. He is supported by a young boy who keeps up a steady rhythm on a bass drum, a girl who bangs a gong and a fantastically costumed person from the play who does a slow Oriental dance on the street. It is Fourth of July weekend, 1971. The air is hot and rancid as only New York City can be. The

252

Bread and Puppet Theatre has left its home at Goddard College in Plainfield, Vermont, traveling the 400 or so odd miles in a red and pink flowered school bus to make their Independence Day stand at Coney Island. The audience they collect is perfectly random, of all ages and races. Some have come especially to see the theatre, but most have just wandered over on their way somewhere else.

To combat the wheezing organ music and the barker's challenges from the shooting booths across the street, Schumann uses his own scratchy fiddle and his own barker. Competing with the gaudy colors are the equally brilliant colors of the theatre. But in place of the capitalistic need to get people in, get their money and get them out that contributes to the flurry of the amusement park, Schumann offers the experience of uncluttered time. In the first place, he is asking for a substantial commitment from his audience: the performance will take nearly an hour. More pertinent, his productions replace the capitalist's credo that "time is money" with a sense that time is unlimited, because only by ignoring its passing, in favor of close scrutiny of the events it reveals, will we understand what there is to know. Repetition is crucial to this theatre. When an action is important or when the puppets strike an attitude that is especially correct, the audience may watch it two or three times. The laconic pace of productions is another way the dismissal of life through the capitalization of time is combatted.

The Bird Catcher is a free adaptation of a Japanese *kyogen*, or satiric intermission play performed classically between Noh dramas. In the prologue to Schumann's piece, three robed personages are growing something. The "something" is three rubber dolls without heads. Each doll is planted in a pile of sand. Then one of the robed actors puts a flower in each doll's neck hole, another waters the sand around each doll and a third hoes it. All the time they are making a subhuman humming sound. Are they bees? Anyway, they are as intense as they are unlikely. The choice of props and the order of activities seem completely off-the-wall, out of Schumann's imagination, or even constructed from the contents of a local garbage can. Their combined sense, however, is undeniably growth and nurture. A hell beast appears; each doll in turn is fried over a fire made of

253

waving strips of red cloth and then devoured by the beast.

Schumann's images are often untranslatable; through the very public form of puppet show he externalizes his own private perception of the world. In *Fire*, his piece to commemorate three Americans who immolated themselves in protest against the Vietnam War, a person inside a large Vietnamese woman puppet laboriously attaches long strips of red tape to her garment. She moves exactly opposite the speed of fire. But the tape sticks like napalm and the deliberateness of her actions makes visible the deliberate nature of the protestors' acts. Their private decisions were arrived at with the same agonizing care with which this masked figure now recreates their furious end.

The repetition of important actions achieves a tension that is wholly other than the rising action-climax-denouement syndrome of popular entertainment.

> As every athlete knows, repetition eventually brings about change: harnessed to an aim, driven by a will, repetition is creative,

writes Peter Brook of his own experiments.* So repetition and the resolute pace of Bread and Puppet productions bring about a change in the way the audience perceives the staged events. Their recurrence is what makes them urgent and important to comprehend, as though until this moment we had skipped applying ourselves to the crucial problem: What exactly is it like to nurture or to destroy life?

The deliberate intrusion of the creator into the creation—Schumann often enters the playing area to bring on a prop, shine a white light or to rearrange the puppets—is another way the slickness fetish of the entertainment industry is destroyed. Schumann, like Brecht, takes great delight in displaying how his theatre works. But his theatre is poor while Brecht's, in terms of stage machinery, is rich. The Berliner Ensemble needs the generous subsidy of a Communist state. Schumann's Bread and Puppet Theatre survives out of the scrap barrel of the affluent society. But this is poverty of a particularly splendid kind. Like Grotowski's it is a deliberate renunciation of goods, allowing for a wealth of invention. It is another example of Schumann's transformation of US reality before he presents it to an audience.

The Empty Space, New York, 1968, p. 138.

254

Schumann trusts his audience to look when there is something important to see and he doesn't mind losing their attention during a performance. He will get it back because at moments when the puppets coalesce around the giving or taking of life they are impossible to ignore. Clearly they have been constructed with these moments in mind, during which their fantastical expressions are most accurate.

The moments are always visual. Schumann's texts have the simplicity, though not the simple-mindedness, of a child's text book. They are usually announced by a narrator, thus freeing the people who operate the puppets from a concern with speaking. The texts' function is to connect the amazing actions on stage to our understanding of reality. They are directional signals into Schumann's imagination.

The Bird Catcher in Hell is an old story adapted to the contemporary situation. A bird catcher arrives in the afterworld where it is decided that he definitely deserves to go to hell. He asks to plead his case before the god of hell, a gigantic gorgon-like head that rises majestically on creaky pulleys above the red curtain. (Everything in the Bread and Puppet Theatre is allowed its own noises. The pulleys creak because it would be violate to oil them.) The bird catcher explains that he was no worse than many. He merely did the bidding of the rich and if he had not killed the small birds for them, someone else would have. A demonstration of his marksmanship and a taste of roasted bird convince the god that, though the bird catcher is fit neither for heaven nor hell, he is the perfect inhabitant of earth. Back on earth the bird catcher is dressed in military uniform and decorated by the rich men he serves. He parades before the audience carrying a sign that identifies him as Sergeant Calley. (The sign changes from performance to performance, after all there are any number of names to choose from.)

But this story, which is bitterly ironic, has less to do with the political force of the work than do certain of its images. Foot-tall people puppets represent the small birds whose bodies are fed to the rich men's hawks. The bird catcher shoots each one as it appears over the red curtain. They fall in a heap on the floor and are fried like the dolls were in the prologue. The god of hell wants to taste a bird and it is handed back to him through a hole in the red curtain. The

255

curtain, manipulated by its two holders, becomes the god's great, greasy mouth; it chops greedily at the bird. When the red curtain is raised, three human-sized, pink-jowled capitalists in top hats and tails are revealed to be literally behind the scenes. Capitalists in formal dress recur sarcastically in nearly every production. They are reminiscent of nothing so much as the angry cartoons that appeared weekly in the *New Masses*, and the truth of this image seems undiminished by the decades.

Costumes, though made of scraps of whatever material is available, are put together with an unerring eye for color and texture. *The Bird Catcher* is costumed completely in reds and oranges. The musicians wear long crimsen costumes and support large grotesque masks and banners decorated with Japanese motifs. Schumann instructs the children in the audience that "this is not a monster play, so don't get scared."

At a time when the movement is an uneasy conglomeration of factions and fads, Schumann's theatre is for everybody. He plays for Third World poor at Coney Island, for the white middle class in the Sheep Meadow in Central Park, for radicals in New York's peace churches, for mid-western college students at Kent State on the anniversary of the slayings there. When he first came to this country he fixed a stage onto a flat trailer behind a car and toured New England towns with a one-man puppet show.

The Bread and Puppet does theatre for children and often with them. The giant Uncle Fatso puppet was constructed with the help of neighborhood children in East Harlem during a workshop there in 1965. The next summer nearly three hundred children from the South Bronx and Central Harlem joined in slapstick shows, performances of "Chicken Little" and the construction of a block-long dragon and the 15-to-20-foot puppets. When they occupied the old courthouse building in Manhattan, the Bread and Puppet Theatre ran open workshops for children. In 1971-72 while Schumann was in residence at Goddard, his co-workers Barton Lane and Brigitte Desrues-Lane continued free weekly workshops at Coney Island and at a nearby hospital. The children made up their own stories and designed and built the puppets needed to act them out.

Schumann's concern with size is child-like; a small boy

who stands belt-high to a policeman has an actual understanding of the enormity of the adult's power. Herod in the 1970 Christmas play was perhaps fifteen feet tall and seemed taller. His huge hands were attached to poles and were moved by two puppeteers in full view of the audience. The people Herod ruled were represented by 8-inch puppets; their plight was implicit in their size.

The biggest puppets, those operated with poles by several people, are always the oppressors. The miniature puppets represent the people. It is from the middle range—actors wearing face masks or carrying heads that make them into figures eight or nine feet tall—that Schumann gets most of the characters for his plays. These middle-range puppets are seldom grotesques, but they are slightly larger than life and their actions seem more important than everyday activities. During the Johnson administration Uncle Fatso was the most accurate representation of the head of state. Nixon, however, has different proportions. In *The Bird Catcher* the title character is played by a smallish actor wearing a pug-nosed face mask. He introduces himself with the statement: "Let me make one thing perfectly clear." Then the narrator takes over his dialogue, leaving him free to gesticulate jerkily.

Schumann's sense of proportion is remarkable. No other people's theatre has used space as effectively or as joyously as the Bread and Puppet. When *The Bird Catcher* was performed at Coney Island the musicians were hidden behind a red curtain; their banners were visible swaying slightly above it. When the same production was done several days later in Central Park, the musicians were not around at all. Schumann had sent them behind the trees at the far end of the Sheep Meadow. There they began a slow stately procession toward the playing area. It took them at least fifteen minutes to reach the stage and by then the play was well in progress. They became visible first out of the corner of an eye: prehistoric beasts swaying across the field.

In the 1972 Easter play *The Fourteen Stations of the Cross*, Jesus is represented by a beatific young man with shoulder-length hair wearing a heavy patchwork dress and work shoes. When He is nailed to the cross, a simple airplane (used in other productions to bomb Vietnamese villages) is lowered from the ceiling and a towering stick figure draped in burlap is raised up and tied to the wings. The actor is thus

257

liberated from the emblem; he is free to perform physical tasks, at the same time that His outrageous suffering is constantly present before us.

Bread and Puppet summer workshops at Goddard College are open to everyone, and the company is made up of constantly changing numbers of people, most of them young. Just as the theatre fits any space and every audience, it has room for anyone who wants to join. The Bread and Puppet is at once the most egalitarian of people's theatres because it is open to everybody and the most elitist because its style has been wholly dependent on Peter Schumann's inspiration. Schumann has found a way to do theatre with untrained actors without sacrificing anything rich from the theatrical experience. A narration frees the actor/puppeteers from having to speak and serves to present the surface reality of the situation. Schumann "uses words, if at all, as caption, as sideshow, as noise or as mirrors of their self-contained idiocy," Jules Rabin writes,* and these are precisely the ways they are used most often in life. It is the puppets and masks that are other than reality, but they are not fantasy creatures. They are moments of inner experience made public and frozen in perfect formation. This is most evident in the gray lady masks that have come to symbolize the Vietnamese struggle: they are compounded of strength and sorrow until it becomes wonderful to look at them. This is why Stephen Brecht has called the Bread and Puppet a "sacral theatre"; they have seized subjective knowledge like a holy object and sculpted it for everyone to see.

For a person inside one of these puppets there is no sense of acting: the heads are ill-fitting, the robes clumsy, sight is limited. The experience is more religious than artistic. I, an average, nondescript person, give my body to this Vietnamese lady mask and robe. I use my energy to move her forward. She, then, becomes a personage worthy of notice. I disappear. It is my disappearance that makes the Vietnamese spirit visible.

There is only one important question for radicals: How can we change the society we live in? But there are many approaches to it. The Living Theatre needs to smash all barricades and so it incites its audience to join in revolution. The Open Theatre uses its ensemble to change the nature of

*Liberation, March 1966.

258

the theatre, expecting that its excellence at this will force the audience to understand the analogy. The Bread and Puppet Theatre extracts what is essential from what already is. Its puppets give witness to shared grace. They are outsized, unlikely, sometimes grotesque but never not human; we recognize them immediately as our own.

The Bread and Puppet Theatre is sometimes criticized by people on the Left because they represent the oppressed as too passive. The Vietnamese, for instance, are never shown with guns fighting back. Yet Schumann's intention is to represent poetically the quality of their resistance—to make them different in size, color, pace and *activity* from their enemy. When his plays are good their visual force leaves no doubt as to the political hippness of the resistance. When they are bad the criticism is understandable.

Sometimes the theatre is funny (they can do slapstick—they cannot, because of the puppets, come close to either high comedy or anything raunchy). It is as often sad. Its thematic freedom has been arrested by the fact of the Vietnam War. The war exists as an atrocity that must be mobilized against and also as a symbol of the recurrent struggle of humanity, of the weak against the powerful, the meek against the loud, of the people against their oppressors. This, for Schumann, is the struggle of good against evil which animates all his productions. The struggle gives rise to the most basic of religious questions: What is the relationship between good and evil? Why does the will to live (profoundly present in Satan's rebellion) often become an act of destruction? This question guides Schumann's major work, *The Cry of the People for Meat**, where meat is at once necessary food and wanton slaughter. It is implicit also in *Fire*, a eulogy for Norman Morrison, Roger LaPorte and Alice Herz. In *Fire*, a self-destructive act and a love for humanity are one, and the imperfection of a world that makes this conjunction possible is apparent.

By asking why it is that some people are good while others are bad, the Bread and Puppet tries to learn how bad people can be changed into good ones. There is nothing simple-minded about these categories. The definition of goodness,

*See Stephen Brecht's excellent analysis of this production: "Peter Schumann's Bread & Puppet Theatre," *The Drama Review*, vol. 14, no. 3, 1970, pp. 44-89.

for example, is clear in the work of the theatre: a revolutionary pacifist stance, a rejection of money, success and competition, an identification with the poor and oppressed and a need to bear witness to their suffering. The Oriental, gray lady mask has become the signature of the theatre. Politically it identifies them with the Third World. Dramatically, its simple and sorrowing lines contrast with the horrific possibilities of the big puppets and the sitting duck quality of the little ones. The mask, like the theatre that created it, represents a new kind of active religious consciousness. The Bread and Puppet Theatre hands out homemade rye bread when it can, plays for free or asks small contributions, goes to the ghettos, colleges and middle class churches because it wants to talk to everyone, and smuggles Daniel Berrigan inside an apostle puppet away from FBI agents, at that moment creating the fugitive priest as actor and the theatre as an actual participant in the revolution.

Peter Schumann

PROBLEMS CONCERNING PUPPETRY AND FOLKMUSIC AND FOLKART IN THE LIGHT OF GOD AND McNAMARA*

Puppet theater is theater of tiny dolls, theater of huge masks which a dancer operates from inside, theater of men on sticks or men hanging from strings. It ranges from half minute nightclub acts and five minute sidewalk shows to the 365 nights that it takes to perform the "Legend of Roland" in Sicily. It seems to have been everything from funmaking, slap-stick, social criticism to the terrible reenactment of a hari-kari on Japan's Bunraku stage. Masks are older than actors, faces of wood and stone are older than mimes. Masked dancers and the effigies they carry are certainly at the origin of theater.

The communion of all, the shape of that communion of all, that which was theater, is no more. Theater is in the present an outlet of spirit, or a check-point of soul of modern society, or, as understood in the USA: show business. In this modern theater puppetry is nothing but an unimportant branch, a low-ranking form of entertainment, which seems to have a comeback right now because some smart people found out how well that little stuff fits the little television screen.

What is left of the great old forms of puppet theater, besides obscure Indian or Persian marionettes and shadow puppets, which very few of us will be lucky enough to see, is the great Bunraku theater of Japan

*Received from Elka Schumann.

260

and the Sicilian puppet theater of medieval legends. Both forms are dying out.

I figure the same can be said of the more familiar Western world Punch-, Kasper-, Guignol-, Petrushka-, Pulcinello- theaters. They still happen to be alive some place, they are sometimes brought back to life with artificial respiration, but their social conditions are no more; you need too many licenses and you are not allowed to play for money in the street, etc., etc. Throwing a baby out of the window is fun, as Punch does even in the days of Batman, but the distinct social and political criticism that went along with many of these wild shows needs a different street, a different audience and different cops than what we have here.

In 1963 I went to a festival celebrating over 300 American and foreign puppeteers. Thanks to this meeting I became acquainted with the Sicilian puppet theater. Everything else was nice or not nice, sweet or not sweet and by all means little, not so much in size as in content and intent. Everything was plush and latex and Walt-Disney-y and basically about funny-and bunny-rabbits. Maybe I should call that the modest approach of this profession and not complain about it, and I should be glad that there were no Hamlet and Faust productions by foam-rubber specialists. But the Kasper of my childhood had been such a beautifully tough, down-to-earth, real and manly little man that I could not help looking for his like, whatever the shape of that likeness might be. From talking to puppeteers then and later on and from articles in the NY Times and other knowledgeable papers I got the impression that in the eyes of the concerned puppetry is on the move, is opening up, is coming back because of foam rubber, because of professional lighting systems, because of television, etc. The saying goes, that when you do in puppet theater what they do in "solid" theater, then you are on the right track: get a switchboard and dimmers, go three years to the Federal Lighting and Lightening School, get a union garbage collector, a cleaning woman, a director, a playwright, a photographer, a bull-fighter for the bullfighting scene, etc. And then by harmonizing all these variants it somehow clicks, you get the magic and the audience claps hands when you want it to.

In Bunraku you have to study for years to be allowed to move a hand. In a Kasper show you play twelve voices, seven puppets, thunder, daylight, devil and dragon all at the same time. Liszt locked himself up with his piano for more than ten years. Pan plays the flute without Conservatorium. Both those holy ghosts: the ghost of Pan and the ghost of the intensely concentrating hermit are altogether missing in modern puppetry, as well as in modern theater.

I don't want to lament about that but I want to ask: how are gods brought back to life? The fact is, they are dead, nobody brings them back to life; our life, the life that we lead, buries them.

Safford Cape, the Belgian builder of beautiful, authentic medieval

261

musical instruments plays beautiful, authentic medieval music on the concert stage. Shakespeare is reproduced in Shakespeare-style, Sophocles in Sophocles-style and so on. But the life of people and the language and art which their life brings forth has nothing to do with style. The historian, the thinker and the reflective mind invent style, not the producer. The artist is caught in the current of events and thoughts of his time. If he is concerned with the issues that need his sensitivity and concern, he is necessarily unconscious of style. Sophocles had no choice of style; the decisions that Antigone and Kreon had to make forced a style upon him. Early medieval music had harsh and pure tone and rhythm, was fierce, not cautious, you can hear rust and cracks in the instruments, and babies crying and men shouting in the background. I don't want to hear such music in Lincoln Center, and any garbage can drum solo by any kid in New York is more medieval music to my ears.

I have heard lovely fiddling for dancing in the barn in Nova Scotia last summer. Thank God there are some remnants. Professionalism and its pride, the many spirits and dwarfs that take care of our tiny talents, the salesmen of all those talents, the importance of every little bit of production, all this ridiculous self-concern makes for the kind of show business that we have inherited. I mean that kind that doesn't make any sense. It doesn't make sense because it doesn't even want to make sense. It wants to make something, it's hard to describe what, something tremendously smooth and balanced and fitting the occasion and fitting the enlightened stage or just the upholstered seat. There are puppet plays with 150 solved technical problems but no spirit, and folk singers with a vast repertory of anti-war, pro-grass, anti-washingmachine, pro-river songs and there is just a few times in your life a man singing a truthful song of his own, a song that you might need. And many such potentially good singers are brainwashed by the State Department of Folk-Singing. They start singing outwardly instead of inwardly. All good folk music, like Beethoven or the Nova Scotia barn fiddlers make a lot of mistakes and can afford them and don't care much for mistakes, because 1) God is more important, and 2) if you get the big red color of the thing that you want, the holy spirit, you need not care so much for the finesse.

I think a good man is both a man who is able to be good in detail and a man who wants to learn at least to fly, or to solve all the problems of the world, or to beat death finally, or to arrange for the second coming. Michelangelo or Rembrandt or all the ever unknown Bavarian, Russian, Mexican painters of the world have been truthfully trying out if our human pains make sense, if we are allowed to happily die, or if we are condemned to unhappily struggle against the fate of all dying and suffering. They have not mixed their colors for the sake of the salesmen, the historians and museums that possess them now.

Still, I was always under the impression that puppeteers and circus people are closest to God and mankind because they don't deal with false gold, because they carry their gifts in their hands, they make fun, they point out some things and not much more, and I think that God likes that attitude better than the ordinarily pretty messed up human ambitions, the complicated ways of heartbreaking compositions, or the withholding and condensing intellect.

But that kind of holy simpleton and ruffian puppetry is dying out and is not likely to come back, as I have pointed out. At the present it is obviously replaced by the Union of the Professional Puppet and Gag Institutes and these institutes have money behind them and the simpletons don't have money behind them and so they are going to lose. On the big commercial and Life-magazine surface the simpletons will lose. For the recording of time and for the coming revolution the simpletons are the avant-garde. And this is my prophecy: new simpletons are going to grow up all over the world; puppeteers with more puppets than tears and puppeteers with more tears than puppets;—folksingers who don't necessarily have voices or guitars but maybe just clap-hands or some kind of rattles;—painters who don't care so much how their pictures look on the wall;—and theater directors who give up Broadway and Off-Broadway and Off-Off-Broadway and train cows to balance baseballs on their tails. Nowadays, they find that out in every business, among the shoemakers as well as among the Presbyterian churches: we have neglected the stuff that life is made of so long and the whole cart is on the wrong track so much, that we simply have to get out and start walking.

The masses of audiences are moved in various directions. Certainly in this country the masses of audiences are moved in the directions of the mass media. The mass media are commercial. Their commercialism means that under the cover of free expression of the participating forces gold is being made, and ways of how to make more gold are being explored. Mr. Folksinger and Mrs. Puppeteer hardly realize that with the help of their harmless contribution of good throat and skillful fingers, marines are being sent around the world and lipstick is being sold to grandmothers who need exactly the opposite of lipstick. The masses of the audiences, the Pop, the success, are in the moment, for example, very useful to Mr. McNamara and his H-bombs. The biggest schmalziest chamber-and-kitchen-orchestra and-chamber-and-kitchen-orchestra audience is thoroughly taken care of. You can see the most wonderful things in the world on a screen about as big as a behind and you don't even have to pay taxes for it.

The world may not win this time. McNamara or Wall Street or somebody like that may win this time, but that destiny is being weighed on the scales of justice high above the clouds on some unknown star where Greek gods hold residence. If the world loses, then there is little sense to talk about puppetry. But assuming that the good old world succeeds against McNamara and his like, then the simpletons

263

and demons of puppetry are also going to win in their hidden fight against show business. The Stomachache Movement will fight The Big Hunger of the World and The Big Pain of the World; the Heartbeat Movement will set out with lots of music and puppets to beat hearts and to move heartbeats, and we will all be able to work together, puppeteers, folksingers, poets, painters, housewives, everybody, because we are all tired, oh tired of books, like Jack, and long for meadows green and woods where shadowy violets nod their cool leaves between, and we are tired of show and show-off business and we long for better soap and better operas, and we are tired of appetizers and surplus food and we long for nectar and ambrosia, and we are tired of spray guns and machine guns, we want fiddle bows and love instead.

Such is the sitaution of puppetry today. Thank you.

BREAD AND PUPPET THEATRE*

MISSISSIPPI**

puppets: *mother* grey lady puppet who weeps crystal tears

son
teacher (in top hat)
students
½ people
other ½ people

are all played by Crucifixion/Last Supper puppets, 6-8 ft. tall, no arms, ochre burlap bodies, yellow or brown faces.

soldier: grey, spiked soldier puppet with built-in gun
president: Uncle Fatso
man I: Crucifixion puppet
man II: Crucifixion puppet

props: chair and table for mother
chair for son
chair for Uncle Fatso
six chairs for students
one chair for teacher
signs, held up one after another by sign man

sound: a two-tone flute call for beginning of every scene except 4, 5, and 6.

---

*In this and the following play, Peter Schumann's text is indicated in italics. The non-italicized descriptions were written by Elka Schumann as a record of the performances.

**First played at Coney Island, June 1970.

264

bell for doorbell

text is spoken over mike in a wierd, drawn-out, incomprehensible way, accompanied by washing-machine agitator
trumpet, creating muffled, hollow unintelligible sounds,
while dialogue signs are held up.

metal click for gun

toy piano for end: O Mary don't you weep don't you
mourn . . . .

(text from newspaper, undated: a barrage of police gunfire left two
dead and several wounded yesterday. All the casualties were black.
The highway patrol refused to comment. The university was closed.
James Gibbs, age 17, worked six hours a day to help support his
widowed mother and three brothers and sisters. Philip Green was
married and had a son who was nine months old the following week.)

I) *flute call*
doorbell

mother:	*come in*
son:	*good evening, mother*
mother:	*good evening, son*
son:	*here are $5*
mother:	*thank you*
son:	*. . .*
mother:	*the rent is not paid*
son:	*I will go again*
mother:	*thank you*
son:	*good by, mother*
mother:	*good by, son*

II) *flute call*
doorbell

mother:	*come in*
son:	*good evening, mother*
mother:	*good evening, son*
son:	*here are $5 more*
mother:	*thank you*
son:	*. . .*
mother:	*the light is not paid*
son:	*I will go again*
mother:	*thank you*
son:	*good by, mother*
mother:	*good by, son*

III) *flute call*
teacher and students file in and sit down

teacher:	*what did you learn?*

265

son:	*I studied hard, I am tired.*
teacher:	*try again*
son:	*yes.*
teacher:	*good*

IV) *president:*   *we have enemies far away. they are bad. we will go into their country and shoot them*

       ½ people: *yes*

       ½ people: *no*

V) *soldier trembling*

       soldier: *the president says we have enemies far away; they are bad; we will go into their country and shoot them*

       students: *no*

       soldier: *be quiet*

       students: *no*

soldier shoots. one student falls

VI) *enter soldier*
      enter son
      son turns to go
      soldier shoots; son falls

VII) *flute call*
      doorbell

      mother: *come in*

enter two men carrying son (empty son puppet)

      man I: *he is dead*

      man II: *he is dead*

      mother: *he is dead?*

      men: *yes*

men exit
mother cries. crystal tear slowly rolls down her face

      toy piano: *O Mary don't you weep, don't you mourn.*

Bread and Puppet Theatre

THE DEAD MAN RISES*

Puppets: *The Woman*
           The River
           The Night
           The Morning

---

*Plainfield, Vermont, March 1971.

The Dead Man
(The puppets are all over life-size, white masks and long
black robes, except the Woman, who is all in white.)

An Attendant in a black shirt and hood

Props: Bridge (a large wooden block or foot-stool)
             One pair white women's shoes
             Length of cloth or cord
             Pillow
             Piece of dark fabric
             Silver leaves

Backdrop: Three screens showing greyish landscapes, mounted in
             cinderblocks

Instruments: Bell
             Soft horn (length of common garden hose) (violin,
             cello, rattle, ocarina also used)

Other Equipment: Ladder
                      Three Flashlights
                      Microphone
                      Amplifier
                      Speaker
                      Floodlight
                      Dimmer

Darkness. Then a small, dim floodlight gradually illuminates the
playing area which is established by three grey-toned paintings on
fabric, hung separately from standing poles at right, left and center
stage upstage; and by a large circle on the floor, outlined by green
branches or sea shells. The Attendant, in black hood and shirt, kneels
at SR.

A tall puppet figure all in white, the Woman, appears from behind a
screen, pauses, then slowly starts to circle the playing area. As she
reaches the center downstage, a whispered, amplified voice is heard:

WHERE ARE YOU GOING? (Bell)
I AM GOING TO THE RIVER. (Bell)
WHY ARE YOU GOING? (Bell)
THE RIVER IS COLD. (Bell)
WHERE IS THE RIVER? (Bell)
THE RIVER IS FAR AWAY.

Breathing sound is heard while Woman completes circle. (Bell)
Silence. Then whispered voice:

HERE IS THE BRIDGE. (Bell)

Attendant steps into the circle and places bridge at the feet of the
Woman, then returns to original place. (Bell) River puppet enters and
stands center stage.

267

THIS IS THE RIVER.
ARE YOU THIRSTY?
YES. (Bell)

The Woman kneels and drinks.

THE WATER IS COLD. (Bell)

The Woman stands up.

I WANT TO TAKE MY SHOES OFF AND WADE IN THE RIVER.

The Attendant steps in, removes the Woman's shoes and places them downstage center; then he returns to his original position.

The Woman steps behind the River and the two puppets circle the stage together in a gentle, gliding motion. Two handheld flashlights illuminate their faces, following them as they move very slowly. Soft horn wail sounds with this movement. (Bell) They turn. (Bell) The Dead Man puppet enters and lies down. Flashlight shines on his face. He is blindfolded (masking tape over his eyes). (Bell) Then the whispered voice:

THERE IS A DEAD MAN LYING IN THE RIVER.
WHAT WILL YOU DO WITH THE DEAD MAN?
I WILL TIE THE DEAD MAN TO THE BACK OF THE RIVER AND TAKE HIM TO MY HOUSE. (Soft horn)

With the help of the Attendant, the Woman raises the Dead Man and places him behind the River puppet, supporting him with her body and clasping the River. The Attendant ties the three figures together with a cord or strip of cloth, and returns to original position. The three figures circle the stage together. (Soft horn throughout this movement; then bell) Whisper:

HERE IS THE BRIDGE.

The Attendant brings in the bridge, puts it down, unties the puppets, and returns to original position with the cord. The River exits. Whisper:

FROM HERE I HAVE TO CARRY THE DEAD MAN TO MY HOUSE.

The Woman carries the Dead Man on her back, circling the stage. (Bell; heavy breathing; bell) Whisper:

DID YOU GO TO THE RIVER?
YES.
WAS THE WATER COLD?
YES. (Bell)
DEAD MAN, I WILL PUT YOU INTO MY BED.

The Woman puts the Dead Man down on the floor. The Attendant enters and places a pillow under his head. The Dead Man lies on his side, facing the audience. (Bell)

The Night puppet enters and stands behind and at the head of the Dead Man. Whisper:

THIS IS THE NIGHT.

The Night covers the Dead Man and the Woman with a dark cloth, then exits. (Bell) There is almost no light on the stage. A flashlight shines on the two puppets. The Morning puppet, which entered during the darkness, rises behind them. Whisper:

THIS IS THE MORNING. (Bell) Full floodlight on.
DEAD MAN, I WILL OPEN YOUR EYES. (Bell)

The Attendant removes the blindfold, takes the pillow, and returns to original position. The Dead Man and the Woman rise. (Bell rings often) Now they dance, face to face, arms outstretched, rocking and circling the stage, and the bell continues to ring. When they reach the back curtain area, silvery leaves flutter down on them from over the top of the back screen. They exit. The River enters and walks slowly to downstage center. A flashlight shines on his face. He kneels before the Woman's shoes. The Attendant enters, ties the shoes on the back of the River, and returns to original position. The River rises, turns and exits slowly. A flashlight shines on the shoes. (Soft horn throughout) Whisper:

THE RIVER FINDS THE LADY'S SHOES AND CARRIES THEM ON HIS BACK. (Softhorn)

The flashlight shines on the backdrop, then goes out.
The End.

THE RADICAL PLAYWRIGHT

... in the East the work of art is evaluated according to
its practical function. The formal experiment, the interi-
or monologue, the poetic image are held to be sterile if
they are not useful in the work of changing society.

To us, who have grown up with a belief in absolute
freedom of expression, this seems to restrict our projects—so long as we esteem the intrinsic value art more
highly than its purpose. But if we find the goal, we can
then struggle to achieve the most audacious forms, for
we know that to a revolution in the social order belongs
a revolutionary art.

Peter Weiss

The radical or would-be radical playwright's position is
becoming increasingly precarious. Temptation to compromise
with the demands of the commercial theatre increases according to the quality of his work: If ensembles will not present
plays they have not evolved, where else but in a commercial
situation can an adequate production be assured? More
crucial: lacking a reciprocal relationship with like-minded
actors, it is almost impossible to work free of realistic concepts of character and of linear plot. The solitary playwright's invention is therefore limited and the kind of dialectical richness simultaneous texts provide is missing from
almost all the political plays of writers who work in
Amerika's fragmented theatre.

Jack Gelber's *The Cuban Thing* and Daniel Berrigan's *The*

270

Trial of the Catonsville Nine are exceptions to the general rule (there are others, no doubt). In entirely different ways (and with totally different degrees of commercial success) both writers allowed radical perceptions to give new dimension to the traditional domestic and documentary modes. If the individual playwright proves himself less innovative than the theatre collective there are still no other recent works that explore so well the family within a revolutionary situation or the current necessity for civil disobedience.

Ideally, ensembles should seek such playwrights out and writers should be able to come to their creative identity within a communal situation, as Megan Terry, Jean Claude van Itallie, and Suzan Yankowitz have been able to do at various times with the Open Theatre. The solution—which is a substantial number of healthy ensembles and the destruction of the commercial theatre—is easily imaginable. Like the solution to every organizational problem of our culture, it is very far from achievable under the current capitalistic system. In the meantime we have to hope for the perseverance and integrity of our writers amidst the amazing pressure of critical/financial success/failure that attends each of their moves. And we continue to suffer through productions that lack the poetry and clarity of an inquiring intelligence while we continue to lose the people who might provide these elements to pursuits other than the theatre or to theatres which are not radical.

THE CUBAN THING

It was a tribute to American freedom that a pro-Castro play should be produced in New York.

Clive Barnes

Jack Gelber's fourth play opened at Henry Miller's Theatre in New York on September 24, 1968. A phalanx of city policemen surrounded the theatre "protecting" first nighters from about one hundred anti-Castro Cuban exiles protesting the play's presentation. Inside, along with Barnes, Edwin Neuman and the other men who pass public judgment on Broadway productions, were the more militant protesters who with catcalls, jeers, and stink bombs meant to stop the play. It was closed the following morning by producer Ivor

271

David Balding, partly in response to unanimous critical pans—the critics seemed offended that Gelber had equated sexuality and the Cuban revolution, instead of using sex for titilation or laughs—partly because the demonstrators promised to return each performance and police told Balding and Gelber that future audiences might not be safe because they could not be expected "to do this every night." It has not been produced again.

The Cuban Thing is Gelber's most politically radical play. It strikes me, along with *The Connection*, as his best work. Because it deals with what happens to people after a revolution, it occupies an essential position in the continuum of people's theatre. It is his favorite play, too: the artistic issue of a lasting commitment to revolutionary Cuba. The number of favorite plays that have been commercial failures is probably alarmingly high. Authors tend to make these their most uncompromising statements and then they are always the hardest to produce well. Gelber directed *The Cuban Thing* himself (he is a talented director) but he never found an entire cast that shared his knowledge of the monumental nature of the events in Cuba. Probably he wasn't looking for one, being more concerned with each person's ability to act, as if that could be separate in this play from his sympathy with Cuba. The thought of going on Broadway (which was a fatal mistake, for who could take seriously a radical play produced there?) created a production too lavish for this work, which is neither slick nor empty-headed.

It is difficult to imagine a successful production of *The Cuban Thing* without an interplay between documentary film and domestic realism, but the film sequences used in New York were never adequately related to the activities on the stage (they were edited from Lee Lockwood's footage by a commercial ad agency and seemed to Gelber not intimate enough, which is his general criticism of the entire production). He needed a comprehensible juxtaposition of filmed and staged events because that would put into perspective the impact of revolutionary reality on individual imaginations that determines the play's structure, a structure sympathetic to Gelber's own relationship as playwright to the events in Cuba, and one which corresponds to the measure against which the Cuban revolution will finally have to stand: Has the condition of socialism created a new man?

272

The documentary film sequence before each scene describes to the audience the historical situation against which it is played. The political world (that world most alien to domestic realism) enters the play itself through the televised trial of Sosa Blanco that the characters watch in Act II, but mainly, it enters through their dreams and their imitations of political figures, both of which allow them to transcend family roles in order to work out their own relationship to the revolution. The act of imitating is not new to these characters and neither is the place (the living room). But the words they imitate after the revolution no longer reflect the logic of domination unchallenged. Imitation which is an ungenerative assertion of equality gives way to creation at the moment that the colonized man becomes the subject of his own perceptions.

The imaginative center of the play is Act II, scene two. Roberto (the father) had given money to the revolutionary forces, but since their victory he has been dislocated. His business is gone and in spite of his eagerness to work the government has not yet assigned him a job. The ex-prostitutes who have been moved into his house also have ambivalent reactions to the revolution. Fidel is at once their savior and the cause of their distress:

This is no life for me. I don't even want to be rehabilitated. Cleaning away like a grandmother. If Fidel could see me. If Fidel would come this bad dream would end.

Roberto comes home after an aimless day. Cuqui begins to dress him as Fidel and tries to excite him sexually. Roberto accepts the disguise; his wig company began to manufacture the Fidel beards shortly after the victorious revolution. Roberto is good at imitations and his position at the moment, as a jobless, impotent middle-aged man, indicates the revolution deserves to be mocked. So he tosses revolutionary phrases about, but while doing so he discovers a use for them: they stall the girls and keep them from noticing that he does not have an erection. As the slogans become useful they also become interesting. Roberto drops his mocking manner and begins to revel in their luscious sounds:

Behind locked doors, in repugnant bargainings, Yankee

imperialists devote days to crushing us. Years of planning to murder us.

The moment he allows himself to be drawn just this far into the revolution he gets an erection. He stops the girls from undressing him; he removes the disguise himself. He begins to recite one of Fidel's actual speeches. But this is no longer an imitation. For the first time the revolutionary rhetoric defines his own sense of well being within the world:

> The transition from one life is very difficult . . . great humanity has cried "Enough!" That revolution is possible. That revolution is inevitable. Patria o muerte. Venceremos.

What do these glorious words mean in Roberto's mouth? That he is ready to lay one, maybe two, of the girls if his luck holds before his wife comes home. But also that he is a man again. He has made his peace with the revolution (the ease with which personal/sexual, public/revolutionary puns are made is indicative of their real connection). Roberto is changed the moment that his impotency contacts the force of the revolution. The change is both lasting and immediate.

The long and complicated scene that precedes this one includes a personal withdrawal which is accomplished in much the same way as Roberto's revitalization. Paco, who had fought with Fidel, has heard that his friend, Carlos, is in a camp for homosexuals. The trial of the ex-chief of police, Sosa Blanco, has just been televised and Paco begins to imitate Blanco's defense. Halfway through the speech the outrageousness of Blanco's excuses collides with and reinforces Paco's own fear that revolutionary justice is becoming absurd, everyone is turning everyone else in. The revolution is demanding more and more energy and he has no more to give. He decides to leave Cuba.

Both these scenes assert the potency with which revolutionary reality intrudes into private lives and reshapes them. Roberto's daughter's nervous breakdown is caused precisely because she won't allow this natural intrusion to happen. Her dreams of revolutionary glory keep her apart from the struggles of revolutionary reality. She is caught in a bourgeois dilemma where the reality does not equal the intensity of her

274

desires. But this split, which keeps Alicia from being changed by the revolution, can no longer be maintained, and she breaks down.

The family that begins *The Cuban Thing* watching dirty movies together, has by its end expanded to include the prostitutes who were once its source of titilation and the servant who was once its mark of privilege. The boundaries of domestic realism have also been upset, though again the form itself has not been replaced. Neither of these occurrences adequately visualizes the effect of the revolution on the Cuban people. But they both recognize that the revolution's real power to change lives is proportionate to how deeply it penetrates the living room, making its goals inseparable from the domestic tasks necessary to sustain life. Sex, eating, housework are the ones that recur here. Maybe they seem prosaic in light of the massive educational and agricultural battles going on off stage. Yet the way they are performed by each character at each point is an accurate indication of where his head is at in regard to the revolution, which is another way of saying where the revolution is at in terms of a new world.

INTERVIEW WITH JACK GELBER

KT: It's hard to separate your play from what happened to it; it caused the most hostile political reaction of any play I can remember.

JG: I still have nightmares about it and you must realize that even though I believed in it and believed in it a lot, it is not a play that is done. I don't know what would happen if it were done again.

KT: Had any Cuban exiles read the play?

JG: Some came to read for parts and one or two I seriously considered. And I told them it was a pro-Fidel play and if they wanted to read, fine. Some of them said, "I'm an actor first and a Cuban second," which is a terrific actor's remark. And some said "no." And then this dyed-blond lady of about 220 cherubic pounds who has a talk show on channel 47 in New Jersey began to lead an anti-Jack Gelber drive. I don't know how she got the play or why she reacted the way she did. Why, for example, wasn't Saul Landau's film, *Fidel*, ever attacked or bombed or its life threatened?*

KT: Why did you first go to Cuba?

JG: In 1957 my wife and I had just enough money to take a trip

---

*In the summer of 1971 the New York movie theatre where *Fidel* was being shown was bombed. The film was withdrawn immediately, but it is still available to be seen.

somewhere. We got a ride to Miami from a fellow I worked with at the UN where I was a mimeograph operator. Then we went to Key West where we could get a cheap night flight to Havana. And all the way we said, "We're not going to be hustled; we're not going to be hustled." And what happened—the first thing we got hustled. We stayed in a hotel in old Havana and we walked up five flights of stairs and we thought, "Oh my God. We're being pushed around and we're in this horrible place and we don't know the language and all these guys have little mustaches—it's awful." And then we opened the window and saw the city. I thought it was terrific. The cock started crowing. The sidewalks looked wavy with mosaics and I thought it was great. We stayed six or seven days. I knew Fidel was in the hills and the revolution was going on, but I didn't know what that meant. In the street I had to start speaking German, which was really more Yiddish, to protect us against the terrible onslaught of the walking dollar bill. And people were very kind then. I suppose if I had been rich I would have done what the rich kids did—gone to the nightclubs and the houses of prostitution. But that was repulsive to me and later on I was so sympathetic to the Cubans when they thought of themselves as a floating whore house. We took a bus across the island to Santiago so we could get a cheap flight to Haiti, where I wrote *The Connection*. Fidel had promised to attack Santiago on the day of the festival and the essential flavor was a town taken over by the Cuban army and marines. There were six correspondents staying in the swankiest hotel in town, Jack Gelber and his wife, a kid from Staten Island who turns up in my play who was a real killer (he had missed the Korean War and had come to kill). The day we left a very terrible thing happened that I didn't find out about until we got to Port-au-Prince. Thirty students, including the urban guerilla "David," who was the chief connection for all information, were rounded up and shot.

KT: Did you decide then to write a play about Cuba?

JG: No. The second time I went to Cuba was after the missle crisis. I went as a journalist for the *Saturday Evening Post.* I spent a month here and found it an extremely vital place to be. I went everywhere. Talked to everyone and they told me everything I wanted to know, much more than I wanted to know because I usually didn't want to know anything. But the article I tried to write was very dull and when I got home I found the things I read about Cuba were unsatisfactory and my response was unsatisfactory and I decided to write a play. I had many false starts. Then I wrote the scene where Roberto [the father] pretends to be Fidel and it came like a piece of poetry. I felt I had to go back to Cuba to verify my feelings and I asked to serve on a jury to give away a prize for Latin American drama. And I decided that I wasn't going to write a play about Cuba. That Cuba was a state of my mind and not a play. And I gave up. I suppose that freed my imagination to work because the whole thing came very quickly. Before I wrote the play I had an idea of doing a Cuban Action Night with dancing and slides and movies and have a play going on that would eventually take over the entire building. I went all over and couldn't find any foundation to support the idea and I'm sure it was for political reasons. The funny thing is that opening night of *The Cuban Thing*, with police cordoning off the street and crowds shouting, was very close to my vision of this action night.

KT: How high on your list of priorities was historical accuracy?

JG: It was right below poetic truth. Without the conceptual condensation of ideas into images nothing could have happened. Certainly I wanted all the facts to be correct in so far as I could use them. I jumped the persecution of homosexuals up a few years because I wanted to end the play in 1964 when the situation was in a way less exciting and more solidified. I wanted the facts to transcend their mere factness. There is a part of the play in which I have the servant know all the facts about Cuba. He tells the supposed reporter from the *New York Times* much more than anyone else does about Cuba. What does he tell his boss? Gossip. That's all they want to hear. They don't want to know that 75 percent of the electric company is owned by US investors.

KT: Why did you decide to use imitations as a way of bringing the events of the revolution into the living room?

JG: Imitation is the colonized people's point of view. There's hardly a Cuban party that you will go to where people do not imitate their friends or their enemies for you. They enjoy it and do it in a big way. They are terrific at it. And I thought this was an essential part of the personality that they wanted to escape. Early in the play when Roberto imitates Batista he says, "We are monkeys, we ape ideas of beauty, we have a language that is not our own."

KT: There are certain issues that radical plays must deal with. For instance, how do you overcome your middle class privilege, or, conversely, how does the working class take on part of that privilege to become a new man?

JG: That is part of this play, certainly. How does Chan the former servant take over his responsibility? He has a breakdown in front of everybody.

KT: And it is curious that his breakdown motivates Barbara's [the mother's] radical transvaluation of values.

JG: Is that true? The first breakdown is Paco's. He feels everyone is turning everyone in. His sexuality is tied up completely with this paranoia. He is worried about his own being, which is his sexual being. They calm him down and Chan has heard all this noise and he comes in and he tells them in a very calm way that he is trying to keep the house together. And everybody starts to bait him. He has a very humble attitude. The mother doesn't want him around because she feels the government should have put her in charge of the house. She is completely tripping out about this guy. Roberto is trying to calm everybody down. He has had his balls chopped off by the revolution and by his wife. He is doing the housework, which is something no Cuban man would ever do. And then Barbara talks about her dream.

KT: Yes, and the dream is partly sexual—she dreamt she was a man— but she also realizes she does not need a fur coat because her arms were covered with fur. The dream represents her turning away from American values of luxury.

JG: True enough. What I think is most remarkable is the difficult transformation of the older parents as opposed to the willing transformation of the younger generation. Barbara has to get rid of an awful lot of crappy ideas. She has to be broken down and in fact is broken down by having her daughter marry Chan, by trying to accommodate her feelings of nationalism to the loss of the consumer items that had formed her life. To be able to join Chan as he begins to smash the materialism around them is a real breakthrough. Of course they pay for that and the Cubans payed for that, too. The business of hating the very thing that was so conspicuously theirs for so long didn't work. In that case it was sugar, it was the night clubs, the flashy stuff. Then like I tried to show these things have other uses. It is not the material object itself that is evil, but what people do to it. They have to rebuild them in some way; even the nicknacks have to be rebuilt by the family in this play. I was severely criticized by Clive Barnes for that. He said how can we believe a play where all the nicknacks broken in one scene are being put together in the next scene several years later.

KT: Why do you have Barbara take up smashing the nicknacks after Chan stops?

JG: I don't really know if I can explain it. I thought it was "right" that she should be the one to make this offer. Even before the father. What she is doing is clear enough, but why I selected her instead of someone else, I don't know.

KT: I do not like the title and I think its ambivalence might have put some people off.

JG: I meant the title sexually. The play is an elaborate pun on sex and politics on one level. I think the Cubans take the revolution sexually. How else could you have a leader who is an intellectual, a father figure and a sex symbol? But I see what you mean. It is an askew statement instead of a right-on statement, and I think that is true about the play in general: it has right-on statements in it but the statements it makes are not right-on. They are askew to the political facts as viewed by political observers. And that is probably the only way I could have gotten this play written. This comes from being a

278

child of the fifties. I have a revulsion for political activity and yet an absolute need for it. But, when you say the title is not right on—what would it mean to have a play that reaffirmed your own ideas about the Cuban revolution? Sort of a celebration?

KT: I was drawn to your play because it did confirm my ideas about the Cuban revolution. I identify with Alicia and think it is very shrewd that you make her have a nervous breakdown. I think that is infinitely possible. I also identify, as you said you did, with Juan, the artist who changes his art to make it serve the revolution. But there are moments of celebration in your play. You have pointed some of them out. And the kind of celebration changes as the celebrants change. The final dance is very different from the frenzy when they smash the household objects and shout, "Fuck the US."

JG: At one point I was going to open the play with a dance. I wanted a very formal dance, then there is a group dance, and finally a very slow personal dance. I thought the change in the style of dancing would be important.

KT: I think the play is very much in favor of the revolution.

JG: So do I.

THE TRIAL OF THE CATONSVILLE NINE

In prison cell and dungeon high
Our thoughts to them are winging
When friends by shame are undefiled
How can I keep from singing.

Quaker song

On May 17, 1968, nine Catholics, two of them priests, and an ex-nun and ordained priest composing the one married couple among them, took 375 files from the 1-A Qualified drawer of the Catonsville, Maryland, Selective Service Office and burned them in the parking lot next door with a mixture of homemade napalm. Their intentions were public and there were newsreel cameras on hand to film the fire. They did not resist arrest. On October 7, 1968, the Catonsville Nine were brought to trial by the United States of Amerika. They pleaded innocent to three counts: that they "did willfully injure and commit depredation against property of the United States; did willfully and unlawfully obliterate records of the Selective Service System . . . and did willfully and knowingly interfere with the administration of the Military Selective Service Act in 1967."

They were given sentences ranging from two years to three and one-half years imprisonment—this last for Father Philip Berrigan and Thomas Lewis, artist, to run concurrently with previous six-year sentences for pouring blood on draft files.* In October 1969, one of the defendents, David Darst, was killed in an automobile crash. In April 1970, John Hogan, Thomas Lewis, Thomas and Marjorie Melville surrendered to the authorities. Fathers Philip and Daniel Berrigan, George Mische, and Mary Moylan went underground. All of them except Mary Moylan were subsequently captured and taken to federal prison.

The Trial of the Catonsville Nine is Daniel Berrigan's factual theatre-piece taken from twleve hundred pages of trial proceedings. It was first performed at the Mark Taper Forum in Los Angeles in August 1970, shortly before Berrigan was captured on Block Island by FBI men posing as "bird watchers." A new production was staged off-Broadway in the spring of 1971. It was also directed by Gordon Davidson, but because Berrigan was then in Danbury Prison the script was prepared by Saul Levitt from Berrigan's published text. (It is now a feature-length film which I have not seen.) The production was standard, though well above average for New York, employing conventional acting techniques, a platform set, simple lighting and contemporary costumes. It did not threaten, harangue, celebrate, revel, shock or otherwise disturb a single notion of proper theatrical decorum. And this might make it difficult to accept if you think that radical art must offer in one form or another a definite affront to bourgeois tastes.

Yet for all its apparent acquiescence to the norms of the bourgeois theatre *Catonsville Nine* undermines them in much the same way as the Catholic Left undermines the Catholic hierarchy. The Left is earnest while the bishops are merely pious. This play can effect the way men live while the bourgeois theatre can only affect realism. There is a sensationalism about even the best documentary plays (I am

---

*Father Philip Berrigan was tried again as one of the Harrisburg Seven accused by the government of planning to kidnap Henry Kissinger and blow up heating ducts in Washington. The Seven were acquitted of all but one minor count: smuggling letters into and out of prison. Father Daniel Berrigan was released on parole after serving a year and a half because of poor health.

thinking of Weiss's *The Investigation* and Hochhuth's *The Deputy*) that makes them akin to the popular crime shows on television. Whether or not they are actually set as trials, they have been conceived as startling exposes of scandalous historical situations. But about *Catonsville Nine* there is only the slightest trace of this. So though the play does not offend bourgeois expectations, neither does it live up to them.

Catonsville Nine is not about history (and therefore not concerned with reversing its interpretation) so much as it is an extension of (recent) history into the present moment. The Nine wanted to hinder the working of the war machine by destroying its access to human lives. Then they wanted to present the illegality of the war in a court of law. By acting heroically, they established a situation in which a Federal judge and jury could also act heroically. But the judge refused to admit the question of the war into his court: "The jury may not decide this case on the basis of the conscience of the defendants. They are to decide this case only on the basis of the facts presented by both sides." The jury, following the judge's order, ruled the Nine guilty, though the US Court of Appeals, in reversing the conviction of Dr. Spock, had already shown that juries do have the right to question the content of laws.

The jury and the judge were cowards, but the play does not recreate the instance of their cowardice. The judge, in real life a Catholic who cried as he handed down the sentence, might in a more conventional design (by Arthur Miller, for instance) have become a central character, a man torn between his duty as he conceived it and his sympathy with the anti-war position of the Nine. In this play he is reduced, as is the prosecuting attorney, to a mere device for facilitating the delivery of the testimonies. The jury is also reduced to anonymity: they were represented in New York by twelve members of the audience seated to the right of the stage. The defense attorney's role is also minimized, though his summation is reproduced at some length. Only the Nine have names and the play is mainly composed of their testimonies, dealing not with the actual events at Catonsville but with the personal experiences in Latin America, in Hanoi, in US ghettos that dictated their presence there.

"It was my hope to induce out of the density of the matter an art form worthy of the passionate acts and words of the Nine," Berrigan writes in his introduction. He began by working "in the manner of the 'factual theatre,'" a form which is nearly objective because the author controls the selection but not the composition of material. But the testimonies he emphasized are essentially subjective, recalling intensely personal moments of awareness. Berrigan responded to their content by editing and arranging them to stand like poetry, thereby increasing their subjectivity. By making factual theatre out of a cummulative series of personal impressions his art form corresponds to the notion of humanity inherent in the lives of the defendants. In contrast, the judge and jury are nearly nonentities because anyone who perceives horror and does not act to halt it loses all sense of himself in the gulf between what he knows and what he does.

There is minimal suspense and no dramatic conflict in this arrangement just as there was neither hopelessness nor fear, nor discord among the defendants, because all these feelings were changed by their act into a coherent revolutionary passion. The play moves forward by the accumulated force of this passion. *Catonsville Nine* becomes a necessary adjunct to the act committed at Catonsville because it re-opens what the judge and jury closed: an arena where the courage generated by the Nine can be applied by the people who come into contact with it to their own lives.

Catonsville Nine has actual power to move each member of the audience closer to breaking the law. (I know it was one reason I went to Washington for May Day '71.) Shock, guilt, complacency, even anger, are useless responses to the war when confronted with the force of these testimonies:

I could not announce the gospel
from a pedastal
I must act as a Christian . . .
I was threatened with verbalizing
my moral substance,
out of existence.

Daniel Berrigan

No sir you did not hear
I was trying to say
that the style of one's action
must coincide with the style of his life
and that is all.

George Mische

282

In a sense it was a choice
between life and death
It was a choice between
saving one's soul and losing it
I was saving my soul

Thomas Lewis

THE SAN FRANCISCO MIME TROUPE

We try in our own humble way to destroy the United States.

SF Mime Troupe

Ronny Davis founded the SF Mime Troupe (it rhymes with "cream") in 1959 as a cultural alternative to the San Francisco Actors Workshop where he worked for three years. In the fifties the Actors Workshop was the flagship of the regional theatre movement. It had Ford Foundation money, a loyal, if small, university-educated audience, an expansive repertoire extending from the classics to Pinter and Beckett and including the European radicalism of Genet and Brecht (the first US production of *Mother Courage*). Its standards were high and its productions more daring than Broadway's. This is the company whose remains are currently interred at Lincoln Center (upon this wreck I will build my ship?).

Davis left the workshop for two reasons: they hadn't found a style and they lacked the morality a style would have signified; their work was separate from the needs of society, even though as intelligent people they recognized those needs, and so the person was still separate from his work. "Yes, we have a style . . . Naturalistic vague Americana with some presentational leanings, but for me this is not quite satisfying," he wrote director Herbert Blau.* The workshop was the liberal solution; Davis was after a radical one.

The guerilla theatre concept as it exists today is mainly the

*Herbert Blau, *The Impossible Theatre,* New York, 1964, p. 177.

284

result of the Mime Troupe's work. "There are hundreds of people looking for something to do, something that gives reason to their lives, and these are the guerillas," Davis wrote in 1965. In "Cultural Revolution U.S.A.—One Step Forward" (1968) he elaborated:

> The key to the arch of imperialism, for the cultural guerilla, is the bourgeois value structure . . . . If we can destroy this . . . the monster may withdraw from aggressive suppression . . . .
>
> Individualism is one of two enemies the cultural guerilla, almost invariably of bourgeois origin or at least education, has to combat in himself. The other is elitism, an extension of the first: me with my talents and extraordinary awareness, or our group with its hot line, must be replaced as ultimate values by the job to be done. Once these enemies are destroyed the individual is really free, to play any of the roles he is called upon by history to fulfill: to be an actor, today, a director tomorrow and next week a writer; a writer today, a publisher tomorrow and next year a book salesman.*

The Mime Troupe's politics are Marxist, unusual among contemporary people's theatres, and since 1962, when they abandoned silent comedy skits and began to do updated commedia dell'arte plays in the parks and streets, their theatre has been directly and militantly related to movement issues. They play for free (taking a collection afterwards) and they move their shows to where the people are. They are also indigenous to San Francisco, and therefore they reflect the West Coast combination of pragmatic politics and impudent showmanship (the Free Speech Movement metamorphosing into the Dirty Speech Movement, for instance) instead of the East's intellectual and avant-garde associations. The Bread and Puppet Theatre does *Fire* as a memorial to three US citizens who immolated themselves in protest against the war. The Mime Troupe is influenced by Schumann's juxtaposition of people and puppets to produce Gutter Puppet skits like *Meter Maid* which, David Kolodney wrote in *Ramparts* (August, 1970), "offered, in addition to Anti-Parking Meter

Guerrilla Theatre Essays: 1, San Francisco, 1970. Available from the Mime Troupe, 450 Alabama Avenue, San Francisco, California.

propaganda (somewhat superfluous), a specific plan of attack: the Aluminum Tab-Top Strategy. The pear-shaped tab-tops are inserted in the meter in place of a coin, either priming the meter clock or rendering it out of order." Or *Ripping Off Ma Bell* (1970), with detailed instructions (now obsolete) of how to make free station-to-station credit card calls from telephone booths around San Francisco: "S-any number-158."

The Mime Troupe has assumed an increasingly utilitarian relationship to the movement, just as people in the movement have become more sure of the significance of the emerging counter-culture. In 1970, troupe members inserted the word "collective" between "non-profit" and "corporation," and they decided to put their performance skills at the service of radical organizations needing a public way to explain specific causes.

Davis left the troupe early in 1970, after having staged a Chinese Opera version of Brecht's *The Congress of Whitewashers*. "I really forced it on them," he says, and his reasons for leaving are linked to the troupe's unwillingness to experiment with more Brechtian performance techniques. Joan Holdon, who in 1967 had turned Goldoni's *L'Amant Militaire* into an anti-war play, wrote a melodrama about women's liberation: *The Independent Female (or, a Man Has His Pride)*. It was performed before San Francisco activist women and then rewritten and redirected to comply with their criticism that the feminist character was too individualistic and self-serving (qualities, after all, that are endemic to characters in melodrama).

In the winter of 1971 the troupe compiled their first non-comic work, *Seize the Time*, a documentary based on Bobby Seale's book and the transcript of the Chicago Eight trial. The piece was written for the Oakland chapter of the Black Panther Party and later played at Panther benefits across the country, often on the same bill with lawyer William Kunstler. *The Dragon Lady's Revenge* (1971) is a melodramatic account of the US government's involvement in heroin traffic in South East Asia, based on articles that appeared in *Ramparts* magazine. After a summer performing *Dragon Lady* in parks around the Bay Area, the troupe planned to tour it to GI coffee houses in the South.

So far the ideological strictness of the collective has not

286

significantly altered Mime Troupe style, although they seem to prefer melodrama to commedia currently. Troupe members take regular voice, movement and circus classes as well as attending a political education program based on the works of the great Communist revolutionaries. Actually, the troupe was always concerned with the correctness of its political interpretations and the new collective is still adamant about keeping up the quality of its productions.

The Mime Troupe approach allows them to do both. It is adaptable to all movement fronts, from fostering the rip-off mentality to the Panther defense, and to a variety of movement people (as of 1970 one-time troupe members numbered about 340). Like all popular forms it is immediately available to any impulse. When the hippy-priest Tom Drooly, employed by the US army as part-time drug counselor, part-time drug dealer, appears on stage in *Dragon Lady*, the Gorilla Band strikes up a few notes of "Jesus Christ Superstar." Drooly's crucifix is a disguised hypo: a cruci-*fix*. In the Minstrel Show which got the troupe busted for obscenity numerous times during a cross-country tour in 1966, the line "I'm coming, I'm coming, though my head is bending low" from the Stephen Foster melody is the occasion for a mimed masturbation. A film, "O Dem Watermelons," interrupts the show halfway through to provide a graphic account of the oppression of the watermelon.

In *L'Amant Militaire*, while the general tries to wheedle information out of the servant girl, she mimes a turnstile and he slips through without paying: it is an image irrelevant to the play but very relevant to the daily survival tactics of the audience. Act II, scene three of the same play shows the lieutenant regress from melancholy lover to child of seven, to child of four, to straight-thinking military hero. It includes a spoof of flower children, some Shakespeare and a bit of the ABC evening news.

The Mime Troupe's style is a coalition of commedia dell' arte theory, mime techniques, Amerikan vaudeville, minstrel show, melodrama. They scoff at realism but they have liberated their stage in these ways only: they are not bound by time or space and so do not have to proceed in linear order, they know the value of presenting separate visual and verbal images simultaneously, they can construct props with their bodies (a turnstile in *L'Amant Militaire*, swinging doors and a urinal in the *Minstrel Show*). While they are extremely physically adept they are not concerned with exploring how their bodies relate to one another (with the possible exception of *Congress of Whitewashers*, which I did not see). Their mobile stage is small and narrow, inhibiting ensemble movements so their acting, very broad and comic, is also self-exhibitionistic. Their scripts, always distinguished for political clarity, are seldom distinguished as literature. So while there is a pragmatic truth to their actions, there is seldom that reconciliation of opposites which art at its most necessary level is about.

How politically useful is the Troupe, for this is what they pride themselves on being first of all? At the University of Wisconsin in 1966 where they were up against already well-defined spacial, formal and administrative boundaries, they were truly disruptive. They were touring cross-country with a civil rights show that echoed Imamu Amiri Baraka and Jean Genet by exposing the predatory nature of black/white sexual relationships and liberal-Tom political ones. But instead of considering their productions as serious art (which might have been acceptable to university officials, though I don't know of any who booked the touring company of *The Blacks* or whose drama departments had yet staged Baraka's plays) they flagrantly advertised an obscene minstrel show. At Wisconsin the Mime Troupe's booking was arranged by radical graduate students, not by the undergraduate theatre committee. Word of their obscenity busts preceded them to campus and administrators calmed themselves by expecting an artless show that would turn off everyone it did not manage to offend. No one was prepared for the mimetic skill of the all-male cast or for the way the hokey melodies and comedy routines threw the serious scenes into powerful relief, or for the inflamatory relationship between the words to "Massa's in the Col', Col', Groun'" we were asked to sing along with, and the movie scenes of violent destruction of watermelons.

The Dragon Lady's Revenge, in Golden Gate Park in 1971, was not as effective. Melodrama has nothing to say about the criminal complicity of the US government with heroin traffickers. It is not, like the minstrel show, a genre developed precisely as a cover for this exploitative relationship. So it becomes cheerfully anachronistic, conducive to nothing so

288

much as a pleasant afternoon in the park. While it is good to be entertained with material that makes political sense, it would be foolish to assert that the conjunction of melodrama with this information contributes to the formation of minds that function in a radical way.

Perhaps *Seize the Time* is their most significant recent work. The dialogue is particularly strained but it has some important images in it, such as Bobby Seale gagged and bound while his words are unrolled on a banner. It also freed the Troupe from its dependence on commedia and melodrama while leaving them with all the useful physical and comic techniques these genres provide.

R. G. Davis and Saul Landau

THE MINSTREL SHOW, OR
CIVIL RIGHTS ON A CRACKER BARREL*

Final Scene

GIMME: How come you always talkin about missionaries, mercenaries. What do you know about what's goin on right here in de ol U.S. ob A.?

INKSPOT: All right, what is going on right here?

GIMME: Well, I'll tell you. You takes me. I works in dis restaurant washin dishes an dere are two kinds of people in dat world. De ones dat works in de kitchen, like de lowly dog, and de ones dat comes in and eats de lowly slop.

INKSPOT: But surely you must meet a nice integrated clientele?

GIMME: Why, sure I meets em. For your edification, I'm going to show you how we meets. Let's say dis area here am de men's room.

BONES: (laughing) He thinks he's LeRoi Jones.

GIMME: I said de men's rooms not de boy's room. Now looks here. Inkspot, I want you to play de white man.

KLINKER: Let's see how you do this time, Inkspot.

INKSPOT: Oh, dat's all right. I takes any character part.

BONES: And what about me, what am I gonna play?

GIMME: Well, Bones, I saved you de big part (Bones ad libs interest and then excitement here) de strongest part, de biggest part. You can see it now, your name in blazin lights, in three feet high letters, up on Broadway—MIDDLE CLASS NEGRO!

BONES: And what are you going to play?

GIMME: I shall merely (English accent) endeavor to play truthfully and sincerely my own natural self.

---

*©1965. Used by permission.

289

INKSPOT: Come on, nigger.
(All three exit, come on with signs: "Nigger" apron and "White" and "Negro" vests. Two minstrels set up door and one is a flushing toilet. Negro and white approach the bathroom door:)
WHITE: After you.
NEGRO: No, after you.
WHITE: Oh, go ahead, I can wait.
NEGRO: No, you were here first, I insist—
WHITE: No—(more ad libbing by both)
NIGGER: (Enters, listens to debate, anxious to get inside, pushes through.) After *me*. Shit, you goin to stand there and debate who is going to take de first piss?
NEGRO: (Enters bathroom) Where's your manners? You're the kind that gives our race a bad image.
NIGGER: In dat case, I moves on over since you have to go so bad. Dere's room enough for two.
NEGRO: That's not what I meant.
NIGGER: Oh, who gives a damn what you meant. (Flushes toilet, pantomimes combing hair.)
WHITE: Maybe I should leave and that way it would be less crowded.
NIGGER: Wait a minute, boss, you mean you didn't even have to go? What de hell you come in here for and cause all dis trouble? You one of dem peeverts?
NEGRO: (To white) Pay no attention, sir. He's probably drunk.
NIGGER: Fuck you. Why you got to kiss de white man's ass?
NEGRO: Watch your language. Remember where you are.
NIGGER: I know where I am. I'm in de pissin room and I come in here to take one. I don't know what you come in here for, but it sure wasn't for pissin.
NEGRO: If you were any kind of civilized human being, you would move aside and let the customers use the facilities first. I'm going to report you to the manager.
NIGGER: If you like de manager so much you can go ahead and piss in his room.
WHITE: I can see what you're up against. It's very difficult to deal with an uneducated person.
NEGRO: I agree.
NIGGER: (To white) Shit, man—you need an education to learn to piss more than one in a commode. And you (to Negro)—you need an education, you white ass kisser.
NEGRO: I resent that, you street nigger! (Goes to punch him. White man intervenes.)
WHITE: Now wait a minute, let's be reasonable about this. Use some reason.
NIGGER: (Pulls out razor) Here's my reason. I'm gonna settle something with Mr. Ass Kisser. (Negro hides behind white.) You chicken

290

shit Mr. Ass Kisser, you ain't no nigger no more. Don't even carry a blade to defend yourself. Mighty educated.

NEGRO: Cool it, baby—we're brothers! Dere's de white man!

WHITE: Don't kill me, I didn't say anything. Honest.

NIGGER: Yeah, no one says nothin to me except clean dis and do dat. Well, now I'm saying something. One of you is going to get it, maybe both. All I gotta do is figure out which one of you I hates the most. (Freeze)

INTER: (After 15-25 seconds) Well, we can't wait all night for you to decide. Remember, this is a Minstrel Show!

ALL: (Action) Oh, yeah!

INTER: Let's "Jump Jim Crow!"

(The following verse is sung once solo and then repeated by all the minstrels.)

> "Come, listen all you gals and boys, I'se just from Tuckyho;
> I'm going to sing a little song, my name's Jim Crow.
> Wheel about and turn about and do jus so.
> Every time I wheel about, I jump Jim Crow."

(Banjos sequel into "O, Dem Golden Slippers" while interlocutor recites and minstrels dance:)

INTER: Oh, the Minstrel show it's coming to a close, so we're gonna dance on our heels and toes, with tambourines and tappin shoes we're gonna have a ball. Now Bones does the shuffle while Gimme claps, and Inkspot wobbles and Klinker claps, and the whole troupe sings and romps about, dancing till de morning.

O, Dem Golden Slippers

O, dem Golden Slippers! O, dem Golden Slippers!
Golden Slippers I's gwine to wear, because dey look so neat.
O, dem Golden Slippers! O, dem Golden Slippers!
Golden Slippers I's gwine to wear, to walk de golden street.

1. O, my Golden Slippers am a'laid away,
   Cause I don't spect to wear em till my weddin day,
   And my longtailed coat, dat I loved so well,
   I will wear up in de chariot in de morn.

2. And my long white robe—dat I bought last June,
   I'm gwine to get changed cause it fits too soon,
   An de ol gray hoss dat I used to drive,
   I will hitch him to de chariot in de morn.

CHORUS: O, dem Golden Slippers! O, dem Golden Slippers!
Golden Slippers I's gwine to wear, because dey look so neat.
O, dem Golden Slippers! O, dem Golden Slippers!
Golden Slippers I's gwine to wear, to walk de golden street.

291

ALL: Oh, de white folks loves to sing dis song,
FIRST THREE: Dey do, dey do.
SECOND THREE: Dey do. (Echo)
   Listen to de darkies all night long,
   Cause it's so relaxin . . .
   (Three minstrels sing in three part harmony as interlocutor speaks:)

In de Evenin

   In de evenin by de moonlight
   You can hear de darkies singin.
   In de evenin by de moonlight
   You can hear dose banjos ringin.
   How de old folks did enjoy it,
   Dey would sit all night and listen
   As we sang
   In de evenin by de moonlight.

INTER: That's it, ladies and gentlemen, the end of our Minstrel Show, reminiscent of the old Christy Minstrels and Daddy T. D. Rice and his entertainers. From 1830 to 1920, Minstrel Shows played from coast to coast across this great land. I'm sure we brought back the old memories of the good old-fashioned American Minstrel Show.
   (Into "O, Dem Golden Slippers")
   O, dem Golden Slippers! O, dem Golden Slippers!
   Golden Slippers I's gwine to wear, because dey look so neat.
   O, dem Golden Slippers! O, dem Golden Slippers!
   Golden Slippers I's gwine to wear, to walk de golden street.
(Minstrels take bows two at a time, then interlocutor, then musicians. Whites take off gloves, showing color, and exit; blacks take off gloves and shuffle. Clean-up ad libs: whites re-enter, taking off blackface, ask blacks to sweep up, etc. Full company bows and rioting.)

—END—

EL TEATRO CAMPESINO

Attempts to organize farm workers were made by the
IWW before World War I, by the Southern Tenant Farmers Union during the grim depression years when black
and white sharecroppers fought Delta plantation owners, and by the National Farm Labor Union in the
1940s. None succeeded and all were ultimately broken
by terror and violence.

Thomas R. Brooks

In September 1965 6,000 Filipino and Chicano migrant
farm workers struck against grape growers in Delano,
California. In 1966 a march of 8,000 on the capital at
Sacramento culminated in the signing of the first contract
with a major grower, Schenley. A year later, DiGiorgio, one
of the country's biggest grape growers, signed a similar contract. The strike continued against a majority of holdout
companies supplemented by a national boycott of non-union
table grapes instigated by the brilliant labor leader Ceasar
Chavez. It was not until 1970 that other area growers capitulated to union demands, bringing 25 percent of the state's
vineyard acres under United Farm Workers Organization contract.

El Teatro Campesino, the leading member of some eighteen Chicano theatres that form *Teatro Nacional de Aztlan*,
was founded in 1965 to support the *Huelga* (strike) and
bolster the morale of the *huelgistas* whose picket signs were
being sprayed with bullets and insecticides. Its first produc-

tion was *The Conscience of a Scab*, involving two characters: a scab, and a striker who quotes Jack London's definition of a strikebreaker: "After God had finished the rattlesnake, the toad and the vampire, he had some awful substance left with which he made a strikebreaker . . . ."

The union struggle was the most potent manifestation of a liberation movement that has come to include Chicanos in the *barrios* (neighborhoods) as well as in the *campesinos* (fields). The Campesino grew up because of the union, but it has expanded in order to define the Chicano's role in the entire movement and hopefully to ensure that organized farm workers do not repeat the right-wing path other union members followed in the forties and fifties. The Campesino does anti-war actos, *Vietnam Campesino* and *Soldado Razo*; actos that poke holes in the *gavacho* (white) attitude toward the Chicano, *Los Vendidos* and *No Saco Nada de la Escuela*; and actos that show how movement ideals become corrupted, *The Militants*.*

The Campesino's director and chief playwright, Luis Valdez from Delano, is a graduate of San Jose State College, where he majored in drama and wrote plays. He went to Cuba in 1964 and for the first time saw theatre being used for social purposes. In 1965 he joined the San Francisco Mime Troupe. "A version of *Tartuffe* was the first thing I saw the Mime Troupe do and it really impressed me because of their on-the-spot references to what was happening right there in the street. They had restructured a classical drama and given it new life." Valdez worked with the Troupe about eight months before the Heugla broke out and "conditions left no other choice. I had to go to Delano."

El Campesino took off from the general premises of the Mime Troupe. It was free, it went where the people were, it was lively, bawdy, comic. It was expansive and literally applicable to political situations. Characters wore signs to identify themselves and they changed personality by the assumption of a new mask or prop.

Valdez explained the Mime Troupe influence in an interview in 1967:

There's a dramatic theory—we used to talk about it in

---

*These actos are available for $3.00 from El Teatro Campesino, P. O. Box 2302, Fresno, California 93720.

the Mime Troupe. I think we've put a different use to it in the Teatro just out of necessity, but it is that your dramatic situation, the thing you're trying to portray on the stage, must be close to the reality that is *on* the stage. You take the figure of DiGiorgio standing on the backs of two farm workers. The response of the audience is to a very real situation of one human being standing on two others. That type of fakery is not imitation. It's a theatrical reality that will hold up on the flatbed of a truck.*

El Teatro Campesino productions are less slickly staged, less well designed and frequently not as well acted as the Mime Troupe's. The first performers were farm workers; now most of them are young and very politically aware sons and daughters of Chicano workers. The Campesino's development has been in an opposite direction—from *actos* concerned with a specific cause, the Huegla, and the mechanics of social change to current experiments with two new forms, *los corridos* and *los mitos*, which are ceremonial in inspiration and mean to effect a subjective change in the audience.

The Mime Troupe audience is basically white, middle class, dropped-out and fairly radical. This had led the troupe to acknowledge its function as "cheerleaders for the revolution." Its audience has already been affected by an acid-stoned vision of the new world but it is less committed to the daily grind of radical organizing or even to the economic deprivations of a radical life style.

El Campesino's audience is poor and Catholic with social aspirations toward the middle class. The theatre has to change ideas both about the Chicano's place in society and about the kind of society Chicanos should want a place in. By necessity the actos deal with a radical transvaluation of values and this creates a tension (as yet not wholly realized) between subjective and objective worlds which has moved the Campesino toward the ritualistic mitos.

Valdez explains this development:

I spend more time in the theatre than on politics now because I have more confidence in what we are doing. We have to go very deep before we effect a change in

---

The Drama Review, vol. 11, no. 4, September 1967.

people. That means a spiritual change, a reorganization of concepts about life. We have to be able to recapture the whole different concept of reality that is predicted in the Mayan books. We can't lay a total claim to it because we are Spanish also. But we lay claim to the Mayan achievement as something that has been left in the dust and needs to be uncovered. So the mitos will try to deal with some of these things.

You know in Delano the farm workers used to call us los bufons, which means clowns, and they used to call the theatre the circo. And I suspect some of them thought it wasn't the most masculine thing to be doing. But that hasn't happened in years. Now people come up and very seriously say "never stop what you're doing." And I suppose they mean it. These are very genuine remarks. We don't get them all the time, of course, but enough to keep us going. And I guess the biggest change is that theatre has become a way of life. It is one of the ways to define life. And this has happened for Chicanos. There are so many Chicanos now who have seen teatros as a way to live, not as a career in the commercial sense, but as a way to work within their life times: to work politically, socially, culturally, spiritually. And all of that has made new forms possible with us and has created all these other groups [which form Teatro Nacional de Aztlan].

Luis Valdez

NOTES ON CHICANO THEATER*

What is Chicano theater? It is theater as beautiful, rasquachi, human, cosmic, broad, deep, tragic, comic, as the life of La Raza itself. At its high point Chicano theater is religion—the huelguistas de Delano praying at the shrine of the Virgin de Guadalupe, located in the rear of an old stationwagon parked across the road from DiGiorgio's camp #4; at its low point, it is a cuento or a chiste told somewhere in the recesses of the barrio, puro pedo.

Chicano theater, then is first a reaffirmation of LIFE. That is what all theater is supposed to be, of course; but the limp, superficial, gringo seco productions in the "professional" American theater (and the

*©1971. Reprinted by permission.

college and university drama departments that serve it) are so antiseptic, they are antibiotic (anti-life). The characters and life situations emerging from our little teatros are too real, too full of sudor, sangre, and body smells to be boxed in. Audience participation is no cute production trick with us; it is a pre-established, pre-assumed privilege. "Que le suenen la campanita!"

Defining Chicano theater is a little like defining a Chicano car. We can start with a low-rider's cool Merc or a campesino's banged-up Chivi, and describe the various paint jobs, hub caps, dents, taped windows, Virgin on the dashboard, etc. that define the car as particularly Raza. Underneath all the trimmings, however, is an unmistakable production of Detroit, an extension of General Motors. Consider now a theater that uses the basic form, the vehicle, created by Broadway or Hollywood: that is, the "realistic" play. Actually, this type of play was created in Europe, but where French, German, and Scandinavian playwrights went beyond realism and naturalism long ago, commercial gabacho theater refuses to let go. It reflects a characteristic "American" hang-up on the material aspect of human existence. European theater, by contrast, has been influenced since around 1900 by the unrealistic, formal rituals of Oriental theater.

What does Oriental and European theater have to do with teatro Chicano? Nothing, except that we are talking about a theater that is particularly our own, not another imitation of the gabacho. If we consider our origins, say the theater of the Mayans or the Aztecs, we are talking about something totally unlike the realistic play and more Chinese or Japanese in spirit. *Kabuki*, as a matter of fact, started long ago as something like our actos and evolved over two centuries into the highly exacting artform it is today; but it still contains pleberias. It evolved from and still belongs to el pueblo japones.

In Mexico, before the coming of the white man, the greatest examples of total theater were, of course, the human sacrifices. *El Rabinal Achi*, one of the few surviving pieces of indigenous theater describes the sacrifice of a courageous guerrillero, who rather than dying passively on the block is granted the opportunity to fight until he is killed. It is a tragedy, naturally, but it is all the more transcendant because of the guerrillero's identification, through sacrifice, with God. The only "set" such a drama-ritual needed was a stone block; nature took care of the rest.

But since the Conquest, Mexico's theater like its society has had to imitate Europe and, in recent times, the United States. In this same vein, Chicanos in Spanish classes are frequently involved in productions of plays by Lope de Vega, Calderon de la Barca, Tirso de Molina and other classic playwrights. Nothing is wrong with this, but it does obscure the indio fountains of Chicano culture. Is Chicano theater in turn, to be nothing but an imitation of gavacho playwrights, with barrio productions of racist works by Eugene O'Neill and Tennessee Williams?

297

Will Broadway produce a Chicano version of "Hello, Dolly" now that it has produced a Black one?

The nature of Chicanoismo calls for a revolutionary turn in the arts as well as in society. Chicano theater must be revolutionary in technique as well as content. It must be popular, subject to no other critics except the pueblo itself; but it must also educate the pueblo toward an appreciation of *social change*, on and off the stage.

It is particularly important for teatro Chicano to draw a distinction between what is theater and what is reality. A demonstration with a thousand Chicanos, all carrying flags and picket signs, shouting CHICANO POWER! is not the revolution. It is theater about the revolution. The people must act in *reality* not on stage (which could be anywhere, even a sidewalk) in order to achieve real change. The Raza gets excited, simon, but unless the demonstration evolves into a street battle (which has not yet happened but is possible) it is basically a lot of emotion with very little political power, as Chicanos have discovered by demonstrating, picketing, and shouting before school boards, police departments, and stores to no avail.

Such guerrilla theater passing as a demonstration has its uses, of course. It is agit-prop theater, as white radicals used to call it in the '30's: agitation and propaganda. It helps to stimulate and sustain the mass strength of a crowd. Hitler was very effective with this kind of theater, from the swastika to the Wagneresque stadium at Nuremburg. At the other end of the political spectrum, the Huelga march to Sacramento in 1966 was pure guerrilla theater. The red and black thunderbird flags of the UFWOC (then NFWA) and the standard of the Virgen de Guadalupe challenged the bleak sterility of Highway 99. Its emotional impact was irrefutable. Its actual political power was somewhat less. Governor Brown was not at the state capitol, and only one grower, Schenley Industries signed a contract. Later contracts have been won through a brilliant balance between highly publicized events which gained public support (marches, Cesar's fast, visits by Reuther, Robert and Ted Kennedy, etc.) and actual hard-ass, door to door, worker to worker, organizing. Like Delano, other aspects of the Chicano movement, must remember what is teatro, and what is reality.

But beyond the mass struggle of La Raza in the fields and barrios of America, there is an internal struggle in the very corazón of our people. That struggle, too, calls for revolutionary change. Our belief in God, the church, the social role of women—these must be subject to examination and redefinition on some kind of public forum. And that again means teatro. Not a teatro composed of actos or agit-prop but a teatro of ritual, of music, of beauty and spiritual sensitivity. A teatro of legends and myths. A teatro of religious strength. This type of theater will require real dedication; it may, indeed, require a couple of generations of Chicanos devoted to the use of the theater as an instrument in the evolution of our people.

298

The teatros in existence today reflect the most intimate understanding of everyday events in the barrios from which they have emerged. But if Aztlán is to become reality, then we as Chicanos must not be reluctant to act *nationally*. To think in national terms: politically, economically and spiritually. We must destroy the deadly regionalism that keeps us apart. The concept of a national theater for La Raza is intimately related to our evolving nationalism in Aztlán.

Consider a *Teatro Nacional de Aztlán* that performs with the same skill and prestige as the Ballet Folklorico de Mexico (not for gavachos, however, but for the Raza). Such a teatro could carry the message of La Raza into Latin America, Europe, Japan, Africa—in short all over the world. It would draw its strength from all the small teatros in the barrios, in terms of people and their plays, songs, designs; and it would give back funds, training, and augmented strength of national unity. One season the teatro members would be on tour with the Teatro Nacional; the next season they would be back in the barrio sharing their skills and experience. It would accommodate about 150 people altogether, with 20-25 in the *National* and the rest spread out in various parts of Aztlán, working with the Campesino, the Urbano, the Mestizo, the Piojo, etc.

Above all, the national organization of teatros Chicanos would be self-supporting and independent, meaning no government grants. The corazón de la Raza cannot be revolutionized on a grant from Uncle Sam. Though many of the teatros, including El Campesino, have been born out of pre-established political groups—thus making them harbingers of that particular group's viewpoint, news, and political prejudices —there is yet a need for independence for the following reasons: objectivity, artistic competence, survival. El Teatro Campesino was born in the Huelga, but the very Huelga would have killed it, if we had not moved 60 miles to the north of Delano. A struggle like the Huelga needs every person it can get to serve its immediate goals in order to survive; the Teatro, as well as the clinic, service center, and newspaper being less important at the moment of need than the survival of the Union were always losing people to the grape boycott. When it became clear to us that the UFWOC would succeed and continue to grow, we felt it was time for us to move and to begin speaking about things beyond the Huelga: Vietnam, the barrio, racial discrimination, etc.

The teatros must never get away from La Raza. Without the palomía sitting there, laughing, crying and sharing whatever is onstage, the teatros will dry up and die. If the Raza will not come to theater, then the theater must go to the Raza. This, in the long run, will determine the shape, style, content, spirit, and form of el teatro chicano.

Pachucos, campesinos, low-riders, pintos, chavalonas, familias, cuñados, tios, primos, Mexican-Americans, all the human essence of the barrio is starting to appear in the mirror of our theater. With them come the joys, sufferings, disappointments and aspirations of our gente.

We challenge Chicanos to become involved in the art, the life style, the political and religious act of doing teatro.

Luis Valdez
Summer, 1970
Fresno, Califas

Luis Valdez

LOS VENDIDOS*

First performance, Brown Beret Junta, Elysian Park, East Los Angeles, 1967.

Scene: HONEST SANCHO'S *Used Mexican Lot and Mexican Curio Shop. Three models are on display in* HONEST SANCHO'S *shop: to the right, there is a* REVOLUTIONARIO, *complete with sombrero, carrilleras, and carabina 30-30. At center, on the floor, there is the* FARM WORKER, *under a broad straw sombrero. At stage left is the* PACHUCO, *filero in hand.*

HONEST SANCHO *is moving among his models, dusting them off and preparing for another day of business.*

SANCHO: Bueno, bueno, mis monos, vamos a ver a guien vendemos ahora, no? (TO AUDIENCE) Quihubo! I'm Honest Sancho and this is my shop. Antes fui contratista pero ahora logre tener mi negocito. All I need now is a customer. *(A bell rings offstage.)* Ay, a customer!

SECRETARY: *(entering)* Good morning, I'm Miss Jimenez from—

SANCHO: Ah, una chicana! Welcome, welcome Senorita Jimenez.

SECRETARY: *(anglo pronunciation)* JIM-enez.

SANCHO: Qué?

SECRETARY: My name is Miss JIM-enez. Don't you speak English? What's wrong with you?

SANCHO: Oh, nothing, Senorita JIM-enez. I'm here to help you.

SECRETARY: That's better. As I was starting to say, I'm a secretary from Governor Reagen's office, and we're looking for a Mexican type for the administration.

SANCHO: Well, you come to the right place, lady. This is Honest Sancho's Used Mexican lot, and we got all types here. Any particular type you want?

SECRETARY: Yes, we were looking for somebody suave—

SANCHO: Suave.

SECRETARY: Debonair.

SANCHO: De buen aire.

SECRETARY: Dark.

SANCHO: Prieto.

SECRETARY: But of course not too dark.

SANCHO: No muy prieto.

SECRETARY: Perhaps, beige.

SANCHO: Beige, just the tone. Así como cafecito con leche, no?

SECRETARY: One more thing. He must be hard-working.

SANCHO: That could only be one model. Stop right over here to the center of the shop, lady. *(They cross to the* FARMWORKER.*)* This is our standard farm worker model. As you can see, in the words of our beloved Senator George Murphy, he is "built close to the ground". Also take special notice of his 4-ply Goodyear huaraches, made from the rain tire. This wide-brimmed sombrero is an extra added feature—keeps off the sun, rain, and dust.

SECRETARY: Yes, it does look durable.

SANCHO: And our farmworker model is friendly. Muy amable. Watch. *(Snaps his fingers.)*

FARMWORKER: *(Lifts up head.)* Buenos días, señorita. *(His head drops.)*

SECRETARY: My, he's friendly.

SANCHO: Didn't I tell you? Loves his patrones! But his most attractive feature is that he's hardworking. Let me show you. *(Snaps fingers.* FARMWORKER *stands.)*

FARMWORKER: El jale! *(He begins to work.)*

SANCHO: As you can see he is cutting grapes.

SECRETARY: Oh, I wouldn't know.

SANCHO: He also picks cotton. *(Snap.* FARMWORKER *begins to pick cotton.)*

SECRETARY: Versatile isn't he?

SANCHO: He also picks melons. *(Snap.* FARMWORKER *picks melons.)* That's his slow speed for late in the season. Here's his fast speed. *(Snap.* FARMWORKER *picks faster.)*

SECRETARY: Chihuahua . . . I mean, goodness, he sure is a hardworker.

SANCHO: *(Pulls the* FARMWORKER *to his feet.)* And that isn't the half of it. Do you see these little holes on his arms that appear to be pores? During those hot sluggish days in the field when the vines or the branches get so entangled, it's almost impossible to move, these holes emit a certain grease that allow our model to slip and slide right through the crop with no trouble at all.

SECRETARY: Wonderful. But is he economical?

SANCHO: Economical? Señorita, you are looking at the Volkswagen of Mexicans. Pennies a day is all it takes. One plate of beans and tortillas will keep him going all day. That, and chile. Plenty of chile. Chile jalapenos, chile verde, chile colorado. But, of course, if you do give him chile *(Snap.* FARMWORKER *turns left face. Snap.* FARMWORKER *bends over.),* then you have to change his oil filter once a week.

SECRETARY: What about storage?

SANCHO: No problem. You know these new farm labor camps our Honorable Governor Reagen has built out by Parlier or Raisin City? They were designed with our model in mind. Five, six, seven, even ten in one of those shacks will give you no trouble at all. You can also put him in old barns, old cars, riverbanks. You can leave him out in the field overnight with no worry!

SECRETARY: Remarkable.

SANCHO: And here's an added feature: every year at the end of the season, this model goes back to Mexico and doesn't return, automatically, until next Spring.

SECRETARY: How about that. But tell me, does he speak English?

SANCHO: Another outstanding feature is that last year this model was programmed to go out on STRIKE! *(Snap.)*

FARMWORKER: HUELGA! HUELGA! Hermanos, salganse de esos files. *(Snap. He stops.)*

SECRETARY: No! Oh no, we can't strike in the State Capitol.

SANCHO: Well, he also scabs. *(Snap.)*

FARMWORKER: Me vendo barato, y qué? *(Snap.)*

SECRETARY: That's much better, but you didn't answer my question. Does he speak English?

SANCHO: Bueno . . . no, pero he has other—

SECRETARY: No.

SANCHO: Other features.

SECRETARY: NO! He just won't do!

SANCHO: Okay, okay pues. We have other models.

SECRETARY: I hope so. What we need is something a little more sophisticated.

SANCHO: Sophisti—que?

SECRETARY: An urban model.

SANCHO: Ah, from the city! Step right back. Over here in this corner of the shop is exactly what you're looking for. Introducing our new 1969 JOHNNY PACHUCO model! This is our fast-back model. Streamlined. Built for speed, low-riding, city life. Take a look at some of these features. Mag shoes, dual exhausts, green chartruese paint-job, dark-tint windshield, a little poof on top. Let me just turn him on. *(Snap. JOHNNY walks to stage center with a pachuco bounce.)*

SECRETARY: What was that?

SANCHO: That, sẽnorita, was the Chicano shuffle.

SECRETARY: Okay, what does he do?

SANCHO: Anything and everything necessary for city life. For instance, survival: he·knife fights. *(Snap. JOHNNY pulls out switchblade and swings at SECRETARY.)*

SECRETARY SCREAMS

SANCHO: He dances. *(Snap.)*

JOHNNY: *(Singing)* "Angel Baby, my Angel Baby . . . ." *(Snap.)*
SANCHO: And here's a feature no city model can be without. He gets arrested, but not without resisting, of course. *(Snap.)*
JOHNNY: En la madre, la placa. I didn't do it! I didn't do it! *(JOHNNY turns and stands up against an imaginary wall, legs spread out, arms behind his back.)*
SECRETARY: Oh no, we can't have arrests! We must maintain law and order.
SANCHO: But he's bilingual!
SECRETARY: Bilingual?
SANCHO: Simon que yes. He speaks English! Johnny, give us some English. *(Snap.)*
JOHNNY: *(Comes downstage.)* Fuck-you!
SECRETARY: *(gasps)* OH! I've never been so insulted in my whole life!
SANCHO: Well, he learned it in your school.
SECRETARY: I don't care where he learned it.
SANCHO: But he's economical!
SECRETARY: Economical?
SANCHO: Nickels and dimes. You can keep Johnny running on hamburgers, Taco Bell tacos, Lucky Larger beer, Thunderbird wine, yesca—
SECRETARY: Yesca?
SANCHO: Mota.
SECRETARY: Mota?
SANCHO: Lēnos . . . MARIJUANA. *(Snap.* JOHNNY *inhales on an imaginary joint.)*
SECRETARY: That's against the law!
JOHNNY: *(big smile, holding his breath)* Yeah.
SANCHO: He also sniffs glue. *(Snap.* JOHNNY *inhales glue, big smile.)*
JOHNNY: Tha's too much man, ese.
SECRETARY: No, Mr. Sancho, I don't think this—
SANCHO: Wait a minute, he has other qualities I know you'll love. For example an inferiority complex. *(Snap.)*
JOHNNY: *(to* SANCHO*)* You think you're better than me, huh ese? *(Swings switchblade.)*
SANCHO: He can also be beaten and he bruises, cut him and he bleeds, kick him and he—*(He beats, bruises and kicks* PACHUCO.*)* would you like to try it?
SECRETARY: Oh, I couldn't.
SANCHO: Be my guest. He's a great scape goat.
SECRETARY: No really.
SANCHO: Please.
SECRETARY: Well, alright. Just once. *(She kicks* PACHUCO.*)* Oh, he's so soft.
SANCHO: Wasn't that good? Try again.

303

SECRETARY: *(kicks* PACHUCO*)* Oh, he's so wonderful! *(She kicks him again.)*

SANCHO: Okay, that's enough, lady. You ruin the merchandise. Yes, our Johnny Pachuco model can give you many hours of pleasure. Why, the LAPD just bought 20 of these to train their rookies cops on. And talk about maintenance. Señorita, you are looking at an entirely self-supporting machine. You're never going to find our Johnny Pachuco model on the relief rolls. No, sir, this model knows how to liberate.

SECRETARY: Liberate?

SANCHO: He steals. *(Snap.* JOHNNY *rushes the* SECRETARY *and steals her purse.)*

JOHNNY: Dáme esa bolsa, vieja! *(He grabs the purse and runs. Snap by* SANCHO. *He stops.)*

SECRETARY *runs after* JOHNNY *and grabs purse away from him, kicking him as she goes.*

SECRETARY: No, no, no! We can't have any *more* thieves in the State Administration. Put him back.

SANCHO: Okay, we still got other models. Come on, Johnny, we'll sell you to some old lady. *(*SANCHO *takes* JOHNNY *back to his place.)*

SECRETARY: Mr. Sancho, I don't think you quite understand what we need. What we need is something that will attract the women voters. Something more traditional, more romantic.

SANCHO: Ah, a lover. *(He smiles meaningfully.)* Step right over here, senorita. Introducing our standard Revolucionario and/or Early California Bandit type. As you can see he is well-built, sturdy, durable. This is the International Harvester of Mexicans.

SECRETARY: What does he do?

SANCHO: You name it, he does it. He rides horses, stays in the mountains, crosses deserts, plains, rivers, leads revolutions, follows revolutions, kills, can be killed, serves as a martyr, hero, movie star—did I say movie star? Did you ever see Viva Zapata? Viva Villa, Villa Rides, Pancho Villa Returns, Pancho Villa Goes Back, Pancho Villa Meets Abbott and Costello—

SECRETARY: I've never seen any of those.

SANCHO: Well, he was in all of them. Listen to this. *(Snap.)*

REVOLUCIONARIO: *(scream)* VIVA VILLAAAAA!

SECRETARY: That's awfully loud.

SANCHO: He has a volume control. *(He adjusts volume. Snap.)*

REVOLUCIONARIO: *(mousey voice)* Viva villa.

SECRETARY: That's better.

SANCHO: And even if you didn't see him in the movies, perhaps you saw him on TV. He makes commercials. *(Snap.)*

REVOLUCIONARIO: Is there a Frito Bandito in your house?

SECRETARY: Oh yes, I've seen that one!

SANCHO: Another feature about this one is that he is economical. He

304

runs on raw horsemeat and tequila!

SECRETARY: Isn't that rather savage?

SANCHO: Al contrario, it makes him a lover. *(Snap.)*

REVOLUCIONARIO: *(to* SECRETARY*)* Ay, mamasota, cochota, ven pa'ca! *(He grabs* SECRETARY *and folds her back—latin-lover style.)*

SANCHO: *(Snap.* REVOLUCIONARIO *goes back upright)* Now wasn't that nice?

SECRETARY: Well, it was rather nice.

SANCHO: And finally, there is one outstanding feature about this model I KNOW the ladies are going to love: he's a GENUINE antique! He was made in Mexico in 1910!

SECRETARY: Made in Mexico?

SANCHO: That's right. Once in Tijuana, twice in Guadalajara, three times in Cuernavaca.

SECRETARY: Mr. Sancho, I thought he was an American product.

SANCHO: No, but—

SECRETARY: No, I'm sorry. We can't buy anything but American made products. He just won't do.

SANCHO: But he's an antique!

SECRETARY: I don't care. You still don't understand what we need. It's true we need Mexican models such as these, but it's more important that he be *American*.

SANCHO: American?

SECRETARY: That's right, and judging from what you've shown me, I don't think you have what we want. Well, my lunch hour's almost over, I better—

SANCHO: Wait a Minute! Mexican but American?

SECRETARY: That's correct.

SANCHO: Mexican but . . . *(a sudden flash)* AMERICAN! Yeah, I think we've got exactly what you want. He just came in today! Give me a minute. *(He exits. Talks from backstage.)* Here he is in the shop. Let me just get some papers off. There. Introducing our new 1970 Mexican-American! Ta-ra-ra-ra-ra-ra-RA-RAAA!

SANCHO *brings out the Mexican-American model, a clean-shaven middleclass type in a business suit, with glasses.*

SECRETARY: *(impressed)* Where have you been hiding this one?

SANCHO: He just came in this morning. Ain't he a beauty? Feast your eyes on him! Sturdy US STEEL frame, streamlined, modern. As a matter of fact, he is built exactly like our Anglo models except that he comes in a variety of darker shades: naughahide, leather, or leatherette.

SECRETARY: Naughahide.

SANCHO: Well, we'll just write that down. Yes, señorita, this model represents the apex of American engineering! He is bilingual, college educated, ambitious! Say the word "acculturate" and he accelerates. He is intelligent, well-mannered, clean—did I say clean? *(Snap.* MEX-

305

AM *raises his arm.)* Smell.

SECRETARY: *(smells)* Old Sobaco, my favorite.

SANCHO: *(Snap.* MEX-AM *turns toward* SANCHO*)* Eric? *(to* SECRE-
TARY*)* We call him Eric Garcia. *(to* ERIC*)* I want you to meet Miss
JIM-enez, Eric.

MEXICAN-AM: Miss JIM-enez, I am delighted to make your acquaint-
ance. *(He kisses her hand.)*

SECRETARY: Oh, my, how charming!

SANCHO: Did you feel the suction? He has seven especially engineered
suction cups right behind his lips. He's a charmer allright!

SECRETARY: How about boards, does he function on boards?

SANCHO: You name them he is on them. Parole boards, draft boards,
school boards, taco quality control boards, surf boards, two by fours.

SECRETARY: Does he function in politics?

SANCHO: Señorita, you are looking at a political MACHINE. Have you
ever heard of the OEO, EOC, COD, WAR ON POVERTY? That's our
model! Not only that he makes political speeches.

SECRETARY: May I hear one?

SANCHO: With pleasure. *(Snap.)* Eric, give us a speech.

MEXICAN-AM: Mr. Congressman, Mr. Chairman, members of the
board, honored guests, ladies and gentlemen. *(*SANCHO *and* SECRE-
TARY *applaud.)* Please, please. I come before you as a Mexican-
American to tell you about the problems of the Mexican. The
problems of the Mexican stem from one thing and one thing alone:
He's stupid. He's uneducated. He needs to stay in school. He needs to
be ambitious, forward-looking, harder-working. He needs to think
American, American, American, AMERICAN, AMERICAN, AMERI-
CAN. GOD BLESS AMERICA! GOD BLESS AMERICA! GOD
BLESS AMERICA!! *(He goes out of control.)*

SANCHO *snaps frantically and the* MEXICAN-AMERICAN *finally
slumps forward, bending at the waist.*

SECRETARY: Oh my, he's patriotic too!

SANCHO: Si, señorita, he loves his country. Let me just make a little
adjustment here. *(Stands* MEXICAN-AMERICAN *up.)*

SECRETARY: What about upkeep? Is he economical?

SANCHO: Well, no, I won't lie to you. The Mexican-American costs a
little bit more, but you get what you pay for. He's worth every extra
cent. You can keep him running on dry Martinis, Langendorf bread,

SECRETARY: Apple pie?

SANCHO: Only Mom's. Of course, he's also programmed to eat Mexican food on ceremonial functions, but I must warn you: an overdose
of beans will plug up his exhaust.

SECRETARY: Fine! There's just one more question: HOW MUCH DO
YOU WANT FOR HIM?

SANCHO: Well, I tell you what I'm gonna do. Today and today only,
because you've been so sweet, I'm gonna let you steel this model

306

from me! I'm gonna let you drive him off the lot for the simple price of—let's see taxes and license included—$15,000.

SECRETARY: Fifteen thousand DOLLARS? For a MEXICAN!

SANCHO: Mexican? What are you talking, lady? This is a Mexican-AMERICAN! We had to melt down two pachucos, a farm worker and three gavachos to make this model! You want quality, but you gotta pay for it! This is no cheap run-about. He's got class!

SECRETARY: Okay, I'll take him.

SANCHO: You will?

SECRETARY: Here's your money.

SANCHO: You mind if I count it?

SECRETARY: Go right ahead.

SANCHO: Well, you'll get your pink slip in the mail. Oh, do you want me to wrap him up for you? We have a box in the back.

SECRETARY: No, thank you. The Governor is having a luncheon this afternoon, and we need a brown face in the crowd. How do I drive him?

SANCHO: Just snap your fingers. He'll do anything you want.

SECRETARY *snaps.* MEXICAN-AMERICAN *steps forward.*

MEXICAN-AM: RAZA QUERIDA, VAMOS LEVANTANDO ARMAS PARA LIBERARNOS DE ESTOS DESGRACIADOS GABACHOS QUE NOS EXPLOTAN! VAMOS—

SECRETARY: What did he say?

SANCHO: Something about lifting arms, killing white people, etc.

SECRETARY: But he's not suppose to say that!

SANCHO: Look lady, don't blame me for bugs from the factory, He's your Mexican-American, you bought him, now drive him off the lot!

SECRETARY: But he's broken!

SANCHO: Try snapping another finger.

SECRETARY *Snaps.* MEXICAN-AMERICAN *comes to life again.*

MEXICAN-AM: ESTA GRAN HUMANIDAD HA DICHO BASTA! Y SE A PUESTO EN MARCHA! BASTA! BASTA! VIVA LA RAZA! VIVA LA CAUSA! VIVA LA HUELGA! VIVAN LOS BROWN BERETS! VIVA LOS ESTUDIANTES! CHICANO POWER!

The MEXICAN-AMERICAN *turns toward the* SECRETARY, *who gasps and backs up. He keeps turning toward the* PACHUCO, FARM-WORKER *and* REVOLUCIONARIO, *snapping his fingers and turning each of them on, one by one.*

PACHUCO: *(Snap. to* SECRETARY*)* I'm going to get you, baby! VIVA LA RAZA!

FARM WORKER: *(Snap. to* SECRETARY*)* Viva la huelga! Viva la Huelga! VIVA LA HUELGA!

REVOLUCIONARIO: *(Snap. to* SECRETARY*)* Viva la revolución! VIVA LA REVOLUCION!

The three models join together and advance toward the SECRETARY, *who backs up and runs out of the shop screaming.* SANCHO *is at the other end of the shop holding his money in his hand. All freeze. After a few seconds of silence, the* PACHUCO *moves and stretches, shaking his arms and loosening up. The* FARM WORKER *and* REVOLUCION-ARIO *do the same.* SANCHO *stays where he is, frozen to his spot.*

JOHNNY: Man, that was a long one, ese. *(Others agree with him.)*

FARM WORKER: How did we do?

JOHNNY: Perty good, look all that lana, man! *(He goes over to* SANCHO *and removes the money from his hand.* SANCHO *stays where he is.)*

REVOLUCIONARIO: En la madre, look at all the money.

JOHNNY: We keep this up, we're going to be rich.

FARM WORKER: They think we're machines.

REVOLUCIONARIO: Burros.

JOHNNY: Puppets.

MEXICAN-AM: The only thing I don't like is—how come I always got to play the godamn Mexican-American?

JOHNNY: That's what you get for finishing high school.

FARM WORKER: How about our wages, ese?

JOHNNY: Here it comes right now. $3,000 for you, $3,000 for you, $3,000 for you and $3,000 for me. The rest we put back into the business.

MEXICAN- AM: Too much, man. Heh, where you vatos going tonight?

FARM WORKER: I'm going over to Concha's. There's a party.

JOHNNY: Wait a minute, vatos. What about our salesman? I think he needs an oil job.

REVOLUCIONARIO: Leave him to me.

The PACHUCO, FARMWORKER *and* MEXICAN-AMERICAN *exit, talking loudly about their plans for the night. The* REVOLUCIONAR-IO *goes over to* SANCHO, *removes his derby hat and cigar, lifts him up and throws him over his shoulder.* SANCHO *hangs loose, lifeless.*

REVOLUCIONARIO: *(to audience)* He's the best model we got! Ajua! *(Exit.)*

FIN

ADDITIONAL DOCUMENTS

Guerilla Theatre

TRIP WITHOUT A TICKET*

Our authorized sanities are so many nembutals. "Normal" citizens with store-dummy smiles stand apart from each other like cotton-packed capsules in a bottle. Perpetual mental out-patients. Maddening sterile jobs for strait-jackets, love-scrubbed into an insipid pacifier. Everyone is kept inside while the outside is shown through window advertising and manicured news. And we all know this. How many TV specials would it take to establish one Guatemalan revolution? How many weeks would an ad agency require to face-lift the image of the so-called "Viet Cong?" Slowly, very slowly, we are led nowhere. Consumer circuses are held in the ward daily. Critics are tolerated like exploding novelties. We will be told which burning Asians to take seriously. Slowly. Later.

But there is a real danger in suddenly waking a somnambulistic patient. And we all know this.

WHAT IF HE IS STARTLED RIGHT OUT OF THE WINDOW. No one can control the single circuit-breaking moment that charges games with critical reality. If the glass is cut, if the cushioned distance of media is removed the patients may never respond as normals again. They will become life-actors.

THEATRE IS TERRITORY. A space for existing outside padded walls. Setting down as a stage declares a universal pardon for imagination. But what happens next must mean more than sanctuary or

---

*Anonymous, *Haight-Ashbury Tribune*, 1968.

preserve. How would real wardens react to life-actors on liberated ground. How can the intrinsic freedom of theatre illuminate walls and show the weak spots where a breakout could occur?

GUERILLA THEATRE INTENDS TO BRING AUDIENCES TO LIBERATED TERRITORY TO CREATE LIFE-ACTORS. It remains light and exploitive of forms for the same reasons that it intends to remain free. It seeks audiences that are created by issues. It creates a cast of freed beings. It will become an issue itself.

This is theatre of an underground that wants out. Its aim is to liberate ground held by consumer wardens and establish territory without walls. Its plays are glass-cutters for empire windows.

The diggers are hip to property. Everything is free, do your own thing. Human beings are the means of exchange. Food, machines, clothing, materials, shelter and props are simply there. Stuff. A perfect dispenser would be an open automat on the street. Locks are time-consuming. Combinations are locks.

So a store of goods or clinic or restaurant that is free becomes a social art form. Ticketless theatre, out of money and control.

First you gotta pin down what's wrong with the West. Distrust of human nature, which means distrust of Nature. Distrust of wildness in oneself literally means distrust of Wilderness.

Gary Snyder

Diggers assume free stores to liberate nature. First free the space, goods and services. Let the theories of economics follow social facts. Once a free store is assumed, human wanting and giving, needing and taking become wide open to improvisation.

A sign: IF SOMEONE ASKS TO SEE THE MANAGER TELL HIM HE'S THE MANAGER.

Someone asked how much a book was. How much did he think it was worth? 75 cents. The money was taken and held out for anyone, "Eh, Who wants 75 cents?" A girl who had just walked in came over and took it.

A basket labeled FREE MONEY.

No owner, no manager, no employees and no cash register. A salesman in a free store is a life-actor, Anyone who will assume an answer to a question or accept a problem as a turn-on.

QUESTION: (whispered) Who pays the rent?

ANSWER: (loudly) May I help you?

Who's ready for the implications of a free store? Welfare mothers pile bags full of clothes for a few days and come back to hang up dresses. Kids case the joint wondering how to boost.

Fire helmets, riding pants, shower curtain, surgical gowns and WWI boots are parts for costumes. Nightsticks, sample cases, water pipes, toy guns and weather balloons are taken for props. When materials are free, imagination becomes currency for spirit.

Where does the stuff come from. People, persons beings. Isn't it obvious that objects are only transitory subjects of human value? An object released from one person's value may be destroyed, abandoned or made available to other people. The choice is anyone's.

STREET EVENT: BIRTH OF HAIGHT-FUNERAL FOR MONEY NOW?

Pop Art mirrored the social skin, happenings X-rayed the bones. Street events are social acid Heightenings.

Pop Art mirrored the social skin, happenings X-rayed the bones. Street events are social acid heightening consciousness of what is real on the streets. To expand eyeball implications until the facts are established through action.

The Mexican Day of the Dead is celebrated in cemetaries. Yellow flowers are falling petal by petal on graves. In moonlight, favorite songs of the deceased and everybody gets loaded. Children suck deaths-head candy engraved with their names in icing.

A digger event. Flowers, mirrors, penny-whistles, girls in costumes of themselves, Hell's Angels, street people. Mime Troupe.

Angels ride up Haight Street with girls holding NOW signs. Flowers and penny-whistles passed out to everyone.

A chorus on both sides of the street chanting UHH!—AHH!— SHH BE COOL! Mirrors held up to reflect faces of passers-by.

Penny-whistle music, clapping, flowers thrown in the air. A bus driver held up by the action gets out to dance a quick free minute. No more passers-by, everybody's together.

The burial procession. Three black-shrouded messengers holding staffs topped with reflective dollar signs. A runner swinging a red lantern. Four pallbearers wearing animal heads carry a black casket, singing *Get Out of My Life Why Don't You Babe* to Chopin's Death March. Members of the procession give out silver dollars and candles.

No more reality. Someone jumps on a car with the news that two Angels were busted. Crowd, funeral cortege and friends of the Angels fill the street to march on Park Police Station. Cops confront 400 free beings: a growling poet with a lute, animal spirit in black, Candle-lit girls singing *Silent Night*. A collection for bail fills an Angel's helmet. March back to Haight and street dancing.

Street events are rituals of release. Re-claiming of territory (sundown, traffic, public joy) through spirit. Possession. Public NewSense.

Not Street=theatre; the street *is* theatre. Parades, bank robberies, fires and sonic explosions focus street attention. A crowd is an audience for an event. Release of crowd spirit can accomplish social facts. Riots are a reaction to police theatre. Parades, bank robberies, fires and sonic explosions focus street attention. A crowd is an audience for an event. Release of crowd spirit can accomplish social facts. Riots are a reaction to police theatre. Thrown bottles and overturned cars are responses to a

311

dull, heavy-fisted, mechanical and deathly show. People fill the street to express special public feelings and hold human communion. To ask "What's happening?" The alternative to death is a joyous funeral in company with the living.

WHO PAID FOR YOUR TRIP?

Industrialization was a battle with 19th century ecology to win breakfast at the cost of smog and insanity. Wars against ecology are suicidal. The US standard of living is a bourgeois baby blanket for executives who scream in their sleep. No Pleistocene swamp could match the pestilential horror of modern urban sewage. No children of White Western Progress will escape the dues of peoples forced to haul raw materials.

But the tools (that's all factories are) remain innocent and the ethic of greed isn't necessary. Computers render the principles of wage-labor obsolete by incorporating them. We are being freed from mechanistic consciousness. We could evacuate the factories, turn them over to the androids, clean up our pollution. North Americans could give up self-righteousness and expand their being.

Our conflict is with job wardens and consumer-keepers of a permissive looney-bin. Property, credit, interest, insurance, installments, profit are stupid concepts. Millions of have-nots and drop-outs in the US are living on an overflow of technologically produced fat. They aren't fighting the ecology, they're responding to it. Middle class living rooms are funeral parlors and only undertakers will stay in them. Our fight is with those who would kill us through dumb work, insane wars, dull money morality.

GIVE UP JOBS SO COMPUTERS CAN DO THEM: Any important human occupation can be done free. Can it be given away?

Revolutions in Asia, Africa, South America are for humanistic industrialization. The technological resources of North America can be used throughout the world. Gratis. Nor a patronizing gift, shared.

An event for the main business district of any US city. Infiltrate the largest corporation office building with life-actors as nyphomaniacal secretaries, clumsy repairmen, berserk executives, sloppy security guards, clerks with animals in their clothes. Low key until the first coffee break and then pour it on. Secretaries unbutton their blouses and press shy clerks against the wall. Repairmen drop typewriters and knock over water coolers. Executives charge into private offices claiming seniority. Guards produce booze bottles and playfully jam elevator doors. Clerks pull out goldfish, rabbits, pigeons, cats on leashes, loose dogs. At noon 1,000 freed beings singing and dancing appear outside to persuade employees to take off for the day. Banners roll down from office windows announcing liberation. Shills in business suits run out of the building, strip and dive in the fountain. Elevators are loaded with incense and a pie-fight breaks out in the cafeteria.

Theatre is Fact/Action.

Give up jobs. Be with people. Defend against property.
Theatre is Fact/Action.

Berkeley Radical Arts Troupe

BUILD RAT AND SERVE THE PEOPLE*

Start a guerrilla theater troupe! It's a good way to get the politics of
SDS across in an entertaining, non-rhetorical fashion to masses of
people. (Besides, it's fun.) Here are some suggestions gathered by RAT
(Radical Arts Troupe) from experience at Princeton and Berkeley.

Politics

Politics is primary. This means that the political purposes of RAT are
more important than the artistic; though the better the artistry, the
clearer the politics will be to the audience. Our plays are designed
primarily to spread SDS ideas and only secondarily to entertain. For
instance, male chauvinist jokes must be excluded, no matter how funny
they may appear to some (and no matter how popular they can be
expected to be). RAT is not Hollywood, and politics is not a popularity
contest.

In particular, we must fight the tendency towards opportunism—'we
know that liberalism is just as bad as conservatism, but most students
don't, so let's not mention it, and we won't alienate them.' If our ideas
are correct, we should be able to convince large numbers of students.
Theater provides us with a forum which appeals to everybody and
allows us to present our politics in a principled way. For instance, the
Berkeley RAT play 'RLTC' (Reserve Liberal Training Corps) was criticized at first by some members of the chapter as 'sectarian' and
'isolating.' Once it was performed, the audience understood and enjoyed it.

It is sectarian to attack an idea without explaining what's wrong with
it. In the 'RLTC' play, for instance, an incorrect way of attacking
student power would be:

Misleader: Hooray for student power!
Leader: Down with student power!
Masses: Yeah! Down with student power!

It is also sectarian to attack people who hold wrong ideas instead of
attacking the ideas themselves. Example:

Some students: Let's have student power!
Leftists: Get lost, counter-revolutionaries!

---

*SDS Radical Arts Troupe skits and songs pamphlet.

313

Still another incorrect approach is to have lengthy dialogue. Experience shows that after about twenty seconds of speech without action, an audience will begin drifting away. Shun the 'reading from leaflets' and 'three speakers for, three speakers against' formats.

Illustrate your points. For example, Berkeley's Chancellor Heyns is a director of Hunt's Foods. A high school radical theater group exposed Hunt's racist exploitation of Chicano tomato-pickers with the following scene: one of them mimed tomato picking while Heyns was sucking his blood through plastic tubing, and spitting it in a Hunt's Catsup bottle. A third character poured the Catsup over fourth character's hamburger. The fourth character: 'This isn't catsup, it's blood!' All actors were mechanical, like well-oiled machines. The scene was repeated several times, and was really powerful.

Keep it simple: Avoid cluttered, complicated stories requiring subtle acting and elaborate props. It will only detract from the value of the play. Eliminate all superfluous lines and gestures. Instead, rely on good politics, simple jokes, and sight gags.

Stock characters will emerge after a few plays—the fat, avaricious businessman, his various lackeys, deans, profs, pigs, etc., and on the other side the people and some leftists. An effort should be made to identify those characters with some symbolic costume (Uncle Sam hat, play money, pig mask). If this is impossible, it may be necessary to wear signs.

Use music and other noisemaking to add to your dramatic effects. Anything will do. Tambourines, bongos are easy to borrow. Kazoos are cheap. Voices can be used, too, and all sorts of simple instruments can be improvised (fill an empty coke can with pebbles and shake it, for example). Again, keep it simple. Background music can create an atmosphere (e.g. military fanfare) and smooth over transitions from one scene to the next. Finally, a good song is always appreciated by the audience.

Useful gimmicks:

- plots based on a parody of well-known stories and plays. We've used Hamlet, Little Red Riding Hood.
- commercials. (e.g. the play is interrupted for a word from the sponsors: 'Be the first kid on your block to kill a communist with the new Mattel toy gun. War may be hell, but with Mattel, it's swell!')
- flashbacks, instant replays, plays within the play.
- court scenes in which the enemies of the people are tried (and convicted!) of their crimes.
- the 'machine' view of the world: having a few people do some interrelated actions in a mechanical fashion, as though they were

314

cogs in a machine—often a highly effective way of describing the working of society or of an institution. (e.g. students standing in line, turning pages and nodding, while a dean or professor keeps up the cadence by screaming rhythmically 'Read! Read! Learn! Learn! Learn!')

Putting the Play Together

Casting: Our plays have had 6 to 12 'actors'. The fewer actors, the more flexibility and mobility you have. Avoid type-casting. Fight racism and male chauvinism by not casting according to sex or race. Casting should be decided upon primarily in terms of building the troupe and the play. That is, new people should take key parts to develop aggressiveness and responsibility; a girl struggling against male chauvinism should take the part of a left-wing leader. Avoid building up stars—RAT is a collective of radicals struggling together, not a road to fame or an ego trip.

This does not mean that available talent should not be used. There is always someone around who is particularly able to make good jokes or puns. There is always someone who has had some experience in bourgeois theater, or someone who can play some musical instrument. But beware of the tendency to rely on the 'specialist'. 'Ordinary' people will display greater creativity.

Collective creation: Avoid having one person write, direct, and star in the plays. The whole troupe should collectively discuss the politics of the play. This serves a dual purpose. On the one hand, it will provide for political struggle with new recruits; quite a few people become committed SDSers through RAT. On the other hand, a clear understanding of the politics helps enormously in figuring out scenes.

Combine spontaneity and discipline. Usually most ideas and jokes in a play originate by ad-libbing during the first meeting (or outside the meetings). An occasional ad-lib during a performance will keep everyone's spirits high and improve the acting. Good performances are only possible with a spirited, enthusiastic troupe, but avoid chaos during rehearsals. One experienced member of RAT (not necessarily always the same one) should direct each rehearsal. It is often helpful to write out the script, but it is essential always to have at least a clear outline in mind. Be flexible in removing from and adding to the play.

Fight defeatism. RAT is hard work, and the play won't write and perform itself. Experience shows that the first production of a troupe is the toughest—so don't get discouraged, especially by rehearsals that seem to fall flat. Remember that your performance will almost invariably be better than the rehearsals.

The Performance

Start with a bang to attract an audience. In one play in which we tried the Chancellor for his crimes, we started with the whole troupe chasing him around Sproul Plaza, screaming and yelling.

Experience shows that a run-through before each performance is important for ensuring RAT's success.

The play itself can last any length of time (ours usually last 7 to 15 minutes). The only limitations are imposed by the time you want to spend working on it. Bigger chapters can afford longer plays and a greater variety of productions than smaller ones.

You can perform anywhere, anytime—during classbreak, at demonstrations, rallies, sit-ins, take-overs, etc.—whenever and wherever a lot of people will gather to watch. Performing before a seated audience is more difficult than performing before passers-by because a seated audience will expect a higher degree of technical proficiency.

Different audiences will react differently to the same scene. For example, in one play, striking students drown a scab. When we performed this on the Berkeley campus, the response was rather weak. But when we performed it for striking oil workers at a union meeting, we got an enthusiastic reception. After many performances, a few people will come to congRATulate you—try to recruit them! And ask the audience for donations.

In performance, always remember the purpose of RAT—to communicate the politics to the audience—and that this purpose must outweigh our fears of performing before the public. Try always to reach out to the people!

Toward People's Art

The basic difference between guerrilla theater and 'regular' theater is a class difference. Specifically, guerrilla theater seeks to serve the people. It draws its inspiration from the struggles of oppressed peoples, not from the visions of an alienated poet. Our plays come from 'ordinary' people with political consciousness, not from 'gifted' actors and directors who are in a hurry to get away from the people.

A director in RAT is responsive and responsible to the troupe and the public. A director in bourgeois theater is often a despot. A guerrilla theater actor is in it to build SDS and the left in this country; an actor in bourgeois theater is on an ego trip. Our plays are intended to reach hundreds and thousands of people, most of whom never 'go to the theater'.

People's art has an enormous potential for growth in this country. If we build our commitment to serve the people, it will reach rarely attained heights. New Left Notes can be a good vehicle for discussion of these ideas. Chapters and individuals should send in articles about their experiences in radical art, along with scripts, posters, poems, etc.

Berkely Radical Arts Troupe

316

Jeriann Badanes

BURNING CITY STREET THEATRE: THE ECOLOGY PLAY*

Six people (Russian Jews) cried over our performance of the Berkeley play. They said we were the hope of the world.

Burning City Journal Entry

At the end of June 1969, eight members of Burning City went to Clesson Valley Farm in East Hawley, Massachusetts to live and work for the summer . . . .

The Ecology Play—The Pillage of Capitalism

The terrible pollution of oceans, rivers, lakes, streams. The murder of birds, animals, trees, people. The desire to make profit instead of life . . . Everyday we read in newspapers, magazines, books about the subject . . . We covered the walls of our rehearsing room with paper so that we could paste up articles, make drawings, images, synopsis of plays, outlines, poems about ecology. We looked backwards to the place where chants, rituals, natural catastrophes took place. We knew that good ecology was being concerned with our own health. How can we change and stop the dying? By eating healthy, organic food together we were making a start in developing our own awareness.

Tracing back the actual step by step development of the Ecology Play is like digging in old ruins and finding once in a while an identifiable bone. It becomes painfully clear that much of what is really powerful between us, spontaneous, revealing and meaningful is never experienced by our audience. For in the process of putting together a playable play, coming from all of us, much is lost and forgotten. In the loose way that we work added to the fact that members are always going and coming back and that we move around a lot, sometimes because we want to and sometimes, because we are undesirables (people in a group are a threat), research takes on a new meaning. Some graduate student in 1995 is going to have a formidable task writing about Street Theatre. Good. But the scraps, the old outlines, the notes and what we remember by talking tell me something else. We are not only changing our lives and the lives of people we are able to touch, but almost unwittingly, unknowingly, we are also changing the whole concept of theatre, destroying all the accepted definitions. There used to be a building called a theatre. A man bought two tickets, one for himself and one for his wife, to a performance that had been repeated now for three years, exactly the same play. They sit in row 2E, laugh a

*This is an excerpt from a longer work, "Burning City Street Theatre—An Analysis of a Theatre Commune," by Jeriann Badanes. Burning City, like Pageant Players, another influential street theatre of the sixties, is now defunct. But many of its former members continue to work in people's theatre.

317

couple of times; at intermission the man pisses and the wife powders her nose. They return and laugh two more times. At the end, the author comes out and takes a bow; it is the 500th performance. That man and that woman don't know that outside in the parks something else is going on. People are sitting around in a circle clapping their hands in rhythm to a play they have just seen.

The plays we create are a vehicle for saying something that we want to say. The parts we play come out of ourselves. You are not going to forget a line if you're saying something you need and want to say. We are then acting out our lives for ourselves and for others. So our scenarios are written down usually after the fact, the fact of creation. God created the earth and then that creation was recorded in the Bible. What we are able to write down serves as a record of what we have already performed . . . .

GENESIS CHAPTER 6: verse 4-8
There were giants in the earth in those days; and also after that, when the sons of God came in unto the daughters of men, and they bare children to them, the same became mighty men which were of old, men of reknown.
And God saw that the wickedness of man was great in the earth, and that every imagination of the thoughts of his heart was only evil continually.
And it repented the Lord that he had made man on the earth, and it grieved him at his heart.
And the Lord said, I will destroy man whom I have created from the face of the earth; both man, and beast, and the creeping thing, and the fowls of the air; for it repenteth me that I have made them.
But Noah found grace in the eyes of the Lord.

During a two-week period in mid-summer it rained and we acted out the story of Noah and the flood. We gathered in the Yurt [a large wooden circular building on the farm] and one of us read the story, while the rest of us using a rotation method acted out the story. It was a perfect performance. We relived the story by being these people, animals and the boat. We added other dimensions. Noah was acted out by a man and a woman at the same time. We became and knew what it was to be animals and when Noah found the skeletons on the land, death was in the room with us. But no one else saw this performance. It was our own ritual, a one shot drama.

The next day we improvised on the story. The arc was transformed into a modern luxury liner, taking people to a better land, another country, the America we wish we lived in. One actress rebelled. She put on a mask, improvised a song and asked the rest of us to get off that ship and join her right now, be in her band, like make it happen right now between us. Ideas of what *could* happen all seemed like a cop-out. So that day we turned Noah's arc upside down and made it relate to us.

318

The boat became a bridge, a rainbow, which gave us light. We dropped the Noah story and next day concentrated only on one image from the preceding workshop. The creation of giants. How can we look like giants? And from this work we developed the theme of the play. The birth of the earth, seen as a giant, vitalized by the sun, his body parts becoming trees, rocks, rivers, stars through the suggestion of chanting. He discovers his shadow, but is left alone when the sun goes down. Alone and cold he transforms into a bum looking into a store window of warm coats. In anger he breaks the window and the falling mannikins (actors) become the tumult of an earthquake. They make a totem formation and through their legs animals, birds, beasts and all living creatures are born. The actors transform into all types and utterances of animals and birds. One animal says, "And among the animals was man." Man appears, a large colored masked figure. The earth giant is shown to need man by the small man creature who carries the earth giant away on her back. This image is broken into by the discovery of America by Columbus, and actor with a drum and fife corp who parade to a halt, where upon Columbus pinches America, an Indian woman with a head band. Freeze, and then Governor Rockefeller enters claiming America as his. Pushing Columbus away and removing her headband he ties it around her waist and shoulder, and claims her Miss America. Fife and drum corp now become a cheering crowd as Rocky and Miss America parade down 5th Avenue. Kiss and ass pinching. Suddenly an image of the building of cities. Boxes of scraps and garbage are thrown around the playing area. Chaos, pollution and an uptown chic is dry fucked in the midst of crazy name calling and throwing garbage at each other. The giant earth reappears now as the guy cleaning up the mess. He admonishes the fucking couple, "That's not the way to do it."

This image of destruction is broken into by a scene of growth, which serves both as a historical ritual of how people in America (Indians) used to grow their food and live in harmony together and also a portrayal and vision of the communal-tribal life of young people sharing their lives. The growing of our own food. The ritual occurs when one person as a seed is blown to a fertile spot, takes root and begins to grow. The others begin a chant-work-dance motion around the seed. "Plow, plant, rain, sun, grow." Bending, grasping, pulling, rising and opening into a joyous rhythmic work motion circling around the seed until fatigued they fall asleep. As the seed grows to a series of drum beats until in full flower she bends to the sleeping figures, wakens them and gives them food. They begin to chant as food is taken in. They are fed until everyone is singing. The seed is now a cornstalk who is joined by two others and they transform into a beautiful flowing river. Music. Two other figures slowly move automatically, carelessly, ruthlessly park near the river and start tying it up with rags from their boxes. Gradually all motion of the river is stopped and the three river figures are covered up with newspapers. The two employees called

"Bill" and two versions of the same man born of capitalism, "Management" and "Labor," carry on a schizophrenic conversation about family, college, vacation, better jobs, more money, etc. While they talk, another voice names the corporations causing this pollution. The giant monopolies rape our land. They finish up by putting a layer of newspapers on, then leave, but come back shortly with another actor, and all three wearing grotesque faces are introduced as the Rockefeller brothers. We are name calling. The Rockefeller brothers talk politics: "South American tour, profits, surplus, sensitive concepts, progress," until they suddenly notice the "river," the 3 figures tied under newspapers. "We must clean this mess up. Urban renewal, a new Standard Oil Company can be built here." So they proceed to burn it up. Bodies and burning. Vietnam. And the river people burn in slow motion, while the three Rockefeller boys seem satisfied.

But the giant-earth comes back, wearing a white gentle mask. The persistent Vietnamese face. In pain he goes to help the river. He sees the Rockefellers: "Who do you think you are? Do you think you own the earth?" They say, "As a matter of fact, yes." They grab him, map out sections and build companies, South American oil wells, sugar plants, etc. They fight with each other about who owns what. The giant struggles back, crying, "The earth needs help." He is joined by all the other actors who chant and overcome the Rockefellers. They call out to the audience, "The earth needs our help. The earth is being destroyed. The earth belongs to everyone and it needs our help now." The end.

In this Ecology play, as in the Berkeley play about the storming of People's Park by the Police, many images are created in a circle form. It is an important symbol and formation for us. The audience seated all around can, like us, see all the other people there too. It allows for intimacy as well as ritual formality. It's the form that joins people as a completion unto itself. The fact that theatre was pushed frontally and put up on a stage, just like judges in courtrooms, forcing people to stare straight ahead, ignorant of who is behind them, seems to fit right in with the process of man's separation from man.

Naledi Nnakintu Alexander*

REPORT ON THE NATIONAL BLACK THEATRE

The National Black Theatre is a four year old community-oriented theatre group that makes its home in the heart of Harlem. It was conceived, organized and is now directed by Barbara Ann Teer, actress and directress. Its purpose is to lead the Black community toward awareness of its problems and its potential on as many levels as possible. It has performed on nationwide television on the "SOUL"

*The author is a member of The National Black Theatre.

320

Show, repeatedly on Black Solidarity Day, at Pan African Conferences, in Bermuda, in many colleges and universities throughout the country, and at the Apollo Theatre in Harlem.

The group which is structured like a very well organized family, has about 46 members. Some members had been in casts of off-Broadway plays, and some still are in shows, occasionally. Some members, most of them, in fact, have never been in an off-Broadway or off-off-Broadway play, and have no desire to expend their energies in that direction. Quite a few of the "family" are now attending, or have at one time attended college. Some are taking graduate studies. Some have never attended college.

There is of course a wide range of personalities, personal incomes, and vocations within the group. The main uniting factor, and the prerequisite for membership, is a commitment to raising the level of consciousness of Black people. One of the tenets of the institution is that the truth—political, economic, social and spiritual—and the strength/ability to deal with it constructively must/will set black people free.

The theatre's physical plant is a 1,000 foot loft at 9 East 125 St., in the heart of Harlem. Originally, it was a huge, unpainted, unheated factory in desperate need of repair. The members of the theatre, some members of Imamu Amiri Baraka's Spirit House in New-Ark, and some friends, tore down, swept, washed, rebuilt, painted, decorated, curtained, sanded, furnished and redesigned the loft into a theatre.

Around 1966-67, Barbara Ann Teer decided that the theatre of mainstream America was ruthless and degraded even white actors and actresses. In addition to the fact that this system dehumanized black people who participated in it, it generally did nothing for black people who might happen to be in the audience. The American culture obviously did not care to see images of itself including honorable, proud, humane African-Americans realistically in its mainstream. Typical shows did not reflect, recharge or recreate black people. They denied the living culture and way of life of a huge minority.

In 1967, Teer gathered a group of people for a production in behalf of the LeRoi Jones [Baraka] Defense Fund, when he was arrested for his activities in New-Ark. This group later produced "We Sing a New Song" for *Onyx* Magazine and began to call itself the National Black Theatre Workshop. The workshop was supported by dues and donations. Its first production was a film celebrating the existence of Malcolm X, called *RISE: A Love Poem for a Love People*. The film was made with *no* budget. The next production was a compilation of workshop member's poetry, songs and chants—in which the audience physically participated. The production was entitled "What Does It Take to Make You Really Want to Be Free?"

Using a new form/system of black images involved changes in language, style, character background and action, music, rhythm, plot and

321

form—there is no need for a simple thought to be divided by intermissions or separated by acts. The form was designed not only to entertain, but to teach/reach black people and help them regain a sense of humanity hard to retain in a society where it is seldom rewarded.

Specifically, this new art form is based on the study of the categories of systems of reactions of black people to life around them. These systems are called the five cycles of evolution.

The first cycle is called the "Nigga" cycle. People in this cycle need to feel a sense of self. They feel degraded on all sides by an inhuman system of employers, social workers, uncaring teachers and indifferent landlords. The "Nigga" man is taught to see himself as worthless and to hate himself. His main concern is his own survival. He is generally very skilled in the arts of survival, but may possess very few marketable skills, which creates problems as far as legal employment is concerned. His reaction to this oppressive situation is rage and rebellion.

There are subtle forms of rebellion against the system, such as the freedom of movement displayed when "Nigga" men and women are walking or dancing. They have the audacity to use the English language in an incredibly creative way as a very complex system of communication, in which one word can have a variety of meanings, shades and nuances unrivaled in mainstream America. They know the average white American is hung-up and trapped in his own repressive culture and they have no desire to be like him.

There are more overt forms of rebellion, such as refusing to join in the mainstream work force and finding more creative ways to survive. The rage builds up daily and since revenge against mainstream America usually meets severe reprisals, it is often vented against the people around them—other black people.

The next cycle is the "Negro" cycle, in which people feel acutely the need to be accepted by the mainstream society. Their reaction to oppression, degradation, and learned self-hatred is to try to join those whom they feel are not oppressed or degraded. They seek to acquire power and self-worth by identifying with those who have power, and who set the standards for self-worthiness. They restrain, restrict themselves in all things that are natural—swaying when walking or snapping their fingers. They change themselves to fit the images and ideals of people they imagine are free—those people in mainstream America. They cannot allow themselves to see that the unoppressed group they are imitating is, in many cases, the oppressor from whom they are so desperately fleeing.

They make their hair straight, their noses and eyebrows thin, their hips flat and their skin dry and light, not for fashion, but out of shame. They refrain from using creative expressions in their language—"If it isn't in the dictionary, it isn't a word." They stop using bright colors and wear more subdued tones. They are careful to follow all rules and regulations and they attain their goals only by accepted and standard

322

procedures. Generally, they learn very important skills, which are necessary for them to enter the mainstream and to progress in the system.

The "Militant" cycle, the third in the series, is composed of people who have realized the futility of imitating the mores and morays of an oppressive system. The militant's most urgent need is revenge and acceptance by society on his terms. He would still like the things that this culture offers to those who succeed—cars, clothes, money, travel, beautiful women, etc., but he realizes that they cannot be obtained by changing himself. His is a good person in his perception. He doesn't need changing to get into the system; the system needs changing so that he can enter it, through the front gate, at last. His primary interest is his own survival, however, and he is only interested in whatever change is necessary to get *him* in. In impatient fury, he rages at the system without any real plan for permanent change. He desperately wants to inflict pain on those who have injured and humiliated him. His vendetta is against all who do not share his beliefs—those blacks whom he feels still have warped perceptions of themselves, the "handkerchief heads" and "Uncle Tom niggas," and those whites whom he feels are keeping him from the "good life," the "honkies."

The black person in the "Nationalist" cycle, the fourth one, has realized that until all his people are ready to wage war on the system, he will be outnumbered in the battle. His strongest needs are for unity among black people and a change in the value system that they adhere to. He learns to love himself for the strong person he is, and in so doing, learns to love his people, because they are all part of his "family," and they are therefore reflections of him. Most of his energy is spent, not in spouting invectives at the system, but in trying to restructure the black community and subculture so the inhabitants can be both natural and unashamed at the same time. He must reflect on his own value system and readjust it if necessary so that he can be an example. The Nationalists organize black businesses and find other ways to establish higher economic standards. They encourage blacks to hire blacks and to change their values so that the good will received from the community will be more important than unfair profits that they could squeeze from poor people. They organize buildings and block associations so that black people will see that they themselves have the power to change their lives—to get more services for the rent, or pay less rent; to get the garbage collected or wreak havoc with the sanitation department. They serve as directors and organizers of black people.

The "Revolutionary" cycle, the highest state of spiritual and mental evolution in the cycles, encompasses all the rest. The revolutionary recognizes the existence of each of the cycles within himself—he has the freedom of the Nigga, the skills of the Negro, the rage of the Militant, and the love of the Nationalist. He can identify with and motivate all cycles of black people, teaching by example, word and deed the

323

potential that black people have. A Revolutionary knows his special abilities and does the most for his people that he can in that area. He realizes that some people are good in politics, some in armed struggle, and some in cultural revival, etc. He realizes that a revolution, or a complete change on all fronts requires that the people involved change on all fronts, and that no aspect of this change is less important than another. He has a thorough knowledge of himself and is motivated by all-consuming love for his people.

In order to become an official member of the National Black Theatre, each person must successfully complete a three-month course of exercises involving each of the cycles. Those who finish their apprenticeship become members. Because the function of the members is not to "act" in the theatrical sense, but to liberate the audience from some of its self-imposed restrictions, and to get them to feel unity, love and purpose, the members are called liberators. Liberators must always continue with classes in order to continue to develop in understanding of the cycles and in the ability to communicate to black people.

The theatre holds classes in its ideology, in meditation and spiritual release, in evolutionary movement (dance), and there is a liberation school for children. The adult liberation course is open to all black, Puerto Rican, or Third World people who apply. Each Sunday there is a free symposium open to the black community with speakers such as Stokely Carmichael, Ossie Davis, Ben H. Jochannan and others. Dance companies, singers and other black people are featured who can educate and enlighten the community.

The best-known production of the National Black Theatre, so far, is *Ritual: To Regain Our Strength and Reclaim Our Power*. It is the ritual cleansing of a black woman in the Nigga cycle. The liberators make wishes for her, explain to her that there is a more human value system, and teach her about her proud African heritage. There are chants in which the audience participates, songs and poetry. All the cycles are represented in the ritual. At the end of the ceremony, the woman is claimed by the new value system and cleansed of her self-hatred.

Through her transformation, all the black people in the audience see the possibility for change. The audience participates in the transformation—helping with chants, standing and affirming the fact that black people *do* "have power," and finally, when the woman and the audience are "saved," everybody participates in a victory celebration. All the black people in the room join hands and form one chain bound together by love for each other. Then everybody—liberators and congregation/audience—dance together in a celebration of victory. All present should now be more aware of the potential that black people have to care about each other enough to unite for the one common goal—freedom from oppression.

The *Ritual* has been successful whenever it has been performed. At

324

Howard University, the audience/congregation rose and continued chanting for 15 minutes after the company had left the building. The group has been asked to return to most places where it has performed.

A more structured presentation is being worked on called *The Revival: What You Gonna Do on Monday, Blackman?*, in which a community is cleansed of drugs by organizing itself.

The National Black Theatre is attempting to establish a tradition of theatre by Black people, not in imitation of European forms, but for black people, based on black life styles, using Black people to communicate its thoughts in theatres where black people can easily attend, where Black people will be comfortable, and where black people can easily afford the prices.

IT'S ALL RIGHT TO BE WOMAN THEATRE

Whereas theatre has been, to date, a combining of specialists, the essence of our theatre is to convey the collective experience. Only part of the message is in the content—the other part is that eleven women are working together to create new forms—a theatre without separation of roles (e.g. director, actress, musician), a theatre without a stage to separate audience and players . . . We feel that we are demystifying first for ourselves, and then for others, the whole concept of art and creativity and theatre, at the same time that we are de-mystifying the concept of privacy in our lives.

—Application for a Foundation Grant

[What follows is an interview with eight of the eleven members of It's All Right To Be Woman Theatre. At their request the remarks of individuals have not been differentiated. Therefore each answer is a combination of comments, sometimes conflicting, from most of the women present. The theatre tours college campuses and plays for women's groups in New York City where its members live. I saw them perform at the New School for Social Research before an all-women audience in the spring of 1971. Many of the women who founded this theatre late in 1970 had previously performed with other people's theatres, such as the Pageant Players and Burning City. A few had no theatre experience but had been active in various areas of the movement.]

KT: What was the turning point in your own lives that made you want to speak to women?

IARTBW: We all came out of the women's movement. I was in a theatre with men and women and the women started to work only with women. I was turned on to theatre and then I was turned on to women's theatre. I think women's culture is really happening, too.

325

I think that's a pretty important question, at least for me, why I'm working with women and talking with women. I was working with a supposed collective street theatre group where what Roberta said was just right, women didn't get a chance. And when the women started working by themselves it so freaked out the men that it caused a split in the group. So then I felt it was really important for me to work with women. The plays we made were twenty times better than the ones the whole group worked on because they were plays from our lives. We were portraying ourselves instead of Vietnamese. And then we'd go out and talk to women. I'm a woman and I was turned on to myself because of the woman's movement. I began to change because of it. And I think that other women seeing the things we're doing will be helped to change.

KT: In your application for foundation funds you say we are all actors, we are all directors. That's very nice and very hard to believe.

IARTBW: We know. The women's movement has always talked about trying to break down indirect manipulation. I came from a position of some authority in the movement and was sick of it and wanted to break all that down. I was sick of seeing movement organizations set women against each other. So we decided not to have that happen. That was the starting point. I really feel that this is the first time I've experienced a process of making decisions and working things out that was part of all our feelings. And everytime you get a little closer to what that feels like, you know you never had it before. That's been disturbing, too, to realize that I never had it before.

> We make theatre out of our lives, our dreams, our feelings, our fantasies. We make theatre by letting out the different parts of us that we have pushed inside all our lives and left to sneak and crouch inside us—the nightmares and the ugly feelings we try to hide, the screams or terror, the emptiness of feeling suddenly alone. We make our music out of the tunes we hum to ourselves and the beats we tap out on a table top. Making theatre out of these private parts of ourselves is one way we are trying everyday to take our own experiences seriously, to accept our feelings as valid and real and to believe in our own ideas. To believe that what happens to us or what we feel or dream is important enough to share with each other and with other women, that it is, in fact, the most important thing we have to share.
>
> **Foundation Application**

KT: When you take stories from your lives and adopt them to what is a non-realistic theatre, how do you do it? How do you find images or ways of doing that?

IARTBW: I think what we do is emotionally realistic and that's the

326

connection. The first thing we did as a group was to go away for a weekend and spend an entire three days telling each other the story of our lives. So we had a basic knowledge of each other. Then we spent four months not being pressured to put together anything. We said certain things like, "Everyone here shares the responsibility for whatever happens. Whether you have or have not had that experience." That made a difference I've never seen in any other group I've worked with. We found that people who had absolutely no theatre experience were getting in there and trying things out and had just as much to say as anyone else. Which is what we're about, also. The exercises we do come from any class any of us ever went to.

One problem we have is that we're trying to be direct and simple and people's lives are not that direct. So you have to find a line, some kind of feeling line or something. It usually happens that the woman whose story it is has the most room to act out her feelings, the people watching respond to her feelings the most and the other people in the story become a little bit shadowy. Also we don't do very long things. I don't feel that we have to. Maybe the whole idea of drama, developing a long story with one character going through many things, maybe that's something we want to get away from. I really like the way we are working where you focus in on one specific subject and just do short segments that show similarities. I really like that way of working right now.

KT: The assumption is that the personal experiences you have are very much like the personal, but as yet unconfronted experiences of the people in your audience?

IARTBW: Of us, too. What we're doing is confronting our own experience. I've been very concerned with my whole experience as an artist. You know, the starving painter in the garret. Even though that's not the experience of every woman, nevertheless the *act* of confronting it is the important part, this is important to all women. Because women have never really taken themselves seriously. Especially white middle class women. Women in the movement were told that their problems were not really important, were not of the first priority. I became more and more aware of the need to think of my own psyche.

> One of the ways we share our performance with the audience is by spontaneously acting out dreams. Someone from the audience will narrate a dream, and we will act it out simultaneously. For example: "I dreamed I was being chased down the stairs by a man with a knife . . ." and someone immediately becomes the dreamer, the man, the knife, several women become stairs, and as the dream is unfolded the actors move through it, and the objects transform. Usually the motion is slow and dreamlike.

Foundation Application

327

KT: At the New School performance one of you told the audience that you had had problems because you felt the first subjects for plays that you thought of were much too universal. You like dream plays because they are very personal?*

IARTBW: I think Roberta said that dream plays are very liberating because other forms try to make some kind of collective moral statement. And I don't think we feel that we know what that statement is. But a dream play is much easier to work with, because you really can't help it. You just dreamt it. It's not a line, but it is something that you know is important.

KT: Does someone from the audience usually offer a dream right away?

IARTBW: Yes. In Boston we had a twelve year old girl come up. We've always just done one dream of our own and then asked for someone from the audience.

KT: How do you feel your work relates to the other liberation struggles, of black, gay, Chicano, poor people?

IARTBW: At this point I don't think I do relate. It's a pretty huge task to adjust myself to what I am, even if it's just white middle class women I can relate to, it's a pretty huge task. And if other people can do it with who they relate to—I'm not chasing after other people. I can't solve all the problems of the movement. But still, I do feel the need to expand. The other day I thought we had to do a play about the war. So my own feelings on this fluctuate and change. It's not something that is clear.

For years I felt it was my responsibility to think of all the oppressed groups together. I just don't feel that way anymore. I don't feel that is my responsibility any more. What I really want to do is to understand myself and this theatre group and then how it fits together in the end, but we are not there yet. I think in the meantime it makes it easier for me to understand other people's oppressions the more I understand my own. I also feel the question is a little bit like saying, "What's the revolution going to be like?" What we are doing is trying to focus intensely and personally. It's a tall order. It means pulling in all the various feelings I've had about the women's movement right into a real experience. And I somehow feel that just our existence is a kind of political statement. We are exploring the ways we've been taught to feel powerless so that we can take power over our own lives. I think many groups are approaching the same problem. We're approaching one small piece of it and they are approaching another.

CONVERSATION WITH ENRIQUE VARGAS

In all practical work of our Party, all correct leadership is neces-

---

*As far as I know, Dream Plays were first performed by the Pagent Players.

sarily 'from the masses, to the masses.' This means: take the ideas of the masses (scattered and unsystematic ideas) and concentrate them (through study turn them into concentrated and systematic ideas), then go to the masses and propagate and explain these ideas until the masses embrace them as their own, hold fast to them and translate them into action, and test the correctness of these ideas in such action.

Chairman Mao

Enrique Vargas worked with Luis Valdez who, he says, taught him more than anyone about how to take images from the people's religious and folklore and give them back to them in a revolutionary way. In New York he founded the Gut Theatre, which later turned into the Third World Revelationists. At the radical theatre festival in 1968 two groups from the Gut Theatre performed. I still remember vividly the nine, ten, and eleven year olds who acted a play about their club house, involving drugs, a shooting and a favored moll. "Powerful, eh," Vargas smiles. He likes to work with kids and he has a genius for it. He says he begins by playing games with them. "Cops and Junkies"—the Cowboys and Indians of the inner city.

Sometime during 1971 Vargas has a falling out with the Third World Revelationists. He says doing theatre no longer seemed organic to him. He had to force himself to get ready for a performance and then he knew it did not come from the people. He points to a drawing over his desk: a man, arms upstretched with a fantastic tree growing out of his mouth. He began to seriously redefine his place in the struggle. He sees the need for various groups to be liberated, "women, Blacks, Latins, even gay people, though I probably won't come to grips with that easily," but he feels all these isolated groups have begun to get oppressive. And I agree with him.

When I arrived Enrique was finishing a letter home to Columbia. He gave me two books to read while I waited. From *Some Quotations Concerning Methods of Leadership* I copied the above quotation. Later we agree that if theatre has a place in Mao's formulation it is to concentrate the people's ideas into images. The other book is more puzzling, *Epidemics of the Middle Ages*, a graphic account of the great plagues. Enrique waves his hand toward the window: "We will have a kind of plague soon. We are going to have to be very physical," to cope with what's happening in the cities. We are in an apartment on Columbus Avenue in the West 90s in a building Vargas and others have been squatting in for several months. The City wants to tear this block down to make way for high-rise projects. Some residents and white and Third World organizers refuse and they are now trying to get themselves together into an illegal community, supplying free medical care, a free store, and when I was there, getting ready for a street festival.*

---

*In the summer of 1971 the City agreed to relocate all the families to their satisfaction and they vacated the buildings.

By "physical" Vargas does not mean a performance style, but a life style. "As long as you are afraid to die, they can hold power over you." For the revolutionary who works among the people and for them, each action is proof of his wholeness. In this context death becomes one more proof. "One more step that had to be taken," I think are Enrique's words. He tells me about being in a Jesuit school and how once as a child he climbed a mountain on his knees, a gesture symbolic of his supplication before Christ. He needs a kind of earnest for the revolutionary struggle, too. Something constant, not glamorous, and all connected. At Operation Move-In he wants to work with the men to learn plumbing and how to care for the building and the lives the building shelters. But it's not easy and there's some doubt as to how long he will stick it out. "I need patience," he says.

We go outside to the 104th St. Post Office which is halfway between our two apartments. Enrique can hardly walk more than two yards without getting stopped by someone with something urgent to say to him. We have to dodge a long-winded woman and then someone on the run whips around a corner and into us. "You can get killed in this fucking City," Enrique says. It is this random violence that is so fearsome to us both.

Enrique is writing a book and this occupation makes the difference between the life on the street and the life of the mind more apparent. "How do you make our writing seem necessary," he asks me? Then answers: "It has to be a reflection of our actions. In an exploitive society the natural tension between action and reflection has been destroyed. The intellectuals are given sole power to reflect and the workers to act. The workers' actions are controlled by the bosses and the intellectuals' reflections are made meaningless because they have no power to act."

He is holding an image in his mind that embodies his own sense of dislocation in the city and his need to find a course of action up to and including death to oppose it. He wants to build a labyrinth out of cardboard boxes. It will travel from neighborhood to neighborhood.

"There will be people guarding it outside. One person at a time will go through. Hopefully, it will be taken seriously and not be just one more thing to fuck up. Maybe that's asking too much. But I want it to be taken seriously."

The labyrinth is about making choices. Enrique feels it's a central image in Western culture. There will be a single entrance. You go through it and find that there are two ways to continue and you have to make a choice. Then you see that your next choice is conditioned by the first choice. Everything you do is connected. It's a matter of recognizing this. You can choose to take power over your life or you can choose to wander randomly through it. The labyrinth is apt, too, because it does not minimize the difficulty of making choices. It is still a maze, still torturous and uninviting. Very like New York City. Yet it is also a way out.

SOME STORIES ABOUT THE NATURE OF PEOPLE'S THEATRE

1. David and I said we would help Bart, Joe, John and Tom from Coney Island do a Bread and Puppet Theatre pageant* at the State University of New York at New Paltz. We drove a Rent-a-Truck up from the city packed with puppets. We needed 150 people to present the story of how Mr. Smallman became Mr. Bigman by eating all the people of the world. It was late Sunday morning when we arrived; nobody was around. We had not been announced. We started to unload the truck while a rock band began to play (it was "Spring Weekend"). By the time we were done there were 300 people sitting on the grass listening to the music and looking at the puppets. About ten people had started to help us unload. The band finished. Bart got a bullhorn and climbed a ladder: "We need twelve people to be inside the dragon." "Who wants to carry the world (a spherical puppet with lots of people growing out of it)?" "We need six capitalist friends of Mr. Smallman's." "Someone has to carry the hot dog Mr. Smallman eats." "Who wants to hold Mr. Bigman's cigar?" We lowered Mr. Bigman's head with its Uncle Sam hat onto his body from the top of the truck. Some of the men pulled the 30-foot devil puppet up on its stand; the afternoon sun was caught behind its scarlet robe, casting horrific shadows. Twenty-five women put on Vietnamese lady masks. Twelve people raised the apostles up, as the whole earth between the dormitories at New Paltz continued to erupt with a fantastical puppet pageant.
2. A friend was hiking. He met another person who had already made camp by the stream. He was invited to camp there also. His companion took out a drum and began to play. It got dark. From the woods they began to hear a flute improvising in perfect harmony with the drum. A person they had never seen before walked into the camp playing the flute. He sat down and continued to play until they all got tired and went to sleep.
3. Marc Estrin and some friends do Infiltration Pieces.** They go to a skin flick in San Francisco, flash lights on different parts of their bodies and talk about them:

...My breast is young, yet heavy as if filled with milk. It's a lover and a mother. I nourish it, and it nourishes. Someday it will fill the mouth of a child ....

And

My penis tells no lies. If I am trying to screw someone for my

---

*The Coney Island branch of the Bread and Puppet Theatre has since become autonomous. They call themselves the Puppet Theatre of War, Dragons and Children.

**Scripts, vol. 1, no. 5, March 1972.

own pleasure and not for love, my penis wants no part of my acting and I come quickly and without joy . . . .

Jeannie, singing:

> Bright morning stars are rising
> Bright morning stars are rising
> Bright morning stars are rising
> Day is a-breaking in my soul.

4. Question: If you help people to a little happiness do you think they'll demand their liberation?
   Answer: I think that's the only way they'll demand their liberation.